NIETZSCHE'S *ON THE GENEALOGY OF MORALITY*

On the Genealogy of Morality is Nietzsche's most influential, provocative, and challenging work of ethics. In this volume of newly commissioned essays, fourteen leading philosophers offer fresh insights into many of the work's central questions: How did our dominant values originate and what functions do they really serve? What future does the concept of "evil" have – and can it be revalued? What sorts of virtues and ideals does Nietzsche advocate, and are they necessarily incompatible with aspirations to democracy and a free society? What are the nature, role, and scope of genealogy in his critique of morality – and why doesn't his own evaluative standard receive a genealogical critique? Taken together, this superb collection illuminates what a post-Christian and indeed post-moral life might look like, and asks to what extent Nietzsche's *Genealogy* manages to move beyond morality.

SIMON MAY is Visiting Professor of Philosophy at King's College, University of London. His monographs include *Nietzsche's Ethics and His War on "Morality"* (1999), a book of his own aphorisms entitled *Thinking Aloud: A Collection of Aphorisms* (2009), and *Love: A History* (2011).

D1195698

NIETZSCHE'S
On the Genealogy of Morality
A Critical Guide

EDITED BY

SIMON MAY

King's College, University of London

CAMBRIDGE
UNIVERSITY PRESS

CAMBRIDGE
UNIVERSITY PRESS

University Printing House, Cambridge CB2 8BS, United Kingdom

Cambridge University Press is part of the University of Cambridge.

It furthers the University's mission by disseminating knowledge in the pursuit of education, learning and research at the highest international levels of excellence.

www.cambridge.org
Information on this title: www.cambridge.org/9781107437234

© Cambridge University Press 2011

First published 2011
First paperback edition 2014

A catalogue record for this publication is available from the British Library

Library of Congress Cataloguing in Publication data
Nietzsche's On the genealogy of morality : a critical guide / [edited by] Simon May.
p.   cm. – (Cambridge critical guides)
ISBN 978-0-521-51880-2 (hardback)
1. Nietzsche, Friedrich Wilhelm, 1844–1900.   2. Ethics, Modern–19th century.   I. May, Simon   II. Title.   III. Series.
B3318.E9N535   2011
170–dc22
2011013187

ISBN 978-0-521-51880-2 Hardback
ISBN 978-1-107-43723-4 Paperback

Contents

Contents

Contributors

R. LANIER ANDERSON is Associate Professor of Philosophy at Stanford University. His papers include "Nietzsche on Truth, Illusion, and Redemption," *European Journal of Philosophy* (2005), "Nietzsche on Redemption and Transfiguration," in Landy and Saler, eds., *The Re-enchantment of the World* (2009), and "What Is a Nietzschean Self?" in Janaway and Robertson, eds., *Nietzsche, Naturalism, and Normativity* (forthcoming).

RAYMOND GEUSS is Professor of Philosophy at the University of Cambridge. He is the author of *Public Goods, Private Goods* (2001), *Outside Ethics* (2005), *Philosophy and Real Politics* (2008), and *Politics and the Imagination* (2009).

EDWARD HARCOURT is University Lecturer in Philosophy at the University of Oxford and a Fellow of Keble College. He has published papers on metaethics, Wittgenstein, the moral emotions, and Nietzsche's moral philosophy, among other subjects.

LAWRENCE J. HATAB is Louis I. Jaffe Professor of Philosophy and Eminent Scholar at Old Dominion University. His books include *Nietzsche's* On the Genealogy of Morality: *An Introduction* and *Nietzsche's Life Sentence: Coming to Terms with Eternal Recurrence.*

NADEEM J. Z. HUSSAIN is Associate Professor of Philosophy at Stanford University. He is the author of "Nietzsche's Positivism," *European Journal of Philosophy* (2004), and "Honest Illusion: Valuing for Nietzsche's Free Spirits," in Brian Leiter and Neil Sinhababu, eds., *Nietzsche and Morality* (2007).

P. J. E. KAIL is University Lecturer in the History of Modern Philosophy at the University of Oxford and Fellow in Philosophy at St. Peter's College. His publications include *Projection and Realism in Hume's Philosophy* (2007).

PAUL KATSAFANAS is Assistant Professor of Philosophy at Boston University. His publications include "Deriving Ethics from Action: A Nietzschean Version of Constitutivism," *Philosophy and Phenomenological Research* (2011), and "The Concept of Unified Agency in Nietzsche, Plato, and Schiller," *Journal of the History of Philosophy* (2011).

BRIAN LEITER is Karl N. Llewellyn Professor of Jurisprudence and Director of the Center for Law, Philosophy and Human Values at the University of Chicago, and also Visiting Professor of Philosophy at Oxford University. He is the author of *Nietzsche on Morality* (2002) and co-editor of Nietzsche's *Daybreak* (1997), *Nietzsche* (2001), and *Nietzsche and Morality* (2007).

SIMON MAY is Visiting Professor of Philosophy at King's College, University of London. His monographs include *Nietzsche's Ethics and his War on "Morality"* (1999), a book of his own aphorisms entitled *Thinking Aloud: A Collection of Aphorisms* (2009), and *Love: A History* (2011), and he is co-editor, with Ken Gemes, of *Nietzsche on Freedom and Autonomy* (2009).

STEPHEN MULHALL is Professor of Philosophy at New College, Oxford. His most recent books are *The Wounded Animal: J. M. Coetzee and the Difficulty of Reality in Literature and Philosophy* (2008) and *The Conversation of Humanity* (2007).

PETER POELLNER is Professor of Philosophy at the University of Warwick. He is the author of *Nietzsche and Metaphysics* (1995) and has published articles on various topics in continental philosophy, ethics, and the philosophy of mind.

BERNARD REGINSTER is Professor of Philosophy at Brown University. He is the author of *The Affirmation of Life: Nietzsche on Overcoming Nihilism* (2006) and articles on nineteenth-century philosophy.

AARON RIDLEY is Professor of Philosophy at the University of Southampton. His books include *Nietzsche's Conscience: Six Character Studies from the* Genealogy (1998) and *Nietzsche on Art* (2007).

CHRISTINE SWANTON is Professor of Philosophy at the University of Auckland. She is author of *Virtue Ethics: A Pluralistic View* (2003) and *Freedom: A Coherence Theory* (1992).

Acknowledgements

I am grateful to Hilary Gaskin, senior commissioning editor for philosophy at Cambridge University Press, for inviting me to undertake this book and for her unstinting encouragement and invaluable counsel; to Anna Lowe, assistant editor at the Press, and her predecessor, Joanna Garbutt, for their superb support; to Christina Sarigiannidou, my production editor, for so efficiently seeing the book through to publication; to Geoff Bailey for creating the index; to Chris Sykes for help in compiling the bibliography; to James Thomas for his careful copy-editing; to Andrew Godfrey for meticulously checking and proof-reading the final text; and, of course, to all my co-authors for their contributions.

SIMON MAY

Note on texts, translations, and references

All authors in this volume refer to Nietzsche's works by the same abbreviations, listed below. References to and citations from *On the Genealogy of Morality* are taken from the English translation by Carol Diethe (Cambridge University Press, 1994), with very occasional departures from it in the form of an author's use of another translation, modification of a translation, or provision of their own. For other works of Nietzsche the particular English translations used by each author are given in a footnote at the beginning of his or her chapter. All secondary literature to which reference is made is listed in the bibliography.

References to secondary literature are made in the Harvard style.

A	*The Antichrist*
BGE	*Beyond Good and Evil: Prelude to a Philosophy of the Future*
BT	*The Birth of Tragedy*
CW	*The Case of Wagner*
D	*Daybreak* (also translated as *Dawn*)
EH	*Ecce Homo*
GM	*On the Genealogy of Morality*
GS	*The Gay Science*
HAH	*Human, All Too Human*
KGW	*Werke: Kritische Gesamtausgabe*
KSA	*Sämtliche Werke: Kritische Studienausgabe in 15 Einzelbänden*
TI	*Twilight of the Idols: or How to Philosophize with a Hammer*
UM	*Untimely Meditations* (also translated as *Unfashionable Observations*)
WP	*The Will to Power*
Z	*Thus Spoke Zarathustra: A Book for Everyone and No One*

Introduction

Simon May

Despite the plethora of writings devoted to Nietzsche's *On the Genealogy of Morality*, the publication of a collection of original scholarly essays on this great book is a rare event.

This volume brings together a broad range of prominent philosophers writing in English, from both sides of the Atlantic and beyond, so giving a sense for the current state of English-speaking scholarship in the field. Most do not limit themselves to close textual exegesis, but rather treat fundamental themes and aims of the work as a whole, freely discussing their philosophical importance.

GENEALOGY AND THE "GENEALOGY"

The theme that recurs, perhaps more than any other, is this: what are the nature, role, and scope of genealogy in Nietzsche's critique of morality? Specifically: if Nietzsche wants to undermine morality, why does he need genealogy to do so? Why not cut to the chase and tell us how he thinks our contemporary values and the functions to which they are *now* put stymie our flourishing and betray the standards for it that he explicitly or implicitly sets?

Paul Katsafanas (chapter 8) claims that most interpretations of the *Genealogy* fail to explain why the work's historical form is necessary to Nietzsche's critique of contemporary morality. He argues that the *Genealogy* employs history in order to show that acceptance of modern morality was causally responsible for producing a dramatic change in our affects, drives, and perceptions. This change, according to Katsafanas, caused us to perceive actual increases in power as reductions in power, and actual decreases in power as increases in power. Moreover, it led us to experience negative emotions when engaging in activities that constitute greater manifestations of power, and positive emotions when engaging in activities that reduce power. For these reasons, modern morality strongly disposes us to reduce our own power. Given Nietzsche's argument that power has a privileged normative status, this fact, Katsafanas concludes, entails that we have decisive reason to reject modern morality.

Peter Kail (chapter 10) investigates genealogy as philosophical method-ology. He discusses what a Nietzschean genealogy might be, how it relates to naturalism, and its normative standing in relation to the project of the "revaluation of values." His chapter begins by arguing for a conception of genealogy *per se* as that of situated psychological explanation of the emer-gence of beliefs and practices, something that Nietzsche has in common with those he dismissively calls his "English" predecessors. Kail then dis-cusses the sense in which Nietzsche's particular genealogy constitutes, or contributes to, a "critique" of morality, and he argues that its function is a *preparatory* one. The genealogy provides a reason to seek further justifica-tion for the central commitments of morality and so prepares the ground for the project of the revaluation of values. It does so by revealing that the sources productive of the relevant moral beliefs are epistemically unreliable, hence depriving such beliefs of their assumed privileged status. Finally Kail compares the conception of genealogy developed here with that of Bernard Williams, and questions not only whether Williams (like Foucault before him) really reflects Nietzsche's approach to genealogy, but also whether there is some distinct method called "genealogy" in the *Genealogy*.

Nadeem Hussain (chapter 7) asks a question that is arguably begged by the *Genealogy*, yet seldom addressed: why doesn't Nietzsche's *own* evalua-tive standard receive a genealogical critique? After all, Nietzsche assesses the value of the value judgments of morality from the perspective of a very particular, substantive conception of what human flourishing comes to. His positive descriptions of the "higher men" he hopes for and the negative descriptions of the decadent humans he thinks morality supports both point to such a conception. So why exempt it from genealogical scrutiny?

Hussain argues that the answer to this puzzle lies in recognizing the centrality of the notion of "life," and its connection to power, in Nietzsche's overall account. The *Genealogy*, he claims, is a genealogy both of the tendency towards power – a tendency towards dominating and growing that is essential to life, including when it might seem that the opposite is happening, as with the ascetic ideal – and of Nietzsche's affirmation of this tendency. Brian Leiter has argued that his "Millian Model" provides the most charitable reconstruction of appeals to a privileged evaluative standard of power; this model ascribes an inference from a strong doctrine of the will to power according to which only power can be desired. Hussain, by contrast, proposes a "Benthamite model" that ascribes an inference from the inescapability of a tendency towards power – and argues that this model avoids the objections that Leiter directs at the Millian model.

But if genealogy, however its nature and scope are precisely to be construed, is so important to Nietzsche's attack on morality, then this raises a very obvious but rather neglected question: Why do noble types end up surrendering to slave morality? Do they accept that there is something wrong with their ethically aristocratic ways? Are they merely overwhelmed by the slaves' cunning and the power of their *ressentiment*? Or is another explanation called for?

Any answers will necessarily be, in considerable part, speculative as Nietzsche provides few clues to why the "slaves" aren't simply dismissed by the "masters," given the latter's "pathos of distance," their original position of social power, and their seeming confidence, indeed delight, in their own values.

Lawrence Hatab (chapter 9) argues that the makings of the surrender are to be found in the growing domestication of culture, an exhaustion of externalized power, and the novel attractions of internalized power (one example of which is Socratic dialectic). The complex ambiguities in Nietzsche's analysis of master and slave morality, Hatab suggests, show that the transition not only endangered but also enhanced cultural life – that the brute power of master types could be refined into higher cultural forms when modified by the slave mentality. The "internalized" power of slave morality represented a weakening of more natural instincts, yet also powered new forms of imagination and thought. And despite the dangers involved, the creative types among the mass of slave types displayed a re-routing of master energies in the direction of reflective cultural works that changed the world.

But, one might reply to Hatab, is there any evidence that the original nobles care about higher culture? And, if not, how do the slaves manage to get them to do so? R. Lanier Anderson's contribution (chapter 2) suggests an intriguing answer to the latter question: they don't. The primary architects of the slave revolt aren't slaves at all: they are nobles. Specifically, they are "priests."

Nietzsche's condemnation of the "*ressentiment* priest" or the "ascetic priest," and of his key role in the slave revolt, might, Anderson suggests, cause us to conclude that Nietzsche's priests are paradigmatic slave types.

And that primary agency in the slave revolt must rest with slavish types. But this cannot be right. Nietzsche is clear, says Anderson (focusing principally on the first essay), that the priests are intended to be *nobles*. Indeed, it is crucial to the argument of the first essay that the priests are *nobler* than certain other noble types whom they oppose. Moreover, there are reasons – tied to Nietzsche's conceptions of the noble and slave types – to think that he introduced the priests into the *Genealogy*'s story of slave revolt in the first place precisely because he needed them to serve as value creators who *invent* slave morality, and thereby set the revolt in motion. If *ressentiment* priests, rather than slaves, have primary agency in the slave revolt, it becomes clearer why Nietzsche thought that a vengeful orientation and troubling self-deception are deeply built into the very values of slave morality, and thus why his genealogy amounts to a serious critique of conventional morality.

RESSENTIMENT

So how can we characterize that psychological condition of *ressentiment* with which the priest so artfully works? In a wide-ranging essay (chapter 6) on the nature, value, and intent of *ressentiment*, Peter Poellner asks, *inter alia*, whether Nietzsche's genealogical account is coherent; if it is, whether he commits the "genetic fallacy"; and what precisely are the grounds of Nietzsche's critique of a morality involving *ressentiment*.

Poellner argues that *ressentiment* should be understood as an intentional *project of object mastery*, although recent critics of intentionalist construals (Wallace, Bittner) are right to insist that it cannot be a reflective strategy. He draws on theories of pre-reflective consciousness associated with the phenomenological tradition to explain how an intentionalist construal of *ressentiment* as a project can avoid the so-called paradoxes of self-deception and the charge of incoherence.

He then outlines some conditions which Nietzsche's theory of *ressentiment* would have to satisfy to be suitable as a critical tool in the manner intended by him. Poellner claims that while this theory is more successful than is sometimes assumed in meeting some of these conditions, it fails to support Nietzsche's radical claim that the morality criticized by him cannot be understood without reference to its supposed psychological origin in *ressentiment*. Though *ressentiment* is a real and important phenomenon, it cannot play the fundamental explanatory role Nietzsche assigns to it. Finally, Poellner turns to the grounds of Nietzsche's criticism of *ressentiment* and concludes that they concern primarily its intrinsic, rather than merely instrumental, disvalue.

GUILT

However the "slave revolt in morals" gains traction over non-priestly noble types, and however we characterize the role of *ressentiment* in this process, there is no doubt that, for Nietzsche, a certain type or use of guilt is central to the operation of slave morality.

In his reading of the second essay of the *Genealogy*, Bernard Reginster (chapter 3) argues that it is not correct to interpret Nietzsche's primary objective there as challenging the non-naturalistic account of the feeling of guilt found in Christian moral psychology (as a manifestation of "the voice of God in man"). Nietzsche's aim, Reginster proposes, is rather to show that the Christian representation of guilt is, in fact, not an account of the ordinary feeling of guilt (the diminution of one's worth as a person when one falls short of certain normative expectations), but a perversion of it, which results from its exploitation as an instrument of self-directed cruelty. Christian guilt is therefore not the ordinary moral emotion of guilt, responsive to reasons, but what Reginster calls a "rational passion." By which he means a passion to which only a rational being is susceptible because it essentially exploits his responsiveness to reason – and which, unlike other passions, not only overrides, but actually corrupts, this responsiveness to reason.

Reginster goes on to argue that the second essay offers important elements of an account of ordinary guilt – but only those elements that are relevant to Nietzsche's diagnosis of Christian guilt as a perverted use of it. It does not intend to offer the complete account of the emergence of the ordinary feeling of guilt that commentators have been at pains to extract from it. For instance, it virtually ignores the role of free will in the feeling of guilt, and does not even attempt to offer a genealogy of the notion of categorical obligation, which it crucially presupposes. Reginster argues that Nietzsche's primary aim is to explain the development of the ordinary feeling of guilt into the Christian notion of inexpiable guilt before God – and that his chief hypothesis is that this development takes place when the feeling of guilt is appropriated by the will to power under social conditions in which the possibilities for its gratification are severely limited. (In this context, Reginster relates it illuminatingly to Freud's account of the origin of guilt in *Civilization and Its Discontents*.)

Reginster's discussion of ordinary guilt and its distinction from the Christian representation of guilt points us towards a large and vexed question: what would a post-Christian and indeed post-moral life look like? A life that is beyond good and evil, though not beyond good and bad; a life that has conquered God and nothingness; a life that has found a meaning no longer structured by the ascetic ideal. Not surprisingly, perhaps, this question elicits a wide and not always compatible range of views in this volume.

"EVIL"

Raymond Geuss (chapter 1) asks what future the concept of "evil" might have in the light of Nietzsche's genealogical investigation, which has revealed "evil" to be how the weak originally characterize the actions of those by whom they feel oppressed and on whom they wish to take revenge, if only imaginary. He warns that replacing or revaluing a moral conception is slow and hard, and is not at all like revising a straightforwardly wrong proposition based on new evidence. Moral conceptions express a kind of person, and so are very deeply ingrained. Indeed, replacing them is slower and harder than revising our tables of vices and virtues. For the concept of "evil" is not like a specific vice: it a structural feature of all vices, a second-order interpretive term, which shows how individual vices are to be understood by reference to some underlying structural feature that they all have; and as such it is likely to have much more staying power than the vices it orders. Moreover, the *ressentiment* that, according to Nietzsche, motivates it cannot be got rid of easily because it arises naturally from weakness, which is in turn simply a fact about oneself.

Interestingly, Geuss remarks that seeing the untenability of the metaphysics on which "evil" is based – for example, the metaphysics of free will – won't cause us to abandon the concept. On the contrary, our continuing need to express our *ressentiment* will be likely to make its use *all the more* "obfuscated, hysterical, and toxic."

The concept of "evil" can, then, be revalued – in other words: its meaning reinterpreted and its extension shifted – only if we somehow get rid of *ressentiment* and its motivations in our own powerlessness, and so no longer need the term "evil" in the same way. If we retain this term we might reserve it, for example, for the intentional and avoidable infliction of great harm, or for especially undesirable traits: traits (analogous to Thomas Aquinas' "capital vices") that are not just undesirable in themselves, but structure an entire life in ways that we consider especially bad. We might also place less emphasis on bad intent and more on the power to carry through bad actions than has historically been associated with the Christian system of morality.

Provided that the new use of "evil" is not connected with imaginary vengefulness – this is the key – it would effectively be a revalued concept. So the question about the future of evil with which Geuss leaves us is this: by what methods, if any, can we control or get rid of our need for vengeance?

AN "AESTHETICS OF CHARACTER"?

It is sometimes said that Nietzsche's ideals are "aesthetic," but Edward Harcourt (chapter 12) is skeptical. He discusses what it is for an ideal of character to be distinctively aesthetic (or for a thinker to have an "aesthetics of character") – and, by way of comparison, makes special reference to some commentators' application of the "aesthetic" label to ideals of character in Aristotle, and to the part played in the regulation of behavior by idealized descriptions of character derived from literary fiction. After examining various interpretations of "aesthetic" as applied to ideals of character, he concludes that the term turns out either to be well motivated but not to mark out a genuine ideal; or else to be poorly motivated, whether as a way of marking out an ideal of a distinctive type, or as a way of marking out what is special about Nietzsche's own ideals, or both. So, tempting as the label may be, if we are to capture what, if anything, is special about Nietzsche's ideals of character, we are unlikely to help ourselves if we continue to reach for the term "aesthetic" to do the work for us.

A "NOBLE" CONCEPTION OF BEAUTY

Aaron Ridley (chapter 14) asks what a noble conception of beauty might be – and, more generally, whether Nietzsche's thoughts about beauty deserve to be taken seriously as a contribution to aesthetics. In other words, do they help us to understand what beauty is, or in what sense beauty is a value for us?

In doing so Ridley argues that the *Genealogy* yields three quite separate conceptions of beauty – two that Nietzsche rejects, with varying degrees of vehemence, and one that he apparently accepts. Least attractive, in Nietzsche's eyes, is the conception of beauty to be found in Kant and Schopenhauer, a conception rooted in a "No" said to the self – in a form of self-denial that eventuates in "disinterestedness" as an aesthetic ideal. Better, he thinks, although still imperfect, is Stendhal's conception – that beauty is a promise of happiness – which is affirmative and "interested" but is also other-regarding, and so holds itself at arm's length from beauty as it really is. The third conception – beauty as, according to Nietzsche, it really is – construes it as one name for, or one dimension of, an erotically intense experience of affirmation, a condition in which value attaches, primordially and essentially, to *the self*. The first two conceptions can, in one way or another, be thought of as slavish: the first is grounded in negation; the second presents the non-self as the originary locus of value. The final conception, by contrast, is *noble*: it is both affirmative and self-regarding. Ridley concludes by suggesting that the second conception – Stendhal's – has at least as much to recommend it as does Nietzsche's preferred alternative.

NIETZSCHEAN EXCELLENCE AND ITS VIRTUES

The egoism of Nietzsche's ideals has given much concern to commentators, partly because it is hard to characterize and partly because it seems so asocial – to put it mildly. Christine Swanton (chapter 13) suggests that this concern is misplaced, and does so by pointing to what Nietzsche calls the "mature individual" who in his terms is an egoist, but of the "mature" sort. She contrasts mature egoism with two forms of immature egoism and with self-sacrificing altruism, all described by Nietzsche. The former are constituted by a faulty conception of one's own good, one concerned with comfort and immediate self-gratification, and by an asocial kind of egoism where one does not respect others. The latter is constituted by an impersonal kind of submersion in the collective or other kinds of altruistic concern where the self "wilts away."

To draw these distinctions Swanton makes some basic points about the nature and structure of virtue as a character trait, in order to help dispel doubt that for Nietzsche we can have virtues (and vices) as well as simply drives. To understand Nietzsche's notion of a virtue, too, she underlines that for him virtues and vices are not constituted merely by "surface" intentions (or even patterns of surface intentions), or by mere tendencies to action. Rather, as he repeatedly emphasizes, to understand humans fully we need to understand their deeper motivations, which inform the patterns of their intentions and behavior. The complexity of the depth-psychological nature of Nietzsche's understanding of virtue and correlative vices is brought out in her chapter by a discussion of several virtues and their correlative vices, as applied to the "mature egoist," and the forms of immature egoism and self-sacrificing altruism, especially as discussed in the *Genealogy*. These virtues and vices include assertiveness (contrasted with cruelty), justice (contrasted with punitive rigorism and what Nietzsche calls scientific fairness), objectivity as a virtue (contrasted with "hyperobjective" and "hypersubjective" vice, particularly in regard to ethics), mature generosity (contrasted with self-sacrificing charity), independence (contrasted with various excesses of independence), and discipline (contrasted with asceticism as a vice).

Stephen Mulhall (chapter 11) sees Nietzsche's concern with the cultivation of human excellence as neither elitist nor incompatible with liberal democratic aspirations. His wide-ranging chapter offers support to the project (initiated by Stanley Cavell and James Conant) of reading Nietzsche as an Emersonian perfectionist, a project that in philosophical terms requires a radical redrawing of the boundaries between the moral, the political, the aesthetic, and the religious dimensions of human thought and practice. In the *Genealogy* these themes are given a specific inflection that is generated by Nietzsche's prefatory identification of himself as one of the men of knowledge who have remained unknown to themselves. The implications of this self-critical stance are worked out in Mulhall's engagements with Wagner's *Parsifal*, with the issue of the origins and nature of language (its cognitive capacities here being represented as inherently evaluative and expressive of commitment in ways epitomized by promise-making), with the task of turning Christian discourse against itself, and with the internalization of the opposition between master and slave.

THE "SOVEREIGN INDIVIDUAL"

When searching for a perfect instantiation of Nietzschean virtue, and indeed of his new ideal more generally, it might be tempting to point to the "sovereign individual," as portrayed in the second essay of the *Genealogy*.

Brian Leiter (chapter 5) takes a fresh look at who this figure is and what he has to do with Nietzsche's conceptions of free will, freedom, and the self. Leiter argues, first, that Nietzsche denies that people ever act freely and that they are ever morally responsible for anything they do; second, that the figure of the "sovereign individual" in no way supports a denial of the first point; and, third, that Nietzsche engages in what Charles Stevenson would have called a "persuasive definition" of the language of "freedom" and "free will," radically revising the content of those concepts, but in a way that aims to capitalize on their positive emotive valence and authority for his readers.

More precisely, Leiter aims to show that the image of the "sovereign individual" is, in fact, consistent with the reading of Nietzsche as a kind of fatalist, which he has defended at length elsewhere. To show that the image of the "sovereign individual" squares with Nietzsche's fatalism, he distinguishes between two different "deflationary readings" of the passage.

On one such reading, the figure of the "sovereign individual" is wholly ironic, a mocking of the petit bourgeois who thinks his petty commercial undertakings – his ability to make promises and remember his debts – are the highest fruit of creation. On another deflationary reading, the "sovereign individual" does indeed represent an ideal of the self, one marked by a kind of self-mastery foreign to less coherent selves (whose momentary impulses pull them this way and that); but such a self and its self-mastery constitute, in Nietzschean terms, a fortuitous natural artifact (a bit of "fate"), not an autonomous achievement for which anyone could be responsible. To associate this ideal of the self with the language of "freedom" and "free will" is, Leiter claims, an exercise in "persuasive definition" by Nietzsche, a rhetorical skill of which he was often the master.

A NEW MEANING FOR SUFFERING?

In the closing sections of the *Genealogy*, Nietzsche looks forward, as he does in concluding the previous two essays, to a world free of morality: to a new ideal and a new type of spirit who might embody it. Specifically he seeks a new meaning for suffering – one no longer structured by the ascetic ideal.

In my own chapter (chapter 4) I claim that the *Genealogy*'s success in undermining morality is limited by Nietzsche's conviction that suffering must be given a meaning – a conviction integral to the very tradition of morality that he wishes to overcome. The meanings that Nietzsche gives suffering – in terms of higher goods, such as creativity in art and values and thought, which it makes possible or of which it is constitutive – might themselves be free of moral presuppositions. But, I argue, as long as he even poses the question of the meaning or purpose of suffering he remains within morality, and so cannot fully affirm life. I advance various reasons for this: for example, that all attempts to give suffering a meaning or justification, including one that is life-affirming, are attempts to eviscerate it of what makes it suffering – notably the helplessness at its core – and to that extent are attempts (absurdly) to eliminate it.

I then propose that genuinely to affirm one's own life is to take joy in its "there-ness" or quiddity as a whole – a whole conceived as necessary (or fated) in all its elements and experienced as beautiful. Crucially, such affirmation is in no way grounded in justifications of suffering. It is also, to take a cue from Nietzsche, consistent with "saying No" to particular experiences or events within the whole – though it is not consistent with seeking alternatives to the actual life we have.

In tracing the movement of Nietzsche's thought on the justification of suffering from *The Birth of Tragedy* to *Ecce Homo*, I attempt to show that he moves towards just such a stance, especially in his desire for *amor fati*; but that at the end of the *Genealogy* he still refuses to go the whole way. The real challenge with which Nietzsche's book leaves us might, therefore, be the opposite of the one he sets: in other words it might be to *resist* the search for a new answer (no longer, of course informed by the ascetic ideal) to the question of the meaning of suffering. Instead we would discover what it would be for our ethics, our sensibility, and our attitude to our life to cease being so powerfully driven by that question. Or perhaps we might experimentally strike it off the agenda altogether.

CHAPTER I

The future of evil

Raymond Geuss

There are fashions as much in vices as in virtues, and these are neither completely dependent on, nor completely independent of, changes in social institutions and transformations of the available moral vocabulary. It is often very difficult to distinguish changes in customs or habits, changes in modes of evaluation, and changes in vocabulary. Do vices become extinct, and if so, how does this occur?

In his *Summa theologiae*[1] Thomas Aquinas discusses the "vice of *simony*" – the desire or attempt to purchase or sell spiritual powers, then by extension the buying and selling of ecclesiastical office – which he classes among the "vices contrary to religion" ("vitia opposita religioni"). Simony still merited a separate topological location among the most serious vices in Dante's *Inferno*, but one would be hard put to find a discussion of it in any contemporary work of virtue ethics. It has probably succumbed to a combination of social and economic changes. Thus there is now widespread skepticism about the very existence of spiritual powers and disinclination to believe that spiritual powers, even if they did exist, could be acquired by purchase. The result of this is that attempts to purchase non-natural powers seem pathetically stupid rather than vicious. In addition, changes in the internal regulatory structure and the relative economic position of the church have caused the market for the sale of spiritual powers to dry up to such an extent that it is difficult or impossible for individuals to develop a fixed disposition to try to buy or sell the power of the Holy Spirit or to purchase or offer for purchase bishoprics, monastic offices, or a place in the College of Cardinals. Simony is not the only vice to suffer. The good old Christian vice of gluttony (*gula*) seems to have disappeared, being reinterpreted as a medical condition or a morally neutral, although perhaps aesthetically repellent, lifestyle choice. In the Middle Ages, too, "curiosity," was often considered a vice; it is now no longer considered at all

---

[1] Secunda secundae, quaestio C.

objectionable, but rather is something which, on the whole, we are inclined to admire.[2] If vices, therefore, can apparently disappear, can new ones also come into existence? Was there always as much "pedophilia" and child abuse as there now seems to be? Have the dissolution of social taboos and the omnipresence of news reporting caused something that always existed suddenly to come to people's attention in a way it did not previously, so that people are forced to make up their minds about its exact evaluation in a way they could have avoided in earlier periods? Was it always there, but accepted or at any rate tacitly tolerated, but now very explicitly and vividly repudiated? Or was it previously "hiding" under some other more general term?

One of the ways in which Nietzsche presents his project in *On The Genealogy of Morality* is as a historical account of the development of contemporary morality, including the development of our virtues and vices and our conceptions of virtue and vice.[3] His account arises, he claims, out of two philological observations about the history of the word "good," or rather about the meaning and history of some earlier terms (καλός, ἀγαθός, *bonus*) that are usually construed as "meaning the same thing" as our word "good."[4] The first observation is that "good" (and its historically existing semantic "equivalents") has had and continues to have two distinct opposites: that which is "bad" is definitely not good, and that which is "evil" is also definitely not good, and yet "bad" and "evil" do not mean the same thing. Furthermore, Nietzsche claims, "bad" and "evil" are not merely semantically distinct because, for instance, "evil" is a subspecies of "bad," so that "evil" means "intensely bad" or "intentionally very bad." If that were the case, "bad" and "evil" would not mean the same thing because everything that was evil would also be bad, but not everything that was bad (for instance, that which was merely mildly or moderately or unintentionally bad) would also count as "evil." This simple kind of difference in meaning is not what Nietzsche intends. Rather, Nietzsche holds that originally "bad" and "evil" were used characteristically by the members of two different groups of people, and that they were used in such a way that their extensions did not overlap. This is a very strong assertion indeed. Nietzsche's second historical observation is that the pair "good/bad" is older than the pair "good/evil," and this stimulates him to the hypothesis to the development of which the first essay of the *Genealogy* is devoted, namely that "good/evil"

---

[2] See Hans Blumenberg, *Die Legitimität der Neuzeit* (1966).
[3] *KSA*, 5.152–78. All quotations are from *Sämtliche Werke: Kritische Studienausgabe*, ed. Colli and Montinari (1980–88), cited as *KSA*, by volume and page.
[4] *KSA*, 5.254–55, 261, 288–89.

should in some sense be seen as arising out of "good/bad" through a revolutionary change in the system of valuation, a "reversal of all values" ("Umwertung aller Werte").

"Evil," of course, is not itself a vice in the normal sense of the term. That is, it is not on the same level of abstraction as proper vices like indolence, cruelty, simony, duplicitousness, envy, or impatience. They seem in the first instance to refer to complexes or patterns of behavior which, to be sure, count as vices only because they form stable constellations which are taken to be the result of persisting psychological states. "Evil," on the other hand, seems not to refer primarily to any externally discernible kind of action, but rather to be a second-order interpretive term, which shows how these individual vices are to be understood by reference to some underlying structural feature that they all have. A very strong philosophical-traditional view would have it that although specific vices might fall into desuetude or die out, "evil" is a structural feature of all vices, and so as long as *any* vice at all remains in existence, "evil" will still exist. Christians, of course, have traditionally held that the possibility of doing evil was an inherent part of human free will, so that even a society which, *per impossibile*, was utopianly good would have a use for the concept of "evil." Since for the Christian "free will" had to stand in the center of any ethical reflection, then as long as humanity continued to exist, the concept of "evil" would retain its relevance and its importance: if Christians and post-Christians are right, its future is assured.

Nietzsche's views on this topic were deeply influenced by his study of the Greek poet Theognis, whom he cites in the *Genealogy* as the "mouthpiece of the Greek nobility"[5] and describes in his unpublished notes as "a poet as philosopher."[6] Theognis was a sixth-century aristocrat from Megara who wrote elegiac distichs of a vaguely ethical character. Many of the verses are addressed to his young boyfriend Kyknus and contain, as is common in works in this tradition of pederastic pedagogy, advice to him about how to live a proper upper-class life.[7] It is perfectly true that Theognis was, as

---

[5] *KSA*, 5.263. I cite Theognis, following *Delectus ex iambis et elegis graecis*, ed. M. T. West (1980).
[6] *KSA*, 7.386.
[7] The poems of Theognis have come to us in collections that seem to comprise various poems by various authors, and it is extremely unclear which of the poems in this collection are really by the sixth-century man from Megara, which are imitations by other people of poems by this sixth-century figure (i.e. poems "in the manner of Theognis of Megara"), and which are completely independent poems by completely different people that simply happened for one reason or another to have been copied together into the collection. This sort of historical-philological detective work – Is this poem *really* by Theognis? Has an imitator added something at the end? If so, where does the genuine "material" end and the added imitation begin? – was exactly the sort of thing which the young Nietzsche was trained

Nietzsche states, a man who formulates in an especially explicit way a certain self-conception of the Greek aristocracy, but what is almost more striking about his work is the way in which it reflects and expresses Theognis' own sense that the world of traditional certainties in which he had been brought up and had lived was being completely transformed in radical ways over which he had no control and of which he deeply disapproved. Nietzsche was obsessed with what he calls the "slave revolt" of morality, by which he meant the process in which old aristocratic values of prowess in war, glory, successful self-assertion, and associated traits were systematically devalued and replaced with virtues of non-aggression, cooperation, benevolence, etc. Theognis' own preoccupation is not exactly the same as Nietzsche's. He is rather sensitive to the destructive effect of new wealth on traditional social hierarchies, but his particular fear is not the devaluation of aggression. He is, however, living through a process of "Umwertung aller Werte," which has some significant similarities to what Nietzsche calls the "slave revolt," and he observes the effect of this transformation of society and its values on language itself; the very meanings of words seem to change.[8]

Thus Theognis writes:

Kyknus, this city is still a city, but the people are different. Those who used to have no knowledge either of laws or judgments, wore clapped out goatskins wrapped around their middles, and wandered about aimlessly grazing outside the city like deer, *they* are now good [ἀγαθοί], and those who used to be noble [ἐσθλοί] are now worthless [δειλοί, "cowards"][9]

and, in what seems to be a separate passage:

Kyknus, those who used to be good [ἀγαθοί] are now bad [κακοί] and those who used to be bad [κακοί] are now good [ἀγαθοί]. Who could stand to see the good [τοὺς ἀγαθαύς] having less honor [ἀτιμοτέρους] and the bad [κακίους] getting honor? A noble man [ἐσθλὸς ἀνὴρ] even goes courting [the daughter of] a bad man [κακοῦ].[10]

I have translated this in a particularly bald way to bring out the apparent confusion of linguistic usage and the crude juxtapositions of opposites that

---

to do, and one of his early published works was an article for a scholarly journal about which bits of the Theognis corpus were genuine (i.e. written by the original sixth-century man from Megara) and which were not. One can see the connection between this kind of enterprise and Nietzsche's later views about "genealogy." So we can be sure that Nietzsche had read and studied his body of poetry with the greatest philological care.

[8] The other classic discussion of the way ethical terms change meaning in extreme circumstances is, of course, Thucydides' discussion of the events in Corcyra during the Peloponnesian War, III.82.

[9] Theognis 53–58.　　[10] Theognis 1109–12.

would be lost in a more idiomatic version. This is a time and a world in which meanings are shifting so radically that it is unclear at first glance what exactly is being said, and contradictory statements seem possible. When Theognis writes that the good are now bad, does he mean that those who were bad (in an agreed-on sense) have now changed their nature and behavior and actually *are* good (in the agreed-on sense), or that those who were (and still are) bad are now *called* "good"? Called by whom? Written Greek of the sixth and fifth centuries BC had practically no punctuation and in particular did not have quotation marks, so one could not distinguish in a text between: "they are good" and "they are 'good'." It is difficult to see how one could try to read passages like these without asking what is meant by "good." Are people good by virtue of having some psychological or behavioral properties, by virtue of coming from a respected stable family, by virtue of their wealth, the honors they receive, their position in society? Does "the bad are now good" mean: "men of good families are now no longer given the positions of honor to which they are entitled," or "men who really have merit are not given appropriate honors," or "good families are no longer producing men of genuine merit" (perhaps because they are ignoring Theognis' own eugenic advice[11]), or something else (or all of the above)?

This passage does not support Nietzsche's specific claims about "evil," but it does indicate a complete dissociation of linguistic usage, with the very same lexical items used to designate that which is completely different, and incompatible. On one usage that was current in Theognis' society, the former wearers of goatskins are "good" (e.g. they are honored in society and get to marry women from the best families); on another they are definitely "not-good" (they are still former wearers of greasy goatskins, and presumably still smell of cheese and garlic and have unattractive personal habits[12]). Nietzsche's first claim is that just as Theognis noticed contradictory uses of "good" (and "bad") in his period, so historically there has been another and philosophically more significant kind of contradictory use of the term "good" in Western moral theory.

In the *Genealogy of Morality* Nietzsche argues that virtually all forms of the moral life in the post-Platonic and post-Christian period in the West, and particularly in the "modern" period, have been inherently both

---

[11] Theognis was keen to ensure that human marriages conformed to the principles of eugenics derived from our knowledge of how to breed the best "rams, asses, and horses"; see Theognis 183–92.

[12] See also a slightly later literary representation in Aristophanes' *Nubes* 41–55 of a similar case to the one envisaged here.

self-deceived and duplicitous in that they *present* themselves as inherently unitary, coherent, and all-encompassing, but are actually a jerry-rigged congeries of potentially incompatible elements. Whatever modern morality is, it is not a form of *Sittlichkeit*, i.e. a coherent form of moral beliefs and habits of individual and social action, much as its representatives might protest to the contrary. The *apparent* unity of "good" as a central concept in morality actually masks the fact that the "good" in question means two very different things: "good" *as the opposite of* "bad" and "good" *as the opposite of* "evil."

The body of the *Genealogy of Morality* gives the well-known development of Nietzsche's historical hypothesis. In the first of three successive treatises he describes the origins of the evaluative pair of concepts "good/evil" out of a process of revaluation of the previously dominant pair "good/bad"; a second treatise treats the way in which humans learned to deal with their aggression by turning it against themselves. The third treatise discusses the role which the ascetic ideal plays in the history of morality in Europe. However, although it is clear that the *Genealogy* is supposed to be an essay in "real" history, of the "grey," dry-as-dust kind, not just a kind of conceptual analysis,[13] it is not so clear what the point of this historical account is supposed to be.

Why is Nietzsche telling us this story? What, if anything, are we supposed to learn from this historical account practically? Is it supposed to change us and the way we live, and, if so, how? In the preface to the *Genealogy of Morality* Nietzsche states that his ultimate aim in undertaking the historical analysis he gives in the body of work was to ask the question of the "value of morality." Western philosophers have for the most part simply *assumed* that morality (in their preferred form) had great or inherent or even absolute value, rather than considering in a spirit of genuine inquiry what kind of value what kind of moral conceptions could be expected to have. One way, then, of seeing Nietzsche's overarching project is as trying to ask two coordinated questions, where previous philosophers asked only one. They asked only "What is the good?," or "What is the final end of human life?," or "What ought I to do?," but really they should have been asking questions of this form *and also* "What value does the good have?," or "What value does doing what I 'ought' to do have?"

To claim, as Nietzsche does, that "modern" morality is not a seamless whole, coherently derivable from a single concept or a single form of valuation, but a disjointed compromise conjunction of various different

[13] *KSA*, 5.254–55.

and potentially incompatible parts might suggest that modern morality is completely chaotic, exhibiting no order or structure at all. The structure it has is not an internal logical order, but a rough-and-ready one imposed on it by one specific element which is dominant, and which coerces the disparate parts into some kind of coexistence. This dominant element has been Christianity. Nietzsche thinks that Christian and post-Christian forms of valuation have had the upper hand historically in the West for a sufficiently long time now for *their* specific form of valuation, which is based on the dichotomy of "good" and "evil," to have a special standing, not just because this is the way in which Western morality has understood itself, but also because moral views based on this dichotomy have had a real effect in making modern Western populations what they are.

Nietzsche does not think that "evil" and the associated conceptions of sin, guilt, etc., are *mere misunderstandings* in the sense in which, say, the belief that I have £1 million in the bank is a simple false belief, of which I can in principle disabuse myself by unprejudiced inspection of my bank statement. Sin and guilt are realities, states of real psychic discomfort rooted in my own somatic constitution. It is merely that these states are not, as Christianity would have it, a universal, necessary part of the human psychic apparatus. Rather they are specific psychic *and somatic* realities that have been produced historically, and have been reinforced, if not generated, by the operation of Christian social institutions which have successfully inculcated them in me. It is extremely important to realize that Nietzsche thinks there is no contradiction between saying that sin has a *somatic* component – it is a state of *physical* discomfort – and also saying that I was caused to acquire this physiological state by the operation of specific historical institutions which were ultimately acting under the guidance of Christian beliefs of various kinds. Hegemonic Christianity, through its institutions, *creates* a kind of person. This means, among other things, that replacing Christian (and post-Christian) moral conceptions will not be as easy as replacing my erroneous beliefs about my financial state with correct ones. Simple observation, the use of empirical methods, and even Socratic dialogue with our own contemporaries – or rather Socratic dialogue between Nietzsche and his contemporaries – won't necessarily do the trick because, by hypothesis, those contemporaries are the fruit of two thousands years of the operation of Christian institutions and have a particular somatic constitution, particular acquired needs, particular forms of feeling, and a particular attachment to certain forms of thinking which one cannot simply suspend or think out of existence. For this reason, Nietzsche thinks, if one wishes to ask his ultimate question about the value of our morality, it is imperative to try to find a standpoint outside our current ordinary language and the usual empirical generalizations we will be inclined to make if we observe our neighbors. He tries to find this in part by studying the "natural history" of moralities, i.e. in a kind of ethnological or anthropological study of other cultures, and also in history. Given his own epistemic situation in the 1870s and 1880s and also his training, the historical approach looms especially large.

Using one of the spatial metaphors which Nietzsche often favors, one might say that to see ourselves and our morality in such a way as to allow us to ask the question about the value of morality, rather than simply reproducing slightly sanitized versions of our own prejudices, requires us to find a position "beyond" that morality, and since good and evil basically structure this morality, a position beyond good and evil. It is, of course, one of Nietzsche's most fundamental tenets that placing oneself beyond "good and evil" does not necessarily mean putting oneself altogether outside the realm of morality – of any conceivable morality. Since "evil," for him, is connected with a highly specific form of negation, being "beyond good and evil" does not necessarily mean being "beyond good and *bad*." In addition, the phrase "put yourself beyond good and evil" is not, for Nietzsche, a universal injunction to all humans telling them how they "ought" to live. First of all, Nietzsche does not believe in a single universal moral code for all humans, secondly he does not believe in a moral "ought," and thirdly he thinks preaching is usually pointless because at the very basic level people don't have much choice in being the sort of person they are. Rather, the injunction ("Forderung")[14] is to *philosophers* to free themselves of the "illusions" of traditional morality. The relation of this philosophical investigation to human practice would need to be further explored, and would repay further discussion.

What about "evil," then? Nietzsche thinks that "evil" is a term which has a complex use:[15]

(a) to designate a certain type of characteristic action which is the natural expression of a certain human type, that is, of human impulses that are associated with the special unreflective vitality of a dominant social group (especially those that inflict harm on a subordinate group);
(b) to interpret actions of the type so designated by relating them to a complex psycho-metaphysics of the soul, freedom, intention, responsibility, and guilt;
(c) to express a contra-attitude (of an appropriate kind) toward actions of that type.

---

[14] *KSA*, 6.98.   [15] *KSA*, 5.270–77.

He also thinks that traditional forms of Christianity-derived moral thinking have made some kind of tacit assumption to the effect that

(d) "good/evil" is not merely *one* evaluative pair, but that it is fundamental, basic, primordial, or definitive.

To put this in terms closer to those developed by some later philosophers, "evil" has an extension or reference, and a meaning, and using the concept expresses an attitude. The extension of the term is archetypically to the actions of a dominant person acting on exuberant human impulses in such a way as to inflict pain, damage, or harm on a weaker subordinate person. The "meaning" is the whole tacit metaphysical theory of human agency which Nietzsche thinks underpins attribution of "evil" to agents. To say that agent X has done something that is "evil" is tacitly to assume that X has an immortal soul which possesses the metaphysical property of freedom of the will, and that X employs this freedom to decide to inflict harm intentionally. It is further tacitly presupposed that X can and should be held responsible for freely acting as he has done, and should feel guilt. In using the term "evil" to designate such an action (or the impulse to perform such an action, or a person who feels such an impulse), I express my own contra-attitude toward it. This "contra-attitude," Nietzsche claims, arises out of my resentment that X is able to act powerfully in ways in which I would like to act myself, if only I did not feel myself too weak to do so successfully and with impunity.

One part of Nietzsche's own detailed account of "evil" is directed at showing that (b) above is a set of untenable beliefs. He takes extremely seriously the fact that, on his view, (b) requires commitment to a full-blown metaphysics of the human subject as fundamentally an immortal soul having a non-empirical property of free will, and he thinks he has shown that no obvious version of that psycho-metaphysics could actually be true. Another part of his discussion purports to show what strong motives people, especially weak members of dominated groups, might have for believing that "evil" is a well-defined and indispensable concept: it allows them to take revenge in thought on those who are stronger than they are, and they in some sense "need" the imaginary sense of power which this conceptual "revenge" gives them. One might think of this account of the motivation for calling some act or some person "evil" as a further part of item (c): the "contra-attitude" was one inherently motivated by a certain kind of vengefulness which arises from a deep-seated need to overcome, even if only in the imagination, one's own sense of comparative weakness.

Let us suppose now for the sake of argument that Nietzsche has demonstrated to our satisfaction that we can no longer hold (b) to be true. One possibility is that "evil" will simply stop being used. After all, the theory on which the application of the concept rests (a metaphysics of human freedom) has been shown to be "refuted." This might conceivably happen, but if Nietzsche's general account is correct it is highly unlikely, given that "evil" refers in a relatively clear way to a recognized set of properties and that its availability and use satisfies a well-entrenched need for a simple way to express our vindictiveness. It is too useful simply to give up. If we did give it up, our underlying need would probably just lead us to create some other lexical items that essentially served the same purpose.

Nietzsche clearly himself thinks that for most people the project of getting rid of *ressentiment* is hopeless, because *ressentiment* arises naturally from weakness and basically one is simply as weak (or as strong) as one is, and there is nothing more to say. "Evil," then will always have a future, at least with the majority of the members of our society. In fact it seems likely that he expects discourse about "evil" to flourish because with the increasing psychological sophistication and devotion to truthfulness which Christianity itself propagates, we will gradually come in some sense to see, or to half-see, the untenability of the metaphysics on which "evil" is based, but will not, because of our need to express our *ressentiment*, be able to give it up. A situation in which we almost-see the internal incoherence of a concept which for deep-seated reasons we simply cannot give up is highly pathogenic. The use of the term "evil" will be likely to become more obfuscated, hysterical, and toxic, as indeed it has.

On the other hand, if we *could* in fact get rid of our underlying need to react to our own powerlessness by venting our aggression on more powerful or uninhibited others through labeling them in this way, we might no longer "need" the term "evil" in the same way. Nevertheless we might think that historically this term has in fact been used to refer to a large number of things that are genuinely especially bad or harmful, although of course they are bad for different reasons from those which would have been cited when Christians characterized them as "evil." The path might be clear for a revaluation of "evil," which might, for all anyone knows, retain the word while reinterpreting its meaning and shifting its extension. Thus we might reserve "evil" for especially serious forms of the bad, or for the intentional infliction of great harm. Or we might have recourse again to Thomas Aquinas and his theory of "capital vices."[16] Thomas held that just as there were (as it were) simple virtues, but also "cardinal virtues," so also there were simple vices and "capital vices."[17] Cardinal virtues were thought to be the

---

[16] *Quaestiones disputatae de malo* Quaestio VIII.
[17] *Quaestiones disputatae de virtutibus* Quaestio V.

"hinges" (*cardo*) on which a good human life turns. That is, they were qualities that were structurally central to the good life, qualities that were not only good in themselves, but that formed the basis of, and brought along in their wake, other good qualities. So, similarly, we might reserve the term "evil" for defects that were not just undesirable in themselves, but also had the property that they tended to bring in their wake many *other* bad things: vices from which other vices arise. Thus, one might think that such things as "censoriousness" or "personal vanity" or "officiousness" were bad human traits, for whatever reason, but also that they did not in themselves generate any further harm; they were simple vices. On the other hand, one might think that "avarice" or "duplicitousness" were both bad in themselves, and also caused those who were afflicted with them to develop other undesirable traits. These were "capital vices." One does not have to find these specific examples convincing to take the underlying general point about certain traits playing a more basic structural role in human life than others. Presenting this theory in a convincing form would, of course, require us to have a view about the good life and its constituents, but Nietzsche would have no objection to that, and we would very likely not call the same things "evil" which our predecessors did. What we would call "evil" under this new scheme would depend on the positive view of the good life which we had formed. Provided that the use of this new term was not connected with imaginary vengefulness, it would effectively be a revalued ("umgewertet") concept, that is a concept based on a form of valuation completely different from that in Christianity. Whether one *calls* this "evil," taking over for convenience the old name, or invents a new name for it, is, for Nietzsche, irrelevant.

So we might carve a niche for a post-Nietzschean concept of "evil" if we meant by that concept simply the idea of intentional action directed at producing something which we thought was especially bad, particularly if we also thought that the agent should have known and prevented the damage or harm in question. We might be extremely open in giving a further specification of what the signal badness in question meant, and also rather open-minded about what "should have known" means. Nevertheless it would not be a foregone conclusion that being "evil" (in the revalued sense) was – hierarchically as it were – the very worst thing there is. Small structural defects in a person's character might not be thought automatically to be worse than anything else one could imagine. An evil but impotent person, that is someone with a psychological disposition to do that which was bad intentionally, but with no particular power to exercise these dispositions, might be thought less of a menace than someone who pursued what he or she genuinely thought was an acceptable political course, but which was in fact very destructive. In that sense "evil" might well have a modest future.

At this point one might be tempted to object that this whole discussion has focused on the *concept* of "evil", or even the term or word "evil," not on the reality. It is one thing to ask whether we will still use the term "polar bear" in thirty years, another to ask whether any polar bears will really have survived the complete melting of the summer ice at the North Pole which we now expect in the near future. This objection misses the point. Evil is not a thing, a substance, or an objective feature of our world; it is nothing like a polar bear or a chemical element or a topographical feature of our earth (such as an isthmus or a promontory). If Nietzsche is right, not only is evil not a thing; it is not originally even an imaginary term that anyone uses to characterize his or her *own* action. The dominant, aggressive masters in Nietzsche's story do not set out to "do evil," and they would originally never have applied the concept at all. "Evil" is an imaginary characterization used by the weak originally to describe the actions of *others* (who are oppressing them) and applied in a spirit of revenge. With the demise of the spirit of vengeance, the monochrome reduction of the world to "good" (light) and "evil" (dark) which it imposed would come to an end, and a world of complex coloration would appear. We would have moved out of the world of bleached white classical statuary into one of highly colored moving images like those in the films of Pasolini or Antonioni. The reflection that many of the "classical" statues were themselves originally clothed in rich fabric and vividly painted might, as Nietzsche hoped it would, help us with the transition. The real question about the future of evil, then, is the question whether we are able to control or get rid of our need for vengeance.

If Nietzsche is right, the traditional Christian ways of trying to get rid of the spirit of vengeance – prayer, fasting, introspection, repentance, sacramental practices, etc. – have shown themselves historically not to work, save perhaps in a few highly exceptional cases. What methods, *if any*, would be effective remains an open question.[18]

---

[18] I should like to thank the members of the audience at the Zeno Lecture which I gave at the University of Utrecht in April 2010 for several clarifying comments which helped me to improve this essay.

CHAPTER 2

On the nobility of Nietzsche's priests

R. Lanier Anderson

This chapter aims to make a limited exegetical point about the first essay of
On the Genealogy of Morality (*GM*),[1] and then to trace its consequences for
Nietzsche's argument about the historical transformation that produced our
current altruistic morality. The textual point is this: the *priests* who figure
importantly in Nietzsche's story are intended to be *unambiguous* instances
of the *noble character type*; they are not to be understood as slaves, or as
inhabiting any ambiguous, intermediate type between noble and slave. My
claim is not new. At least in the context of the first essay, it is a fairly
straightforward textual observation, and it has been marked by commentators (more or less) in passing, with a fair frequency (see e.g. Deleuze [1962]
1983: 126; Nehamas 1985: 121, 120–26; Migotti 1998: 755–56; Ridley 1998a:
44–45; May 1999: 46; Wallace 2007: 122–24; Conway 2008: 33). More
importantly, Bernard Reginster (1997) relied on the observation to do
crucial argumentative work in his path-breaking account of *ressentiment* in
GM, I, which lies in the background of the interpretation I will offer here.
Nevertheless, there remains a tendency to overlook the nobility of

---

[1] In working for this volume, I have largely followed Diethe's translation of the *Genealogy*, but I
sometimes depart from it in the direction of greater literalness or more standard philosophical
usage. I provide Nietzsche's German where my translation choice might be taken to have serious
consequence for the argument, but more often (where they are less decisive) my departures are silent.
In making these adjustments, I was strongly influenced by the choices made in the Clark/Swensen
and Kaufmann translations, which are also listed in the bibliography. For Nietzsche's German, I used
Colli and Montinari 1980–88 (*KSA*). I also made use of the following translations, cited by abbrevia-
tions. Dates of the first German publications appear in square brackets: *Human, All Too Human*, trans.
R. J. Hollingdale ([1878] 1986); *The Gay Science*, trans. Walter Kaufmann ([1882, 1887] 1974); *Beyond
Good and Evil*, trans. Walter Kaufmann ([1886] 1966a); *On the Genealogy of Morality*, trans. Carol
Diethe ([1887] 2007). Also consulted: *On the Genealogy of Morality*, trans. Maudemarie Clark and Alan
Swensen (1998); *On the Genealogy of Morals*, trans. Walter Kaufmann (1968c); and *The Antichrist*,
trans. Walter Kaufmann ([1888] 1954a). Parenthetical citations in the text refer to Nietzsche's section
numbers, which are the same in all editions.

Nietzsche's priests. Our students routinely make the mistake, and even insightful readers of Nietzsche are occasionally drawn into it.[2]

The reasons for oversight here are not far to seek. Classifying the priests as nobles can seem anomalous, given a common account of what is on offer in the first essay. The standard story – it is *so* standard that it amounts to what "everybody knows" about *GM*, I[3] – begins from Nietzsche's claims about a "*slave revolt in morality*" (*GM*, I, 7, 10, *et passim*). Altruistic morality is supposed to have arisen through a revolution against a previously existing "noble pattern of values" that glorified the typical character traits of some privileged class. According to the story, those who were devalued under the "noble" values – the weak, the dispossessed, the "slaves" – resented the privileged class, but, being weak, they lacked the means to strike back at the nobles in any direct way. Eventually, they found a way to revenge themselves *indirectly*, by undermining the basic pattern of values under which the noble way of life was glorified. The resulting "slave revolt" replaced noble values with something close to our current altruistic morality – a set of values demanding respect for the interests of others and equal consideration for all. Morality as we have inherited it is therefore to be understood as a "slave morality," invented in pursuit of this program of "revaluation" (*GM*, I, 7) and motivated by the vengeful desire to deprive nobles of any good conscience in the enjoyment of their privileges and characteristic virtues.

---

[2] Consider, for example, a passing remark of Robert Pippin's, in his important paper on the "lightning/ flash" argument of *GM*, I, 13. The context is Pippin's contention (the general thrust of which I endorse) that Nietzsche's evaluative judgments about the character types he deploys in *GM* (e.g. "noble," "slave," etc.) are more nuanced and qualified than is often appreciated. But as one of his examples, Pippin offers Nietzsche's praise for the priests *as though it constituted a criticism of nobility* (thereby implying that Nietzsche's priests are non-noble):

> Likewise, he [Nietzsche] certainly seems to be criticizing nobility by contrast when he says: "[I]t was on the soil of this essentially dangerous form of human existence, the priestly form, that man first became an interesting animal, that only here did the human soul in a higher sense acquire depth and become evil – and these are the two basic respects in which man has hitherto been superior to other beasts" (*GM*, I:6). (Pippin 2006: 142)

But the priests *are* nobles, not slaves, as Nietzsche makes clear at the beginning of this same section. Thus (*contra* Pippin), praising them cannot count as implicit criticism of nobility via an invidious contrast with non-nobles. The loss of this particular data point does not undermine Pippin's broader conclusions; it is germane to my purposes simply as an example of the tendency for even quite subtle readers of Nietzsche to elide or miss the nobility of the priestly type.

[3] To be clear, the "standard story" I have in mind here is the sort of conventional wisdom we often deploy in shorthand descriptions of Nietzsche's argument in *GM*, I; it is not intended to capture the nuanced variation among different scholarly accounts. That said, some key aspects of the standard story I describe do get quite widespread expression in the literature – notably the idea that primary agency in the slave revolt must belong to the slaves themselves. See the quotations in the text below from Owen 2007 and Leiter 2002, as well as Wallace 2007 and the other references listed in the next two notes.

It is natural, and rather common, to attribute the primary agency in these developments to those Nietzsche describes as "slaves" – after all, it is a *slave* revolt. David Owen offers a clear example of the tendency:

Nietzsche suggests that the slaves' condition is experienced by them as intolerable, generating feelings of *ressentiment*, but since these feelings of *ressentiment* cannot typically (Spartacus notwithstanding) be given outward expression, they turn inward and become creative, which is to say that they seek and find an alternative mode of expression [i.e. the "slave revolt"]. . . . [Through that revolt,] *the slaves have constructed* a general conceptual mechanism . . . *and developed* a general mode of evaluation . . . that allows them to experience a feeling of power. (Owen 2007: 78, 80; my italics)

Even Brian Leiter (despite his general deflationist scruples about agency in Nietzsche; see Leiter 2007) is equally clear that the revolt is the slaves' *doing*: "slaves, unable to take physical action against the sources of their misery (their masters, their oppressors), are driven by their stewing hatred of their masters to do the only thing they can do, create new values, values that devalue the masters, that invert the masters' valuations" (Leiter 2002: 203).

In Nietzsche's own telling of the story, though, it is clear that the priests, too, are supposed to play some important role in the "slave revolt." That is why it seems strange that he classifies them as nobles. Since they are heavily involved in the slave revolt, and since they seem to be so much at odds with the noble values that Nietzsche's genealogy is attempting to bring back to the surface (see *GM*, I, 6), it seems they should be counted as slaves, instead. Commentators are therefore tempted either to write them out of Nietzsche's first-essay story by focusing on the slaves alone, or to count the priests as slaves outright in this context,[4] or else to argue that Nietzsche's treatment of the priests involves some confused, unstable, or ambiguous hybrid of slave and noble characteristics.[5]

I believe that these responses to the apparent anomaly are mistaken, and in fact, that the anomaly is *merely* apparent. The textual evidence makes it quite plain that Nietzsche's priests are intended to be counted as nobles. Moreover, I contend, the *Genealogy* is never confused on the point, and their status was never meant to be ambiguous. On the contrary, the priests'

---

[4] In addition to the example from Pippin (2006: 142), discussed above, see Richardson (1996: 62), whose account of the slave revolt attributes to the slaves something I take to be clearly an achievement of priestly nobles (namely, the Jews' "act of the *most spiritual revenge*," *GM*, I, 7), thereby implicitly counting the priests as slaves.

[5] The most important discussion taking this broad tack is due to Ridley (1998a: 41–63, esp. 45–50), but he is followed in important respects by Janaway (2007: 224–26; see also 81, 92, 99, 101, and 144), and Owen (2007: 78–80, 83–85). I will discuss this subtle interpretive move in section 2.A.

nobility is crucial to their intended role in Nietzsche's account of the slave revolt, which turns out to differ in some subtle ways from the standard story that "everyone knows." Thus, acknowledging the nobility of the priests illuminates the actual structure of the first-essay argument, as well as the nature of Nietzsche's categories "noble" and "slave."

I will begin my defense of these claims by reviewing the textual evidence from *GM*, I, that the priests have to be nobles (section 1). I then explore Nietzsche's motivations for introducing the priests into his first-essay story in the first place, and use that account to clarify the nature of nobility and slavishness for Nietzsche (section 2). Finally, with those results in place, I retell the story with a focus on the role of the priestly nobility, reaching the (perhaps surprising) conclusion that the priestly nobles, so far from being an ambiguous or confused/confusing intermediary type, are supposed to be even *more* noble, in important respects, than the warrior nobles Nietzsche presents as their rivals (section 3).

I. THE NOBILITY OF NIETZSCHE'S PRIESTS: THE TEXTUAL CASE

The textual case for the nobility of Nietzsche's priests is straightforward. Nietzsche initially introduces the priests as nobles (*GM*, I, 6), reinforces that characterization by repetition (*GM*, I, 7), and endorses numerous claims and descriptions that are entailed by it (*GM*, I, 7, 11, 16, *et passim*). I turn now to the details.

Early in *GM*, I, Nietzsche defines nobility through a crucial affective/behavioral marker, plus an associated rule of "*conceptual transformation*" (*GM*, I, 4) that is involved in the birth of noble values. Nobles are characterized by a "*pathos of distance*" (*GM*, I, 2) out of which they create values: "the noble, the mighty, the high-placed and high-minded, who felt and ranked themselves and their actions as good, which is to say, as of the first rank, in contrast to everything lowly, low-minded, common, and plebeian ... claimed for themselves the right to create values" (*GM*, I, 2; cf. *BGE*, 260, 261). Thus, to be noble is to *feel* oneself to be starkly different from, and *higher than*, other people, and then to act on the basis of that affect to posit (and then live up to) standards of achievement proper to one's special, privileged status.

In the beginning, Nietzsche believes, this noble privilege was tied to relatively obvious, externally observable relations of interpersonal dominance or social class standing. But eventually, noble values undergo the "*conceptual transformation*" I mentioned: "the basic concept is 'noble', 'aristocratic' in the class sense [*im ständischen Sinne*], from which 'good' in the sense of 'noble of soul [*seelisch-vornehm*]', 'high-natured soul', 'privileged of soul' necessarily develops" (*GM*, I, 4). Here is the key point: Precisely because the nobles create values *by framing standards of achievement* for themselves, their concepts of praise, which start out as relatively simple social class designations, have a tendency to evolve into normatively loaded terms focalized instead on the "*typical character trait[s]*" (*GM*, I, 5) that enable nobles to do the special things they do and be the special people they are. What begins as merely a set of self-affirmative feelings in a privileged class eventually becomes deepened and internalized into something recognizable as a system of excellences of character, which are typically thought to be united with (and perhaps, a justification for) – but no longer simply identical to – the group's privileged social standing. Nietzsche presents etymological evidence to support his thesis that a conceptual transformation of this sort really did occur, and that it left semantic traces in the evaluative vocabularies of various European languages.[6]

With these ideas about nobility in place, Nietzsche introduces the priests:

> To this rule that the political concept of privilege always resolves itself into a psychological [*seelischen*] concept of privilege, it is not immediately an exception (although it provides occasions for exceptions) when the highest caste is at the same time the *priestly* caste, and hence prefers for its collective designation a predicate that calls to mind its priestly function. There, for example, "pure" and "impure" confront one another for the first time as class designations [*als Ständeabzeichen*], and here too, there comes later the development of a "good" and a "bad" in a sense that is no longer about class [*in einem nicht mehr ständischen Sinne*]. (*GM*, I, 6)

Nietzsche could hardly be clearer about his intentions. From their first appearance in the *Genealogy*, the priests are identified as a noble group ("the highest caste"), and their professed values undergo the same "conceptual transformation" from plain class concepts into virtues of character that Nietzsche sketches for noble values generally. It should therefore come as no surprise when, toward the end of the quoted passage, Nietzsche maps the priestly value judgments about purity and impurity onto the general *noble* pattern of values (based on the opposition, good vs. bad), and not onto the pattern he will attribute to slave morality (good vs. evil). Nietzsche does go on to make various negative rhetorical insinuations about the priestly version of the noble pattern of values: it involves "something *unhealthy*"; the priestly cures offered in response to this unhealthiness are "naïve," or even "dangerous"; the priests are "brooding," "emotionally explosive," and

---

[6] Migotti (1998: 767–70) offers an exploration and defense of this etymological argument.

so on (*GM*, I, 6). None of this, however, detracts from the noble status of the priests or their values. Throughout his discussion, Nietzsche continues to refer to them as a "priestly *aristocracy*" (*GM*, I, 6; my italics), and more importantly, he makes it crystal clear that the priests possess the "*pathos of distance*" that is nobility's official defining mark in *GM*: indeed, "in fact, through them clefts were finally torn open between man and man which even an Achilles of free-spiritedness would shudder to cross" (*GM*, I, 6).

Thus, the priests enter the first-essay story clearly marked as a noble type. Nietzsche never describes a process in which these noble priests lose that status, or degenerate into slaves. On the contrary, his ensuing discussion of the conflict between the priests and the "knightly-aristocrats," or "warrior nobles" – a struggle which results in the priests' rapid and apparently total defeat ("too bad for them when it comes to war!") – only reinforces the point by continuing to refer to the "priestly-*noble* manner of valuation" (*GM*, I, 7; my italics). It is true that Nietzsche quickly pivots to a discussion of "the Jews, that priestly people who in the last resort were only able to gain satisfaction from their enemies and conquerors through a radical revaluation of their values, that is, through an act of the *most spiritual revenge*" – that act being "*the slave revolt in morality*" (*GM*, I, 7). But Nietzsche never asserts that the "priestly people" themselves are slaves in his sense – only that they promoted slave morality in a form which quickly consolidated itself as *another* religion, i.e. Christianity. (His description of the value inversion they promulgated clearly evokes the Sermon on the Mount.[7]) I would be the last to deny that Nietzsche here asserts that the priests make an essential contribution to the slave revolt; indeed, that crucial role of priestly nobles is exactly what sets the interpretive problem of this chapter. But by itself, that contribution is not evidence of their slavishness. To conclude that it was would simply avoid (indeed, beg) my basic question: How (and why) would a group of (priestly) *nobles* promote a slave revolt in morality?

The nature and content of the concepts "noble" and "slave" in Nietzsche's hands is obviously a big part of the issue here. If they were

---

[7] Thus, Nietzsche:

It was the Jews who, rejecting the aristocratic value equation (good = noble = powerful = beautiful = happy = blessed) ventured, with awe-inspiring consistency, to bring about a reversal, and held on to it with the teeth of the most unfathomable hatred (the hatred of powerlessness), saying: "Only those who suffer are good; only the poor, the powerless, the lowly are good; the suffering, deprived, sick, ugly are also the only ones saved, salvation is for them alone – whereas you rich, the noble and powerful, you are in all eternity the evil, cruel, lustful, insatiate, godless, you will also eternally be wretched, cursed and damned!" . . . We know *who* became heir to this Jewish revaluation . . . (*GM*, I, 7; Nietzsche's ellipses)

intended as essentially historical/sociological categories, then the defeat and
subsequent subordination of the priestly caste at the hands of warrior
nobles – however historically underdescribed it remains in Nietzsche's
account – might be sufficient by itself to remove them from the domain
of nobles. In those senses, after all, actual social or political dominance
would arguably be necessary conditions of nobility. But as I just hinted,
Nietzsche's actual first-essay story is characterized by a striking paucity,
perhaps amounting even to a disturbing *absence*, of historical and sociological detail. In fact, he never even quite says outright that the priests *are*
actually defeated by warrior nobles; he leaves that point to our imaginations
("too bad for them when it comes to war!") and our background knowledge
that the main "priestly people" he mentions was in fact conquered by Rome.
Such minimal treatment as he does offer, moreover, deflects attention from
the historical priests and warriors themselves to the contest between
"knightly-aristocratic *value judgments*" and the "priestly-noble *manner of
valuation*" (*GM*, I, 7; my italics). All this suggests rather strongly that for
Nietzsche, the sense of "noble" or "slave" or "priest" that matters is not
historical and sociological, but rather *moral-psychological*. That suspicion is
definitively confirmed by the initial introduction of the noble type canvassed above, which concerned itself centrally with the "conceptual transformation" that mapped strictly class-based terms to characteristically noble
virtues of character. I therefore follow the emerging scholarly consensus
that, in Nietzsche's usage, terms like "noble," "slave," and "priest" are
defined not by their application to concrete social groups, but as *psychological type concepts*, meant to capture characteristic patterns of belief, self-
conception, affect, and (especially) valuing.[8]

But if this is right, then the fact that the priests become "powerless" (*GM*,
I, 7) in a *political* sense after their defeat by the warrior nobles is no evidence
that they have lost nobility. What matters for their psychological type status
is whether they respond to the crisis of powerlessness and subordination in a
noble or a slavish *manner*.[9] A noble, in the grip of the pathos of distance

[8] The point receives essential discussion in Reginster (1997: 285–87, *et passim*), but the influence of this
assumption on discussions of Nietzsche's *Genealogy* has become widespread; see e.g. relevant sections
of Bittner 1994, Ridley 1998a, May 1999, e.g. at 51–52, Leiter 2002, Reginster 2006, Pippin 2006,
Janaway 2007, Owen 2007, Wallace 2007, etc.
[9] Compare the structure of Nietzsche's own concept of "great health" (developed most prominently in
GS, 382; *GS*, Preface; and *EH*, "Why I Am So Wise" and "Why I Am So Clever"). What characterizes
the "great health" is not at all the immediate absence of illness (it is a health "that one does not merely
have but also acquires continually, and must acquire because one gives it up again and again, and must
give it up"; *GS*, 382). Instead, one is healthy in this sense if, *when one falls into illness* (as one inevitably
does), one settles on *reactions* that tend to restore health, rather than deepening the corruption. In this

(and thus a deeply felt conviction of her own superiority), must bridle at any such condition; a slave, by contrast, exhibits acquiescence in subordination. In fact, what *constitutes psychological* slavishness for Nietzsche is precisely the slave's inability to value herself (or in general to adopt beliefs and values that are truly her own), and her consequent adoption of the characteristic values, beliefs, and assessments of the masters who dominate her, even where she is herself devalued by that scheme:

Since time immemorial, in all ... dependent social strata, the common man *was* only what he was *considered*: not at all used to positing values himself, he also attached no other value to himself than his masters attached to him (it is the characteristic *right* of the masters to create values). ... [E]ven now the ordinary man still always *waits* for an opinion about himself and then instinctively submits to that – but by no means always a good opinion; also a bad and unfair one ... (*BGE*, 261)

Now consider, in this light, Nietzsche's description of the priests' reaction to subordination:

Out of this powerlessness their hate swells into something huge and uncanny, into something most spiritual and most poisonous. The greatest haters in world history, also the most ingenious [*geistreichsten*] haters, have always been priests: – compared with the spirit of priestly revenge all the rest of spirit taken together hardly merits consideration. (*GM*, I, 7)

Hyperbole aside – and however different this may seem from some of Nietzsche's more glowing characterizations of other nobles – it must be admitted that this reaction is very far indeed from the submissive acquiescence that is supposed to characterize the slavish mindset. On the contrary, it is the outraged reaction of frustrated nobles, still fully in the grip of their own pathos of distance and railing against the world out of joint that has left them in such a compromised position despite their (self-avowed) *intrinsic superiority*.

One final strand of textual evidence may lead some readers to assimilate the priests of *GM*, I, to slaves, perhaps because it suggests such an invidious evaluation of the priests on Nietzsche's part. The first essay repeatedly describes the priests as "evil." For example, after strenuous complaints about how dangerous they are, Nietzsche "concedes" that

sense, the "great health" is a higher-order condition which includes a sense of one's real needs and dispositions to act on those needs in ways that restore one's healthy equilibrium when it has been disturbed. Likewise here, psychological nobility is construed not as actually exhibited, first-order social privilege, but as a set of attitudes, character traits, and dispositions to react to what happens (including *loss* of privilege) in a noble manner.

with some fairness one could also add that it was on the soil of this *essentially dangerous* form of human existence, the priestly form, that man first became an *interesting animal*, that only here did the human soul in a higher sense acquire *depth* and become *evil* – and of course these are the two basic forms of man's superiority hitherto over other animals! ... (*GM*, I, 6)

He goes on to insist that the priests are "the most evil enemies" (*GM*, I, 7), and that the Christian glorification of love, as the flower of the slave revolt, actually results from the "hatred" proper to the "priestly people," and indeed from "the same impulse with which the roots of that hatred were burrowing themselves ever more thoroughly and greedily down into every-thing that was deep and evil" (*GM*, I, 8).

There is no question that Nietzsche finds the priestly type problematic and dangerous – they promote a moral development he views as cata-strophic – and he clearly intends to pull no rhetorical punches against them in this avowedly polemical book.[10] But it is important to assess his claim that they are "evil" with some care, given the basic argument of the first essay. Recall, noble values, which purport to pick out unequally distributed (and presumably rare) intrinsic excellences of character, are supposed to have been replaced by the slave morality, with its impartial, universal norms of conduct, and Nietzsche captures the two competing evaluative systems through a distinction between the value oppositions good/bad and good/evil. The noble, *good/bad* pattern contrasts the excellent and admirable against the base, contemptible, and worthless, whereas slave morality operates with the *good/evil* opposition between altruistic, other-regarding (moral) goodness, and cruel, selfish, aggressive, desirous *evil*. Since this is the basic rhetorical frame for the entire first essay, Nietzsche keeps the use of these terms under tight control. It is therefore quite striking that he describes the priests as *evil*, rather than *bad*. Why should he adopt the terms of the slave morality to make insinuations about its originators?

The answer becomes obvious as soon as we consider how Nietzsche tries to sharpen up his contrast between the two senses of "good":

---

[10] It is worth noting, in this context, that one of Nietzsche's central rhetorical devices in *GM* is to adapt some of the most manipulative canards and emotionally explosive charges from the literature of anti-Semitic polemics, so as to turn these barbs against the anti-Semites themselves. (The governing thought is that *they* [and their Christian ideology] are among the primary European inheritors and exponents of the *ressentiment*-fueled slave revolt in morals, which is the mother of all secret Jewish conspiracies – the irony of course being that this fact is hidden best of all from them!) The prevalence of this rhetorical strand, and especially its detailed allusions to contemporary anti-Semitic polemical literature, were called to my attention by Elijah Millgram (pers. comm.), who has done important research tracking down these sources in detail. I expect this material will be published in Millgram's future work on *GM*.

[H]ow different are the two words "bad" and "evil," although both seem to be the opposite for the same concept "good"! But it is *not* the same concept "good": on the contrary, just ask yourself *who* is actually "evil" in the sense of the morality of *ressentiment*. Answered in all strictness: *precisely* the "good person" of the other morality, the noble, powerful, dominating one, only re-colored, reinterpreted and re-seen through the poisonous eye of *ressentiment*. (*GM*, I, 11)

With this, the significance of priestly "evil" for our particular question is suddenly transformed. For in this light, the fact that the priests are so consistently described as "evil" (*not* "bad") turns out to be striking evidence *for their nobility*, since the "evil" are "*precisely* the 'good one[s]' of that other morality." Indeed, in the very first description of the priests as evil (the closing lines of *GM*, I, 6, quoted above), Nietzsche clearly intends to *praise* them, despite their dangerousness, exactly because they made humanity "*interesting*," deep, and "*evil*." "Evil" can operate as a term of praise in this context only because it tracks the priests' nobility.[11]

To be clear, it is not my view that Nietzsche himself hereby means to endorse the slave morality or inhabit its judgments "from within" so as to condemn the priestly nobility; on the contrary, once more, he is using "evil" as a term of praise. In addition, I take him to be highlighting a strange form of inner consistency acquired by Christianity under his interpretation. As I have been suggesting, for him the slave morality was invented not by slaves at all, but by priestly nobles – in its paradigmatic Christian form, by the Jews as the archetypal noble priestly people. (He writes, "just compare the peoples with similar talents, such as the Chinese or the Germans, with the Jews in order to feel who are first rank and who fifth rank"; *GM*, I, 16.) But the slave morality consists in the vengeful condemnation of nobility and its pretensions in all their forms. It is therefore only consistent (from Nietzsche's point of view) that the slave morality ought to count the priestly nobility in general, and the Jewish priestly nobility in particular, as evil. Thus, Christian anti-Semitism, steeped as it is in vitriol and extreme *ressentiment*, turns out to be just a consequent expression of the slave morality's hatred of all nobility (as well as a symptomatic manifestation of what is disturbing about that morality). In the inner logic of the slave

---

[11] The passage in question is the same one quoted by Pippin (see note 2, above) in support of his contention that Nietzsche's attitude toward the priests is nuanced and not unqualifiedly negative. Again, I endorse that general conclusion. But as I noted, Pippin himself takes any praise of the priests to involve Nietzsche in a criticism, by way of contrast, directed against nobility as such. This can follow only because Pippin assumes that the priests are not nobles, and there I cannot agree. On the contrary, as we now see, it is *exactly because* Nietzsche is rigorously and consistently construing the priests as nobles that his calling them "evil" can count as any kind of praise in the first place.

morality, it makes perfect (albeit twisted) sense that the quintessential priestly-noble people (and especially its nobility – the high priests, or even the Pharisees[12]) should be condemned as evil, and even that this seed should have been planted in the slave morality in the first place by its Jewish creators themselves. For this very condemnation is a sure marker of the nobility they were so desperate to (re)assert through the vengeful program of the slave revolt![13] Thus, the characterization of the priests as evil, far from suggesting in any way their degeneration into slavishness, stands as simply one final confirmation of their nobility.

2. WHY ARE NOBLE PRIESTS NEEDED FOR THE SLAVE REVOLT?

As we have seen, Nietzsche asserts the nobility of the priests in so many words in *GM*, I, 6–7. Confronted with that evidence, I think most readers will readily concede the *possibility* of a priestly nobility. In that sense, it is probably *mere* oversight that explains why so many scholars (even after Reginster's 1997 discussion) have continued to omit the priestly nobles from descriptions of the slave revolt. That said, the interpretive line I followed

[12] Although the Pharisees might reasonably be taken as an anti-noble party insisting that religious life should not be the special province of the high priesthood, it seems to me likely that Nietzsche would endorse a different interpretation. Focusing on the frequent New Testament depiction of Pharisees as rigorists, he would likely insist that their view especially justifies the idea that the Jewish people *as a whole* (or at least, the law-abiding people) form a nobility, chosen of God, who are pure by contrast to Gentiles (hence the focus of *GM*, I, 7, on the *entire* "priestly people," who [it strikes me] are clearly intended to count as noble, especially in light of *GM*, I, 16). This would feed into Nietzsche's largely cynical interpretation of Saul/Paul, the converted Pharisee (Acts 23:6) who became "Apostle to the Gentiles," thereby infecting *the others* with the slave morality. See following note. (Thanks to Rachel Cristy for historical information and discussion.)

[13] This strand of Nietzsche's view comes out especially clearly in his account of the importance of Paul in *The Antichrist* (see *A*, 24, 40–45, *et passim*), where Paul's interpretation of the significance of Jesus' life and sacrifice is treated as a more or less explicit program for undermining the (fundamentally noble) values and culture of Rome, motivated by revenge on behalf of, and deploying the intellectual resources of, the Jewish priestly nobility in which he was trained. A full discussion of this reading of *A* must await another occasion, but the basic idea is present in *GM*, as well. Consider Nietzsche's treatment of the slave revolt as a more or less explicit, cynical political program for Jewish revenge against Rome in the last few sentences of *GM*, I, 8. These texts convince me that, *contra* Wallace, a "strategic" *element* must be built into our understanding of the slave revolt from the ground up, and not as a secondary phenomenon (see Wallace 2007: 112–26, esp. 122–24, *et passim*). I do concede Wallace's main point, however, that for most of its participants (in my view, *including* most of the priestly-noble *inventors* of the slave morality), the *mechanism* by which the revolt operates is not clear-eyed, cynical, instrumental strategizing, but instead the one he identifies, exploiting indirect, uncon-scious or dimly conscious *expressive* relations between emotional orientation and values. For just this reason, moreover, I believe that the work the slave morality does for the priests themselves involves a certain amount of self-opacity and self-hatred, which seems to me somewhat underappreciated in Wallace's own account.

above also suggests some stronger conclusions – namely, that the *Genealogy* conceives the priestly type *as such* as a special case of noble, and that these priestly nobles played a *large and indispensable* role in framing the slave revolt in morality, *displacing the agency of the slaves* themselves in that development. Insofar as they go beyond acknowledging the bare possibility of priestly nobles based on *GM*, I, 6–7, these claims are more controversial: after all, Nietzsche himself concedes that even though priests *need not* be an exception to the general rule that high castes endorse noble valuation, the type does "provide occasion for exceptions" (*GM*, I, 6).[14] So not all priests are nobles, and perhaps any who contribute to the slave revolt, in particular, should not be counted as (fully) noble.

One strand from the recent literature offers sophisticated resistance along these lines against the stronger implications of my interpretation. Aaron Ridley concedes that the priest is officially presented as a noble type (Ridley 1998a: 44–45, 48, 50), but insists nevertheless that Nietzsche's character-ization of the priests incorporates slavish elements as well, so that his overall view of the priestly type is ambiguous, or even a fundamentally confused amalgam of noble and slave (Ridley 1998a: 45–46, 50, 61). Ridley's inter-pretation has been influential, followed at least in part (or in qualified form) by Owen (2007: 78–80, 83–85) and Janaway (2007: 224–29). Owen, indeed, goes so far as to assert that the sort of Reginster-inspired reading of *GM*, I, that I prefer "goes down something of a blind alley in making the crux of Nietzsche's critical argument hang on the claim that it is the priest who initiates the slave revolt in morality" (Owen 2007: 168, n. 16 to p. 85).

I begin by setting out the key details of Ridley's interpretation of the priests, and raising a few questions about it (section 2.A). I then offer an alternative reading (section 2.B), based on a claim about why Nietzsche felt the need to introduce a priestly nobility into his account of the slave revolt in the first place.

A. *The priest as hybrid of noble and slavish traits?*

I concede from the outset that I find much of Ridley's treatment of the *Genealogy* not just ingenious, but insightful. Indeed, its interpretive care is manifest in the forthright way it confronts the textual evidence for priestly

---

[14] For reasons that will become clear, I presume that some, perhaps many or even most, of the priests who have served at the head of Christian communities once the slave morality was well established should in fact be counted among these exceptions – priests who do not exhibit psychological nobility in the crucial sense of creating values of their own or endorsing their own values in a strong and naïve sense.

nobility, and also (what Ridley takes to be) the evidence for priestly slavishness, without ducking the interpretive problems that result. Still, I find the thesis of noble/slave ambiguity within the priestly character type unconvincing.

Ridley's conclusion – that Nietzsche finds himself backed into character-izing the priests in slavish terms – is motivated in the main by conceptual considerations. As I noted, he concedes the textual point that Nietzsche officially presents the priests as nobles. But he cannot accept the apparent consequence that nobles should take part in the slave revolt on their own account. Instead, he suggests, they might at most be involved in "orches-trating" it, or otherwise promoting it "from the outside":

the priest ought not to be seen as a *participant* [my italics] in the first stage of the revolt ... [since] "the priestly caste and the warrior caste" are identified as two distinct kinds of noble (GM I.7). As a noble, the priest already affirms himself for what he is, and so has no immediate personal interest in overturning the noble scheme of values. So if he does orchestrate the first stage of the revolt, he does so for rather remoter reasons than those of its participants. (Ridley 1998a: 44–45)

The key background assumption motivating Ridley's distinction of the backstage "orchestrating" role from full-fledged "participation" concerns the defining conceptual features of slavishness. Ridley assumes that to be a slave is to have a particular moral psychology whose needs and interests are distinctively served by the *ressentiment* revaluation. Anyone who whole-heartedly assumed an active, creative role in the slave revolt must inhabit that psychology, and the person *thereby counts* as a slave. That is why the quoted passage can take the bare fact that the priests are nobles as *sufficient* to disqualify them as "participants" in the slave revolt. The creative inspira-tion and active prosecution of that development must (by definition) come from slaves. Naturally, since I take the slave revolt to have been conceived by priestly nobles, I reject any conceptual identification of wholehearted participation in that development with slavishness. I offer an alternative conceptualization in the next subsection.

Sensitive to the text as he is, Ridley himself cannot overlook the extensive role played by the priests (and the "priestly people") in Nietzsche's actual first-essay story about the revolt. That role creates serious textual tensions for his conceptually motivated effort to minimize their "participation" in the *ressentiment* revaluation. The difficulty can be stated as a trilemma: the priests are nobles; but they seem to participate essentially in the slave revolt; and full involvement in the slave revolt is sufficient for slavishness (hence, incompatible with nobility). Ridley's response to the difficulty is twofold.

First, to blunt the trilemma's first horn, he suggests that Nietzsche fails to maintain full control over his own conceptual apparatus, and ineluctably slides into treating the priests as slavish when accounting for the their contributions to the slave revolt. Sometimes, this line amounts to no more than a restatement of the conceptual point just rehearsed.[15] But Ridley also suggests some more particular psychological features that the priests are supposed to share with slaves. For example, they react to the "internalization" brought on by living under customs with "thoughtfulness, inwardness" (Ridley 1998a: 47) and "brooding . . . emotional explosions" (*GM*, I, 6), rather than physically acting out their aggressions. This makes them "repressed" (*GM*, I, 7), "sick" (*GM*, III, 15), and filled with *ressentiment*, like the slaves (Ridley 1998a: 49, 50).

I am unconvinced by this line. Ridley's suggestion relies on Nietzsche's discussions (from *GM*, II) of "internalization" and its promotion of complex inner life, but these treatments are never expressly restricted to the slave type (see esp. *GM*, II, 1–3, 16–19). Nietzsche does suggest that the "shapeless population" (*GM*, II, 17) of common people was brought under the "confines of society and peace" (*GM*, II, 16) in an especially rapid and violent way, and therefore suffered from the loss of external outlets for aggression in a very stark form. But the general problem of living under customs applies to *everyone* who "finds himself imprisoned once and for all within the confines of society and peace" (*GM*, II, 16), and Nietzsche makes a special point of indicating ways that paradigmatic *nobles*, too, come to terms with it (see particularly, *GM*, II, 1–2, on the right to make promises; and II, 19, 23, on the noble use of gods to keep bad conscience "at arm's length," which would be unnecessary if nobles simply were not subject to "internalization" at all).[16] *Ressentiment* itself is a separate and more complicated matter and receives attention below; for now, I simply reiterate that the whole question at stake here is *whether* abiding *ressentiment* and its characteristic evaluative reaction against the noble morality is essentially slavish, or whether it might not, as Reginster (1997) argued, come to characterize a noble group under special, unfavorable circumstances.

---

[15] Thus, for example, just after the passage I quoted in the text above, Ridley goes on to complain that Nietzsche's account of the priests ends up being "contradictory" (Ridley 1998a: 45), containing elements of both nobility and slavishness. But the primary element of slavishness cited in that discussion is *just* that they are crucially involved in the slave revolt. That feature counts as slavish only because of the conceptual identification of slave status with contributing to the slave revolt as a "participant." This assumption, of course, makes it a presupposition that anyone who invents and promotes such a slave revolt cannot be a noble. I take this to beg the question I am trying to pose.

[16] See also the following note.

Ridley's second, more important, move in response to the trilemma is to insist that the slave revolt in morality must be understood as a two-stage affair (Ridley 1998a: chapters 1 and 2). In its first, "immanent" phase, the slaves themselves (with or without the help of the priests – Ridley [1998a: 44] thinks it doesn't matter) confront not only their oppression by nobles, but more fundamentally, the basic human problem of living under customs and social rules. As we saw, they are violently "imprisoned within the confines of society and peace" (*GM*, II, 16), and their natural aggressive drives are denied any external outlet. Nietzsche famously conjectures that, as a result, these aggressive drives *"turn themselves inwards"* (*GM*, II, 16), producing exacerbated *ressentiment*, as well as more straightforward forms of psychological self-torture. Nobles are "imprisoned within the confines of society" just as much as slaves, of course, but Ridley argues that they retain access to a release for aggressive instincts, namely, exercising them against "the foreign world" (*GM*, I, 11) – either against those outside the community, or against the slaves, who are not their equals.[17] In nobles, therefore, *ressentiment* "exhausts itself in an immediate reaction," and does not *"poison"* the conscience (*GM*, I, 10). By contrast, the slaves' *ressentiment* does build up under the pressure of undischarged aggression, and eventually it "becomes creative and gives birth to values" (*GM*, I, 10). Ridley identifies three crucial conceptual innovations proper to this immanent phase of the slave revolt: the distinction between doer and deed (*GM*, I, 13), the idea of free will (*GM*, I, 13), and the moralized conception of guilt (*GM*, II, 21). With these notions in hand, he argues, the slaves are able to separate the nobles' particular actions from the *"typical character trait[s]"* that constitute noble virtue, and then hold the nobles responsible for the acts (since they

---

[17] Ridley has in mind the famous passage,

The same people who are so strictly held in check *inter pares*, by custom, respect, habit, gratitude, and still more by mutual spying and jealousy, and who on the other hand in their behavior toward one another show themselves so resourceful in consideration, self-control, delicacy, loyalty, pride, and friendship, – they are not much better than uncaged beasts of prey toward the outside world . . . There they enjoy freedom from every social constraint; in the wilderness they compensate for the tension that comes from being closed in and fenced in for so long within the peace of the community; they *return* to the innocent conscience of the wild beast, as exultant monsters, who perhaps come away from a hideous succession of murder, arson, rape, and torture with such high spirits and equanimity that it seems as if they have only played a student prank, convinced that the poets will have something to sing about and celebrate for years to come. (*GM*, I, 11)

I note, however, that even though these nobles are depicted as gaining some affective compensation for the repression involved in life under customs, it is just not true, on Nietzsche's account, that they are exempt from that repression. On the contrary, it is the source of their primary cultural achievements, as the beginning of the passage makes clear. For this reason, it is implausible to take repression and what Nietzsche calls "internalization" (*GM*, I, 6; II, 16) as markers of the slave type. They are just as characteristic, and maybe in some ways *more* characteristic, of the nobles.

could have done otherwise). The slaves thereby attain a framework within which it is possible to affirm themselves as "good" (since they do not act aggressively like the nobles), and more centrally for Nietzsche, they also gain an expressive outlet for their *ressentiment*, at least in imagination, through condemnation of noble misconduct (Ridley 1998a: 26–40).

The priests enter Ridley's story only in a second, "transcendentalizing" stage (Ridley 1998a: 41ff.). While the first phase of the revolt offered some satisfaction for the slaves' *ressentiment*, the revenge it provides remains largely imaginary, since the two main real sources of the slaves' suffering – oppression by the dominant nobles and the social demand to repress their aggressive instincts – are not at all altered through moralistic indignation by itself. According to Ridley, the priests are able to offer an important additional consolation, based on other-worldly considerations. These, too, do not actually *remove* the slaves' suffering (that would be asking too much), but they at least *explain* it.[18] The explanation as Nietzsche reconstructs it is strange and interesting. In short, the priest proposes that as custom-bound, reflective animals suffering from repressed aggression, we should understand our suffering as a *punishment* for our being the sorts of creatures we are, or even for *existing at all* (*GM*, III, 15). This solution consistently extends the psychological formations built up already in the first phase, since now *ressentiment*, too, is redirected inward just like the rest of our instincts (Ridley 1998a: 56–57). In addition, it has the advantage of offering a *generalized* explanation for all suffering, since it identifies a blameworthy target of *ressentiment* that is bound to be accessible in every single instance – i.e. the sufferer herself (see Ridley 1998a: 53–54). Precisely the universal generalization, however, is what requires transcendentalizing ideas supplied by the priests: If what is blameworthy in me is no longer restricted to some particular acts (in which I perhaps behaved more or less like the aggressive nobles), but instead now extends to encompass everything I do and indeed my existence as such, then, plausibly, I will need to find my whole mode of existence wanting *by contrast* to some other, more perfect way of being.[19] The priest, with his access to transcendent insights, is needed to offer such

---

[18] And Nietzsche insists that such explanations are valuable indeed, since "suffering itself was *not* his problem . . . Man, the bravest animal, . . . does *not* negate suffering as such: he *wills* it, he even seeks it out, provided he is shown a *meaning* for it" (*GM*, III, 28).

[19] This last conclusion that *there must be* another world is plausible, but notice that (*contra* Ridley?) it is not actually required by the argument. Indeed, Nietzsche himself would have been acutely aware of the escape route available in the logical space of possibilities, since it is provided precisely by *Schopenhauer's* pessimism. In that version of the ascetic ideal, the work of condemning our mode of existence is done completely by the negative value judgment leveled against it, *without* the benefit of invidious comparison to some more blessed state. Our life of incessant desiring is globally assessed

an "otherworldly solution to the problem of this-worldly suffering" (Ridley 1998a: 57).

With this two-phase picture of the slave revolt in place, Ridley can reconcile the three commitments that jointly produced tension for his view: (1) the official nobility of the priests, (2) their key role in the slave revolt, and (3) his insistence that active "participation" in the revaluation demands psychological slavishness. For now he is free to suggest that the first phase of the revolt – the one whose essential motivation rests on the psychological consequences of oppression as a slave – involves the priests only in some accidental and remote way, if at all. The priests become essential only in the second, transcendentalizing phase, where they merely build on a psychological foundation already laid down at stage one. Thus, the priests need not inhabit the slave's psychology, or even understand it "from within" so as to invent a value system responsive to its needs. All they need do is to sympathize with the slaves' situation enough to grasp a lack in a value system the slaves have already developed – a lack which the priests fill, moreover, in just the spirit one might expect from nobles, i.e. precisely as a route to establish power for themselves ("*Rule over the suffering* is [the priest's] realm"; *GM*, III, 15).

The solution is elegant, but it goes far beyond anything the *Genealogy* makes explicit. Indeed, it even forces Ridley to take some key moments in the text as simply confused. For example, of the point when Nietzsche introduces the priestly nobles (*GM*, I, 6) and then immediately (I, 7) indicates their participation in the slave revolt, Ridley writes, "I think we should take GM I.7 to mark a moment at which Nietzsche was simply trying to do too much at once. The whole of the slave revolt (both phases) is presented here in the most compressed form, and if distinctions [e.g. between noble and slave] are elided and valuations conflated as a result, one ought not perhaps to be too surprised" (Ridley 1998a: 46).

But if, instead, we rejected the two-phase interpretation altogether and found another resolution for the problem posed by the nobility of the priests, then perhaps there would be no need to find such confusion. And in fact, that problem admits of a far simpler solution. If we simply abandon Ridley's third commitment – the conceptual identification of psychological slavishness with participation in the slave revolt – then matters become much more straightforward. The priests are nobles, just as Nietzsche says; and they not only participate in, but are even primarily responsible for the

as an unmitigated evil, but as the ringing conclusory lines of *The World as Will and Representation* make clear, there is no alternative mode of existence to save us – or perhaps better, the superior alternative to this life is . . . precisely nothing.

slave revolt, just as Nietzsche says; and that is just fine, because being a *creator of slave values* is not the same as *being a slave*. I will try to motivate this alternative by highlighting a different explanation of why Nietzsche introduces the priests into *GM*, I, in the first place, and drawing out its consequences for our understanding of the nature of the noble and slave types.

B. Why did Nietzsche introduce the priests, anyway?

Nietzsche notes in the *Genealogy*, Preface, that the basic idea of some distinction between a "master morality" and a "slave morality" was by no means new to that work (*GM*, Preface, 4). Already in *Human, All Too Human*, he had advanced a similar hypothesis about the "twofold prehistory of good and evil" (*HAH*, I, 45), and the idea gets prominent development in *Beyond Good and Evil* (*BGE*, 260–61). Returning to these earlier statements from the point of view of our present problem, what is most striking is the complete absence of the priests (or any parallel type) from Nietzsche's original conception. Instead, one finds simpler accounts, reminiscent of the standard story I rehearsed at the outset, or Ridley's "first phase" of the slave revolt. Thus, in the "twofold prehistory" of *HAH*, we find a good/bad-type morality originating among noble castes, contrasted against a morality rooted in fear that originated "in the soul of the subjected, the powerless" (*HAH*, I, 45). Or again, simply, "The moral discrimination of values has originated either among a ruling group whose consciousness of its difference from the ruled group was accompanied by delight – or among the ruled, the slaves and dependents of every degree" (*BGE*, 260). In neither case is any room carved out for a priestly caste, and in both cases full agency in the development of slave morality is attributed to the slaves themselves: in these accounts, Nietzsche is asking what happens when "the violated, oppressed, suffering, unfree, who are uncertain of themselves and weary, moralize" (*BGE*, 260).

In light of what we have seen about the *Genealogy*, these older formulations raise a pressing question: *Why* did Nietzsche introduce the priests into the *Genealogy* story at all, and then place such emphasis on their role, when they had no place in his initial conception? What new problem are the priests there to solve? Interestingly, the answer will turn out to provide some compelling evidence about the proper defining marks of the noble and slavish types.

We can take a clue from a second element that goes missing from Nietzsche's early distinction between master and slave moralities. Along with all discussion of the priests, *HAH* and *BGE* lack any account of the *transition* from the noble pattern of valuation to the slave morality. The early accounts perhaps *hint* at the temporal priority of noble to slave values. But in *Human, All Too Human*, the suggestion is thin indeed. (Nietzsche presents his "twofold prehistory" this way: "*firstly* in the soul of the ruling tribes and castes. . . . – *Then* in the soul of the subjected, the powerless" [*HAH*, I, 45]; there is nothing more about temporal order, and even the "first . . . then" structure could be intended to mark a merely discursive, not a temporal ordering.) Temporal priority is more developed in *Beyond Good and Evil*: "It is obvious that moral designations were everywhere first applied to *human beings* [in the form of noble character traits, one assumes] and only later, derivatively, to actions"; and perhaps there is a suggestion that slave morality operates *in reaction to* a noble ethic already in place – "The slave's eye is not favorable to the virtues of the powerful; he is . . . *subtly* suspicious of all the 'good' that is honored there" (*BGE*, 260). But in neither case is there anything like the historical story demanded by the project of genealogy, which aims to explain *how* the radical transition from a dominant master morality to the slave morality could have taken place. Plausibly, then, Nietzsche found it necessary to introduce the priests when he set himself seriously to the task of explaining the transition involved in the revaluation of values, moving from a bare *distinction* between two value patterns to the story of a *revolution* through which one replaces the other.

Why, then, should such a story need priests at all, much less a priestly nobility, with all its complications? After all, as we have seen, the standard story about the slave revolt that "everyone knows" often happily leaves them out (see e.g. Leiter 2002: 202–4). The very next section of *Beyond Good and Evil* reveals the premise that gave Nietzsche trouble. We met it already above, in our efforts to separate questions of sociohistorical or political subordination from the distinctively moral-psychological senses of slavishness or nobility:

Since time immemorial, in all . . . dependent social strata, the common man *was* only what he was *considered*: not at all used to positing values himself, he also attached no other value to himself than his masters attached to him (it is the characteristic *right* of the masters to create values). . . . even now the ordinary man still always *waits* for an opinion about himself and then instinctively submits to that – but by no means always a good opinion; also a bad and unfair one . . . (*BGE*, 261)

The same ideas remain crucial in the *Genealogy*: nobles are defined from the outset as those who "claimed for themselves the right to create values" (*GM*,

I, 2), and slaves as those who accept the values imposed on them from above – for example, the slaves "adapted themselves to the cult of the gods practiced by their masters, whether through compulsion or through submission and mimicry" (*GM*, II, 20). Thus, insofar as the noble/slave distinction detaches itself from external relations of actual political dominance and becomes "spiritualized" into a moral-psychological contrast between character types, the distinction comes to depend *crucially* on the idea that nobles create values for themselves, and slaves submissively accept them from others.

With this premise in place, however, the very idea of a "slave revolt in morality" becomes very hard to explain, or even to understand. For if it is anything, the *ressentiment* revaluation is an episode of value creation: "The slave revolt in morality begins when *ressentiment* itself *becomes creative* and *gives birth to new values*" (*GM*, I, 10; my italics). But if the capacity to create values is constitutive of nobility, then no slave could carry out such a revaluation. Anyone who did *that* would *eo ipso* prove herself to be noble. After all, what matters for moral-psychological nobility is not anything so obvious as birth, or actual political standing, but the deep-going self-confidence that allows one to take one's own new ideas as a standard that must be lived up to: "What is noble? . . . It is not actions that prove him – actions are always open to many interpretations . . . It is not the works, it is the *faith* that is decisive here . . . some fundamental certainty that a noble soul has about itself" (*BGE*, 287) – the sort of faith in oneself that allows one to create new values. For Nietzsche, then, the slave revolt has to be a deep mystery. Only the psychologically noble could ever create values. But why would any noble soul create the sort of values *appropriate for slaves?* Creating such values should be unthinkable. And yet they most certainly exist.[20]

The thrust of my hypothesis will by now be obvious. When Nietzsche set about to explain how slave morality arose through the revaluation of a pre-existing noble pattern of values, he immediately confronted a problem: according to his own theory of value creation – a theory built into his conceptions of nobility and slavishness from the ground up – creating values was incompatible in principle with psychological slavishness. The priestly nobility was introduced to get around exactly this problem, and that is why Nietzsche is so keen to insist that his priests are nobles. As nobles they share the capacity to create values. But as we will see in section 3, the priestly nobility is especially vulnerable to corruption, because they can be

---

[20] As I mention in note 34, this puzzle was first called to my attention by Alexander Nehamas. It was the source of the ideas in this chapter.

conquered with no loss to their nobility.[21] And then their political and cultural subordination by warrior nobles can warp the process of value creation, which would normally ground new values on self-affirmation and self-glorification. Instead, the energy of value creation is diverted to expressing vengeful feelings: "the priestly people ... in the last resort was only able to gain satisfaction from their enemies and conquerors through a radical revaluation of their values, that is, through an act of the *most spiritual revenge*" (*GM*, I, 7). To revenge themselves on their happy foes – or at least to give vent to their frustrations – they invent a new set of values that condemns the noble happiness they are now excluded from, and even aims to corrupt the very values of their enemies by seducing them into valuing something contemptible, something fit for *slaves*. They invent the *slave morality*.[22]

I defer further description of this process to section 3, but the present sketch is already sufficient to suggest a more complete conceptual determination of the noble and slave types. Section 1 pointed to three apparently different ideas. First, I emphasized Nietzsche's initial, official characterization of nobility in terms of the pathos of distance, and then second, the "*conceptual transformation*" (*GM*, I, 4) that mapped noble class concepts into psychologically focalized concepts picking out excellences of character. Later on, I emphasized certain attitudes constituting the (affirmative or negative) relation between a person and her values or key self-regarding beliefs: a person who passively accepts values and self-conceptions thrust on her from abroad is slavish; by contrast, a noble person creates or endorses values of her own.

In fact, all three ideas belong together as a single package. The pathos of distance is in part a feeling of superiority over others, but that superiority is

---

[21] Defeat makes them no whit less *pure*, which is the decisive mark of their nobility. I discuss this point further, below.

[22] I here follow Wallace (2007) in claiming that the motivation for this act of value creation is not strictly strategic, even though (for me) it does include (perhaps more in the mode of hope than of planning) the distant goal of obtaining revenge against the happy. The key work that revaluation does for the slave morality's inventors more immediately is to *express* their frustration and hatred of their enemies, in the form of moralistic condemnation. To gain this benefit, however, the priests have to begin to *internalize* the slave values. To the extent that internalizing those values would corrupt their noble enemies (and thereby count as revenge), it also corrupts them (since they are noble), and in this respect, they *sacrifice themselves* to their project of revenge (and vengeance expression). While Wallace seems to find this consequence (i.e. that the invention of slave morality is self-sacrificing/self-defeating from the ground up) unacceptable, it seems to me both psychologically plausible (as a response of nobles who have *given up hope* of any success or revenge through more conventional open conflict), and to fit with Nietzsche's own description of the *ressentiment* priests, whose revaluation involves a complicated and self-opaque mixture of self-contempt and self-hatred along with noble self-assertion.

clearly supposed to arise out of an attitude of self-affirmation tied to a self-regarding form of value creation: the noble "felt and ranked themselves and their actions as good, which is to say, as of the first rank, in contrast to everything lowly, low-minded, common, and plebeian. It was from this *pathos of distance* they first claimed for themselves the right to create values" (*GM*, I, 2).[23] The conceptual transformation of class concepts into virtues of character is likewise bound to the same underlying attitudes of self-affirmation and value creation. For as we saw, the nobles create values by framing standards of achievement for themselves, and then living up to them, in a process that involves self-directed attitudes of honoring, or self-affirmation. That process drives the conceptual transformation Nietzsche describes. At the deepest level, then, nobility consists in an interconnected set of self-affirmative attitudes that enable the noble person to create values that are her own: again, "It is not the works, it is the *faith* that is decisive here . . . some fundamental certainty that a noble soul has about itself . . . *The noble soul has reverence for itself*" (*BGE*, 287).

What matters for the noble/slave contrast, then, is not (*contra* Ridley) whether a person participates in the slave revolt, or whether she is stuck in the grip of *ressentiment*, but instead, her more basic psychological *capacity* for value creation and self-endorsement. It is not about *which* values govern her life (i.e. which *content* those governing values carry), but rather about her *manner* of relating to those values, about the underlying moral-psychological structure that determines the person's relation to her values. With this way of drawing the contrast, the way is open for a noble (i.e. value-creating) type to invent values that *answer to the needs* and interests of the *slavish* type. The creation of slave values becomes possible. It is now time to turn to a quick account of how and why it happens.

3. THE SLAVE REVOLT, AND THE *SUPERLATIVE* NOBILITY OF THE PRIESTS

My understanding of the slave revolt in morality largely follows Reginster (1997), particularly concerning the nature of *ressentiment* and its place in the moral psychology of the priests.[24] My own telling will focus on specific

---

[23] A parallel discussion is prominent in the *BGE* account of "master morality": "The noble type of man experiences *itself* as determining values; it does not need approval; . . . it knows itself to be that which first accords honor to things; it is *value-creating*" (*BGE*, 260).

[24] Since I can offer only a quick sketch, readers should consult Reginster 1997 for more detail, as well as the extension of the ideas in Reginster 2006: 251–60. My view, like Reginster's (2006) update, has also been strongly influenced by Wallace's (2007) distinction between strategic and expressive

points where the noble status of the priests does argumentative work. It will be useful to begin with a recap of what we have established so far.

In the standard story of the slave revolt, primary agency remains firmly with the slaves themselves, who hatch a clever plot to revenge themselves on their oppressors – or at least express their frustration – through an attack on the value system that glorifies the noble way of life. They invent a new, altruistic value system demanding equal respect for the interests of all – the slave morality. The new values justify sweeping moral condemnation of the nobles, thereby affording expression for the slaves' *ressentiment*, and at the same time they offer the slaves terms on which they can affirm themselves as "good," by contrast with "evil" nobles. Thus, the standard story identifies two distinct motivations for the slave revolt: it gives needed vent to the slaves' vengeful affects, and it permits them a newfound opportunity for self-affirmation.

But as we saw, the standard story conflicts with the theory of value creation Nietzsche built into his psychological conceptions of nobility and slavishness. According to that view, the invention of new values (of the sort paradigmatically involved in the slave revolt) is a constitutive mark of psychological nobility, so Nietzsche's categories cut against the primary agency of slaves in value creation that is at the heart of the standard story. I suggested that Nietzsche introduced the priests for just this reason, as nobles who usher in the slave morality for reasons of their own. But what are those reasons? Why should a class of nobles promote new values so radically different from the noble values through which they could express their own distinctive virtues and "pathos of distance" (*GM*, I, 2)?

The beginning of Nietzsche's answer is apparent from his first introduction of the priests in *GM*, I, 6–7. There Nietzsche is keen to emphasize, alongside the nobility of the priests, *how different* a priestly nobility is from the paradigmatic classes of nobles he appealed to when first describing the noble pattern of valuation. Of course, the priestly nobles have their own specific version of the good/bad value pattern – they value the "pure" over the "impure" (*GM*, I, 6) – but this fact does not yet separate them from nobles in general, all of whom develop some more determinate conception of "good" through which the "main nuance" of their particular, self-conceptualized superiority gains expression (they are "the strong," or "the

interpretations of the slave revolt; I believe it is possible to take on board Wallace's point that the revaluation crucially operates through an *expressive mechanism*, without abandoning the idea that it has certain (suitably opaque and long-term) strategic goals. A full discussion of Wallace's subtle view must await another occasion, but some indications of the direction of my response will emerge here and in the conclusion.

rich," "the truthful," "the courageous," etc.) (*GM*, I, 5). With the priests, however, Nietzsche quickly pivots to some unhappy consequences unique to the priestly version of the pathos of distance: "the very nature of an essentially priestly aristocracy admittedly makes it clear why it was precisely here that contradictory valuations could so soon become internalized and heightened in a dangerous manner"; "From the very beginning there has been something unhealthy about these priestly aristocracies"; "With the priests simply *everything* becomes more dangerous"; and so on (*GM*, I, 6). While all noble valuation involves the internalizing conceptual transformation of class discriminations into "psychological concepts of privilege" (*GM*, I, 6), in the priestly case, this internalization is more extreme, promoting a more "inward" and "brooding" type. It thereby detaches the conception of excellence more decisively from actual class domination and external action. That is supposed to be "dangerous" and "unhealthy" for the priestly nobles themselves. As a result, Nietzsche insists, "One will already have guessed how easy it was for the priestly manner of valuation to split off from the knightly-aristocratic and then develop into its opposite" (*GM*, I, 7). It is open to question how easy this would be to guess,[25] but what matters for us is just this: the priests are *so* different from other nobles that with them, the possibility emerges of a certain kind of *basic incommensurability* operating *within* the domain of noble patterns of value.

A quick and dirty thought experiment can expose the sort of incommensurability at issue. Nietzsche focuses attention on a conflict between priestly- and knightly-aristocratic cultures (*GM*, I, 7), but quite obviously, his framework also envisions conflict between other types of noble groups. Already in his earliest treatments of the idea, Nietzsche emphasized the possibility: in noble morality, "One does not regard the enemy as evil: he can requite. In Homer the Trojan and the Greek are both good" (*HAH*, I, 45). So, imagine a conflict between two groups of "knightly" or warrior nobles who share the same version of the good/bad noble value pattern: each values the strong and has contempt for the weak. Such a conflict will quickly come to blows, and eventually, one side prevails (Troy falls, say, and the Greeks enslave the remaining Trojans). But what transpires at the more abstract level of the two value systems? The defeated Trojans will naturally be

---

[25] I agree here with Ridley (1998a: 45) that it is *not at all* easy or obvious, in fact, how this transition is supposed to work. In fact, the opening sentence of *GM*, I, 7, has always stood in my mind as a textbook example of the interpretive principle that where the philosopher says something of the form, "And now *obviously* we can see that . . ." it tends to be *exactly there* that the real difficulty in the argument under consideration lies – the emphasized "*obviously*" having been wheeled in precisely to smooth over some gap!

disappointed by the actual outcome, but it puts no pressure whatsoever on their *value system itself*, on the contrary, it is reinforced. There was a test of strength, and the stronger side prevailed. By their own lights, things are as they should be; the strong are on top, and the weaker (i.e. they themselves, as was proved in the event) are subordinated and enslaved. Remarkably, there is a certain parallel *in result* between this case and the natural upshot of interactions between warrior nobles and slaves, given what we saw above about the slavish mindset. Slaves, recall, are characterized by submissive acquiescence in the values of their masters, so for Nietzsche, they, too, by their own lights, should simply accept the outcome of their weakness. In neither case is there any internal pressure against the operative value system.

But consider, by contrast, what should happen in the sort of conflict that concerns Nietzsche in *GM*, I, 7, in which "the priestly caste and the warrior caste confront each other jealously and will not come to terms on a price." In Nietzsche's mind, of course, the outcome of the contest is hardly in doubt ("too bad for [the priests] when it comes to war!"); the priestly nobility will be ruthlessly subordinated. But at this point Nietzsche's description shifts its emphasis from the priests and warriors themselves to the contest between their value schemes – it is "the knightly-aristocratic value judgments" versus "the priestly-noble manner of valuation." And at the more abstract level, the outcome is quite different from the previous examples. For it is not at all the case that the priests' value system forces them to recognize the superiority of those who have subordinated them, nor must their own defeat represent any failure in terms of their basic values. On the contrary, surely the priests themselves would judge their warrior adversaries to be decidedly *impure* (i.e. *bad*, on the pure/impure scheme), and *military* defeat need not compromise their own purity in any way. In this sense, the priestly and knightly value systems simply do not "line up." This failure of alignment opens up a striking new possibility: here an entire nobility is systematically subordinated with no hope of returning to social dominance, but in a way that is and remains fundamentally *inconsistent* with its core value system, and so *radically unjustified for them*. For the defeated priestly nobility, therefore, the world is basically "out of joint" in a way it is not for defeated warriors or oppressed slaves.[26]

It is this very situation, as Reginster (1997: 285–89) argues, that gives rise to *abiding*, self-consuming *ressentiment*: the priests cannot resign themselves to subordination in the manner of slaves or defeated warriors, for that situation is patently at odds with their self-defining value system, nor does

---

[26] All quotations in this paragraph are from *GM*, I, 7.

that value system (being of the noble, good/bad pattern) provide any internal resources that could lead the priests by rational steps to a reflective abandonment of their sense of superiority. With no outlet, their frustration climbs to impossible levels, and *ressentiment* becomes, in them, an all-consuming (almost mood-like) affective orientation that orders all their other affective responses, instead of a passing emotion that "exhausts itself in an immediate reaction" (*GM*, I, 10) as it does in ruling nobles.

Notice that the *nobility* of the priests is *crucial* to the relentless, undischargeable character of *ressentiment* in this case: it is precisely because of their self-avowed felt *superiority* (which, unlike that of defeated warrior nobles, has in no way been disconfirmed by events) that subordination is so frustrating for them.[27] I will return momentarily to this key point. The slaves, of course, will eventually come to experience *ressentiment* just as sharply as the priestly nobility, but before they can, they must learn to see their oppression as *unjustified*, and for that, they will need the evaluative insights of the slave morality itself, through which they can slough off the slavish adherence to the values of their masters.[28] In this sense, too, the psychological ordeal of the priests, who can alone invent those "liberating" slave values and pass them on, is strictly prior to that of the slaves in the logic of Nietzsche's argument.

It is in the noble priests, then, that "*ressentiment* becomes creative and gives birth to new values" (*GM*, I, 10). Still, the values in question are supposed to be *slave values*. If nobles and slaves are so different, why would nobles create a "slave morality," and perhaps more perplexingly, how? In what sense are the values that the priests invent *slave* values at all?

The values of the *ressentiment* revaluation are "slavish" in the specific sense that they are apt for slaves and responsive to their interests, in much the way the standard story emphasizes. The good/evil morality glorifies humility, meekness, "self-denying, quiet, patient virtue" – thereby permitting the slavish character to view "the very weakness of the weak – that is to say, his *essence*, his effects, his whole unique, unavoidable, undetachable reality" as though it "were . . . a voluntary achievement, something willed, chosen, a *deed*, an *accomplishment*" (*GM*, I, 13). Even more important in

---

[27] Again, see Reginster 1997: 287, *et passim*.

[28] Here I depart from Wallace (2007: 126–29, *et passim*), who insists that the slave morality is the product of necessarily prior *ressentiment* in the slaves. I agree that the slave morality is the product of prior *ressentiment*, but I take it to have been in the noble priests, not the slaves. I doubt that, absent the evaluative resources of the slave morality, the slaves as Nietzsche understands them (recall *BGE*, 261) would be able – from the deprivation of their conditions alone – to get beyond resignation and perhaps envy of those better situated, to the focalized hatred of the happy that Wallace (2007: 117–19) rightly builds into the notion of *ressentiment*.

Nietzsche's eyes, of course, the slave morality also promotes a spirit of righteous indignation against the happy and fortunate of the world, simultaneously encouraging and giving vent to *ressentiment* in the weak. Thus, the slave morality is justly so called because it answers to the "*needs*" (*GM*, I, 13) of the slave type, and these selling points promote its spread and institutional consolidation.

With this, we can return to the why-question about what the morality does for its creators, the priests. For them, the slave revolt does two key pieces of work. First, as Ridley (1998a: 50–54, 57) rightly noted, the *ressentiment* revaluation and its spread among slavish types immediately serves a perfectly standard ambition of the priests *qua* nobles: it is a *route to power* ("*Rule over the suffering* is his realm"; *GM*, III, 15). But this straightforward function is not the central focus of Nietzsche's concern.[29]

The more important work the slave morality does for the priests, from his point of view, is to open a path toward *revenge*, and the expression of vengeful affect, against the fortunate and happy:

[L]et us turn right to the greatest example. Nothing that has been done on earth against "the noble," "the mighty," "the masters" and "the rulers," is worth mentioning compared with what the *Jews* have done against them: the Jews, that priestly people who in the last resort were only able to gain satisfaction from their enemies and conquerors through a radical revaluation of their values, that is, through an act of the *most spiritual* revenge. (*GM*, I, 7)

Or again,

This [Christian] love grew out of [Jewish] hatred, as its crown, as the triumphant crown expanding ever wider in the purest brightness and radiance of the sun . . . pursuing the aims of that hatred – victory, spoils, seduction . . . Is it not part of the secret black art of a truly *grand* politics of revenge, a far-sighted, subterranean, slow-working and precalculating revenge, that Israel itself should denounce her actual instrument of revenge before all the world as a mortal enemy and nail him to the cross, so that "all the world" . . . could take precisely this bait . . .? (*GM*, I, 8)

And so on, and on. The main aim of the slave morality *for the priests* is to express their vengeful hatred of their enemies through a moralistic condemnation that denies any goodness in them, and even in the very noble type itself. And if the nobles themselves could be seduced by the mysterious appeal of these new values, then the priests would also secure *actual revenge*

---

[29] Indeed, I would argue that this first function is in important ways *instrumental* to the second function. The dominion established by the priests supports the institutional consolidation of the slave morality, and *thereby* ensures that it will remain around long enough to fulfill its central purpose, the *revenge* that I go on to discuss in the text below.

against their oppressors by *poisoning the conscience of the happy*, who (as we saw above) so little deserve their sovereign good fortune according to the value scheme of the priests (i.e. their true, underlying, *noble* value scheme of pure/impure = good/bad). One last time:

> [W]hen would they actually achieve their ultimate, finest, most sublime triumph of revenge? Doubtless if they succeeded in *shoving* their own misery, all misery generally, *into the conscience* of the happy: so that the latter would eventually start to be ashamed of their happiness and perhaps start to say to one another: "It's a disgrace to be happy! *There is too much misery!*" (*GM*, III, 14)

But even this talk of "poisoning the happiness" of their enemies fails to capture the full measure of revenge accomplished through the slave revolt. For what *truly* corrupts the nobles whose values become infected by the *ressentiment* revaluation is that they end up with a set of values that is *fit for slaves*. They become *contemptible*, through being governed by a value system that is contemptible (and thereby corrupting). With that, the revenge of the priests is complete, and *this* revenge is *why* they created slave values in the first place, on Nietzsche's account.[30]

The incommensurability we saw between the priestly-noble and knightly-aristocratic value schemes provides a crucial background for this program of revenge and the underlying affective complex of *ressentiment* that motivates it. There would be no "far-sighted, subterranean, slow-working" program of revenge without the priests' refusal to acquiesce in their subordination in the manner of slaves (or, as we saw, of defeated warrior nobles). Their resolve in that refusal is stiffened by the normative justification it draws from their value scheme, which continues to under-write their feeling of intrinsic superiority even after defeat (as well as their

---

[30] As I noted above (note 22), the priests sacrifice themselves by descending into the same contemptible condition in the pursuit of their revenge. For once they create the slave morality out of the spirit of revenge, the priests do end up being forced to *internalize* its outlook, and this will involve a significant measure of self-contempt. (In this respect, they become the first examples of those Nietzsche hopefully points to in our current culture, who have a "'*higher nature*', a more spiritual nature" because they are "divided in this sense and really and truly a battle ground for these opposites" [*GM*, I, 16] – i.e. the good/bad and good/evil patterns of valuation.) In the priests' case, however, it seems that they are *forced* to take on slave values, for something like the reason Nietzsche later advances to explain philosophers' asceticism: after all, the slave revolt is not to be accomplished in an afternoon, but must take the *long* view, and meanwhile the priest "had to *play* that part [here, the slave morality] in order to be able to be [who he was], [and] he had to *believe* it in order to be able to play it" (*GM*, III, 10). As a result, the slavish good/evil pattern is unhappily integrated into the priest's psychology, and generates all manner of self-deception, self-blindness, mendacity, and internal division – all of which is a major focus of Nietzsche's concern in *GM*, I. For a compelling account of the underlying structure of the priest's internal division, see Reginster 1997.

parallel judgment that the oppressors are bad/impure). Thus again, the priests' *nobility* is crucial to the operation of Nietzsche's argument.

But there is a further, more psychologically telling point, which allows me to conclude by settling an outstanding promissory note. The stability of the priestly value scheme under conquest depends on more than just its failure to align with warrior-noble values in the way we saw. It also matters, as Reginster (1997: 286) notes, that the priests see their subordination as not only unjustifiable, but irremediable.[31] It is because their defeat seems so hopeless that in them *ressentiment* becomes *abiding*, along with a psychological structure involving enormous repression. In order for their value scheme to persist even in the face of such hopelessness and repression, the sense of intrinsic superiority constituting the priests' nobility must be unusually strong. Clearly Nietzsche believes this to be so (*GM*, I, 6–8, *et passim*), but what is more telling for my purposes is his explanation for this fact. Nietzsche thinks the priests are *right*, and all their evidence supports them – they *are* superior to the warriors.

On this point, it is important not to be misled by the reversals in rhetoric demanded by Nietzsche's polemical purposes. Of course Nietzsche complains vociferously about how dangerous and evil the priests are, and the damage that their evaluative innovations have wrought. But as we saw, their "evil" amounts to nobility (*GM*, I, 10), and they are so dangerous precisely *because* they are noble. Indeed they are even more noble than other nobles. He frequently describes them in ways that express or entail this *superlative* nobility: they are the "most spiritual" and "*most evil*" (hence, again, most noble) (*GM*, I, 7); the superlative hatred of the slave morality "burrowed [with its roots] ever more thoroughly and greedily into *everything* that was deep and evil" (*GM*, I, 8; my italics); the so-called "battle of Rome against Judea" is depicted as the contest of the very most noble among the strong and the priestly people of the very first rank – and Judea has been *victorious* over the best (*GM*, I, 16); and of course, we already saw that it was with the priests "that man *first* [my italics] became an *interesting* animal, that only here did the human soul acquire *depth* in the *higher* [my italics] sense and

---

[31] One can imagine, by contrast, other intra-noble conflicts – say, between "the strong" and "the rich" – where the initial outcome left the losers room to imagine that continued prosecution of the fight on essentially the same evaluative terms was feasible. Perhaps, for example, the rich are the initial losers, for much the same reasons proper to the priestly-/warrior-noble conflict, but they retain some of their assets (or more importantly, means of production), and so can hope eventually to co-opt or buy off, and then incorporate, their erstwhile conquerors. In that case, the value systems will continue to confront one another in open contest, and the two value schemes might even adjust toward one another over time. With the priests, by contrast, the conflict tends to be "driven underground" in them, thereby promoting the sort of repression typical of their strategy of *ressentiment* revaluation.

become *evil* . . . the *two basic forms of man's superiority* [my italics] hitherto"
(*GM*, I, 6).[32]

Perhaps most telling of all in this respect, however, is the priests'
experience of the pathos of distance, the official mark of nobility in the
Genealogy. Their pathos of distance is so extreme that they wish to share
nothing at all in common with the ordinary run of (impure, dirty) common
people, not even their bodily nature (see *GM*, I, 6; III, 11–14). As Nietzsche
writes,

the very nature of an essentially priestly aristocracy makes clear why it was precisely
here that contradictory valuations could so soon become dangerously internalized
and *heightened*; and in fact through them *clefts were finally torn open between man
and man* which even an Achilles of free-spiritedness would shudder to cross. (*GM*,
I, 6; my italics)

Nietzsche clearly means to convey here a maximal degree of the pathos of
distance, and given the official definition, that in turn entails that the priests
exhibit a maximal degree of nobility.

To return to the psychological consequence, precisely because they are in
fact *more* noble than other nobles who subordinate them, the priests have
available justifications that strengthen their capacity to cling to their own
value scheme even in the face of radical and total defeat. That in turn
permits the emergence of abiding *ressentiment* and eventually, revaluation. I
take this as one final confirmation that, so far from being a confused,
ambiguous, or intermediate type between noble and slave, Nietzsche's argument *requires* that the priests be counted as nobles – indeed *superlatively* so.

4. CONCLUSION

I have been concerned to argue here for the nobility of Nietzsche's priests, as
he presents the psychological type in the *Genealogy*. The priests' nobility
turns out to be essential to the workings of Nietzsche's first-essay account of
the slave revolt in morality, contrary to the standard story that everybody
knows. By way of conclusion, I offer one final note to suggest the advantages
of the interpretation I have offered over the standard story.

Nietzsche's primary aim in the *Genealogy* is to offer a *"critique"* (*GM*,
Preface, 6) of traditional altruistic morality, and his historical claims serve
that end by making a point about the *meaning* of that morality. In

---

[32] Nor is this way of talking limited to the *Genealogy*. Compare *GS*, 358, which concludes with
Nietzsche's insistence that a church is a *nobler* institution than a state, due to its confident reliance
on spiritual forms of power.

particular, its origin in a slave revolt is supposed to reveal that morality carries the cultural meaning – even for us, its present-day adherents – of a constantly available justification for self-righteously revenging ourselves on those more fortunate and happy.

The account I have offered more plausibly establishes this cultural meaning than the standard story. For on the standard story, recall, there are *two* powerful motivations animating the slave revolt and hence governing the shape of its values: the slaves express their *ressentiment*, true, but they also acquire new means of self-affirmation, through which they come to value their own distinctively moral virtues. The standard story thus leaves Nietzsche's genealogical argument open to a neat countermove; perhaps the *original* slaves were animated by *ressentiment*, but that motive is dispensable precisely because the morality they invented was also motivated by a desire for self-affirmation. Therefore, we present-day moralists should be able to focus on morality's self-affirmative function and ignore the original role of *ressentiment*, thereby purifying morality of its vengeful aspects. We simply need to place all our weight on the positive, self-affirmative work morality does for its adherents, which neither Nietzsche's own values nor the slave morality itself ought to have anything against.

By contrast, the story I have told posits an origin which shapes the content of the slave morality *through and through* as a system for expressing vengeful feeling against, and ultimately taking spiritual revenge upon, the happy. Moreover, the detailed working of that revenge presupposes that the slave morality is itself something contemptible. Thus, its adherents are bound to experience their attachment to it in the self-deceiving and self-opaquely self-hating ways Nietzsche takes such pains to emphasize in *GM*, I. Finally, as Reginster (1997) also notes, for the *ressentiment* priests, their eventual revenge, gained by corrupting the very values of their opponents,[33] was the central aim, without which any other successes they achieve with morality would be pointless and empty. Slave morality's role as a vehicle for

---

[33] I do not pretend to have offered any explanation of *how* the slave revolt proved so successful (i.e. of why *non*-priestly nobles would ever be seduced by it). I take that to be a major lacuna in Nietzsche's first essay. In my own view, the discussions from *GM*, II, emphasized by Ridley – about internalization and life under customs – are intended to fill just this gap. Briefly, while warrior-type nobles *initially* retain some external outlets for their aggressive instincts (*GM*, I, 11), eventually the progress of civilization brings them more and more thoroughly "within the confines of society and peace" (*GM*, II, 16), and they begin to suffer the difficulties associated with internalization. Not being too clever themselves (*GM*, I, 10), they are left vulnerable to the priestly ascetic explanation of that suffering (*GM*, III, 13–22), so their bad conscience is "moralized" into full-fledged guilt (*GM*, II, 21), and they fall under the sway of the priests, or their cultural descendants. Thus, again *contra* Ridley, I take it to be crucial to Nietzsche's overall argument that the "internalization" of *GM*, II, is a *general* phenomenon proper to slave and noble alike, and not a characteristic feature of the slave type.

ressentiment is therefore the core function toward which all its features are oriented. Perhaps it would be possible in principle to purge our morality of the effects this origin has wrought on what morality means to us and the work it does for us, but if Nietzsche's story is really right, such a purification would require a ground-up reframing so extensive that it would amount to a second revaluation of the sort he demands.[34]

---

[34] My first debt is to Alexander Nehamas and a graduate seminar he taught at Penn (probably in 1989 or 1990). It was there that I arrived at the ideas in this chapter and first tried them out in a presentation. One of the members of the seminar was Bernard Reginster, and the way I recall it now, after the course, each of us thought he remembered that the point about the nobility of the priests had been his own discovery. I now believe that the idea must have been due to Nehamas all along; he was the one who posed the key problem for our reflection: "How is a slavish revaluation of values possible when, for Nietzsche, value creation is a constitutive mark of nobility?" We just drew the consequences that he must have seen in advance. And that, after all, is the mark of a truly great graduate teacher: the students all leave the room with the unshakeable sense that they have come to see the ideas (i.e. the ones planted there by the teacher) *by figuring them out themselves*. I also owe thanks to John Richardson, for encouraging me to write up the thought, and to Simon May, for the invitation to contribute to this volume, for his patience, and for comments on the final draft. Rachel Cristy provided comments on the final draft and valuable research assistance tracking discussions in the secondary literature, as did Anne Pollok (with special attention to the German literature); I thank Cristy, Pollok, Joshua Landy, and Katherine Preston for conversations about how to formulate the ideas.

CHAPTER 3

The genealogy of guilt

Bernard Reginster

The second essay of *On the Genealogy of Morality* ostensibly develops an account of the origins of the feeling of guilt, which is marked by the appearance of tight conceptual cohesion: the essay begins with an analysis of the concept of *conscience*, proceeds to an examination of *bad* conscience, and concludes with a view of *moral* bad conscience, or guilt itself, with an emphasis throughout the essay on the crucial influence of socialization on the development of all these phenomena.

Still, there remains much disagreement among commentators over the precise structure of the account Nietzsche develops in that essay. In this chapter, I shall propose a new interpretation of this structure, which keeps to the conceptual resources Nietzsche actually offers in the essay. My objective is therefore primarily exegetical and, in some respects, modest, for although this chapter supplies (arguably) the groundwork for a philosophical exploration of Nietzsche's account by circumscribing its philosophical stakes, it does not engage very far in such an exploration.

It is important to note at the outset that the object of Nietzsche's inquiry in the second essay is *Christian guilt*, or the feeling of guilt as it operates and is understood in the *Christian* moral outlook: this much we can gather not only from the importance of the role played by Christianity in his account, but also from the emphasis he places on the Christian view of conscience in the brief review of the second essay he offers in *Ecce Homo:* "The *second* inquiry offers the psychology of *conscience* – which is not, as people may believe, 'the voice of God in man'" (*EH*, "The Genealogy of Morals").[1]

---

[1] The reference edition of Nietzsche's works is *Sämtliche Werke: Kritische Studienausgabe*, edited by Giorgio Colli and Mazzino Montinari (1980–88). I have used the following translations with customary abbreviations: *Beyond Good and Evil*, trans. Walter Kaufmann (1966a); *Daybreak*, trans. R. J. Hollingdale (1982b); *Ecce Homo*, trans. Walter Kaufmann (1969); *On the Genealogy of Morality*, trans. Carol Diethe (2007); *The Gay Science*, trans. Walter Kaufmann (1974); and *Human, All Too Human*, trans. R. J. Hollingdale (1986).

In contrast to the dominant line of interpretation, I shall argue that Nietzsche's objective in the second essay is not (at least not primarily) to challenge the non-naturalistic account of the feeling of guilt promoted by the Christian outlook (namely, guilt as a manifestation of "the voice of God in man"[2]) but to show that the Christian representation of guilt is not an account of the ordinary feeling of guilt – the diminution of one's worth as a person experienced when one falls short of certain normative expectations – but a perversion of it, which results from its exploitation as an instrument of self-directed cruelty. Christian guilt is therefore not the ordinary moral emotion of guilt, responsive to reasons, but what I shall call a *rational passion*, by which I mean a passion to which only a rational being is susceptible because it essentially exploits his responsiveness to reason, and which, unlike other passions, not only overrides, but actually corrupts, this responsiveness to reason.

I do not mean to suggest, however, that Nietzsche has nothing of particular interest to say about the ordinary feeling of guilt in that essay. On the contrary, his claim that Christian guilt is a peculiar perversion of the susceptibility to this feeling actually *presupposes* an account of it. The second essay explicitly discusses some aspects of this account, which I shall also take up. However, it does not intend to offer the *complete* account of the emergence of the ordinary feeling of guilt that commentators have been at pains to extract from it, simply because it describes only those features that are relevant to his diagnosis of Christian guilt as a perverted use of it, leaving out large issues, such as the origin of the concepts of free will and categorical obligation, which a complete account would surely have to address.

I. CONSCIENCE

Since the feeling of guilt is a species of "bad conscience," Nietzsche begins his investigation with an examination of the concept of "*conscience*." The concept of conscience typically designates an inner *voice* – the voice of

---

[2] This is far and away the most common interpretation of the essay. Representative in this connection is Leiter (2002: 223), who emphasizes the similarity of Nietzsche's account of morality with those of Hume and Freud (Leiter 2002: 10–11). However, Leiter does not note one crucial implication of this comparison: a naturalistic explanation of guilt precludes any appeal not only to "the voice of God in man," but also to Kantian "pure reason." Both Hume and Freud take a "naturalistic" account of morality to derive it from a combination of certain psychological facts – including passions or drives, together with certain cognitive and instrumental or prudential reasoning capacities – with certain naturally occurring circumstances. Thus, Freud's explanation of guilt is supposed to include an account of how, from such a combination of factors, human beings could have become responsive to "categorical imperatives."

conscience – that reminds each of us of our obligations. Nietzsche, who rejects the idea that it is "the voice of God in man," asks how such a structure could have developed in the human psyche. Insofar as it is a voice reminding us of our obligations or commitments, conscience is "the *will's memory.*" Since undertaking an obligation or a commitment is like making a promise, the possession of a memory of the will underwrites "the right to make promises." For we do not have the right to make promises unless we have the ability to keep them, and this ability requires that we be reminded of them. Nietzsche observes that our minds are naturally endowed with an active force of "forgetfulness," by virtue of which it disposes of impressions that would otherwise linger in, and clutter, our consciousness. He infers that the will's memory is not part of our innate natural endowment but constitutes a capacity that must be "bred" into us:

It is by no means a mere passive inability to be rid of an impression once it has made its impact, nor is it just indigestion caused by giving your word on some occasion and finding you cannot cope, instead it is an active *desire* not to let go, a desire to keep on desiring what has been, on some occasion, desired, really it is the *will's memory:* so that a world of strange new things, circumstances and even acts of will may be placed quite safely in between the original "I will," "I shall do" and the actual discharge of the will, its *act*, without breaking this long chain of the will. (*GM*, II, 1)

By defining this memory of the will as a matter of "keeping on desiring what has been, on some occasion, desired," Nietzsche suggests that it is more than the memory of the fact that I once desired to do something, and gave my word that I would do it, as commentators usually suppose; it is rather the perpetuation of *desire* itself. Nietzsche's use of the word "desire" in this context may cause some confusion. For a "memory of the will" is not simply the perpetuation of some wish or inclination I once had: the "will" to be remembered here is an *obligation* undertaken, or a "promise" made – "I will," "I shall do." To define this memory of the will in terms of keeping on "desiring" is simply to indicate that what is to be perpetuated is the *motivation* itself, not the awareness that I was once so motivated. In making a promise, I express the intention – the *desire* in a broad sense – to do what I have promised: the "will's memory" simply is the perpetuation of this desire.

2. INDEBTEDNESS

Nietzsche's inquiry then proceeds to an examination of the concept of "*indebtedness*" because guilt and indebtedness bear a close etymological connection: the German word for guilt – *Schuld* – also means debt, or indebtedness. Nietzsche takes this etymological connection to suggest a *conceptual* one (*GM*, II, 6), and concludes that we stand to learn much about guilt from an analysis of indebtedness. The feeling of indebtedness arises in the context of contractual relationships, which are essentially relationships established by *promising*, and so involve the whole apparatus designed to make promising possible, particularly the recourse to the infliction of pain:

> Precisely here, *promises are made*; precisely here, the person making the promise has to have a memory *made* for him; precisely here, we can guess, is a repository of hard, cruel, painful things. The debtor, in order to inspire confidence that the promise of repayment will be honored, in order to give a guarantee of the solemnity and sanctity of his promise, and in order to etch the duty and obligation of repayment into his conscience, pawns something to the creditor by means of the contract in case he does not pay, something which he still "possesses" and controls, for example, his body, or his wife, or his freedom, or his life. (*GM*, II, 5)

A contractual relationship is established between two parties when one, the "debtor," promises to repay the other, the "creditor," in some fashion for something – a loan, or some kind of service – the creditor agrees to provide. If the debtor fails to keep his promise and repay his debt in kind, he is liable to some form of "punishment." Nietzsche uses quotation marks because "punishment" in this context – or at any rate a practice that looks like punishment, in which pain is inflicted on the delinquent debtor – is not an expression of disapproval, moral or otherwise: it involves no judgment, on the part of either party, that the delinquent debtor has acted in an evil or reprehensible way, which makes him *deserving* of that "punishment." It is merely an alternative form of repayment by the debtor of the debt he contracted.[3]

Nietzsche observes that far and away the preferred form of alternative compensation in cases of delinquency is the infliction of pain: "The compensation, then, consists in a warrant for and title to cruelty" (*GM*, II, 5). He wonders at the strangeness of this idea:

> Let's be quite clear as to the logic of this whole matter of compensation: it is strange enough. The equivalence is provided by the fact that instead of an advantage directly making up for the wrong (so, instead of compensation in money, land or possessions of any kind), a sort of *pleasure* is given to the creditor as repayment and

---

[3] Nietzsche adds that it does not matter either whether the delinquent debtor deliberately refused, or simply proved unable, to discharge his debt. For the point of this "punishment" is only the fulfillment of a contract (*GM*, II, 4).

compensation, – the pleasure of having the right to exercise power over the powerless without a thought, the pleasure *"de faire le mal pour le plaisir de le faire,"* the enjoyment of violating. (*GM*, II, 5; cf. 6)

There are, as it turns out, two strange features in this conception of punishment. One is "the idea that every injury has its *equivalent* which can be paid in compensation, if only through the *pain* of the person who injures" (*GM*, II, 4). In other words, every injury – the loss of possessions, of a loved one, and the like – has its equivalent in a specifiable amount of pleasure. The other strange feature of cruelty is the idea that "*to make* someone suffer is pleasure in its highest form" (*GM*, II, 6). The conjecture Nietzsche offers is that *making* someone suffer is pleasurable because it gratifies the will to power.

I have argued elsewhere that the will to power is the desire to engage in the activity of confronting and overcoming resistance. Cruelty – "*making* someone suffer" – is a paradigmatic manifestation of the will to power in the following way: the prospect of suffering necessarily creates resistance in its intended victim, which the cruel individual *overcomes* simply by managing to *make* his victim suffer.[4] Thus, when Nietzsche notes that "[t]hrough punishment of the debtor, the creditor takes part in the *rights of the masters*" (*GM*, II, 5), he indicates that what the creditor enjoys is not the suffering of the debtor *as such*, but the *overcoming* of the resistance, which the prospect of this suffering is bound to arouse in the debtor, by the very fact that he is made to suffer.[5]

It is crucial to note that original contractual relationships are not relationships of *trust* between individuals who already possess "the right to make promises." This is why the individual who contracts a debt "has to have a memory *made* for him" through the threat of "hard, cruel, painful things," the purpose of which is to "etch the duty and obligation of repayment into his conscience." The original debtor's motivation for keeping his promises is the "dread" of the creditor and his power (see *GM*, II, 20). He does not consider that his worth or standing is at stake in the keeping of his promises, and therefore he does not regard his failure to do so as *wrongdoing*, and his punishment as *deserved*. The fear of the unpleasant consequences of his

[4] Nietzsche observes that "to practice cruelty is to enjoy the highest arousal of the feeling of power [*den höchsten Kitzel des Machtgefühls*]" (*D*, 18). I have argued elsewhere that cruelty affords the highest feeling of power because this feeling is aroused by the activity of confronting and overcoming resistance, and not simply by a state of control or domination (see Reginster 2006: 139–43).

[5] To shore up the connection between power and cruelty, Nietzsche brings out two interesting observations: the pleasure of cruelty is greater for those who are less powerful than those they make suffer (*GM*, II, 5), and lower, or perhaps even inexistent, in those who already are (or feel) more powerful (whence their inclination to mercy) (*GM*, II, 10).

promise-breaking, which constitutes the original feeling of indebtedness ("consciousness of debts"; *GM*, II, 20), is therefore not a feeling of *guilt*, precisely because it does not involve a diminution in his estimation of himself as a person.

Thus, Nietzsche observes that if the delinquent debtor does not *already* feel guilty for this indebtedness, the punishment exacted *cannot* arouse such a feeling, for two reasons. First, "the mere sight of the judicial executive procedures inhibits the criminal himself from experiencing his act, his mode of conduct, as reprehensible *as such:* because he sees the same kind of action practiced in the service of justice and given approval, practiced with a good conscience" (*GM*, II, 14). Second, he can regard the punishment as nothing more than a stroke of bad luck, or the unfortunate consequence of miscalculation:

For millennia, wrongdoers overtaken by punishment have felt . . .: "something has gone unexpectedly wrong here," *not* "I ought not to have done that" – , they submitted to punishment as you submit to illness or misfortune or death . . . If, in those days, there was any criticism of the deed, it came from intelligence, which practiced criticism: we must certainly seek the actual *effect* of punishment primarily in the sharpening of intelligence, in a lengthening of the memory, a will to be more cautious, less trusting, to go about things more circumspectly from now on. (*GM*, II, 15)

The crucial implication of this view of the relation between guilt and punishment is that guilt cannot consist of the *fear* of punishment. If the *fact* of punishment cannot arouse the feeling of guilt in those who do not already regard what they did as wrong, and can only make them more cautious and circumspect in continuing to do what they did, then the *prospect* of punishment will not arouse guilt feelings either, and will amount to nothing more than the apprehension of the unpleasant consequences of further imprudence or miscalculation. One way of bringing out this contrast is to point out that if a delinquent debtor came to believe that he has gotten away with it, and will escape punishment, no "pangs of conscience" would remain; by contrast, if he felt guilty, the conviction that he would escape punishment for his wrongdoing would not make him feel any less guilty. Hence, guilt cannot be fear of punishment.

3. BAD CONSCIENCE

Nietzsche describes the origin of bad conscience in the following terms:

I look on bad conscience as a serious illness to which man was forced to succumb by the pressure of the most fundamental of all changes which he experienced, – that change whereby he finally found himself imprisoned within the confines of society and peace. It must have been no different for this semi-animal, happily adapted to the wilderness, war, the wandering life and adventure than it was for the sea animals when they were forced to either become land animals or perish – at one go all instincts were devalued and "suspended." ... They felt they were clumsy at performing the simplest task, they did not have their familiar guide any more for this new, unknown world, those regulating impulses which unconsciously led them to safety – the poor things were reduced to relying on thinking, inference, calculation, and the connecting of cause with effect, that is, to relying on their "consciousness," that most impoverished and error-prone organ! (*GM*, II, 16)

It is important to note that Nietzsche's conception of the "state of nature," prior to socialization, is not, as it is for Freud, the helpless and dreadful state of individuals ill-suited for solitary life in nature. Nietzsche's presocial individual is, on the contrary, "happily adapted to the wilderness, war, the wandering life and adventure." Nietzsche therefore assumes that it must have taken "an act of violence" to tear him away from this state of happy adaptation (*GM*, II, 17). And he attributes this initial act of violence to a small group of strong individuals – "some pack of blond beasts of prey, a conqueror and master race" – bent on exercising their will to power in "the shaping of a population, which had up till now been unrestrained and shapeless, into a fixed form" (*GM*, II, 17).

Nietzsche is most interested in one particular *effect* of this forced social-ization, namely, a change in the individual's relation to his own instincts: "at one go all instincts were devalued and 'suspended'." In the new social "conditions of existence," the very instincts or "regulating impulses" which were once reliable guides "to safety" become, and come to be seen as, dangerous liabilities. I can no longer trust that the pursuit of an impulse I feel in given circumstances will be in my best interest, and I must instead rely on "thinking, inference, calculation, and the connecting of cause with effect." This first problem caused by forced socialization, that the old instincts could no longer be trusted, is compounded by another, which Nietzsche describes as follows:

meanwhile, the old instincts had not suddenly ceased to make their demands! But it was difficult and seldom possible to give in to them: they mainly had to seek new and as it were underground gratifications. All instincts which are not discharged outwardly *turn inwards* – this is what I call the *internalization* of man: with it there now evolves in man what will be later called his "soul." The whole inner world, originally stretched thinly as though between two layers of skin, was expanded and extended itself and gained depth, breadth and height in proportion to the degree that the external discharge of man's instincts was *obstructed*. Those terrible bul-warks with which state organizations protected themselves against the old instincts of freedom – punishments are a primary instance of this kind of bulwark – had the result that all those instincts of the wild, free, roving man were turned backwards, *against man himself.* Animosity, cruelty, the pleasure of pursuing, raiding, changing and destroying – all this pitted against the person who had such instincts: *that* is the origin of "bad conscience." (*GM*, II, 16)

The origin of bad conscience lies in what Nietzsche calls "the *internalization* of man." I have already noted one aspect of this process of internalization: the emergence of "this really dismal thing called reflection" (*GM*, II, 3), by which the old instincts become objects of reflective awareness. Prior to forced socialization, the individual's point of view is directed "outward": these old instincts frame this point of view, but they are not its objects. Since he is "happily adapted to life in the wilderness," he never has to reflect on, let alone question, those instincts. And when they are frustrated, as they are bound to be from time to time, he is prone to think that the problem is with the outer world, or with his calculations about it, not with those instincts themselves. Under conditions of forced socialization, the frustration of the old instincts becomes *systematic*; this prompts a reorientation of the individual's point of view, which is now directed "inward": his old instincts become objects of reflective awareness and criticism – *they* could be the problem. Not to be "trusted" anymore, they cease to shape the point of view *from which* he thinks about, and evaluates, the world, and become objects *to which* his thought and evaluation are directed.

The remarkable fact, which captures Nietzsche's attention, is that this "internalization of man" does not simply consist of such a reflexive reorientation of his point of view toward the inner world of his instincts. It also involves "a declaration of war against all the old instincts" (*GM*, II, 16), specifically, a "devaluation" of them. It is no doubt true that, given Nietzsche's supposition of an original state of happy adaptation, the individual could only be induced to reflect on his instincts when they become problems or liabilities, as they are in conditions under which their pursuit has become a source of systematic torment and frustration. But it remains to be seen why their frustration actually prompts a *condemnation* of these old instincts themselves, rather than of the new external conditions that make their satisfaction impossible.

The explanation of this remarkable fact is that "the old instincts had not suddenly ceased to make their demands" but, since they can no longer be discharged "outwardly," they "turn inwards," or against themselves. Since, as I noted, Nietzsche singles out cruelty as a paradigmatic instance of the "instinct of freedom," he describes bad conscience as "cruelty turned back on itself" (*GM*, III, 20). Although he sometimes describes bad conscience as cruelty the individual directs "against himself," he means against himself insofar as he harbors cruel impulses: "The *instinct of freedom*, forcibly made latent – we have already seen how – this instinct of freedom forced back, repressed, incarcerated within itself and finally able to discharge and unleash itself only against itself: that, and that alone, is *bad conscience* in its beginnings" (*GM*, II, 17).[6]

Nietzsche does not explain why the instinct of freedom can discharge itself "*only against itself*" in this manner, but his account suggests some hints. We may assume that the original state-builders not only frustrate the will to power directed against them by their superior strength, but interested as they are in creating social cohesion, they must also actively prevent individuals from exercising their cruelty on other members of the community. The only way left to satisfy his cruel instincts, then, will be for the individual to turn them on himself. We may also assume, moreover, that many of an individual's instincts are useful to the community, so that their indiscriminate suppression will also be actively discouraged. And since socialization requires the suppression of cruelty, but cannot eliminate its "demand" for discharge, it makes good "economic" sense (to borrow a Freudian concept) to make its own suppression an occasion for discharge.

Bad conscience is obviously an unpleasant feeling – Nietzsche notes that we speak of the "pang" or the "sting" of conscience – and the individual with a bad conscience feels bad not because his "old instincts" are now denied satisfaction, he feels bad for *having* them in the first place. But one can feel bad for having certain instincts in all sorts of ways. The individual forced into society might regret having cruel instincts, which, by being now denied satisfaction, have become a source of perpetual torment. The individual who subscribes to Schopenhauer's conception of happiness in terms of "will-lessness" will deplore his cruel instincts because he deplores having any instincts at all, since their presence proves to be the main obstacle to his happiness: he feels bad about them much in the way the prisoner who aspires to freedom feels bad about his shackles. Finally, the Christian deplores his cruel instincts because he believes that having them diminishes his worth as a person – he feels bad about them in the way the sinner feels bad about his

---

[6] Note that the issue is not to avoid suffering: there is suffering in the frustration imposed on the will to power of the individual forced into social life by the "artists in violence and organizers" who build the original state; and there is suffering in the frustration this individual imposes on his will to power when he turns it against itself. By "*making* someone suffer," be it another or himself, the individual overcomes the resistance, which the prospect of this suffering is bound to arouse in him. Nietzsche emphasizes this pleasure in overcoming resistance when he describes "bad conscience" as resulting from a "desire to give form to oneself as a piece of difficult, resisting, suffering matter, to brand it with a will" (*GM*, II, 18).

sinful proclivities. The devaluation is *prudential* in the first two cases (cruel instincts make one *unable* to achieve happiness), whereas it is *moral* in the last case (cruel instincts make one *undeserving* of happiness).

Now, the individual who regrets or deplores his instincts on prudential grounds, by recognizing in them an obstacle to his happiness, is not motivated by self-directed cruelty: his purpose in condemning his instincts is not to make himself suffer. It is true that, like the Schopenhauerian ascetic, he might deliberately and systematically deny his instincts satisfaction, but it is to the end of "liberating" himself from them by becoming indifferent to the suffering caused by their frustration. In this case, he will see the war he wages against his instincts as only a *means* to his eventual "liberation" from them. When the war the individual wages against his instincts is motivated by self-directed cruelty, by contrast, it becomes an *end*. He denies his instincts satisfaction not in order to liberate himself from them but in order to enjoy overcoming the very suffering their frustration causes him (which might require him, perversely enough, to keep these instincts alive and well).

There still remains a difference between the deliberate, masochistic frustration of one's cruel impulses, which Nietzsche calls "animal bad conscience" (*GM*, III, 20), and the *condemnation* of these impulses as evil, which makes one feel guilty for having them – or "moral" bad conscience. Changing the direction of cruelty – turning it "inwards" – does not necessarily take the form of a moral condemnation of it. So, although the feeling of guilt may well be a form of bad conscience – self-directed cruelty manifested as moral self-reproach – the analysis of bad conscience alone does not supply an analysis of guilt.

4. THE MORALIZATION OF INDEBTEDNESS

Nietzsche acknowledges that his inquiries into indebtedness and contractual obligation have so far ignored the "moralization" of these concepts (*GM*, II, 21). He defines the "moralization" of *Schuld* and *Pflicht* as "the way they are pushed back into conscience; more precisely, the way *bad* conscience is woven together with the concept of God," or "their relegation to *bad* conscience" (*GM*, II, 21). This definition is less than ideally clear. It suggests that a "moralized" feeling of guilt results from the combination of indebtedness with bad conscience, or more precisely from the use of indebtedness as an instrument of self-directed cruelty. And it also suggests that the possibility of a "moralized" feeling of guilt requires not just the notion of indebtedness, but of indebtedness toward God.

Most commentators suppose that the feeling of indebtedness does not amount to a feeling of guilt because the debtor regards his debt as a merely *prudential* obligation, which does not engage his worth *as a person*.[7] It follows that the feeling of guilt is the feeling of indebtedness when my worth as a person is taken to be at stake in the repayment of the debt. This interpretation is in keeping with Nietzsche's account. He describes the feeling of guilt as a feeling of "personal obligation [*persönlichen Verpflichtung*]" (*GM*, II 8), but he also observes that the failure to fulfill a contractual obligation originally concerns me only because of the unpleasant consequences it might bring upon me, and not because it engages my worth as a person. It arouses a feeling of *guilt* only if I come to see my worth as a person at stake in the fulfillment of my obligations, that is to say, using such non-Nietzschean terminology in a broad sense, when they take on a *categorical*, as opposed to a merely *prudential*, character.

Nietzsche remarks that when my failure to repay a debt is the consequence of negligence or miscalculation, I may criticize myself for my imprudence or my incompetence (see *GM*, II, 15). But feeling imprudent or incompetent, even if I believe that I have no one to blame for it but myself, is not yet feeling guilty: only my worth as a competent, proficient, or capable agent is at stake, not my worth *as a person*. For my prudence matters to me only if the determinate ends it enables me to realize matter to me in the first place. Of course, I may, under certain circumstances, deplore my imprudence not just because of the unpleasant consequences it brings upon me, but also because of what it tells about me as a person. In this case, however, I regard prudence itself, if only implicitly, as a *categorical* obligation.

Most commentators also suppose that the feeling of indebtedness becomes a feeling of guilt when it is associated with "bad conscience," understood as self-directed cruelty.[8] However, this cannot be right: the

---

[7] Here is a representative sampling: "the debtor's attitude toward the fact is primarily prudential; he may regard it as inconvenient, but he does not regard himself as a worse person for his indebtedness" (Ridley 1998a: 32); "guilt presupposes one's commitment to norms, and hence a developed notion of personal accountability" (May 1999: 62); "failing to pay one's debts by no means decreases one's worth as a person" (Risse 2001: 65); the "feeling of debts" becomes "moralized" when it is taken to concern "debts that reflect badly on one's personhood" (Leiter 2002: 241). Janaway (2007: 132) also emphasizes the non-moral character of indebtedness.

[8] Here is a sampling: "'guilt' [is] when one is turning the fact of one's indebtedness back against oneself, as something with which to torment oneself" (Ridley 1998a: 32); "the bad conscience *as a feeling of guilt* arises from an *earlier form of the bad conscience* (which has nothing to do with guilt) and an *indebtedness towards gods*" (Risse 2001: 56); "man's internalized cruelty . . . disposes him to seize upon instruments like the concept of debt to God and turn it into *guilt* before God" (Leiter 2002: 240); Janaway (2007: 134) argues that guilt is what results from the recourse to indebtedness to "legitimize" the pain caused by internalized cruelty.

association of indebtedness with bad conscience does not suffice to produce a feeling of guilt. For the feeling of indebtedness can be "pushed into *bad* conscience," and used as an instrument of self-directed cruelty, already in its purely prudential form: I could imagine that harboring cruel impulses is a breach of contract (say, with God) and torment myself with thoughts of terrific "punishments" for harboring them. But if such a feeling of indebtedness produces no diminution in my estimation of myself as a person, it is hard to see how it could be marshaled to produce *moral* bad conscience, or a feeling of *guilt*.[9]

Emphasizing indebtedness *toward God*, as some commentators propose to do,[10] will not help. If the feeling of indebtedness itself by no means decreases my worth as a person, it is hard to see how making it indebtedness toward God could have this effect. If indebtedness is to affect my estimation of myself as a person, it must be in virtue of its character as indebtedness, and not in virtue of who I am indebted to: being a delinquent debtor *as such* must be what decreases my worth as a person. In that case, however, the feeling of indebtedness would already be a feeling of *guilt*, and indebtedness toward God would only intensify the feeling of guilt (*GM*, II, 20).[11]

This difficulty invites an alternative line of interpretation, according to which the feeling of indebtedness would involve, *prior* to its "moralization," a belief in the *categorical authority* of the obligations I have undertaken, such

---

[9] Leiter (2002: 242) recognizes that something "is still missing" from the explanation of guilt in terms of the association of indebtedness with bad conscience. But what he sees missing is not an account of how internalized cruelty alone could transform debts into things "that reflect badly on one's personhood" (241). Even Freud (1930: 125), with whose enterprise Leiter explicitly compares Nietzsche's genealogy, attempts to explain how what is at first only *prudential* self-criticism could become *moral* self-criticism, answering to "categorical imperatives," by invoking the "internalization" of external authority figures. For a recent critique of the Freudian account, see Velleman 2006. Poellner (1995: 242) nicely brings out the problem; and Janaway (2007: 132–33 and 136) appears to recognize that the merely prudential character of contractual obligations does not suffice to turn bad conscience into guilt.

[10] Risse (2001: 65), in particular, argues that directing the feeling of indebtedness toward God "turns [it] into a deep sense of being a complete failure with respect to what one is first and foremost, namely, God's creature." See also Leiter 2002: 240.

[11] There might be ways to improve this sort of explanation. We might surmise, for example, that in the Christian outlook, God will grant us His favors only if we regard his "Commandments" as *categorical* norms. The commandment to love one's neighbor arguably has this peculiar structure: it is hard to see how one could successfully observe it – love one's neighbors – if one's motivational focus remains on gaining God's favors. In other words, it is a matter of prudence to regard certain requirements as *moral* (or categorical) requirements. Even if we accept this view, however, it still remains unclear how such categorical/moral motivation could emerge in the minds of individuals whose sole motivations up to then were instrumental or prudential – how, that is, it could cease to matter motivationally that the commandment is *God's* commandment. But Nietzsche himself nowhere develops, or even alludes to, this line of thought.

that the failure to repay my debts would cause me to experience a decrease in my worth as a person.[12] This interpretation implies that the feeling of indebtedness could have already developed into a feeling of guilt prior to its association with bad conscience.

This line of interpretation has two main advantages, but faces one major challenge. Its first advantage is exegetical: it allows us to explain how "pushing back" indebtedness into bad conscience could produce a distinctively *moral* bad conscience, namely, self-directed cruelty manifested under the distinctive guise of moral self-reproach, or reproach of myself *as a person*. Self-directed cruelty ("animal bad conscience") could not assume this guise by making use of the feeling of indebtedness, unless I already took my worth as a person to be at stake in my indebtedness. The second advantage is philosophical: self-directed cruelty is not only unnecessary to the understanding of ordinary guilt, it also threatens to distort it. For I become susceptible to experiencing a decrease in my worth as a person when I fail to fulfill certain obligations simply and solely by being committed to their categorical authority, that is to say, to the view that my worth as a person is at stake in them.

The obvious challenge for this line of interpretation is exegetical: if the feeling of indebtedness is already a feeling of guilt, it becomes unclear what the "moralization" of the concepts of guilt and duty could accomplish. The answer to this challenge is hinted at in Nietzsche's insistence on the fact that, as a consequence of their "moralization," the concepts of guilt and duty become the exclusive property of "*bad* conscience" (*GM*, II, 21). This indicates that "moralized" guilt and duty can only evoke a *diminished* self-esteem in the agent who experiences them. It is easy to see how the association of bad conscience with the concept of God, particularly in the notion of indebtedness toward God, could accomplish this: the notion of indebtedness toward God is, in effect, the notion of an "inexpiable guilt," and the contractual obligation that cannot be fulfilled therefore represents a normative standard – a "duty" – designed only to leave man "palpably convinced of his own absolute worthlessness" (*GM*, II, 22). I shall now develop this interpretation of the "moralization" of guilt.

---

[12] May (1999: 76) defends this interpretation: "the debtor-creditor relationship can model the operation of guilt only by itself presupposing the concept of personal accountability – i.e. a strong sense that one's obligations are justified," in virtue of which the accountability one feels for them "is not sustained simply by external threats, rewards, and monitoring" (74). May also notes that Nietzsche's genealogy of moral guilt presupposes, but does not explain, this sense of personal accountability. Although I agree that there is an unmotivated leap in Nietzsche's account, I shall argue shortly that he has more to offer concerning the notion of "personal accountability" than May recognizes.

5. GUILT AND RESPONSIBILITY

According to the interpretation I am proposing here, "moralization" is not the process whereby the non-moral concepts of indebtedness and contractual obligation become the moral concepts of guilt and duty. It is rather a different process whereby the concepts of guilt and obligation, already understood in a generic moral sense, are enrolled in the service of the aims of morality understood in a specific sense, namely, as "slave morality" or "Christian" morality. According to my interpretation, therefore, Nietzsche takes the Christian representation of guilt to be not a particular account of the ordinary feeling of guilt, but a perversion of the susceptibility to that feeling.

Nietzsche argues, in particular, that Christianity perverts the susceptibility to ordinary guilt by turning it into "guilt towards *God*" (*GM*, II, 22). To make his case, he must have in mind a fairly determinate conception of ordinary guilt. He suggests that feeling guilty is feeling indebted in a way that decreases my worth as a person – it is a feeling of "personal obligation" (*GM*, II, 8). What requires explanation is therefore what my worth as a person amounts to, and how it could have come to be at stake in the fulfillment of my contractual obligations.

Some commentators emphasize the role of freedom of the will: the failure to repay a debt arouses a feeling of guilt – decreases my worth as a person – when it is represented as freely chosen.[13] This emphasis ignores one of the most remarkable features of the genealogy of guilt developed in the second essay, namely, that "freedom of the will" plays no significant role in it – it is the object of only one passing mention (*GM*, II, 4). This is not to say that Nietzsche takes freedom of the will to play no role in the account of guilt: it certainly does, even in other parts of the *Genealogy* (see *GM*, I, 13; III, 15). In the second essay, I want to suggest, he recognizes that this freedom of the will is at best a necessary condition of guilt: I could feel responsible in this sense for my imprudence, for example, and blame myself for it, and yet not feel *guilt*. Another necessary condition for guilt concerns the nature of the norms being violated: they must be not merely prudential norms, but norms that have a bearing on my worth as a person. It is on this condition of guilt that Nietzsche focuses in the second essay.

Although the importance of the concept of personal worth for the understanding of guilt is widely acknowledged among commentators (see

---

[13] For example, Ridley (1998a: 32) appears to maintain that a debtor comes to "regard himself as a worse person for his indebtedness" when he interprets it "as freely chosen."

note 7), it is virtually nowhere given an analysis. I take Nietzsche to propose
at least the rudiments of such an analysis in the very beginning of the second
essay. It starts from his hypothesis that the susceptibility to the feeling of
guilt emerges from the original "legal" practice of making contracts: "In *this*
sphere of legal obligations then, we find the breeding-ground of the moral
conceptual world of 'guilt', 'conscience', 'duty', 'sacred duty'" (*GM*, II, 6).
Since Nietzsche insists that the original feeling of indebtedness is *not*
tantamount to a feeling of guilt, we must ask how the former could provide
the conceptual underpinnings of the latter.

The need for contractual relationships motivates the enterprise of breeding an animal with the right to make promises, or with a "conscience." And
this, Nietzsche observes, "is precisely what constitutes the long history of
the origins of *responsibility*" (*GM*, II, 2). The possession of a "conscience" is
what makes me a *responsible* agent. It is crucial to understand what
Nietzsche means by responsibility in this context. Calling someone responsible might denote the fact that he is free, so that his action is imputable to
him, rather than merely to some part of him, or to some event altogether
external to him. But calling someone responsible might also refer to the fact
that he can be trusted or relied upon, that he is someone who truly has "the
right to make promises" because his word, once given, is good and secure.
Nietzsche is interested primarily in this second sense of responsibility: a
responsible agent is one who can be trusted or relied upon. He calls the
individual who has become responsible in this sense the "*sovereign
individual*."

We gain a more precise understanding of the character of the sovereign
individual by examining the process through which he is produced.
Nietzsche claims that conscience – the "will's memory" – is bred through
pain, "the most powerful aid to mnemonics" (*GM*, II, 3): it is the prospect of
the pain incurred for breaking one's promises that ensures the perpetuation
of the motivation to keep them. However, it is crucial to note that the fear of
pain plays a merely *enabling* role in the development of conscience, but is
not *constitutive* of it. For the fear of pain, which initially motivates the
individual to control those among his intervening desires and emotions that
conflict with his promise-keeping, can eventually become replaced by what
Nietzsche describes as a feeling of "power" or "freedom." The frustration of
conflicting intervening desires in order to fulfill a promise is itself a source of
pain, and the individual who learns to overcome this pain in this manner –
that is to say, the resistance opposed by those conflicting desires – comes to
derive a feeling of power and freedom from this overcoming. It is at the end
of this process, when the feeling of freedom or power has replaced the fear of

pain as the motivation for promise-keeping, that we find the "sovereign individual":

> This man who is now free and who really does have the right to make a promise, this master of the free will, this sovereign – ... how could he, with his self-mastery, not realize that he has necessarily been given mastery over circumstances, over nature, and over all creatures with a less durable and reliable will? The "free" man, the possessor of a durable, unbreakable will, thus has his own *standard of value* in the possession of such a will: viewing others from his own standpoint, he respects or despises ... [he] *confers an honor* when he places his trust, ... gives his word as something which can be relied on, because he is strong enough to remain upright in the face of mishap or even "in the face of fate" ... The proud realization of the extraordinary privilege of *responsibility*, the awareness of this rare freedom and power over himself and his destiny, has penetrated him to the depths and become an instinct, his dominant instinct ...: this sovereign man calls it his *conscience*. (*GM*, II, 2)

The "conscience" of the sovereign individual is "an actual awareness of power and freedom." For his mastery over himself is also a "mastery over circumstances, over nature, and over all creatures with a less durable and reliable will," in sum it is a mastery over "fate" itself because, by being able to control the influence his own emotions have over the conduct of his life, he is thereby able to control the influence which circumstances, nature, and fate might have over it, at least insofar as these factors affect his emotions.[14]

So, the driving force behind the conscience of the sovereign individual is not the fear of pain but the enjoyment of the feeling of *power*. Nietzsche does not explain why an agent becomes "responsible" only when the feeling of power is substituted for the fear of pain in motivating his promise-keeping. But we might offer the following surmise. Note that we do not call "responsible" just anyone on whom we can depend to do what he has promised to do. For instance, we will not judge trustworthy or "responsible" an agent who keeps his promises only because he fears the unpleasant consequences of breaking them or desires the rewards expected from keeping them. One plausible motivation for our attitude in this case is the recognition that the agent does not care about keeping his promises *as such*, and would break them the moment the unpleasant consequences of so doing would be either avoidable or outweighed by the pleasures for the sake of which the promises would be broken. This suggests that we consider an

---

[14] Owen (2007: 99) nicely observes that "the point here is not *per impossibile* that the sovereign individual has (or is committed to) mastery over fate in general" but that he shows "prudence" not only by promising "ponderously, seldom, slowly" (*GM*, II, 2), but also by being prepared to accept responsibility in cases where it was impossible to honor the promises he made.

agent trustworthy or "responsible" only if he finds some positive satisfaction in promise-keeping *as such*.

An agent who derives a feeling of "power" or "freedom" from his promise-keeping thereby finds some positive satisfaction in it: it gratifies his will to power. But the pleasure derived from satisfying his will to power could still conceivably be outweighed by the pleasure afforded by the gratification of other, stronger impulses. So, Nietzsche concludes that we consider truly "responsible" or "sovereign" only the individual in whom the "instinct for freedom" – the will to power – has become "the dominant instinct."[15]

Now, Nietzsche goes one significant step further (which the second essay leaves unmotivated): promise-keeping, and the self-mastery it requires, is a source not only of pleasure, but also of "pride" or self-esteem. The possession of a "durable and reliable will" is for the sovereign individual a *"standard of value"* in terms of which he determines what is respectable, honorable, or contemptible. Being "responsible" is therefore not just a pleasant *state*, in which his *desire* for power is gratified, it is a *standing* or a *status*, in which the *value* of power (or freedom) is instantiated. Being "responsible" makes him honorable and worthy of respect.[16]

This notion of responsibility plausibly frames a concept of *personhood* as a standing that warrants respect. Nietzsche appears to suppose that it is already so in the early "legal" framework, which constitutes the conceptual "breeding-ground" for the feeling of guilt; and his concept of responsibility, understood as the ability to govern one's behavior in accordance with obligations or commitments, bears a similarity to the notion of rational autonomy, which has long been thought to distinguish human beings from animals, and indeed "constitutes man's sense of superiority over the animals" (*GM*, II, 8; see 6).[17] On the view I am attributing to Nietzsche, then, once the right to make promises becomes the "proud realization" of a

---

[15] Ridley (2009: 187) emphasizes "whole-hearted commitment . . . to executing the relevant intention come what may" as the distinguishing mark of "sovereign promising," but ignores the motivational role of the will to power in this commitment. I am also in sympathy with Gemes (2009), who takes the "sovereign individual" to represent "agency responsibility," or the responsibility presupposed for someone's doing counting as an *action* (in contrast to "desert responsibility," which bears on whether the agent deserves reward or punishment for it). However, much depends on what is meant by "genuine agency" and Gemes's characterization of it as "a stable, unified, and integrated hierarchy of drives" also ignores the crucial role played by the will to power as the "dominant instinct" of the sovereign individual (*GM*, II, 2).

[16] Acampora (2006: 148–49) usefully notes that the phrase *"with the right to make promises* [das versprechen darf]" is ambiguous between being *permitted* to make promises and deserving *respect* or *honor* for it. Unlike her, I take the strength of the sovereign individual to give him the "right" to make promises in *both* senses.

[17] Hatab (2008: 76) claims that "the sovereign individual names the modern ideal of individual rational autonomy." This is correct if by "autonomy" he means self-constraint or self-command, the ability to

"privilege," or evidence of standing or status, the breaking of a promise will, in and of itself, decrease one's worth as a person in the way characteristic of ordinary guilt since it puts the individual's standing as a responsible agent into question.

6. GUILT AND PUNISHMENT

The conceptual backdrop of "legal" contractual relationships is also supposed to illuminate one of the most puzzling features of ordinary guilt, namely, its relation with punishment, or suffering: "In the same way, it was here that the uncanny and perhaps inextricable link-up between the ideas of 'guilt and suffering' was first crocheted together" (*GM*, II, 6). Some of what is uncanny about this linkup becomes apparent when we consider the guilty agent's experience of his punishment.

The guilty not only accepts his punishment, which he regards as deserved, but also welcomes it as a way of *expiating* his guilt. Now, it is tempting to suppose that punishment expiates his guilt by providing *reparation* for his wrongdoing. But this *reparative* view of punishment faces significant difficulties. In the first place, the punishment is often of such a nature (various kinds of suffering or deprivation inflicted upon the guilty) that it can hardly constitute reparation for the harm done. How can depriving the thief of his freedom compensate his victims for the loss of their wealth? We have already considered Nietzsche's answer to this question: "I ask again: to what extent can suffering be a compensation for 'debts'? To the degree that *to make* someone suffer is pleasure in its highest form, and to the degree that the injured party received an extraordinary counter-pleasure in exchange for the injury and distress caused by the injury: to *make* someone suffer" (*GM*, II, 6).

The deepest difficulty with the reparative view of punishment, however, lies in the supposition that the guilty welcomes his punishment because he wishes above all to repair the particular damage caused by his wrongdoing. But this, as Gabriele Taylor has argued, is not the case:

The important feature of guilt is that the thought of the guilty concentrates on herself as the doer of the deed. Having brought about what is forbidden she has harmed herself. She has put herself in a position where repayment from her is due,

make and keep commitments. This is the sense in which the sovereign individual has "freed itself from the morality of customs" and become "an autonomous, supra-ethical individual" (*GM*, II, 2): he no longer needs the threat of punishment (be it external or internalized) to motivate him to honor his commitments, which remains the basis for the authority of customs (*D*, 9). Hatab goes too far, obviously, if he has in mind the Kantian form of this ideal, as responsiveness to pure rational norms.

but the point of the payment is not, or is only incidentally, that a moral wrong should be righted. This, the righting of a moral wrong, may well be the form the repayment takes, but from the point of view of the guilty person this is only a means towards the end: that she should be rid of the burden, that she should be able again to live with herself. The painfulness of the guilt-feelings is therefore explained by the uneasiness the person concerned feels about herself. (Taylor 1985: 97)

What matters to the guilty is the fact that, by violating her obligations, she has diminished her *standing*, or her worth as a person, and not (primarily) the fact that she has caused harm in doing so. Accordingly, the point of undergoing punishment is to restore her damaged standing, not to repair the harm she has caused, even if the punishment happens to provide such reparation, as it apparently always does for Nietzsche.

Nietzsche's account helps us to see how punishment could have assumed this peculiar significance for the guilty. In his view, the feeling of guilt is a consequence of the breaking of a commitment. He observes that, in the premoral "legal" contractual framework, out of which the concept of guilt emerges, the breaking of a commitment is already wrong in *two* different respects: besides the "immediate damage" done by the agent's breaking of some particular promise, for example, there is the loss of his *standing* as a responsible agent, who has "the right to make promises." And it is the latter loss that matters most: "The immediate damage done by the offender is what we are talking about least: quite apart from this, the lawbreaker is a 'breaker', somebody who has broken his contract and his word" (*GM*, II, 9). In this premoral contractual context, Nietzsche suggests, the standing lost is simply that of a trustworthy, reliable promise-keeper, which presumably matters to the agent on essentially prudential grounds. In losing that standing he deprives himself of the benefits of contractual relationships, particularly those that bind him to a "community."[18] The purpose of punishment, in this case, is not simply to repair the "immediate damage" he has done but to restore his status as a trustworthy promise-keeper. Likewise, in a context in which indebtedness engages one's worth as a person, the wrongdoer's violation of his obligation affects his self-esteem in the manner characteristic of a feeling of guilt. What he welcomes in punishment is the opportunity not to repair the damage his transgression has caused, but to restore his standing as a "responsible" agent. Being a responsible agent in this moral context is not just a matter of being a

---

[18] Hume makes a similar point in the *Treatise of Human Nature*: "When a man says *he promises any thing*, he in effect . . ., by making use of this *form of words*, subjects himself to the penalty of never being trusted again in case of failure" (1960: 522). I am grateful to Peter Kail for bringing this point to my attention.

trustworthy promise-keeper in the eyes of others, but of being an "autonomous" agent – a *person* – who, in mastering his desires and emotions, is able to conduct his life in accordance with the commitments he has undertaken (see *GM*, II, 2).

To restore his standing, the promise-breaker would have, first, to *accept* punishment, or regard it as *deserved*. Such acceptance indicates primarily for Nietzsche, *not* that he believes he could have done otherwise, but that he recognizes the normatively binding character of his contractual obligations ("the solemnity and sanctity of his promise"; *GM*, II, 5), and acknowledges that he was wrong in failing to keep them. This alone, of course, does not suffice to qualify him as a "responsible" agent, who has "the right to make promises." To have this right, he must also have acquired a "memory of the will," that is to say, the ability to maintain his *motivation* to fulfill his promises, regardless of intervening events or desires. In other words, to merit the standing of a "responsible" agent, he must not only sincerely believe that he ought to keep his promises, he must also prove capable of doing so. His ability to endure the punishment would aim to provide precisely such a proof. Keeping one's promises requires the capacity to withstand the suffering caused by the deliberate frustration of conflicting desires and emotions. By welcoming and withstanding his punishment, the wrongdoer would seek to demonstrate that he still possesses this capacity, contrary to what his present wrongdoing may suggest.[19]

7. GUILT AS A RATIONAL PASSION

In the interpretation I am proposing here, Nietzsche's genealogy of Christian guilt exposes it as a *rational passion*, or, as he puts it, a "madness of the will" (*GM*, II, 22). Rational passions are passions to which only a rational being is susceptible, because they essentially exploit his responsiveness to reasons. Even though, like any other passion, rational passions are not themselves responsive to reasons, they differ from other passions in that their *object* is the person's standing with regard to norms or reasons: a rational passion is gratified, or frustrated, by a belief the person forms about his normative standing. It follows that, whereas other passions typically will only *override* or *bypass* reason, rational passions will often end up *corrupting*

---

[19] In so doing the guilty "assumes responsibility" for his violation, which still means, for Nietzsche, that he believes that he could have done otherwise. This, however, amounts not to a recognition of contracausal freedom, which Nietzsche repeatedly and adamantly rejects, but to an assertion of *power*, or the "strength" to overcome the conflicting desires and emotions that motivated his violation (see *BGE*, 21).

it. The narcissistic passion for thinking well of oneself is an instance of rational passion: to be susceptible to such a passion, the narcissist must be responsive to norms and the self-assessment they govern; but in order to ensure its own gratification, his passion might also lead him to corrupt these norms so as to ensure a favorable self-assessment.[20]

The Christian's guilt is another instance of rational passion: it is the passion for thinking ill of himself, or, as Nietzsche puts it, the "*will* to find himself guilty and condemned without hope of reprieve" (*GM*, II, 22). Nietzsche argues that Christian guilt operates with normative expectations that have been distorted by this passion for self-debasement. As he conceives of it, Christian guilt is indebtedness toward God, which is the most extreme development of a particular form of indebtedness – indebtedness toward the ancestors. The individual is justified in feeling indebted only if he believes that God (or the ancestors) has in fact delivered the goods for the possession of which he feels indebted to Him (*GM*, II, 19).

The distinctive feature of Christian guilt is that it is *inexpiable*, because the debt we owe God is of such "transcendence" and "holiness" that "it cannot be paid off" (*GM*, II, 21) by such finite animal beings as we are. The problem this poses is not just that debts cannot be paid off, but that guilt is inexpiable – that is to say, it is not just that the Christian cannot compensate God but that he cannot reclaim his standing as a "responsible" agent. Indeed, insofar as he was never able to fulfill his obligations to God, he could not even *claim* that standing in the first place.

If Christian guilt were responsive to the normative logic of indebtedness, we would expect a loss of belief in the existence or the power of God to result in a loss of guilt: "we should be justified in deducing, with no little probability, that from the unstoppable decline in faith in the Christian God there is, even now, a considerable decline in the consciousness of human guilt" (*GM*, II, 20). But this is precisely *not* what happens: "The facts diverge from this in a terrible way. With the moralization of the concepts guilt and duty and their relegation to *bad* conscience, we have, in reality, an attempt to *reverse* the direction of the development I have described, or at least halt its movement: now the prospect for a once-and-for-all payment *is*

---

[20] Nietzsche's interest in rational passions is far more extensive than commentators have recognized. For instance, he devotes much attention to the "pathos for *possessing* the truth" (*HAH*, I, 630), or the need for "faith" and "certainty" (*GS*, 347). Only beings responsive to norms such as truth and certainty can develop such a passion, but it is itself not necessarily governed by those norms and may well end up corrupting them: "The presupposition of every believer of every kind was that he *could* not be refuted; if the counter-arguments proved very strong it was always left to him to defame reason itself and perhaps even set up the '*credo quia absurdum est*' as the banner of the most extreme fanaticism" (*HAH*, I, 630).

to be foreclosed" (*GM*, II, 21). This leads Nietzsche to surmise that what is at work in Christian guilt is not answerability to existing norms of self-assessment, but their corruption out of self-directed cruelty:

> We have here a sort of madness of the will showing itself in mental cruelty which is unparalleled: man's *will* to find himself guilty and condemned without hope of reprieve, his *will* to think of himself as punished, without the punishment ever measuring up to the crime, his *will* to infect and poison the fundamentals of things with the problem of punishment and guilt in order to cut himself off, once and for all, from the way out of this labyrinth of "fixed ideas," this *will* to set up an ideal – that of a "holy God" – , in order to be palpably convinced of his own absolute worthlessness in the face of this ideal. (*GM*, II, 22)

It is not, in other words, because he happens to believe in a "holy God" to whom he owes more than he can repay that the Christian feels guilty. It is rather because of his "*will* to find himself guilty" that he believes in such a God.

In Nietzsche's view, then, Christianity did not invent the ordinary concept of guilt, but, under the sway of "animal bad conscience," transformed it into a perfect instrument of self-directed cruelty by introducing the notion of guilt toward God: "this man of bad conscience has seized on religious precept in order to provide his self-torture with its most horrific hardness and sharpness. Guilt towards *God:* this thought becomes an instrument of torture" (*GM*, II, 22; cf. 20). It is *self-directed* cruelty insofar as it is precisely in virtue of harboring "animal instincts" (such as cruelty) that man fails to fulfill his obligation toward a "holy God": "In 'God' he seizes upon the ultimate antithesis he can find to his real and irredeemable animal instincts, he reinterprets these selfsame animal instincts as guilt before God" (*GM*, II, 22). And it is a *perfect* form of self-directed cruelty insofar as it represents guilt as inexpiable. Prior to its Christian reinterpretation, the distinctive feeling of diminished self-esteem experienced by the guilty could only be an imperfect instrument of self-torture because guilt could always in principle be expiated: he only had to undergo the appropriate amount of punishment to restore his worth as a person. Once it is conceived as inexpiable guilt toward God, however, the loss of worth as a person becomes absolute, a loss which nothing can redeem short of a radical self-denial, of a total repudiation of one's "animal" nature, which of course leads us to what Nietzsche describes in the third essay as "the aspiration to a quite different kind of existence," that is to say, the *ascetic ideal* (*GM*, III, 11).

CHAPTER 4

Why Nietzsche is still in the morality game

Simon May

Man ... does not deny suffering as such: he wills it, he even seeks it
out, provided he is shown a meaning for it, a purpose of suffering.
(*GM*, III, 28)[1]

I. THEODICY AND LIFE-DENIAL

When Nietzsche tells us that man doesn't repudiate suffering, but even
seeks it, as long as he is given a meaning for it, he does so in a most
significant place: in the concluding section of the concluding essay of *On
the Genealogy of Morality*. He clearly advances this proposition as an indis-
putable truth, rather than as merely a heuristic device intended to disorient,
seduce, and shock his readers into questioning old assumptions. Moreover,
in looking back at this book at the end of his philosophical life, he tells us
that though its three essays all begin in a way that is "*calculated* to mislead"
and "deliberately foreground," nonetheless each of them progresses through
intimations of "disagreeable truths" to posit an entirely "*new* truth."[2]

Nor is this proposition about suffering presented as true just of
"Europeans," or inheritors of Christianity, or those otherwise infected by
slave morality. It embraces "man" – human beings in general. What is local
to the inheritors of slave morality is rather that all the meanings they have
given to suffering are structured by the ascetic ideal. And the ascetic ideal in
turn gives direction to, and expresses, a "*will to nothingness*" – an "aversion

---

[1] The English translations of Nietzsche's works to which I refer are as follows: *Beyond Good and Evil*,
trans. Walter Kaufmann ([1886] 1966a); *Ecce Homo*, trans. Walter Kaufmann ([1888] 1967c); *The Birth
of Tragedy*, trans. Walter Kaufmann ([1872] 1967a); *The Gay Science*, trans. Walter Kaufmann ([1882;
Book V, 1887] 1974); *On the Genealogy of Morality*, trans. Carol Diethe ([1887] 1994); *Thus Spoke
Zarathustra*, trans. Walter Kaufmann, in *The Portable Nietzsche*, ed. and trans. Walter Kaufmann
([1883–85] 1954b); *Twilight of the Idols*, trans. Walter Kaufmann, in *The Portable Nietzsche*, ed. and
trans. Walter Kaufmann ([1889] 1954c); and *The Will to Power*, trans. Walter Kaufmann and R. J.
Hollingdale (1968).
[2] *EH*, "Genealogy of Morals."

to life, a rebellion against the most fundamental prerequisites of life" (*GM*, III, 28). All those diverse meanings of the ascetic ideal, which Nietzsche lists in opening his third essay – the meanings employed by artists, philosophers, women, the disgruntled, priests, and sundry others – are, it turns out, merely guises of, or ways of furthering, this single underlying will.

But exactly what meaning for suffering might there be that, rather than being averse to life, would affirm life? And how might its animating will be characterized? Nietzsche famously doesn't present such an alternative in the *Genealogy* – but equally he doesn't doubt that one will eventually appear, along with its champions. It is just that, as he suggests in all three essays, the time isn't yet ripe. For one thing, the destruction of the existing ideal has a long way to run: it is a drama in several hundred acts, which will occupy the two centuries after Nietzsche himself writes (*GM*, III, 27) – a drama whose central dynamic, the will to truth becoming conscious of itself, is, Nietzsche says, not just *his* problem but the very meaning of his being, perhaps therefore the key task to which his life is devoted.[3] For another, he wonders whether champions of a new ideal that will not be hostile to life and world are "even possible today" (*GM*, II, 24). Though an all too brief incarnation of a noble ideal appeared in Napoleon – this "most isolated . . . man there has ever been" – he was in the end a bizarre exception to the still triumphant instincts of *ressentiment*. Far from resolving the conflict between a noble ethic and herd morality, he left any resolution to the future, and perhaps to an indefinite future (*GM*, I, 16–17, *passim*).

It is striking that each essay of the *Genealogy* concludes with a similar message: the old ideal, or will, still has us in its grip; the time for a new one and a new type of spirit to embody it has not yet come; but eventually it will come, even if we cannot now say precisely when and how. And when it does, morality and its underlying "will to nothingness" will be overcome.

But will they? If suffering is given a new meaning, free of the ascetic ideal and uncontaminated by the will to nothingness, will that be a sign and symptom of morality finally overcome? Will it signal the recovery of a stance of affirmation towards life – the recovery that animates Nietzsche's writing from his first work to his last? I suggest that it will not – until the very insistence on giving suffering a meaning in terms of a higher good that it makes possible, or of which it is constitutive, is itself overcome.

---

[3] "'*What does all will to truth mean?*' . . . and here I touch on my problem again, on our problem, my *unknown* friends (– because I don't *know* of any friend as yet): what meaning does *our* being have, if it were not that will to truth has becomes conscious of itself *as a problem* in us?" (*GM*, III, 27).

For to posit such a meaning for suffering is, of course, to advance a theodicy – and the impulse to do so is inseparable from traditional, life-denying morality. Indeed, even to *search* for such a justification is to remain in morality – including where the hoped-for justification is one that Nietzsche would regard as free of morality: for example, one that, to use oppositions he himself presents in the *Genealogy*, privileges the "rights of the few" rather than the "rights of the majority" (*GM*, I, 16), or the reality of this world and of man's natural inclinations, rather than aspirations to a beyond and ideals that slander this life and world (*GM*, II, 24).

In other words, one of the central truths to which the whole *Genealogy* has been leading – that man tolerates and even wills suffering providing he is shown a meaning for it – is just another expression of moral thinking and its religious roots. So, too, Nietzsche's hope of finding a meaning for suffering that can affirm life and its most fundamental presuppositions rather than express an aversion to them is a symptom of the very despair that he diagnoses in morality. A stance towards life that genuinely affirms it would not, I argue, consider suffering as standing in *any* need of such meaning.

As I will suggest, there are clear signs that Nietzsche intermittently recognizes this – and that he inconclusively strives, above all in his desire for *amor fati*, to find an attitude of affirmation to which one does not need to clamber up by justifying one's sufferings in terms of higher goals to which they are putatively necessary, or otherwise in terms of some whole of which suffering is a part. Though he repeatedly lapses back into precisely such justifications – for example seeing suffering as a precondition for, or con-stitutive of,[4] creativity in art and values, strength, heroism, knowledge, and all the human flourishing he values – the movement of his thought suggests a struggle to escape theodicy and instead to find an affirmation of life that is an ungrounded joy in life's "there-ness" or quiddity.

But before turning to this movement of Nietzsche's thought it is neces-sary to propose the elements of an affirmation of life that is free of theodicy. Specifically we must try to see what *amor fati* really involves – including how we can say Yes to the "piece of *fatum*" that he elsewhere says each of us is (*TI*, "Morality as Anti-Nature," 6), while also accommodating the obvious fact

---

[4] I owe this distinction between suffering as an indispensable condition of supreme goods and suffering as constitutive of them (so that to will these ends is also to will suffering) to Reginster (2006: e.g. pp. 231–33). In any event, it does not rescue Nietzsche from being in the business of theodicy. A central question of affirmation, as I see it, is how to affirm life without anesthetizing suffering by postulating the latter's necessity, whether in a means–end way or constitutively, to a higher goal which we supremely value – a question that the secondary literature does not really take up.

that we all, including Nietzsche himself, find much "nauseating" or "loathsome" in our lives, experiences and encounters. Since Nietzsche's own explication of life-affirmation does not begin to match, in clarity or scope, his diagnosis of life-denial, we need to do this work for him in order to see how far he himself succeeds in affirming life and how far, by contrast, he remains stuck in morality and its life-denial.

Life-affirmation: a theory

(1) To affirm life is to look with joy upon one's life as a whole, conceived as necessary (or fated) in all its elements, without justifying it or desiring an alternative to it.

(2) This joy is a disposition: living – with whatever it brings – thrills to itself. Such a disposition bears no relation in tone and texture to complacency, let alone to tolerance or grudging acceptance. Nor is it grounded in judgments – such as "it is better to live than not to live," "life is precious," or "to affirm my life enables me to have a sense of power over it and its necessity, rather than to feel like its helpless plaything." (All of the latter can quite easily be expressions of despair.) Nor, too, does such affirmative joy feature in an answer to the question "How should I live"? No ends or projects can ground it, not even Nietzschean ones. For example, I might be better off saying No to all my mediocre valuings and doings if I want to flourish in the commitments I most care about. But, at the same time as I am doing this, my disposition to affirm will do something quite different: it will say Yes to my life in all its quiddity.

(3) To affirm one's life as a whole is consistent with loathing, regretting, or "saying No" to, particular experiences or events in it – including some of one's sufferings. These experiences or events can be affirmed only *qua* inextricable parts of the whole life conceived as fated – this whole life being the primary object of affirmation (and every event in it making up the person I am).

(4) Though Nietzsche does repeatedly suggest that to affirm life is to welcome all its suffering, I suggest that to "welcome suffering" is a kind of contradiction. What is actually "welcomed" is no longer the original suffering, since all attitudes that succeed in welcoming suffering remove its essential sting, which is its unwantedness and the overwhelming helplessness it engenders. Such attitudes tend to be directed at eliminating precisely this sting – and therefore the essence of

suffering – by seeing some sort of goodness or beauty in it: deeming that what was unwanted was actually a blessing, that its helplessness has in fact made one stronger or better, that what one could hardly bear should really be a matter for gratitude, that one has discovered beauty where one initially experienced only horror.

In particular, justifications of suffering in terms of higher goods to which it is essential aim at just such mastery; and, as a stance, justification involves standing back from its object. In addition it is usually an *ex post* stance ("without that suffering I couldn't have achieved X," etc.), which removes the stance still further from the actual experience. This is quite appropriate when we are reflecting on the value of our goods or practices; but such a standing back in order to justify does not belong to the experience of life-affirmation (think of affirming the lives of our children).

(5) The suffering that poses the greatest challenge to affirming one's life is, in any case, precisely that which *cannot* credibly be justified – and which goes on stubbornly resisting all attempts to discover its blessings or beauty. It cannot be denied that such suffering exists, whether it is the result of natural causes – such as earthquakes and tsunamis and illness of a sufficient order to destroy the conditions for flourishing – or man-made ones – such as the gas chambers at Auschwitz and the intentions of those who devised and operated them. The whole challenge of affirmation ultimately exists because of, and in relation to, the existence of such horrors.

(6) Moreover, since affirmation as joy cannot be a purely cognitive matter but is primarily affective, it cannot ultimately depend upon finding a satisfactory meaning in suffering, or be a product of justifying suffering – whether my own suffering or suffering as intrinsic to life.

Only such affirmation – that takes joy in one's life's there-ness without seeking to justify its suffering as constitutive of one's supreme goods[5] or as otherwise essential to their attainment – moves decisively beyond the impulse to theodicy.

II. THE RADICALISM OF NIETZSCHE'S ACCOUNT OF LIFE-DENIAL

To see what a mountain has to be climbed to get from where we are now, as Nietzsche diagnoses it, to genuine life-affirmation we need to consider the

---

[5] Goods such as artistic creativity – or love, involving as it does the inevitable possibility of loss.

extraordinarily radical account of life-denial that emerges from the *Genealogy*. The will that has turned against life on account of its potential for suffering thereby denies everything about the world of which suffering is constitutive – including nature, growth, the human, and transience (*GM*, III, 28). At the same time it posits supreme goods, whether conceived in transcendent or secular terms, that are insulated from the contingency, loss, and destruction from which suffering arises. But to seek such a state of affairs supposedly purified of suffering and the causes of suffering, and so of the only world that, for Nietzsche, can exist, is to seek what does not exist, what is nothing.[6]

Crucially, the will to nothingness, as Nietzsche portrays it in the *Genealogy*, is in no way diminished by loss of faith in God – in other words by the "death of God" conceived as atheism (*GS*, 125).

Before the death of God, the goods posited by the will to nothingness explicitly involved a transcendent deity: suffering is a path to God, in whose realm death, loss, and transience are abolished; it is redeemed by the sacrifice of his son; it is punishment for disobeying him. And of course, in the traditional theodicy, suffering and evil are the price to be paid for the blessing of metaphysically "free will."

After the death of God, the underlying will remains perfectly intact. All that changes is that the goods posited by this will are no longer structured by overtly supernatural or otherwise dualistic categories. Instead, the same hope is pursued in ways that don't appeal to these now discredited categories. For Nietzsche's rare spirits it is, for example, pursued through goods like truth and truthfulness conceived as unconditionally valuable (e.g. *GM*, III, 27). For the masses, as he sees them, it is sought through intense commitment to comfort, predictability, and convenience: the goals of the "last man"; or through the ethos of industrial civilization: hard work, neatness, the search for technical means of making life ever safer, the "positivist" mindset to which the "industrious race of machinists and bridge-builders" (*BGE*, 14) foreseen by Nietzsche is so competently devoted. Or there is the form of life of the peace-loving scholar – of orderly experimentation and wide-ranging curiosity, but strictly within bounds that avoid risk and danger and instead stabilize and calm one's life. All are expressions of *"the religion of comfortableness"* (*GS*, 338).

---

[6] *GM*, III, 28; cf. the idea of life denying itself in *GM*, Preface, 5, and *GM*, III, 11. Or, as Nietzsche puts it in *TI*, "Reason in Philosophy," 6: "The criteria which have been bestowed on the 'true being' of things are the criteria of not-being, of *naught*."

The people who hear the madman announce the death of God don't realize that this event, insofar as it is conceived merely as atheism, does nothing to overcome the governing will to nothingness. An unheroic, ethically unambitious, risk-averse civilization that laughs at supernatural ideas (for example, at their empirical unverifiability, their childlike hopes for absolute security, their licensing of religious bigotry, or the supposed logical impossibility of former articles of faith, such as God being both omnipotent and all-good) sees man as nothing more than a sophisticated animal, and takes it for granted that life and its goods can be conceived only in naturalistic terms – such a down-to-earth naturalism does not by these tokens affirm life.

How God's death might intensify life-denial

On the contrary, as morality undermines itself – loses faith in unconditioned values, in a saving Father, in a metaphysically free will that enables us to "choose" good and say No to evil, and in the other consolations of crude metaphysical dualism – the fear of suffering and so the will to nothingness are set to become *more* intense. The danger – as Nietzsche correctly prophesies – is that losing the old comforting beliefs will make us ever more squeamish about suffering and invest ever more effort in eliminating it.

The result of the death of God (in the limited sense of atheism) is therefore not to liberate individuals boldly to pursue their own destinies, but to erect an array of conceptual and ethical barricades against the risky and the unexpected, to empty life of heroism in thought and deed. As suffering becomes ever more successfully mastered, it also becomes (as many challenges become when we have little or no experience of them) ever more frightening.

Atheistic pessimism, like Schopenhauer's, arises, Nietzsche says, not from the experience of misery but from the fear of misery; not from actual suffering but from squeamishness about suffering:

The general lack of experience of pain of both kinds [of the body and of the soul] and the relative rarity of the sight of anyone who is suffering have an important consequence: pain is now hated much more than was the case formerly; one speaks much worse of it; indeed, one considers the existence of the mere *thought* of pain scarcely endurable and turns it into a reproach against the whole of existence. (*GS*, 48)

Of course the life of comfortable predictability that this squeamishness seeks can become boring, and there might be times when one craves escape from it through any activity that will stimulate desire and sensation – including suffering. But this is a craving to suffer that stems merely from "a craving to do something" of those "who cannot endure their boredom and themselves, who need neediness" (*GS*, 56). It is not the suffering to which the self-respecting individual intrepidly taking the risk of seeking his or her own path is open – not the suffering that one risks when one maximally opens oneself to, and seeks power over, the world. It looks for monsters to slay (*GS*, 56), but in the sense of forays undertaken from a nondescript position of comfort, rather than in the sense of a lifelong and courageous throwing of the self into a world which it wishes to find an individual way of mastering.

III. LIFE-AFFIRMATION IS NOT A SIMPLE REVERSAL OF THE VALUES AND CONCEPTS OF LIFE-DENIAL

This ethical, conceptual, and affective apparatus of life-denial – pre and post the death of God – has been well analyzed in the secondary literature. Intense effort has been devoted to reconstructing Nietzsche's portrayal of the values and concepts structured by slave morality, their motivation by *ressentiment*, and their search for transcendence of time, causality, fate, becoming, and, in the life of the "last man" or the "small man," all risk and danger.

But we return to the question: what would it be to affirm life? How can we characterize the stance of "[s]aying Yes to life even in its strangest and hardest problems" (*TI*, "What I Owe to the Ancients," 5)? As I have already suggested, naturalism and the repudiation of metaphysical dualism in its various guises are not, *in themselves*, expressions of life-affirmation. On the contrary, thoroughgoing naturalism – for example one that has abandoned belief in metaphysically free will and sees human beings as animals in a universe with no *telos* – can be as life-denying as the overt supernaturalism that preceded it.

Thus life-affirmation is not vouchsafed even by a thoroughgoing reversal of the concepts and values that characterize life-denial. So that instead of valorizing being we would valorize becoming; instead of seeking permanence we would welcome the natural impermanence of all things; instead of praising pity and weakness we would praise cruelty and strength; instead of denying the body and natural instinct we would glorify them; instead of caution and risk-aversion there would be dangerous living and *Rausch* – that "over-fullness of spirit" out of which new values and new art forms would be forged.

Though these are all *expressions* of the life-affirming spirit, as Nietzsche depicts it, they are the cart not the horse. The reversals on which they depend – be they characterized in terms of their affects, cognitions, or valuings – cannot be achieved directly. They can be achieved only by those who are no longer dogged by the "problem of suffering."

If the problem of suffering is still in the driving seat, these expressions of life-affirmation will be faked – and a tremendously powerful and creative individual will fake them tremendously powerfully and creatively; but sooner or later the individual concerned will revert to type. (Though I cannot go into it here, this is precisely the case of Wagner, as Nietzsche presents it, and especially of Wagner's gathering obsession with the redemption of suffering, culminating in *Parsifal.*)

The question then is what attitude to our life we would have if the "problem of suffering" were not to arise in the first place. How would we characterize this attitude phenomenologically – in other words, not simply in terms of its cognitive and axiological commitments but in terms of how it is experienced?

IV. DISPOSITIONS OF THE LIFE-AFFIRMER

Affirmation is not a product of justification

As I remarked earlier, a key feature of the will that has turned against life on account of its suffering is to demand that suffering – one's own, or in general – be justified in terms of supreme goods of which it is a precondition or else constitutive. My central claim in this chapter is that a will that affirms one's own life or life in general – that looks with joy upon it as a whole, conceived as necessary (or fated) in all its elements – seeks no such justification; indeed, I claim that such justification *does not occur to it.*

Affirmation, in other words, doesn't involve assuring ourselves that suffering is essential to these goods, either as the condition of their attainment or as constitutive of them. And it certainly doesn't involve a calculus of welfare that issues in an all-things-considered attitude to life – whether of my own life or of life "as such."

On the contrary it is a stance that is all the stronger for demonstrating no wish to engage in such assurances – for simply taking joy in the existence and reality of its object, joy that cannot be mitigated by the object's failings, however painful or unsightly or regretful we find them. One motive, after all, for seeking to justify something is that we are unsure of our commitment to it. The will to justify involves, experientially, detachment from, perhaps even mistrust of, its object (essential though that is when we are reflecting on the worth of our goods and practices, how to live our lives best, and so on). It is the position of the observer who stands back and reaches judgments. Crucially it presupposes that there is the alternative of saying No, even if it rejects that alternative.

When, for example, we affirm the life of our child we don't do so only after evaluating him, weighing his positive against his negative qualities, and then settling, all things considered, for who he actually is. It isn't that we fail to see and even dislike his faults; rather our joy in the reality or there-ness of his life is neither diminished by these faults nor reached by justifying or even explaining their value to his whole life. The same will be true for any of our deep commitments – for anything that, as Nietzsche puts it in his late statement on *amor fati* (to which I will turn in a moment), we do not merely bear but *love*. Even if I should justify those commitments or my life as such, this would, at best, issue in cognitive affirmation, with some allied affective affirmation – but not in enthusiastic, unhesitating Yes-saying.

This illustrates my suggestion that life-affirmation is not a matter of merely reversing the valuations of life-denial. The pose of assuming that "life" or its suffering can be evaluated and justified is the pose of the life-denier, *even if* he should end up giving it a positive valuation. The desire for justification is inconsistent with the spirit of affirmation. Prior to our evaluations of the world are the positions from which we make them, and these positions can still be the product of the will to nothingness even when they end up saying Yes to all the things to which previously one said No.

But the reason why the life-affirmer has no desire to justify suffering does not just have to do with the relation between affirmation and justification. It also has to do with the nature of suffering, which at its heart is about helplessness, vulnerability, uncertainty, lack of control. Why did it strike? Why me? How bad will it get? What consequences will it have? Will it ever end? To interpret suffering as Nietzsche comfortingly does – as constitutive, say, of creative activity, so that to will the latter *is* to will suffering – is still to be in the business of abolishing precisely the helplessness, the interpretive vacuum, that gives suffering its sting, by telling ourselves that we have in fact willed it, that its consequences are desirable, and indeed not merely desirable but among the greatest goods of which we can conceive. And to that extent, it is still to be in the business of abolishing suffering itself – an ambition that Nietzsche elsewhere deems "insane" (*BGE*, 225). For suffering interpreted is no longer suffering.

If Nietzsche wishes to revalue our attitude to suffering he would need to dissolve the problem altogether – to cease to make vindications of it so

vitally important to ethics and to the affirmation of life. Suffering cannot be
revalued merely by giving it a new justification that is free of the metaphysical or teleological categories of Christianity and its secular successors.

* * *

Nonetheless, if we look at Nietzsche's propensity to justify suffering, we see
an interesting movement in his thought, one which suggests that he is
tending towards such a dissolution of the problem. In his early work,
notably *The Birth of Tragedy*, he is overtly in the business of theodicy,
despite his gathering hostility to the pessimism (Christian and atheist/
Schopenhauerian) that fuels it. In his middle to late period, beginning
with *The Gay Science*, he, on the one hand, still invokes or justifies suffering
as a necessary condition of his supreme goods – great art, great men, heroic
deeds, knowledge,[7] the creation of new values, creativity in general[8] – and
looks for ways of "seducing" even his higher human beings to life; while, on
the other hand, moving powerfully towards a more ungrounded affirmation
of life in his first statement of both *amor fati*[9] and "eternal recurrence."[10]
Finally in his last two active years and especially in his concluding published
work, *Ecce Homo*, he seems to make a decisive further move away from
grounding life-affirmation in justifications of suffering.

Thus in *The Birth of Tragedy* (1872), affirmation is explicitly presented as
the result of justification, indeed *as a justification*: "only as an *aesthetic
phenomenon* is existence and the world eternally justified" (*BT*, 5 and 24).
It matters little that the terms in which Nietzsche is seeking to justify
existence and its horrors are aesthetic – by contrast to the various religious
and non-religious theodicies that justify existence in moral terms, such as
the necessity of free will to striving for goodness and salvation and yet also to
the possibility of evil. The very terms in which this famous pronouncement
is couched – the observer's stance of evaluating "existence" or "the world" as
a whole, the search not just for justification but for "eternal justification" –
are the terms employed by precisely the pessimism that Nietzsche comes to
repudiate. (And in his late preface to *The Birth of Tragedy*, his "attempt at a
self-criticism," he criticizes his younger self as a "pessimist" – marked by
"deep hatred against 'the Now', against 'reality' . . . believing sooner in the
Nothing . . . than in 'the Now'" [*BT*, "Attempt at a Self-Criticism," 7]. Which

---

[7] The thought of "life as a means to knowledge" was, Nietzsche says, his "great liberator" – *GS*, 324.
[8] For example, Nietzsche has Zarathustra posit creation as "the great redemption from suffering."
Indeed "that the creator may be, suffering is needed" (*Z*, II, 2, "Upon the Blessed Isles").
[9] *GS*, 107.
[10] Paradigmatically formulated at *GS*, 341, and in *Thus Spoke Zarathustra* (*Z*, III, 2, "On the Vision and
the Riddle," 13, "The Convalescent" – from 1883–85).

is consistent with the equation that I am suggesting: namely that the very desire to justify suffering is a mark of pessimism.)

By contrast, in *The Gay Science* (1882)[11] he recasts this same thought and pointedly drops the idea of justification. "As an aesthetic phenomenon existence is still *bearable* for us," he now says (*GS*, 107).[12] We see here that Nietzsche in no way affirms existence unconditionally: after all, only under the aspect of its aestheticization is existence bearable. Indeed, in the same passage he remains unable to affirm existence without the "counter-force" that art provides against the "nausea and suicide" that honest looking at the nature of things would induce (*GS*, 107). The same is true when he says that "we possess *art* lest we *perish of the truth*" (*WP*, 822, from 1888), and speaks of art as "the great seduction to life, the great stimulant of life . . . *the redemption of the man of knowledge . . . the redemption of the man of action . . . the redemption of the sufferer*" (*WP*, 853, §2).

That Nietzsche's approach to affirmation in this middle period remains residually structured by the conceptual form of theodicy is seen, moreover, in the fact that the referent of his affirmation is "existence," which, from the context, seems to be existence as such rather than my individual existence. Yet in Book V of *The Gay Science*, a late work published in 1887, he pours scorn on the whole standpoint of evaluating existence as such:

the whole pose of "man *against* the world," of man as a "world-negating" principle, of man as the measure of the value of things, as judge of the world who in the end places existence itself upon his scales and finds it wanting . . . (*GS*, 346)

And in *Twilight of the Idols* (1888), he makes a similar point:

One would require a position *outside* of life, and yet to have to know it as well as one, as many, as all who have lived it, in order to be permitted even to touch the problem of the *value* of life: reasons enough to comprehend that this problem is for us an unapproachable problem. (*TI*, "Morality as Anti-Nature," 5; cf. *TI*, "The Problem of Socrates," 2)

Yet in suggesting that an existence not experienced as an aesthetic phenom-enon would be unbearable, or that life (and specifically truth-seeing) not buttressed by art would warrant suicide, Nietzsche is very much involved in "the problem of the value of life." And this involvement means, not surprisingly, that he adopts a standpoint – that from which he assesses the bearableness of "existence" – remarkably similar to the "pose" of placing

---

[11] In fact only Books I to IV of *The Gay Science* are from 1882, and as we will see Book V, published in 1887, attempts to move away from overall attitudes towards existence.

[12] Young (1992: 157 n. 16) connects this later formulation with Apollonian art.

existence itself upon the scales that he diagnoses in traditional morality and dismisses as a "monstrous insipidity" (*GS*, 346). As a standpoint it is just as absurd if it issues in a positive evaluation of existence or deems existence to be "bearable" as if it issues in the traditional negative evaluation or deems it to be unbearable. For it is still nothing but a vainglorious fiction dreamed up by the will to nothingness – by the sufferer who imagines he can arrogate to himself the power of judgment over the tolerability of existence or life, and thereby over the suffering that is constitutive of it.

In stark opposition to these searches for an aesthetic theodicy, when Nietzsche first presents *amor fati* and wishes it for himself, he seems to be speaking of an ungrounded Yes-saying to our life as a whole just as we find it:

> I want to learn more and more to see as beautiful what is necessary in things; then I shall be one of those who make things beautiful. *Amor fati*: let that be my love henceforth! I do not want to wage war against what is ugly. I do not want to accuse; I do not even want to accuse those who accuse. *Looking away* shall be my only negation. And all in all and on the whole: some day I wish to be only a Yes-sayer. (*GS*, 276)

Looking away was clearly not about to be Nietzsche's only negation: in the following year, 1888, he was to write, among other diatribes, *The Antichrist*, *Twilight of the Idols*, and *The Case of Wagner*. In that extraordinarily productive last year, we see a continuation of his ambivalent position on the justification of suffering. On the one hand it is still the driving force behind thoughts like this:

> . . . all becoming and growing – all that guarantees a future – involves pain. That there may be the eternal joy of creating, that the will to life may eternally affirm itself, the agony of the woman giving birth *must* also be there eternally. (*TI*, "What I Owe to the Ancients," 4)

This echoes the statement in the slightly earlier *Beyond Good and Evil* (1886) in which Nietzsche says of "*great* suffering" that "only *this* discipline has created all enhancements of man so far" (*BGE*, 225). (And such a view of suffering is in turn prefigured in one of the most ancient Christian theodicies, dating back to the Greek-speaking Father of the Church, St. Irenaeus [*c.* CE 130–202], and before him to St. Paul, in which hardship and pain are seen as needed for soul-making, for the self-creation of human beings so that they may attain more perfect states of being.[13] St. Paul says: "we rejoice in our sufferings, knowing that suffering produces endurance, and endurance produces character, and character produces hope . . ."[14] – a thought

---

[13] Hick 1966: 211–15, 253–55.   [14] Romans 5:3–4; cf. II Corinthians 12:7–10. Cited in Hick 1966: 357.

that, despite the fundamentally different values structuring it, bears more than passing resemblances to Nietzsche's, not least in its concern with averting despair.[15])

On the other hand the stances of affirmation (which, perhaps, also function as tests of affirmation) that Nietzsche advances in his later philosophy – *amor fati* and the capacity to will "eternal recurrence" – are formulated in a manner that neither appeals to nor presupposes any such justification:

> *amor fati*: that one wants nothing to be different, not forward, not backwards, not in all eternity. Not merely bear what is necessary, still less conceal it . . . but *love* it. (*EH*, "Why I Am So Clever," 10)

Elsewhere in this last work that looks back over his life he speaks of "Saying Yes unconditionally";[16] he singles out the idea of eternal recurrence, with its pure, unjustified desire for the infinite repetition of one's life, as the "highest formula of affirmation" and "the fundamental conception of" *Thus Spoke Zarathustra*;[17] and he remarks of *Dawn*:

> This Yes-saying book pours out its light, its love, it tenderness upon ever so many wicked things; it gives back to them their "soul," a good conscience, the lofty right and privilege of existence. (*EH*, "Dawn," 1)

Moreover, we now see Nietzsche value the capacity to look at unvarnished reality without resorting to art (in the sense either of creativity or of seeing things as beautiful) as a counter to the horrors of doing so: "How much truth does a spirit *endure*, how much truth does it *dare*? More and more that became for me the real measure of value . . . error is *cowardice*" (*EH*, Preface, 3).

It is a progress of fits and starts, but there is a clear direction of movement away from theodicy and towards an affirmation of life that does not invoke a supreme good to which suffering is essential.[18]

---

[15] See, for example, *GS*, 107, *WP*, 822 and 853, §2, cited above.

[16] *EH*, "The Untimely Ones," 2.   [17] *EH*, "Thus Spoke Zarathustra," 1.

[18] This movement in Nietzsche's thought is, in general, not captured by the secondary literature – though what Gemes (2008) calls Nietzsche's "naïve affirmation" makes no appeal to any sort of justification. More typically, Reginster proposes an interpretation of Nietzsche's view of affirmation that, while avoiding narrow means–end instrumentalism, suggests that "to affirm life we must therefore *show* that suffering is good for its own sake" (Reginster 2006: 15; my emphasis). He goes on: "Suffering can therefore be truly redeemed by creativity only if it is essentially necessary for it, that is to say, only when the suffering is an enabling necessary condition of the very possibility of creativity. What this proposal needs is an account of the way in which suffering is essentially necessary for creativity." In a similar vein Reginster seeks a justification of destruction or of negation in terms of the creation to which it might lead, negation "that will be felt as leaving something valuable behind" (Reginster 2006: 246). But to show that suffering is good for its own sake, or to seek an account of the

Life-affirmation is not to consider alternatives to the particular life we have

In addition to not being grounded in such justifications, affirmation does not involve a search for alternatives to the individual life we have – and for similar reasons. The will that has turned *against* life is the will that posits alternatives to life's suffering – and, specifically, repudiates those aspects of existence that cause suffering. Whether conceived in religious or secular terms, these alternatives crave peace and security: the redeeming God, the comfortable predictability of the "last man," unconditional values, and other forms of insurance against loss and transience – all, for Nietzsche, ways of emptying life of its richness, all ways of willing *das Nichts*. When Augustine talks of *quies*, or eternal rest, both as the nature of God and as the highest good for which, in his ethics, life can strive, he perfectly expresses the target against which Nietzsche takes aim. In seeking *quies* in God, we seek perfect and immutable rest in another world, which is entirely free of the contingency and loss that are constitutive of this life. This is well expressed in Augustine's famous words at the beginning of his *Confessions*: "you have made us for yourself, and our hearts find no peace until they rest in you."[19]

In general the disposition to consider alternative lives to the one we have reflects – and creates – an uncertain relation to this one, just as a disposition to consider what it would be like to have more pleasing children than the ones I have would cast doubt on my affirmation of the latter. The Nietzschean affirmer, if asked to entertain the idea of an alternative life, would consider it otiose, without interest, and, incidentally, given a determined world,[20] unintelligible.

Ascetically ideal thinking is the paradigm of thinking that imagines radical alternatives of this sort. The superior domain that it posits – God, permanence, unconditioned values, and the like – is the alternative to the inferior domain in which we actually live; and only striving for the superior can justify, redeem, and give acceptable meaning to, the inferior. And that supreme impresario of the ascetic ideal, the "ascetic priest," is, Nietzsche tells us, "the incarnate wish for being otherwise, being elsewhere, indeed, he

---

way in which suffering is essentially necessary for creativity, or to demonstrate that destruction is to be welcomed *because* it leaves something valuable behind, is still to be in the old game of justification. This is not the spirit of *amor fati*, nor, as I have suggested, of any genuine affirmation.

[19] Augustine 1961: Book I, 1.

[20] I will not supplement the already considerable weight of argument in the secondary literature for Nietzsche's deterministic view of history. This interpretation is well supported by his talk of "fate," "necessity," the interlinking of all events such that "if ever you wanted one thing twice . . . then you wanted *all* back" (*Z*, IV, 19, "The Drunken Song," 10), and his suggestion that the individual is "the whole single line of humanity up to himself" (*TI*, "Skirmishes of an Untimely Man," 33).

is the highest pitch of this wish, its essential ardour and passion. . ." But if I am free of concepts and values structured by the ascetic ideal and do not believe in, hope for, or seek an order other than the (deterministic) one in which I necessarily live – the one characterized by what Nietzsche calls "necessity" or "fate" – then the thought of an alternative life that is superior in value to this one wouldn't occur to me.

Life-affirmation is consistent with despising particular events in our life

But now we must return to a central and rather obvious question, which I raised before but too briefly answered: how are we to affirm life, precisely if we do not or cannot justify its most horrific events or see anything beautiful in them?

The first point to make here is that to affirm one's life is not at all the same thing as – and nor does it require us – to find everything *good* or indeed beautiful about it. As a "Yes-sayer" I can, like Nietzsche, detest the "small man," the operations of slave morality in me and others, the actions of my sister, the racism of my compatriots, and other events and experiences of my life, while not wishing to have lived another life free of those events and experiences.

Nietzsche is not saying that ultimately everything is, and can only be, good in one way or another (and so affirmable). Not only does he, as just mentioned, disvalue a great many things; but, more fundamentally, his revaluation of all values presupposes such a No-saying – an ethical No-saying and an aesthetic No-saying – to much of the world that he finds himself in. Indeed he explicitly recognizes this, speaking of the task he had set himself in *Beyond Good and Evil*:

> After the Yes-saying part of my task had been solved, the turn had come for the No-saying, *No-doing* part: the revaluation of our values so far . . . (*EH*, "Beyond Good and Evil," 1)

There is, therefore, room within a Nietzschean ethic of affirmation for detesting, repudiating, and regretting particular events and experiences, providing such valuations and sentiments are not structured by the ascetic ideal. That is: providing the relevant phenomenology has no room for thoughts of an alternative life or world purified of suffering and the causes of suffering.

* * *

Nietzsche himself knows that the question of how it is that one can say No and yet be an affirmer cannot be avoided. Indeed he poses it forcefully in his retrospective take on the character of Zarathustra:

The psychological problem in the type of Zarathustra is how he that says No and *does* No to an unheard-of degree, to everything to which one has so far said Yes, can nevertheless be the opposite of a No-saying spirit; how the spirit who bears the heaviest fate . . . can nevertheless be the lightest . . . how he that has the hardest, most terrible insight into reality . . . nevertheless does not consider it an objection to existence, not even to its eternal recurrence – but rather one reason more for being himself the eternal Yes to all things . . . "Into all abysses I still carry the blessings of my saying Yes." – *But this is the concept of Dionysus once again.* (*EH*, "Thus Spoke Zarathustra," 6)

This passage poses the question . . . only to beg it: for what is the "reason" for being the eternal Yes to all things – "all things" necessarily including those to which Zarathustra has already said No?

To some extent Nietzsche employs concepts like "overcoming" and "creativity" and "seeing beauty" to answer this sort of question. Life, as he conceives it, is a continuous overcoming: the assertion of power over things, including those we loathe and reject (but also those we admire and respect), by interpreting, incorporating, transforming, and destroying them. Creativity is just this: forging, for example, new forms of art, or thought, or statecraft out of the world we inherit, incorporating what we might loathe or fear or despise into a whole that we affirm. One who destroys, repudiates, overcomes, or transforms the old in new creations by that token affirms it. He can affirm it as something he nonetheless respects in its own right and as essential to his own creativity (say Einstein's attitude to Newton; Newton's to the "giants" on whose shoulders he stood; Kant's to Hume; to some degree, Nietzsche's to the creative energies of slave morality). And he can respect it simply as something to be overcome (say Nietzsche's welcoming of hardship) – where overcoming is what life is and how power is measured (e.g.: one's "tablet of the good" – one's values – is the tablet of one's overcomings: *Z*, I, 15, "On the Thousand and One Goals"[21]).

And yet there are two reasons why concepts like "overcoming" and "creativity" do not really suffice for answering Nietzsche's question about Zarathustra. First, their value in grounding affirmation is limited by the fact

---

[21] The central importance of "overcoming" (and related concepts like "becoming") to Nietzsche's ethic means that the *Übermensch* is, if an ideal at all, then one whose final attainment is undesirable by Nietzsche's own standards; for it would leave nothing further to overcome and strip life of all becoming. For similar reasons, the perfect achievement of the "sovereign individual" cannot be Nietzsche's new ideal. Perhaps the reason why Nietzsche, though searching for new ideals, ultimately seems to mistrust the very notion of an ethic structured around them, is not only that they abstract from the rich detail of life and so risk impoverishing our ambitions, but, even more importantly, that the wish to fulfill them is tantamount to a wish for stasis. Cf. May 1999: 116–18 and 86, where I argue that the *Übermensch* as well as the perfectly sovereign individual are neither attainable nor desirable ideals.

that they still smack of a theodicy, where, as I discussed above, what we repudiate is justified by a higher good of which it is constitutive or a necessary condition. Whereas we have said that the purest affirmation dispenses altogether with the crutch of justification.

Second, these concepts are useless when faced with the question: how does the agent affirm her suffering when, as far as anyone can tell, it isn't expressed in any creativity on her part, and is such that she cannot possibly find beauty in it? For example, suffering that eliminates her entire family in a natural or man-made disaster? Or suffering that destroys the creative opportunities of precisely the sort of supremely gifted individual whom Nietzsche would respect? Say, hypothetically, the situation of a Picasso[22] entirely paralyzed just before the execution of a work that would have expressed his highest will to power and now unable to turn this suffering – or any that preceded it – into further creative acts. How is the subject of such experiences to affirm them in Nietzsche's ultimate sense – that of *amor fati* and willing eternal recurrence – if he or she cannot redeem the loathsome in terms of a higher good which it makes possible?

Such examples point, I suggest, to an inescapable feature of life-affirmation: the proper object of affirmation is *not* the particular event as such but rather my whole life of which the particular event is an inextricable part. This helps us see how saying Yes to the whole and No to the particular can be reconciled.

The object of affirmation is the whole, not the particular

When Nietzsche talks of affirming everything about one's life to the extent of wanting nothing to be different, "not forward, not backward," he does not mean, of course, that we reach this position by aggregating separate affirmations of each event in our life over its whole span. "Life," for him, is not the summation of a series of distinct events or experiences. And so life-affirmation is not the summation of a series of distinct affirmations. It is

---

[22] Picasso is the paradigm of the individual that Nietzsche most highly values. As John Richardson (2007) portrays him, he relates cannibalistically to people and things and events and his great predecessors – all of them grist to his creative mill; Picasso himself compares his protean artistry and prodigious experimentation to God's; he worships Dionysus; and he is entirely unconcerned with others' sufferings, especially if the latter are needed for his own work. Pity, altruism and any sort of egalitarianism do not feature in his axiological repertoire as Richardson presents it. He is generous, kind, and tender when the spirit takes him, but never in any moral sense. He seems even more of a Nietzschean hero than Goethe and, possibly, than Napoleon, whose promotion of equal rights for citizens under the law is something about which Nietzsche, for all his antipathy to equality, is strangely quiet.

rather the other way around: life – my whole lived life until now – is what is affirmed, and in affirming my life I *ipso facto* affirm particular events insofar as they are inextricable parts of the whole.

Admittedly in Nietzsche's characterization of the affirmer of eternal recurrence individual events indeed seem to be the objects of their own separate affirmations: "The question in *each and every* thing, 'Do you desire this once more and innumerable times more?' would lie upon your actions as the greatest weight." But, as so often with Nietzsche, things aren't necessarily as clear as any single utterance might suggest. The very next sentence seems to claim that what is affirmed is my own self and life as a whole: "Or how well disposed would you have to become to *yourself* and to *life* to crave nothing more fervently . . ." (*GS*, 341, my italics).

Regardless of what Nietzsche intends in this paragraph, I do not see how individual events can possibly be self-standing objects of affirmation. There are surely some events that destroy the agent's flourishing however it is conceived and calibrated – such as the Picasso and Auschwitz examples above – and to which those experiencing them, including those with Nietzschean intuitions about the good for them, cannot be well disposed, including in any aesthetic sense. There are many events and experiences to which Nietzsche does, in fact, "say No" (as would, perhaps, any flourishing individual) and on which, again, he does not look with anything remotely like delight.

Moreover, fundamental philosophical positions that Nietzsche adopts – especially on the individuation of events and on determinism – also suggest that the individual event is a less suitable candidate for affirmation than the whole life in which it is situated. For him all individuation of "actions" or "events" or "experiences," all chopping up of life, with its unfathomable complexity and myriad interconnections, into these discrete chunks, about whose nature, significance, and value we then deliberate as if they were meaningfully isolatable from the whole, is deeply arbitrary. Here two key aspects of his thought come together: his determinism means that an event is always embedded in a chain of cause and effect and so to delineate it as a unit of affirmation (or indeed evaluation) is always artificial. And his account of human action and the intentions behind it as inscrutably complex means that any description of a particular action or event would be hopelessly incomplete, and its consequences impossible to gauge more than superficially.[23]

---

[23] Elsewhere I have argued in some detail why, for Nietzsche, individual actions – their nature, causes, and consequences – are inscrutable and their value unknowable. An action, he says, is always "unique and irretrievable" (*GS*, 335), "open to many interpretations," "unfathomable" (*BGE*, 287), and, at least

A whole lived life is the most viable object of affirmation we have (ideally it would be the entire history in which that life is embedded, which at the limit is the whole of existence – but seen, as it were, from the inside and so not guilty of placing existence as such upon the scales[24]). Particular events or experiences can therefore be affirmed only in the act of affirming the whole lived life – to which, on Nietzsche's deterministic view, they are inescapably necessary.[25]

And, let us note in passing, it seems to be the opposite with Nietzsche's priest: he says No precisely to the whole – a No that enables him to say Yes, or somehow to conjure a Yes, to the particular: "His 'no' that he says to life brings a wealth of more tender yeses to light as though by magic" (*GM*, III, 13).

So a rough answer to Nietzsche's question about how Zarathustra can be both a Yes- and a No-sayer is this: If we despise particular experiences – here we return again to the Auschwitz example; or to Zarathustra's somewhat more rarefied revulsions – we nonetheless affirm them in affirming our life, and its fatedness, as a whole.

Nietzsche explicitly says as much when – in discussing one of his highest types, Goethe, and "the highest of all possible faiths," that of Dionysus – he identifies the core stance of this "faith" as follows:

> only the particular is loathsome, ... all is ... affirmed in the whole. (*TI*, "Skirmishes of an Untimely Man," 49)

in more complex cases like artistic creation, subject to "thousandfold laws" that "defy all formulation through concepts" (*BGE*, 188). For "even the firmest concept is, compared with [these laws], not free of fluctuation, multiplicity, and ambiguity" (ibid.). Since concepts have this inevitable vagueness – indeed, through being necessarily shared, they are also too general to succeed in denoting accurately what is ineluctably private and personal – "each of us will always succeed in becoming aware only of what is not individual but 'average'" (*GS*, 354). This idea that our actions follow laws that cannot be conceptualized seems to contain two thoughts: first, something like a Wittgensteinian "private language argument" that concepts can refer only to what is publicly shared and hence to nothing that is strictly individual; and, second, the supposition that empirical concepts, being shared and therefore general, pick out predicates of a level of generality and ambiguity several notches cruder than the finely grained events and mechanisms that underlie our every action (cf. May 1999: 112).

[24] Thus even a complete summation of the actions of an individual's life would still constitute an incomplete, and arbitrary, unit of affirmation since strictly speaking the only complete unit of affirmation would include every event that has ever occurred – and it is, of course, precisely this totality that Nietzsche says "Yes" to in affirming the "Eternal Return" – cf. May 1999: 113. (To put this point in Quinean language: our actions must face the tribunal of our affirmations collectively and not singly – and, ideally, the unit will comprise every interrelated event and so constitute a sample of infinite size.)

[25] The inscrutability of our actions and of their value to us suggests a further reason why affirming life cannot depend upon justifying it: quite simply, that life cannot, as a practical matter, be justified. It is important to emphasize, however, that these practical problems with achieving theodicy constitute a less important objection to making the affirmation of life depend upon its justification than the argument, suggested above, that the very *desire* to justify life is incompatible with the spirit of affirmation.

And he goes further: one who has this faith (that the loathsome is affirmed in the whole) "*does not negate any more*" (ibid.).

So we have it in black and white: the particular may be loathsome *precisely* to one who "*does not negate any more.*" Here we see, as clearly as we can, that affirmation and positive valuation are not the same; and that we can affirm our life – indeed affirm it in the "highest possible" way – while finding particular events and experiences within it "loathsome."

And we find confirmation that affirmation is not the product of a justification: for, as Nietzsche himself says, it is an act of "faith."

Affirmation is the new redemption

The whole life that is, I have claimed, the primary object of affirmation can be referred to in various ways. Sometimes, Nietzsche portrays it as a narrative, as when he speaks of being "poets of our lives" (*GS*, 299). Or, in a similar vein, he thinks of it as a work of art, or aesthetic unity, in the whole of which we can find beauty or take joy *without* needing to do so in every one of its individual parts. At other times he designates it with the word "fate." Or he conceives the whole as the expression of my specific "will to power" within the myriad contingencies of a lived life. To affirm the whole under whatever description is, he suggests, to see beauty in it – and specifically in its *necessity.*[26]

However the whole is described, in affirming it we redeem it – in a new sense of "redemption" to which Nietzsche points us: one that makes all those events that we find loathsome affirmable as integral to a whole lived life; one that, unlike its Christian predecessor, neither involves any form of justification nor thinks of the redeeming whole in teleological terms or as deriving value from a transcendent good (e.g. "the Kingdom of Heaven").

Thus in affirming Auschwitz in the only way in which it can, perhaps, be affirmed – within the whole life to which it belongs – the particular despised experience is redeemed.

In the passage just cited Nietzsche, in fact, makes this clear. It reads, more fully, like this:

... only the particular is loathsome, ... all is *redeemed* and affirmed in the whole. (*TI*, "Skirmishes of an Untimely Man," 49; my italics)

---

[26] As we saw in *GS*, 276, for example, he links the seeing of beauty in things with their necessity – and regards these attitudes as integral to *amor fati.*

In saying that "all is redeemed and affirmed in the whole" Nietzsche does not mean that redemption is distinct from affirmation, for example that the one makes possible the other. He means that to achieve one *is* to achieve the other. This is confirmed by an often-cited passage from *Zarathustra* about redemption:

"... to re-create all 'it was' into a 'thus I willed it' – that alone should I call redemption. ... All 'it was' is a fragment, a riddle, a dreadful accident – until the creative will says to it, 'But thus I willed it ... thus shall I will it'." (*Z*, II, 20, "On Redemption")

Again, what is painful about the past – in this case our impotence in the face of it, and specifically in the face of time (which I argue elsewhere is the ultimate object of *ressentiment*[27]) – becomes redeemed when we will, which means when we affirm, that past. Here, Nietzsche has overcome ascetically ideal thinking insofar as redemption no longer involves escape from what causes us suffering in this life – such as loss and transience – into another life that is supposedly free of those causes of suffering. Rather redemption is affirming everything that has happened in our past, including the suffering, by "willing" it.

It is worth noting that in this picture determinism, in the full sense in which Nietzsche thinks of it, becomes a redemptive concept[28] – just as in the old order "free will" was such a concept. Back then, the capacity freely to choose a life dedicated to God over a life dedicated to profane goods, to pursue good rather than evil or *caritas* rather than *cupiditas*, and to atone for one's sins, were all part of the conceptual apparatus of redemption. Whereas now the deepest possible acceptance of the determined necessity of life, an acceptance marked by seeing that necessity as beautiful, is what redeems the past, including all its losses and sufferings.

V. CONCLUSION: THE STANCE OF THE LIFE-AFFIRMER

In summary, I suggest that affirmation of life is joy in the "there-ness" or quiddity of one's own life as a whole conceived as necessary in all its elements and experienced as beautiful.

And the principal disposition of the life-affirmer is to take such joy in the whole without any impulse to justify its sufferings as constitutive of, or otherwise essential to, its supreme goods, and without being "seduced"

---

[27] May 2009.   [28] I thank Ken Gemes for pointing this out to me (in discussion).

to life by seeing beauty in it. (In other words, the affirmer does not take joy in his life as a whole *because* he has seen goodness or beauty in it.)

The stance of the life-affirmer can be further characterized as follows:

- The primary object of affirmation is the individual's lived life as a whole.
- To affirm my life is consistent with loathing, or "saying No" to, particular experiences or events in it.
- Those experiences or events can nonetheless be affirmed *qua* necessary or inextricable parts of the whole.
- Despite saying No to particular events or experiences the life-affirmer has no will to consider alternatives to the actual life he has.

I have therefore suggested that affirmation of one's life involves going beyond a revaluation of suffering that merely posits new goods (such as artistic creativity) to which suffering is deemed essential or constitutive – even if these goods are no longer structured by metaphysical dualism or the search for comfortableness. *And* it goes beyond the stance of seeking beauty in one's life – or specifically in its necessity – in order somehow to be seduced to it. Instead it involves the far more radical step of ceasing to make the whole question of suffering – how do we affirm our life despite its suffering? – such a central concern.

To recast this point in the terms of the concluding section of the *Genealogy*:[29] the real challenge is not to find a new answer, no longer informed by the ascetic ideal, to the question of the meaning of suffering – an answer that, as Nietzsche repeatedly suggests, might be couched in terms of enhancing one's creativity or finding beauty in necessity. The real challenge is to stop being obsessed with the question itself. The very preoccupation with this question remains a symptom of life-denial – even if it results in a revaluation of suffering that now hails as good what was previously condemned as bad, or deems beautiful what was once denigrated as ugly. In many ways Nietzsche regards that preoccupation as part and parcel of the will to nothingness that has driven European morality and sensibility since Plato. And yet so much of his thinking remains enslaved to this very question. One wonders what our ethics and sensibility would look like if the question were to be demoted – or even experimentally struck off the agenda altogether.[30]

---

[29] "The meaninglessness of suffering, *not* the suffering, was the curse that has so far blanketed mankind, – *and the ascetic ideal offered man a meaning!* Up to now it was the only meaning . . ." (*GM*, III, 28).

[30] I thank Julia Annas, Ken Gemes, Edward Harcourt, Chris Janaway, Peter Kail, Sabina Lovibond, David Owen, Bernard Reginster, Aaron Ridley, Simon Robertson, and Michael Slote for comments on an earlier draft of this chapter, which was presented to audiences in London, Oxford, and Southampton.

CHAPTER 5

Who is the "sovereign individual"? Nietzsche on freedom

Brian Leiter

Most readers of Nietzsche's *On the Genealogy of Morality* over the last century would, one suspects, be astonished to discover the prominence recent scholarship has given to the enigmatic figure of the "sovereign individual," who appears just once, in section 2 of the second essay (*GM*, II, 2), and never appears again, in the *Genealogy* or indeed anywhere else in the corpus.[1] Yet according to Keith Ansell-Pearson, for example,

> The overriding aim of the *Genealogy of Morals* is to show that what Kant and the modern liberal tradition of moral and political thought simply take for granted, the sovereign individual in possession of a free will and conscience, is in reality the product of a specific historical labour of culture or civilization. (Ansell-Pearson 1991: 277)

If this were really the "overriding aim" of the *Genealogy*, one would have expected Nietzsche to be a bit clearer about it and to have more to say about this "sovereign individual." Ansell-Pearson's claim is, to be sure, rather extreme, but his is, nonetheless, on a recognizable continuum with more sober assessments. John Richardson, for example, describes *GM*, II, 2, as "a dramatic statement of [Nietzsche's] positive view" of freedom (Richardson 2009: 128). For Peter Poellner, the sovereign individual gives expression to "the constitutive conditions of full-fledged, autonomous rather than heteronomous selfhood" (Poellner 2009: 152). Ken Gemes thinks the "sovereign individual" illuminates "genuine agency" (2009: 37), the question, "what is it to be a self capable of acting" (39), indeed, "what exactly it is to be a genuine self" (40).

So who is this "sovereign individual" of *GM*, II, 2, and what does he have to do with Nietzsche's conceptions of free will, freedom, or the self? I shall argue for what would have been, at one time, a fairly unsurprising view,

---

[1] I have generally started with the translations of Nietzsche's works by Clark and Swensen, Hollingdale, and/or Kaufmann, and then made changes based on the Colli and Montinari edition of the *Sämtliche Werke* (1980–88), though in some cases the translations are entirely mine.

namely, that (1) Nietzsche denies that people ever act freely and that they are ever morally responsible for anything they do; (2) the figure of the "sovereign individual" in no way supports a denial of the first point; and (3) Nietzsche engages in what Charles Stevenson (1938) would have called a "persuasive definition" of the language of "freedom" and "free will," radically revising the content of those concepts, but in a way that aims to capitalize on their positive emotive valence and authority for his readers.[2]

More precisely, I aim to show that the image of the "sovereign individual" is consistent with the reading of Nietzsche as a kind of fatalist, which I have defended for many years (Leiter 1998; 2002: 81–87; 2007). On the fatalist interpretation, Nietzsche thinks that persons have certain essential psychological and physiological traits over which they have no autonomous control and which, together perhaps with environmental influences like values, causally determine their life trajectories. In particular, Nietzsche thinks that the *feeling* of free will is, at bottom, an epiphenomenon of a process in which conscious thoughts that are consistent with and temporally proximate to succeeding actions are misinterpreted as causal, when, in fact, both the thoughts and the actions themselves are causally determined by non-conscious, perhaps neurophysical aspects of the person (see Leiter 2007). The upshot is that our actions are neither *causa sui*, nor caused by any conscious state with which we might identify, and so our actions cannot bear ascriptions of responsibility, that is ascriptions of justified praise and blame. To the extent, then, that Nietzsche continues to use the language of "freedom" and "free will" – and he does so in a variety of passages that we will consider – he must use those concepts in revisionary senses unrecognizable to either of the two major traditions of thinking about free will in the modern era: on the one hand, the broadly Kantian identification of freedom with autonomous action, meaning action arising from rational self-legislation (or guidance), which grounds moral responsibility; and, on the other, the broadly Humean equation of freedom with acting on the basis of effective, conscious desires with which we "identify" (in some sense to be specified). Neither traditional concept of freedom or free will is available to or embraced by Nietzsche the fatalist.[3]

---

[2] "A 'persuasive' definition is one which gives a new conceptual meaning to a familiar word without substantially changing its emotive meaning, and which is used with the conscious or unconscious purpose of changing, by this means, the direction of people's interests" (Stevenson 1938: 331).

[3] Rutherford (2009) makes a *prima facie* plausible case that Nietzsche's view is closer to Spinoza's conception of freedom, but as Rutherford notes, Spinoza's is a "neglected" conception in the history of philosophy, and so has little or no resonance with those ideas of freedom that are culturally important. (Rutherford also discusses the Stoic view of freedom as a possible antecedent, but given Nietzsche's

To show that the image of the "sovereign individual" squares with Nietzsche's fatalism, I distinguish, in what follows, between two possible "deflationary readings" of the passage. On one such reading, the figure of the "sovereign individual" is wholly ironic, a mocking of the *petit bourgeois* who thinks his petty commercial undertakings – his ability to make promises and remember his debts – are the highest fruit of creation. On another deflationary reading, the "sovereign individual" does indeed represent an *ideal* of the self, one marked by a kind of self-mastery foreign to less coherent selves (whose momentary impulses pull them this way and that), but such a self and its self-mastery is, in Nietzschean terms, a fortuitous natural artifact (a bit of "fate"), not an autonomous achievement for which anyone could be responsible.[4] To associate this ideal of the self with the language of "freedom" and "free will" is an exercise in "persuasive definition" by Nietzsche, a rhetorical skill at which he was often the master. I am inclined to think the second reading is probably the correct one, though the somewhat ridiculously hyperbolic presentation of the "sovereign individual" makes the first reading attractive. But either reading allows us to understand how and why Nietzsche, the fatalist and arch-skeptic about free will, would have created the figure of the "sovereign individual."

NIETZSCHE ON FREEDOM AND RESPONSIBILITY

We do well to begin by reminding ourselves of what Nietzsche actually says about free will and responsibility in the many passages – from many different books that span his entire philosophical career – that must inform any interpretation of the section on the "sovereign individual."

Even if we put to one side *Human, All Too Human*, a work of the late 1870s in which Nietzsche clearly accepted a straightforwardly incompatibilist picture in which the determinism of our universe rules out free will and moral responsibility,[5] evidence of Nietzsche's skepticism about freedom and responsibility remains plentiful in his mature corpus of the 1880s. Thus, at the start of the decade, in *Daybreak*, he writes:

explicit hostility to the Stoics and his many substantive differences with them – over the role of "assent" in the causation of action, the possibility of correct judgments about "the good," and compatibilism [all noted by Rutherford] – this pedigree for Nietzsche's view seems less likely.)

[4] The Spinozian view that Rutherford ends up ascribing to Nietzsche – according to which "[t]he person who becomes free is the person whom fate favors with the ability to regiment in herself a principle of acting that is expressive of her inherent power" (Rutherford 2009: 35) – comes to the same thing, though Rutherford does not remark upon the radically revisionary notion of freedom involved.

[5] E.g. *HAH*, I, 106. But see *HAH*, I, 39 for a statement of skepticism about free will and responsibility echoed in later work.

Do I have to add that the wise Oedipus was right that we really are not responsible for our dreams – but just as little for our waking life, and that the doctrine of freedom of will has human pride and feeling of power for its father and mother? (*D*, 128)

Belief in freedom of the will is to be explained by the ulterior motivations we have for accepting it, not by its reality: we are as little responsible for what we do in real life as for what we do in our dreams. It is hard to imagine a more bracing denial of freedom and responsibility. The same themes are sounded in one of his very last works, *The Antichrist*:

Formerly man was given a "free will" as his dowry from a higher order: today we have taken his will away altogether, in the sense that we no longer admit the will as a faculty. The old word 'will' now serves only to denote a resultant, a kind of individual reaction, which follows necessarily upon a number of partly contradictory, partly harmonious stimuli: the will no longer "acts" [*wirkt*] or "moves" [*bewegt*]. (*A*, 14)

Denial of the causality of "the will" (more precisely, what we *experience* as willing) is central to Nietzsche's skepticism about free will (Leiter 2007) and also explains why he frequently denies "unfree will" as well: what we experience as "will" does not, in fact, cause our actions, so the causal determination or freedom of *this* will is irrelevant. In *Daybreak* (124), he writes:

We laugh at him who steps out of his room at the moment when the sun steps out of its room, and then says: "*I will* that the sun shall rise"; and at him who cannot stop a wheel, and says: "*I will* that it shall roll"; and at him who is thrown down in wrestling, and says: "here I lie, but *I will* lie here!" But, all laughter aside, are we ourselves ever acting any differently whenever we employ the expression "*I will*"?

If the faculty of the will "no longer 'acts' or 'moves'" (*A*, 14) – if it is no longer causal – then there remains no conceptual space for the compatibilist idea that the right kind of causal determination of the will is compatible with responsibility for our actions. If, as Zarathustra puts it, "thought is one thing, the deed is another, and the image of the deed still another: the wheel of causality does not roll between them" (*Z*, I, 6, "On the Pale Criminal") – a pithy statement of the point of the *D*, 124, passage – then there is no room for moral responsibility: I may well identify with my "thoughts" or my will, but if they do not *cause* my actions, how could I possibly be responsible for them?

In the central discussion of free will and responsibility in the *Genealogy*, Nietzsche writes:

For just as common people separate the lightning from its flash and take the latter to be a *deed*, something performed by a subject called lightning, so popular morality also separates strength from the expressions of strength as if there were an indifferent substratum behind the strong person which had the *freedom* to manifest strength or not. But there is no such substratum ... [T]he suppressed, hiddenly glowing affects of revenge and hate exploit this belief [in the subject] and basically even uphold no other belief more ardently than this one, that *the strong are free* to be weak, and the birds of prey are free to be lambs: – they thereby gain for themselves the right to hold the bird of prey *accountable* [zurechnen] ... [The weak] *need* the belief in a neutral "subject" with free choice, out of an instinct of self-preservation, self-affirmation, in which every lie is sanctified. (*GM*, I, 13)

The "will" that was denied as a faculty in the other passages is now here dubbed a "substratum" that stands behind the act and chooses to perform it, or not. But there is no such faculty, whether we call it "will" or substratum, choosing to manifest strength or weakness: there just is the *doing*, no doer who bears the responsibility for it. The discussion of "The Four Great Errors" in *Twilight of the Idols* is to the same effect. As he concludes there,

Today we no longer have any pity for the concept of "free will": we know only too well what it really is – the foulest of all theologians' artifices, aimed at making mankind "responsible" in their sense ... [T]he doctrine of the will has been invented essentially for the purpose of punishment, that is, because one wanted to impute guilt. (7)

Once again, denial that the will is a causal faculty – the central argument of this chapter of *Twilight* – is juxtaposed with a psychological explanation for why people would nonetheless be motivated to believe in freedom and responsibility. Once we abandon this "error of free will" we should, in turn, abandon the reactive concepts whose intelligibility depends on it, concepts like "guilt." Zarathustra well describes the required revision to our thinking about freedom and responsibility that results: "'Enemy' you shall say, but not 'villain'; 'sick' you shall say, but not 'scoundrel'; 'fool' you shall say, but not 'sinner'" (*Z*, I, 6, "On the Pale Criminal"). The abandoned concepts – that of villain, scoundrel, and sinner – are all ones that require freedom and responsibility that would license blame, while the substitute concepts (enemy, sick, and fool) merely describe a person's condition or character, without supposing anything about the agent's responsibility for being in that condition or having that character.

Any account of what is going on in the passage on the "sovereign individual" (*GM*, II, 2) must show how it is consistent with these pervasive themes in the Nietzschean corpus.

THE SOVEREIGN INDIVIDUAL

Nietzsche begins the second essay of the *Genealogy* with a characteristically naturalistic question:[6] how to "breed an animal [*ein Thier heranzuzüchten*]" which is able to make and honor a promise? The assumptions underlying this question are twofold. First, and most obviously, human beings are certain kinds of animals. And second, as with other animals, one explains what they do (e.g. promise-making) not by appeal to their exercise of some capacity for autonomous choice and decision, but in terms of the causal mechanisms (e.g. breeding) acting upon them which yield certain steady behavioral dispositions. Nietzsche identifies two preconditions for the behavioral disposition at issue here, namely, promise-making: first, *regularity* of behavior and, second, reliable *memory*. Regularity is necessary because a promise-maker must be "answerable for his own *future*" (*GM*, II, 1), and one cannot be answerable for a future that is utterly unpredictable. Memory is essential for the obvious reason that only someone who can *remember* his promises can possibly honor them.

Two factors are singled out by Nietzsche as formative for the human animal in its development of regular behavior and a memory: the "morality of custom" and the role of pain in mnemonics. With "the help of the morality of custom and the social straitjacket, man was *made* truly predictable [*berechenbar*, or calculable]" (*GM*, II, 2). Nietzsche here alludes to his own earlier discussion in *Daybreak* (esp. 9), which, drawing on the etymological connection between *Sittlichkeit* (morality) and *Sitte* (custom), advanced "the plausible hypothesis that customs constituted the first morality, that traditional ways of acting played the same role during early human life that 'rarefied and lofty' moral codes, rules, and principles play today: that is, they provided criteria for moral right and wrong" (Clark and Leiter 1997: xxix–xxx). In this earlier discussion, however, Nietzsche's goal was a certain naturalization of the (implausible) Kantian account of moral motivation as a matter of reverence for the moral law: Nietzsche proposes instead that it is "obedience to tradition" (and fear of the consequences of deviation from tradition) that really constitutes moral motivation – not some fictional "reverence" for a moral law (cf. Clark and Leiter 1997: xxx).

By the time he writes the *Genealogy*, Nietzsche is now more interested in the role of custom ("the social straitjacket") in making humans "truly predictable," i.e. regular in their behavior. This development eventually

---

[6] On Nietzsche's naturalism and its role in the *Genealogy*, see Leiter (2002: 3–26) and Leiter (forthcoming).

yields the individual with a conscience, whom Nietzsche refers to variously as a "sovereign" or "autonomous" individual (*GM*, II, 2). Here is the crucial passage:

[W]ith the help of the morality of custom and the social straitjacket, man was *made* truly predictable. Let us place ourselves, on the other hand, at the end of this immense process where the tree actually bears fruit, where society and its morality of custom finally reveal what they were simply *the means to*: we then find the *sovereign individual* as the ripest fruit on its tree, like only to itself, having freed itself from the morality of custom, an autonomous super-ethical individual (because "autonomous" and "ethical" are mutually exclusive), in short, we find a man with his own, independent, durable will, who has *the right to make a promise* – and has a proud consciousness quivering in every muscle of *what* he has finally achieved and incorporated, an actual awareness of power and freedom, a feeling that man in general has reached completion. This man who is now free and who really does have the right to make a promise, this master of the *free* will, this sovereign – how could he remain ignorant of his superiority over everybody who does not have the right to make a promise or answer for himself, how much trust, fear and respect he arouses – he *"merits"* all three – and how could he, with his self-mastery, not realize that he has necessarily been given mastery over circumstances, over nature and over all creatures with a less durable and reliable will? The "free" man, the possessor of a durable, unbreakable will, thus has his own *standard of value*: in the possession of such a will: viewing others from his own standpoint, he respects or despises; and just as he will necessarily respect his peers, the strong and the reliable (those *with the right* to give their word), – that is everyone who makes promises like a sovereign, ponderously, seldom, slowly, and is sparing with his trust, who *confers an honour* when he places his trust, who gives his word as something which can be relied on, because he is strong enough to remain upright in the face of mishap or even "in the face of fate" –: so he will necessarily be ready to kick the febrile whippets who make a promise when they have no right to do so, and will save the rod for the liar who breaks his word in the very moment it passes his lips. The proud realization of the extraordinary privilege of *responsibility*; the awareness of this rare freedom and power over himself and his destiny, has penetrated him to the depths and become an instinct, his dominant instinct – what will he call his dominant instinct, assuming that he needs a word for it? No doubt about the answer: this sovereign man calls it his *conscience*.

Let us start at the beginning. The "sovereign individual" is said to be the "fruit [*Früchte*]" of the long tradition of the morality of custom, but the tree bears this fruit at the point when the morality of custom is left behind: this individual is "autonomous" or "supra-ethical" (*übersittlich*) in the quite precise sense of being no longer bound by the morality of custom (*Sitte*). He is the perfected animal, the one so perfected by the breeding of the morality of custom that he no longer needs the discipline of *Sitte* to perform his "trick," as it were. And what exactly is the "trick" of this well-trained animal? Surely it bears emphasizing that he is described as having one and only one skill: he can actually make and keep a promise! And why can he do that? Because he can remember that he made it, and his behavior is sufficiently regular and predictable, that others will actually act based on his promises. This might explain why Nietzsche gives this self-important animal, the so-called sovereign individual, a suitably ridiculous and pompous name: he refers to him, in the original, as the *"souveraine Individuum,"* a mix of French and (perhaps) Latin, meaning, literally, a sovereign atom – a phrase he never uses again, anywhere, in the corpus.[7] And the "conscience" of this self-important creature, as Nietzsche makes clear, consists in nothing more than the ability to remember his debts. One might, then, be tempted to conclude that this whole passage is little more than a parody of the contemporary bourgeois who thinks that he has achieved something "unique" – something *individual* – just because he is steady enough to make a promise and honor it. Capitalism, as everyone knows, destroys customary practices. Yet after their demise there remains the upright bourgeois who fancies himself the highest fruit of creation simply because he can remember his contractual obligations!

I am not persuaded that the preceding captures all there is to the passage, but the preceding interpretive possibility ought to give pause to the often flat-footed literalism about *GM*, II, 2, characterizing much recent scholarship. Yet there is, admittedly, more to the passage than what we have called attention to so far. In a recent, vigorous challenge to deflationary readings of the passage (including my own), Thomas Miles (2007) has argued that "self-mastery" is central to the image of the sovereign individual, and that "[t]his self-mastery consists of a self-affirming conscience that guides the sovereign individual to take on great tasks and fulfill his commitments to them" (2007: 12). As we have already noted, however, the only "great [*sic*] task[]" concretely on offer by Nietzsche is that the sovereign individual can make a promise and keep it. This is not nothing, to be sure, but it seems *prima facie* hard to square with the overblown rhetoric of *GM*, II, 2, rhetoric to which Miles himself calls attention (2007: 13); for example:

---

[7] Nietzsche never uses the possible cognate expressions anywhere in the corpus either – phrases like *souveränes Individuum* or *souverainer/souveräner Mensch*. Nor does Nietzsche ever employ again in the corpus any of the distinctive phrases he uses to characterize or refer to this *souveraine Individuum*: e.g. *das autonome übersittliche Individuum* or *Herr des freien Willens* or *Privilegium der Verantwortlichkeit* or *der Inhaber eines langen unzerbrechlichen Willens*; these phrases appear only in *GM*, II, 2, and never again in the corpus. (I am indebted to Nicholas Koziolek for research assistance on these points.)

The proud realization of the extraordinary privilege of *responsibility*, the awareness of this rare freedom and power over himself and his fate [*Geschick*], has penetrated him to the depths and become an instinct, his dominant instinct: – what will he call his dominant instinct, assuming that he needs a word for it? No doubt about the answer: this sovereign man calls it his *conscience*. (*GM*, II, 2)

But Nietzsche, as we have already seen, denies – and not just once – that anyone has "freedom and power over himself and his fate" or that anyone has, as *GM*, II, 2, also claims, "mastery over circumstances [*Umstände*]." The conclusion of "The Four Great Errors" from *Twilight of the Idols* is as clear as any passage in Nietzsche on the subject:

[N]o one *gives* people their qualities, not God or society, parents or ancestors, not even *people themselves* (– this final bit of nonsense was circulated by Kant – and maybe even by Plato – under the rubric of "intelligible freedom"). *Nobody* is responsible for people existing in the first place, or for the state or circumstances or environment they are in. (*TI*, "The Four Great Errors," 8)

That means, of course, that the sovereign individual, whose "privilege of *responsibility*" extends to "himself and his fate," indeed, to his "circumstances," is delusional, at least if he *really* believes any of this. He may well *feel responsible*, but his feeling is unwarranted.

Such a conclusion is exactly what one should expect given Nietzsche's most important discussion of the phenomenon of "self-mastery" from *Daybreak*, a passage to which I have called attention before as striking evidence of Nietzsche's fatalism (cf. Leiter 1998). In section 109 of that book, Nietzsche canvasses six different ways of "combating the vehemence of a drive [*eine Triebe*]," for example, by avoiding opportunities for gratification of the drive, thus weakening it over time; or by learning to associate painful thoughts with the drive, so that its satisfaction no longer has a positive valence. More significantly, Nietzsche is also concerned to answer the question as to the "ultimate motive" for "self-mastery." He explains it as follows:

[*T*]hat one *wants* to combat the vehemence of a drive at all, however, does not stand within our own power; nor does the choice of any particular method; nor does the success or failure of this method. What is clearly the case is that in this entire procedure our intellect is only the blind instrument of *another drive*, which is a *rival* of the drive whose vehemence is tormenting us ... While "we" believe we are complaining about the vehemence of a drive, at bottom it is one drive *which is complaining about the other*; that is to say: for us to become aware that we are suffering from the *vehemence* of a drive presupposes the existence of another equally vehement or even more vehement drive, and that a *struggle* is in prospect in which our intellect is going to have to take sides.

Even if the intellect must "take sides" (*Partei nehmen*) there is no suggestion that the intellect determines which side prevails: to the contrary, the intellect is, on Nietzsche's picture, the mere "blind instrument [*blinde Werkzeug*]" of another drive. Thus, the fact that one masters oneself is *not* a product of autonomous choice by the person, but rather an effect of the underlying psychological facts characteristic of that person, namely, which of his various drives happens to be strongest. There is, as it were, no "self" in "self-mastery": that is, no conscious or free "self" who contributes anything to the process. "Self-mastery" is merely an effect of the interplay of certain drives, drives over which the conscious self exercises no control (though it may, as it were, root for one side or the other). The "conscious self" and its body is simply an arena in which the struggle of drives is played out; how they play out determines what the self believes, values, becomes. But, *qua* conscious self or "agent," the person takes no active part in the process. To be sure, some "higher types" – Goethes and Nietzsches, for example – exemplify a unified hierarchy of drives that Nietzsche occasionally dubs as exemplars of "freedom" (we'll return to that, below). But we do not honor Nietzsche's admonition to read him free of moral prejudices if we then try to reconstruct this as a moral ideal (Kantian or Humean) of autonomy and responsibility.

In sum, we can agree with the emphasis of Miles on the "self-mastery" characteristic of the "sovereign individual," and still acknowledge that, given Nietzsche's conception of self-mastery, it is wholly compatible with his denial of free will and moral responsibility in so many other passages.[8]

"FREEDOM" AND "FREE WILL" IN NIETZSCHE

How is this account of the "sovereign individual" passage, which shows it to be of a piece with his fatalistic skepticism about freedom and responsibility, to be reconciled with what Nietzsche says elsewhere in his work when he talks of "freedom" and "free will"?

Poellner (2009) suggests that one important "positive" view of freedom in Nietzsche represents it as a kind of "substantive ideal" (152).[9] As Poellner describes it:

---

[8] Miles also makes the good point (2007: 15) that the description of the "sovereign individual" in *GM*, II, 2, resembles the characteristics I argue Nietzsche associates with the higher type (Leiter 2002: 116–22). But there is no reason in Nietzsche to think being a "higher type" is anything other than a fortuitous natural fact – as Nietzsche took it to be in *his very own* case! See Leiter 2002: 157–59.

[9] Poellner also thinks there is an account of "freedom" in Nietzsche that is concerned with "a *transcendental* question: the constitutive conditions of full-fledged, autonomous rather than

[Freedom as a substantive ideal] is what seems to be at stake in many of those remarks where Nietzsche expresses admiration for people who, as he sees them, have succeeded in integrating an unusually great multiplicity of "drives" and evaluative commitments into a long-lasting, coherent whole. (2009: 152)

I think this is the best reading of what Gemes (2009) has recently been arguing as well.[10] When he speaks of Nietzsche as wanting to understand "genuine agency" (40) and wanting to change "his preferred readers from being mere conduit points of a vast array of conflicting inherited drives into genuinely unified beings" (45), I take him to see Nietzsche as presenting us with an ideal of agency, one involving a kind of unity of the drives. Perhaps the "sovereign individual" is meant to represent such an ideal as well, albeit opaquely. Yet the ideal itself does seem to be a recognizably Nietzschean one.

The question, however, naturally arises why this ideal should be associated with "freedom" or "free will" or "autonomy": why not just say that Nietzsche's ideal agent has a certain pattern of coherent drives or dispositions (the pattern to be specified, of course) and leave it at that? "Freedom"

---

heteronomous, selfhood" (2009: 152). As Poellner explains it: "Nietzsche . . . seems to be interested, like Kant, not just in minimal agency, but in autonomous or free agency in a sense which it would be inappropriate to ascribe to a compulsive subject, or to an addict or acratic person – a slave of momentary affect and desire [*GM*, II, 3] – or to a very young child . . . What emerges from [*GM*, II, 2, on "the sovereign individual," and *GS*, 335, 347] is that autonomy or freedom in the relevant sense is a matter of 'having a protracted will' and 'mastery over oneself' under the aegis of a 'conscience'" (*GM*, II, 2). The last bit makes the account sound like a "substantive ideal," the reading I focus on in the text, which I think is the best reading of Poellner's point, especially since I do not see any textual evidence that Nietzsche is interested in Kant's transcendental question or in the problem of akrasia.

[10] I find Gemes's terminology and discussion somewhat confusing. He contrasts what he calls "deserts free will" with "agency free will." According to the latter, "the free will debate is intrinsically tied to the question of agency: what constitutes an action as opposed to a mere doing?" (2009: 33). To be sure, no one thinks that there can be free will or free agency if there is not a difference between *actions* and "mere doings," for example, mere bodily movements. But there are lots of ways to mark that distinction that have no bearing on any issue that anyone in philosophy, now or in the past, identifies with the issue of "free will." Perhaps actions require *intentions to act*, whereas "mere doings" – such as reflexive bodily movements – lack them. That would still leave wholly open every familiar issue about *freedom* of the will.

Gemes employs other formulations for his idiosyncratic category of "agency free will." He says that it is concerned with the question of "what makes for autonomy" (33), and then says later that "agency free will" is concerned with "the profounder question, 'What is it to act in the first place, what is it to be a self capable of acting?'" (39). Unfortunately, there is no textual evidence that these are Nietzsche's concerns. Gemes also says, without, once again, any evidence or citation, that those interested in "deserts free will" "tend to write as if we already have a notion of self and action more or less firmly in place and are only raising the question of whether such selves are ever to be held morally responsible for their actions" (39). It is true that writers on free will, both historically and at present, typically assume that they have a handle on the distinction between actions and "mere doings" (to use Gemes's terminology), but the "notion of self" is often precisely what is at issue for those Gemes would put in the "deserts free will" camp: is the self, for example, to be identified with our second-order desires, or is the self, or "will," merely an effect of other causes?

is, after all, a promiscuous concept. In ordinary language, we say that someone just released from prison is a "free man," and we also say that someone who shuns conventional expectations – about careers or styles of dress or other social norms – is a "free spirit." But being unconstrained by physical limits (as in prison walls) or social conventions (as in expectations about career or appearance) does not raise philosophically interesting points about freedom of human agency, for Nietzsche or anyone else. We need much more evidence than an occasional use of the term "freedom" to conclude that Nietzsche has a philosophically important *positive* conception of freedom or free will.

Readers of Nietzsche know that he often employs familiar concepts in revisionary or highly deflationary senses. Such is ultimately the case with Nietzsche's view of "freedom" and "free will," I suggest. I agree with Gemes and Poellner that Nietzsche sometimes (though not nearly as often as they think) associates the language of "freedom" with certain kinds of persons – agents whose psychic economy has a certain kind of coherence – but in so doing he has engaged in what Charles Stevenson would have called a "persuasive definition" of "freedom": he wants to radically revise the content of "freedom" while exploiting the positive valence that the word has for his readers. This is because Nietzsche recognizes that to *really* transform the consciousness of his preferred readers he must reach them at an emotional, even subconscious level, and one way to do so is to associate Nietzschean ideals with values in which his readers are already emotionally invested. And as Nietzsche notes in *The Gay Science*, values are "among the most powerful levers in the involved mechanisms of our actions" (*GS* 335). Thus by associating an ideal of the person with the evaluatively (i.e. emotionally) laden word "freedom," Nietzsche increases the likelihood that he can activate the causal levers of at least some readers that will lead them towards this new ideal. Yet from a purely descriptive point of view, he might just as well have called his new ideal agents "causally coherent," since his picture really has nothing to do with "freedom" at all: Nietzsche's ideal "unified" agent is just a kind of natural artifact, one whose drives interact constructively rather than destructively. But with regard to his rhetorical aims, Nietzsche is shrewd to sometimes describe such natural artifacts as exemplars of "freedom."

Both Gemes and Poellner, like other writers in this genre, rely on a very small number of passages to support what they claim is Nietzsche's positive account of freedom. I want to examine these passages with some care – I have already dealt with *GM*, II, 2, in this regard – since I think it will turn out that they do not generally bear the readings Gemes and Poellner want to give them. To be clear, I am not denying that Nietzsche highly values persons who, by natural fortuity,[11] exhibit the kind of agency picked out, I take it, by Gemes's notion of "genuine agency" and Poellner's notion of "full personhood." But none of this has anything to do with any concept recognizable as "freedom" to the two most influential modern traditions of thought, the Humean and the Kantian.

What better place to start than with *Twilight of the Idols*, "Skirmishes of an Untimely Man," section 38, which Nietzsche explicitly titles "My Conception of Freedom." Here is how he introduces and explicates that concept:

Liberal institutions cease to be liberal as soon as they are attained: later on, there are no worse and no more thorough injurers of freedom than liberal institutions. Their effects are known well enough: they undermine the will to power; they level mountain and valley, and call that morality; they make men small, cowardly, and hedonistic – every time it is the herd animal that triumphs with them: Liberalism: in other words, herd-animalization.

This introduction to "My Conception of Freedom" seems clear: one undermines *freedom* in Nietzsche's sense by making "men small, cowardly, and hedonistic." Philosophical and religious traditions have had many views of freedom, to be sure, but I am not aware of any in which being big, brave, and indifferent to suffering loomed large, yet that appears to be precisely the concept of freedom Nietzsche invokes here. This passage continues:

These same [liberal] institutions produce different effects while they are still being fought for; then they really promote freedom in a powerful way. On closer inspection, it is war that produces these effects, the war *for* liberal institutions . . . [W]ar educates for freedom. For what is freedom? That one has the will to assume responsibility for oneself [*den Willen zur Selbstverantwortlichkeit hat*]. That one maintains the distance which separates us. That one becomes more indifferent to difficulties, hardships, privation, even to life itself. That one is prepared to sacrifice human beings for one's cause, not excluding oneself. Freedom means that the manly instincts which delight in war and victory dominate over other instincts, for example, over those of "happiness." The human being who has *become free* [*der freigewordne Mensch*] – and much more the *spirit* who has become free – spits on the contemptible type of well-being dreamed of by shopkeepers, Christians, cows, females, Englishmen, and other democrats. The free man is a *warrior* [*Der freie Mensch ist Krieger*].

---

[11] I use "fortuity" in its colloquial sense, since as the account in Rutherford (2009) makes clear, both Spinoza and Nietzsche view such persons as products of natural *necessity* – a point to which we will return.

Assuming "responsibility" for oneself is not quite the same thing as actually being responsible for one's actions. The former is an attitude, a disposition – that of the warrior it turns out, since the attitude is immediately equated by Nietzsche with the characteristics of the warrior, e.g. "indifference to difficulties, hardships, privation, even to life itself," and so on. Philosophical and folk Humeans and Kantians, needless to say, do not think "freedom" means pleasure in warfare – though warriors are, to be sure, usually thought to be big, brave, and indifferent to suffering! This is, quite clearly, "persuasive definition" in the sense Stevenson identified many decades ago.[12]

In section 41 of the same chapter from *Twilight*, Nietzsche then describes the "Freedom Which I Do *Not* Mean," namely,

... abandonment to one's instincts ... [Today] the claim for independence, for free development, for *laisser aller* is pressed most hotly by the very people for whom no reins would be too strict ... [T]hat is a symptom of decadence: our modern conception of "freedom" is one more proof of the degeneration of the instincts.

In other words, Nietzsche renounces one of the colloquial connotations of the idea of "freedom," namely, freedom from constraints. The point here is of a piece with the concern in *Beyond Good and Evil*, section 188, where Nietzsche says:

[E]verything there is, or was, of freedom, subtlety, boldness, dance, or masterly assurance on earth, whether in thinking itself, or in ruling, or in speaking and persuading, in artistic just as in ethical practices has only developed by virtue of the "tyranny of such arbitrary laws" ... Every artist knows how far removed this feeling of letting go [*laisser aller*] is from his "most natural" state, the free ordering, placing, disposing and shaping in the moment of "inspiration" – he knows how strict and subtly he obeys thousands of laws at this very moment, laws that defy conceptual formulation precisely because of their hardness and determinateness [*Bestimmtheit*].

So freedom in Nietzsche's sense does not mean "freedom from constraint," but its opposite: being subject to "hard" and "determinate" laws! Section 213 of *Beyond Good and Evil* continues this line of thought:

---

[12] There must be some limits, of course, on "persuasive definitions" if they are to persuade – one could not persuasively define "dishwasher," for example, as "pleasure in warfare"! But "freedom," as we have already remarked, is a promiscuous concept, and Nietzsche exploits this fact in passages like the one from *Twilight* we are considering. He also employs, to good effect here and elsewhere, the device of persuasively redefining a concept by first equating it with a commonsensically cognate concept but then equating that one in turn with others, until we end up with a radical revision of the original. (Thanks to Gabriel Zamosc for pressing me on this issue.)

Artists . . . are the ones who know only too well that their feeling of freedom, finesse and authority, of creation, formation, and control only reaches its apex when they have stopped doing anything "voluntarily" [*willkürlich*] and instead do everything necessarily [*notwendig*] – in short, they know that inside themselves necessity and "freedom of the will" have become one.

Notice that *freedom of the will* is placed in quotes by Nietzsche himself in this passage: it is not, after all, *real* freedom of the will, since it involves nothing voluntary, only action which is necessary, actions bound, as he says, by hard laws.

These passages resonate, in turn, with the famous section 335 of *The Gay Science*, which appears to suggest that people can "create" themselves. Here is the bit of the passage emphasized by Poellner and Miles: "We . . . want to *become who we are* – human beings who are new, unique, incomparable, who give themselves laws, who create themselves!" Yet this passage then continues as follows – a continuation about which most scholars are, alas, silent:[13]

To that end [of creating ourselves] we must become the best learners and discoverers of everything that is lawful and necessary in the world: we must become *physicists* in order to be *creators* in this sense [*wir müssen Physiker sein, um, in jenem Sinne, Schöpfer sein zu können*] – while hitherto all valuations and ideals have been based on *ignorance* of physics . . . Therefore: long live physics! (*GS* 335)

Creation "in this sense" is, then, a very special sense indeed: for it presupposes the discovery of what is "lawful and necessary" as revealed by physical science. (This recalls the earlier theme about the equivalence of freedom and necessity.) In context, what Nietzsche has in mind becomes clearer (cf. Leiter 2002: 96–97): for in the preceding part of *GS* 335, he explains that while the particular cause of any action is "indemonstrable" [*unnachweisbar*], we do know that values are "among the most powerful levers in the involved mechanism of our actions." Thus the task for the sciences is to discover the laws of cause and effect governing particular values and particular actions, a more refined version of the task that Nietzsche later calls for in the "Note" at the end of *GM*, I: namely, for the human sciences to examine the *effects* of different kinds of valuations on different kinds of people (on "the good of the majority" and "the good of the minority," as he puts it in the "Note").

---

[13] Rutherford (2009) is an illuminating exception, connecting the passage with Spinozian themes and offering an alternative reading (indeed, the most plausible alternative I have seen) to the one I sketch in the text.

So what textual evidence of Nietzsche's putative "positive" view of freedom remains? Section 347 of *The Gay Science* – which equates "freedom of the will" with *freedom from* the need for certainty, the need that drives people, Nietzsche says, to "faith" and "fanaticism" – obviously tells us nothing about agency or free will, and is a wholly revisionary usage of the concept. There is, in addition, the openly revisionary account of freedom in the first chapter of *Beyond Good and Evil*, according to which,

"Freedom of the will" – that is the word for the multi-faceted state of pleasure of one who commands and, at the same time, identifies himself with the accomplished act of willing. As such, he enjoys the triumph over resistances, but thinks to himself that it was his will alone that truly overcame the resistance. (*BGE*, 19)

As I have argued elsewhere (Leiter 2007), the analysis of the will and freedom in this chapter is fully of a piece with his general denial of free will and moral responsibility (as even Gemes [2009: 48] has acknowledged).[14] That leaves us, then, with just two passages in the published corpus that interpreters of his "positive" theory of freedom rely upon. In one passage, *GM*, III, 10, in which Nietzsche considers how the ascetic ideal validates the conditions under which philosophers can flourish, he concludes by noting that even in the modern world, the obstacles to being a philosopher remain great: "Is there [even now] enough pride, daring, courage, self-confidence, will of spirit, will to take responsibility, *freedom of will* [emphasis in original], for 'the philosopher' on earth to be really – *possible?*" This passing reference to "freedom of will" is revealing, since it makes clear that Nietzsche views it as interchangeable with dispositions of character like pride (*Stolz*) and courage (*Tapferkeit*) and self-confidence

---

[14] Clark and Dudrick (2009) challenge my reading of *BGE*, 19, and so I should say something briefly about why I find their alternative unpersuasive. The crux of their argument is to deem Nietzsche's "phenomenology [of willing] simply implausible" (251), which then opens the door for them to reread the passage as limited to "actions performed in opposition to temptation," and thus as implicating "one's commitments or values" (251). This reading, alas, finds no support in the text at all, and is motivated entirely by the claim that as a phenomenology of willing *simpliciter*, Nietzsche's account is implausible, *and so must be read otherwise*. I do not find the account implausible (phenomenology does require careful introspection!), but even if one concurred with Clark and Dudrick about this, it would not follow that the passage has a meaning not to be found in the text: perhaps it is just bad phenomenology. But the evidence that Nietzsche holds the view of the will I attribute to him (Leiter 2007) is overwhelming, and *BGE*, 19, as I read it fits nicely with the view that Nietzsche articulates elsewhere in his work (Clark and Dudrick confine their attention to this *BGE* passage). Curiously, Clark and Dudrick make an issue (251, n. 3) out of my translation of "ich bin frei, 'er' muss gehorchen" as "I am free, 'it' must obey" instead of "he" must obey. While Kaufmann follows Clark and Dudrick on this point, Judith Norman (in the Cambridge edition) translates it as I do ("it"), and she is surely right to do so, for contrary to Clark and Dudrick's claim that there is "no masculine noun in the passage for which the masculine pronoun substitutes," it is, I would have thought, obvious in context that the "er" that obeys is *the body* (*der Körper*), which of course is a masculine noun.

(*Selbstgewissheit*), all traits one can possess without being responsible for having them, without, in short, having developed them *freely*.

That brings us to perhaps the most interesting Nietzschean passage mentioning freedom, from chapter 8 of *Twilight of the Idols*, a passage on Goethe. It bears quoting at some length:

> Goethe – not a German event but a European one: a magnificent attempt to overcome the eighteenth century by returning to nature, by coming towards the *naturalness* of the Renaissance, a type of self-overcoming on the part of that century ... He made use of history, science, antiquity, and Spinoza too, but above all he made use of practical activity ... [H]e did not remove himself from life, he put himself squarely in the middle of it; he did not despair, and he took as much as he could on himself, to himself, in himself. What he wanted was *totality*; he fought against the separation of reason, sensibility, feeling, will (– preached in the most forbiddingly scholastic way by *Kant*, Goethe's antipode), he disciplined himself to wholeness, he *created* himself ... In the middle of an age inclined to unreality, Goethe was a convinced realist: he said yes to everything related to him, – his greatest experience was of that *ens realissimum* [the most real thing] that went by the name of Napoleon. Goethe conceived of a strong, highly educated, self-respecting human being, skilled in all things physical and able to keep himself in check, who could dare to allow himself the entire expanse and wealth of naturalness, who is strong enough for this freedom ... A spirit like this who has *become free* stands in the middle of the world with a cheerful and trusting fatalism in the *belief* that ... everything is redeemed and affirmed in the whole ... *he does not negate any more* ... But a belief like this is the highest of all possible beliefs: I have christened it with the name *Dionysus*. (*TI*, "Skirmishes of an Untimely Man," 49)

There are two striking *motifs* in this passage: first, the emphasis on an ideal of *naturalness* and *realism*, which is explicitly associated with Napoleon; and second, the equation of commitment to this ideal with "freedom," an attitude of fatalism, and ultimately Dionysus. How are we to understand these motifs and their relation?

The immediately preceding section ("Skirmishes of an Untimely Man," 48) of *Twilight* in fact concerns Napoleon, and his "high, free, even terrible nature and naturalness" – indeed, Napoleon is declared by Nietzsche to be "a piece of 'return to nature', as I understand it" – exactly the "return" Nietzsche attributes to Goethe. If we understand the sense in which Napoleon returns to "nature" and exemplifies the "natural," we will understand something about the meaning of "freedom" in the following section. Now Napoleon's "return to nature" in section 48 is explicitly contrasted with Rousseau's conception of man's "natural" state, which Nietzsche deems the "idealistic" fantasies of the rabble, meaning, in particular, their "doctrine of equality." "No poison is more poisonous than this," says Nietzsche, and section 48 concludes that "only one person ... perceived it correctly: with *disgust*," namely Goethe. Since "this freedom" for which Goethe is strong enough is equated with "the entire expanse and wealth of naturalness" of which Napoleon is the exemplar, it would seem to follow that the *freedom* of a Goethe is, *in part*, an acceptance of the reality of the natural inequality between people and a renunciation of the Rousseauian illusions about what persons are like in a truly natural state.

But Goethe's kind of "freedom," his "becom[ing] free," is also explicitly equated with an attitude of "cheerful and trusting fatalism," which, in turn, is equated with the Dionysian attitude that is clearly recognizable as *amor fati*, that is, acceptance and affirmation of the way things *really* are, rather than falling prey to the fantasies of the "idealist and rabble rolled into one," namely, Rousseau. To be free, in this sense, then, is to be free of the wish that reality be other than it is – that is, unequal, terrible, and cruel (as Napoleon, of course, was). It is not, needless to say, to be a free agent as conceived by Kant or Hume. Nietzsche would rather persuade select readers to the fatalism of a Goethe by co-opting the language of freedom itself to commend to them an attitude that is premised on the profound denial of one liberal ideal of freedom: namely, a denial of the Enlightenment hope that men, through free will and their rational capacities, can all become equal. Like the illiberal idea that *der freie Mensch ist Krieger* or that to be free is to be big, brave, and indifferent to suffering, this key passage from *Twilight* persuasively redefines "freedom" in the service of Nietzschean values: in this case, the illiberal idea that to be *truly* free is to be not just reconciled to, but to affirm the essential inequality of persons.[15]

CONCLUSION

If Nietzsche really says so little that suggests he holds out the hope of a freedom or free will that would be recognizable to the philosophical tradition, or common sense, as such; if his skepticism about freedom and responsibility is so resolute; if what he *actually* says about freedom and free will is so clearly revisionary, so plainly an exercise in persuasive definition that means to exploit his readers' antecedent emotional investment in "freedom" on behalf of very different Nietzschean ideals, even quite illiberal ones – then how are we to explain the recent scholarly "consensus" (if that is

---

[15] Rob Sica correctly points out to me that the account of "free" death in the immediately preceding section of *Twilight* is comparably revisionary of the idea of freedom, though with a different cognitive import. I suspect such examples could be multiplied.

what it is) with which we began? It is, I fear, a manifestation of the fault against which Nietzsche often railed, and which we have seen so many times before in the Nietzsche literature, in Heidegger's transformation of Nietzsche into the last metaphysical philosopher, in Kaufmann's rendering of him as a harmless secular humanist, in Nehamas's defanging of him as an aestheticist (cf. Leiter 1992). In each case, the aim is to make Nietzsche less appalling to we delicate modern readers than he really is: for Nietzsche does *not* believe in freedom or responsibility; he does not think we exercise any meaningful control over our lives; he does not think that his revisionary sense of "freedom" – the "long, protracted will" as he puts it in the passage from *GM*, II, 2, with which we began – is in reach of just anyone, that anyone could "choose" to have it; indeed, in the important passage from *Twilight* with which we concluded, "freedom" is rather clearly invoked on behalf of Nietzsche's illiberal vision of the inescapable reality of human inequality. The resistance to these points in the recent scholarly literature, I conclude, reflects the continuing malign influence of moralizing readings of Nietzsche, of the failure to remember what he says about his conception of Renaissance virtue, namely, that we understand it, and him, "moraline-free" (*A*, 2).[16]

[16] An earlier draft benefited from the discussion of it at a plenary session of the annual meeting of the Friedrich Nietzsche Society at St. Peter's College, Oxford, in September 2009. I am especially grateful to Peter Kail for pressing on me the need to think about Spinoza, which led me in turn to the illuminating paper by Rutherford (2009), whom I thank for permission to cite it and for his comments on the penultimate draft.

CHAPTER 6

Ressentiment *and morality*

Peter Poellner

I. INTRODUCTION

It is widely acknowledged that there is an intimate connection between Nietzsche's ostensibly historical diagnosis of the vicissitudes of *ressentiment* in the second and third essays of *On the Genealogy of Morality* and his critique of contemporary European morality. Commentators often quote his remarks, in the *Genealogy*'s preface, that his historical analysis of the "*origin* of our moral prejudices" (*GM*, Preface, 2; translation modified) is to serve a deeper, philosophical and critical purpose:

I was preoccupied with something much more important than the nature of hypotheses, mine or anybody else's, on the origin of morality (or, to be more exact: the latter concerned me only for one end, to which it is one of many means). For me it was a question of the *value* of morality. (*GM*, Preface, 5)[1]

[W]e need a *critique* of moral values, *the value of these values should itself, for once, be examined* – and *so we need to know* about the conditions and circumstances under which the values grew up, developed and changed. (*GM*, Preface, 6; last emphasis mine)

Nietzsche's suggestion, in the preface and throughout the text of the *Genealogy*, is that there is a tight link between a correct understanding of the origin of "morality" and a proper appreciation of at least some of the grounds warranting a negative judgment of its value. But, as has often been remarked by critics, *prima facie* this confidence seems quite misplaced. Even if Nietzsche succeeds in showing that morality owes its original emergence to disreputable motivations, this would only impugn its value

---

[1] The following editions of Nietzsche's writings will be used in this essay: *Human, All Too Human*, trans. R. J. Hollingdale (1986); *The Gay Science*, trans. W. Kaufmann (1974); *Thus Spoke Zarathustra*, trans. R. J. Hollingdale (1969); *Beyond Good and Evil*, trans. R. J. Hollingdale (1982a); *On the Genealogy of Morality*, trans. C. Diethe (2007); *Twilight of the Idols and The Anti-Christ*, trans. R. J. Hollingdale (1990b); *The Will to Power*, trans. W. Kaufmann and R. J. Hollingdale, ed. W. Kaufmann (1968); and *Werke: Kritische Gesamtausgabe*, eds. G. Colli and M. Montinari (1967–77).

if it could be shown that morality cannot have, or at any rate has not, acquired in the course of its history sufficient rational authority that is independent of those putative original motives for its adoption and propagation. Barring such a demonstration, one might charge Nietzsche with having lapsed into a version of the genetic fallacy: a conflation of the question of the causes or grounds of the original adoption of some practice with the question of its current justification. There are two ways in which Nietzsche might respond to this worry. He could either abandon or at least qualify as hyperbolical his claims about the importance of the genealogical method, and concede that genealogy can at best serve as a propaedeutic, loosening our psychological allegiance to morality by highlighting its *pudenda origo*, while the real reasons for rejecting it are to be found elsewhere, for example in its instrumental disvalue with respect to ends Nietzsche happens to rate highly. His remark that a correct diagnosis of the "origin of morality" is only "one of many means" towards a "critique of moral values" might be thought to relativize the importance of genealogy in something like this spirit, as do some passages in the notebooks (*WP*, 254, 257; *KGW* VII.3.34.69).[2] Alternatively, Nietzsche could stick by his stronger pronouncements in the preface of the *Genealogy* and insist that the link between the allegedly disreputable psychological origins of morality and the content of that morality is not merely causal but constitutive, so that the content simply cannot be understood apart from those motives. To have understood the original motives would on this account be tantamount to grasping an omnipresent, essential feature of morality, and assuming that those original motives are justifiably exposed by genealogy as disreputable or odious, genealogy would indeed be, as Nietzsche claims, more than mere history; it would simultaneously be an instrument of critique. A third interpretive option would be to attribute to Nietzsche the view that certain features of morality's origin which make its original manifestation particularly objectionable, while not constitutive of morality *tout court*, are nevertheless frequently or typically associated also with its later manifestations, and wherever this association is present, this gives us further grounds for rejecting it, in addition to whatever other objections we or Nietzsche may have against morality even where it has emancipated itself from its original motivations. In this chapter I want to examine the philosophical basis of the second and third lines of response, which seem to me to capture most of

---

[2] For readings which, based on these disclaimers, have tended to downplay the critical potential of genealogy or its centrality for Nietzsche's critical project, see Leiter 2002: 177–78; and Reginster 2006: 197–200.

Nietzsche's explicit characterizations of his enterprise in the *Genealogy* and elsewhere: "You can look behind every family, every corporate body, every community: everywhere, the struggle of the sick against the healthy ... These ... are all men of *ressentiment*, ... [which is] inexhaustible and insatiable in its eruptions against the happy" (*GM*, III, 14). In this and many other passages Nietzsche asserts the persistence of a psychological pattern that figures centrally in his account of the origins of morality, and such a psychological continuity is necessary for genealogy to be relevant as a form of critique. Since Nietzsche claims that morality has its origins in the complex psychological condition of *ressentiment*, my first aim in this paper will be to articulate a reconstruction of what this condition involves (section 2). The challenge is to produce an interpretation of *ressentiment* that is coherent and can plausibly be attributed not only to those individuals and societies among which morality initially took hold, but also to (some or many of) its later adherents. Moreover – and this makes such a reconstruction even more challenging – it should tell us something about why *ressentiment* is objectionable. This issue will be addressed in section 3.

There can be no question but that Nietzsche considers morality as we know it to have its roots, in some way, in the condition of *ressentiment* (*GM*, I, 7, 9, 10). What is that morality, as Nietzsche understands it? Like many commentators, I think that the morality which is the object of Nietzsche's critique is not a manifestly unified set of beliefs or practices. Nietzsche rather uses the term to refer disjunctively to a range of superficially quite different phenomena which are, however, said to be unified, at least in part, by their putative common "origin" in *ressentiment*. Firstly, "morality" in Nietzsche designates a range of ostensible virtues of motives, actions, and character, considered as non-instrumental goods: including prominently humility, compassion, and justice (*GM*, I, 14). With respect to the last of these, Nietzsche makes it plain that he considers the distinctively modern ideal of justice – involving the idea that "every will should regard every other will as its equal" (*GM*, II, 11), i.e. that every rational agent has a justified claim to equal consideration as an end merely *qua* rational agent – to be a product of *ressentiment* (ibid.). Secondly, "morality" includes a certain metaethical conception of the good as involving unconditional demands on every human or every rational being, independently of their actual motivational structures (*A*, 11; *BGE*, 187). Finally and most generally, the morality which is the target of Nietzsche's critique finds expression in all versions of the *ascetic ideal* – roughly, the idea that a special or overriding value resides in a domain other than the empirical, contingent, conditioned, time-and-space-bound, essentially affect-involving circumstances of our phenomenal "life" (*GM*, III, 11). Each of these valuations, then, falls under Nietzsche's concept of morality and they all have their "beginning . . . when *ressentiment* itself turns creative and gives birth to values."

But what is *ressentiment* and how, precisely, does Nietzsche envisage this process of value creation? Interpretations of both in the secondary literature still differ widely and the differences between these readings have implications both with respect to the plausibility of Nietzsche's story and with respect to its critical potential. If we turn to Nietzsche's explicit account, in *GM*, I, 10–14, and *GM*, III, 14, we find, however, also a number of features that are largely uncontested among interpreters.

(1) *Ressentiment* as Nietzsche presents it in these passages is a psychological condition which has at its core an experience of pain, or discomfort, or frustrated desire. This pain or discomfort, in the situation Nietzsche considers primary or fundamental, is experienced or interpreted by the subject of *ressentiment* as caused by *other* subjects (call them the objects of *ressentiment*).[3]

(2) This interpretation of a "not-self" (*GM*, I, 10) as the cause of one's suffering motivates a negative affective response, resentment in a non-technical, everyday sense – Nietzsche calls it hatred – towards those Others.

(3) The original pain and the negative affect towards its presumed cause jointly motivate a desire for mastery or superiority in the subject of *ressentiment*. Here we encounter the first of several ambiguities: the subject of *ressentiment* desires mastery, power, over *something* – but over what? Does the subject seek mastery (a) merely over *his own suffering* or discomfort, or (b) over *those others* taken as the causes of his suffering? Let us call (a) the *self-therapy* or *self-affirmation* reading, and (b) the *object-mastery* reading. A desire for self-therapy or self-affirmation does not entail a desire for object mastery. An employee might suffer from being routinely humiliated by her boss, might desire to overcome the pain this causes her, and might as a result of this desire internalize an ethic of self-denial or stoic indifference. If successful, she would have achieved her desire by having removed her pain. The fact that, by making herself invulnerable to insult, she would also have shown herself to be, if her boss actually intended to hurt her, *superior* to him in a certain sense, might not matter to her – that might for her be merely an

---

[3] In this essay I shall largely have to disregard *introjected ressentiment*, which takes as its object a part or aspect of the empirical, embodied, subject himself, and which Nietzsche considers to be a *derivative* phenomenon (cf. *GM*, III, 15–16). See section 2 for some brief remarks on this.

unintended side effect of her emotional self-immunization. Her newly gained psychological resilience might perhaps be called, with some terminological liberty, a kind of self-affirmation. On the other hand, the woman might only be able to overcome her feeling of humiliation by showing herself, or her boss, that *he* is powerless to affect her psychic well-being – in this case, her internalizing of an ethos of stoic indifference would be a means toward the desired end of what I have called object mastery. The difference between the self-affirmation and the object-mastery accounts of *ressentiment* has large implications for the critical potential of Nietzsche's story.

(4) The final element of the dynamic of *ressentiment* is the subject's hitting upon a new evaluative framework that allows him to remove his pain or discomfort by making possible either self-affirmation or mental mastery over the external source of pain. In the *ur*-scenario presented in the first essay of *GM*, members of the oppressed populace in an archaic feudal warrior society, suffering both from being physically and politically dominated and from being incapable of self-affirmation in terms of the dominant ethical code of that society, adopt a new ethical code that simultaneously makes it possible to affirm themselves as what they are – politically powerless, incapable of outward self-assertion – and confers on them an evaluative distinction relative to their rulers. That new ethical code includes the ostensibly intrinsic values of humility, compassion, forbearance, and justice. The modes of comportment which are thus newly conceptualized as *virtues* need not themselves be novel; on the contrary, they are likely to be previously prevalent among the powerless slaves, since they are particularly appropriate to their predicament. What is being "created" by *ressentiment* is thus not necessarily a new type of comportment, but a different way of conceptualizing an existing one in evaluative terms.

Many commentators have thought that this final element in Nietzsche's description of *ressentiment* presents us with a second ambiguity. Are the new values adopted as the result of an *intention* on the part of the *ressentiment* subjects to produce an evaluative code that would permit either self-affirmation or (mental) mastery of the hated Other (the rulers, in this case), or do the slaves, as a result of their desires (for either self-affirmation or object mastery), simply *find themselves*, unintentionally, with a new set of values answering to these desires? On the first, the intentional reading, the slaves' "creation" of a new ethics, "morality," is subject to a form of instrumental rationality: the new values are embraced by them because the slaves are aware of them *as* useful instruments for achieving their desires, and this awareness explains why they are adopted by them. On the second, non-intentional, interpretation, there is no instrumental intention involved: the new values, as it were, obtrude themselves into the slaves' consciousness, because (in a purely causal, non-rational sense) they answer to their desires. These pairs of interpretive options along two dimensions – self-affirmation vs. object mastery, intentional vs. non-intentional – yield four possible combinations and thus four distinct readings of the relation between *ressentiment* and morality. In my view, only one of these combinations – *ressentiment* as the intentional adoption of a new set of values *with an instrumental motive*, and as concerned with object mastery (mastery of a "not-self") – fully preserves the critical potential Nietzsche attributes to his diagnosis (see section 3 below). It is the interpretation most clearly consistent with his own utterances but it is also beset with daunting philosophical difficulties.[4]

2. *RESSENTIMENT* AS AN INTENTIONAL PROJECT OF OBJECT MASTERY

The *ressentiment* subject's initial suffering or discomfort and the negative affect it generates result in some way in, as Nietzsche puts it, "*ressentiment* itself turn[ing] creative and giv[ing] birth to values" (*GM*, I, 10). The subject develops a commitment to certain general, overriding standards of appraisal – the *ressentiment* values – which permit an ostensibly impartial, negative judgment on the offending agents, the objects of *ressentiment*, for violating them. The *ressentiment* values can achieve this only by being taken as having legitimate authority also over those who are not motivated to recognize them, and this presumption is one typical feature of the morality system which is the target of Nietzsche's attack. It is clear that Nietzsche thinks that this emergence of a new set of values permitting blame of the offending Others is at least partly *successful* in transforming the original negative hedonic state of the *ressentiment* subjects by making possible their "self-affirmation" (*GM*, I, 13). The new values allow them to "construct their happiness artificially by looking at their enemies" and by "talking themselves into it, *lying* themselves into it" (*GM*, I, 10). What is this peculiar "happiness" that the new values engender in their adherents? Implicit in

---

[4] In view of these difficulties, some recent interpreters have tended to construe *ressentiment* as a non-intentional, "expressive" process not driven by instrumental motives, e.g. Bittner 1994; Wallace 2007. For some brief critical remarks on R. Jay Wallace's subtle version of this reading, see notes 5 and 9 below.

Nietzsche's diagnosis here is the thought that a subject's *belief* in her orientation towards what she considers to be a good end is *itself* a source of satisfaction; this idea is what underlies the traditional talk of "virtue being its own reward." Nietzsche explicitly accepts this idea. In *The Gay Science* he writes:

Important as it may be to know the motives that actually prompted human conduct so far, it may be even more essential to know the fictitious and fanciful motives to which men ascribed their conduct. For their inner happiness and misery has come to men *depending on their belief in this or that motive – not* by virtue of the actual motives. (*GS*, 44, first emphasis mine; also *HAH*, II, 91)

The peculiar "artificial" happiness and self-affirmation characteristically made possible by *ressentiment* exploits precisely this difference between one's actual motives and the beliefs one has about them. But there is a further twist here. The belief in the goodness of one's own motives may in certain circumstances give rise to an additional, different kind of satisfaction when the subject *contrasts* his or her own virtue with its absence in others. When accompanied by a belief that others lack the virtues one believes onself to possess, this can engender a sense of a particular kind of superiority over those others – call it moral superiority. The texts are unequivocal that it is this particular sense of superiority over a hated Other that constitutes the initial and primary end of the psychic dynamic of *ressentiment* (although it need not be its only or "ultimate" end; cf. *GM*, III,14) and it is also the core of the *ressentiment* subject's newly found "artificial" happiness and "self-affirmation":

They have taken out a lease on virtue to keep it just for themselves . . . there is no doubt about it: "Only we are good and just" is what they say, "only we are the *homines bonae voluntatis*" . . . The will of the sick to appear superior in *some* way . . . – where can it not be found, this will to power of precisely the weakest! (*GM*, III, 14; translation modified)

This supplies an answer to the question of whether the need that is served by *ressentiment* as Nietzsche conceives it is merely for self-affirmation, or instead for a more complex kind of self-understanding that essentially involves object mastery – the belief to be in some way superior to the offending "not-self." It is clearly the latter. And this explains a central feature of it which would otherwise be puzzling. Nietzsche stresses that a special sort of reactiveness is essential to *ressentiment*:

[S]lave morality says "no" on principle to some "outside," "Other," "not-self": and *this* "no" is its creative deed. This reversal of the evaluating glance – this *essential* orientation to the outside . . . is a feature of *ressentiment*: in order to come about, slave morality first has to have an opposing external world . . . – its action is basically a reaction. (*GM*, I, 10; translation modified)

What does Nietzsche mean when he says that an "orientation to the out-side," to an "Other" that is apprehended as "opposing," is *essential* to *ressentiment?* This obviously means more than the fact that this psycholog-ical process contingently has its origin in a confrontation with a not-self that is interpreted as different and hostile. Nietzsche gives us a clue to what else is involved here when he imagines the slaves exhorting one another "let us be different . . ., let us be good" (*GM*, I, 13). This indicates that it is essential to the function of the new values that their *content* be *in opposition* to whatever values and desires happen to be manifest in the behavior and beliefs of those Others who are resented on prior and independent grounds (for example, because of their power or their possessions). Where the targets of *ressenti-ment*, like the nobles in Nietzsche's example, esteem ostensible virtues such as agonistic prowess, pride, unreflective impulsiveness, and respect for hierarchies of birth, the "reactive" values of *ressentiment* will include puta-tive virtues and goods opposed to these, such as peacefulness, humility, reflective prudence, and an egalitarian idea of justice. But it is easy to think of this situation all but reversed. In a modern secular enlightenment con-text, where the dominant values include a liberal universalist conception of justice, reflective prudential rationality, and individualism, a *ressentiment*-motivated ideological revolt among individuals who feel themselves disad-vantaged or marginalized might valorize, for example, an ethnically based notion of justice, pre-reflective instinct, and the individual's subordination to the collective. *Ressentiment* cannot even partly be identified in terms of a specific set of value contents. And the reason for this flexibility of *ressenti-ment* with respect to the values it may end up with is precisely that, whatever values are embraced from these motives, are embraced "reactively" in Nietzsche's sense: they owe their appeal in the particular case to their being understood as *opposed to* and underwriting a negative judgment of whatever evaluative framework is represented by the respective not-self – the individual or group who is resented on prior and independent grounds.

If the adoption of the *ressentiment* values essentially involves the reactive pattern just described, this implies that the need it satisfies is not simply one of self-therapy or straightforward self-affirmation in the sense sketched earlier.[5] This is what, according to Nietzsche, distinguishes *ressentiment*

---

[5] Nor, by the same token, is that need simply for a vindicatory self-understanding in Wallace's sense, i.e. for the ability to make sense of one's affective experience as *appropriate* to its objects. Cf. Wallace 2007: 118–19.

from the irenic, anti-aristocratic ethos of the Nazarene, whom in *The Anti-Christ* he calls the "only Christian" (*A*, 29–30). That ethos is, Nietzsche insists, free of *ressentiment*, despite its novel, non-orthodox, anti-establishment character (*A*, 40), for it is not based on an "*essential* orientation" to an "opposing external world." By contrast, the inverse dependence of the *ressentiment* values on another, opposing evaluative framework shows that the desire they answer to is one for self-empowerment through a certain kind of object mastery. The unacknowledged function of the adoption of these values is to make possible blame, disparagement, diminution in thought, of the Other who is the object of *ressentiment*. The purpose of this process is thus a special sense of superiority – moral superiority – and this is at the heart of what Nietzsche means when he sometimes speaks of it as an "imaginary revenge."

If this analysis is right, then two questions become pressing. Firstly, the adoption of the *ressentiment* values serves an instrumental function, but are they also adopted with an instrumental *intention*? Are they, in other words, adopted with the aim of achieving what I have called object mastery? Secondly, are the *ressentiment* values genuinely internalized, or do the subjects merely have a motivated false belief that they are committed to them? Nietzsche is unequivocal on both questions: it is essential to *ressentiment* that its values are *not* really internalized by its subjects, who are therefore not motivated by the contents of those values for their own sake, but merely avow them with an instrumental intention:

And what mendacity to avoid admitting this hatred as hatred! . . . What do they really want? At any rate to *represent* justice, love, wisdom, superiority, that is the ambition . . . And how skilful such an ambition makes them! In particular, we have to admire the counterfeiter's skill with which the stamp of virtue . . . is now imitated. (*GM*, III, 14; cf. III, 11)

Nevertheless, the subjects do not merely cynically lie about their own conscious motivations, they are genuinely self-deceived about them, having motivatedly false beliefs about them:

[T]he man of *ressentiment* is neither upright nor naive, nor honest and straight with himself. His soul *squints*. (*GM*, I, 10)

I call a lie: wanting not to see something one does see, wanting not to see something *as one sees it* . . . The most common lie is the lie one tells oneself. (*A*, 55, my emphasis; cf. *A*, 46)

The picture of the emergence of morality that Nietzsche asks us to contemplate seems to be as follows. The *ressentiment* subjects adopt a set of values enjoining a negative judgment of other subjects who are resented on grounds quite independent of these values. The belief that they are motivated by these values for their own sake makes possible for these subjects a "reduction in thought" of the resented Others and consequently a particular sense of superiority – "moral" superiority – over them. This reduction in thought of the Other, which Nietzsche calls an imaginary revenge, is the *aim* that the subjects consciously pursue in subscribing, at the level of conscious, though mistaken, belief, to the *ressentiment* values. We may therefore say that their actual motive, which explains their false beliefs about their own mental state, is fundamentally detractive and superiority-craving – a will to power which is disguised also from themselves. Again, Nietzsche could hardly be more sarcastically explicit:

"We good people – *we are the just*" – what they are demanding is not called retribution, but "the triumph of *justice*"; what they hate is not their enemy, oh no! They hate "*injustice*," "godlessness." (*GM*, I, 14)

Nietzsche's talk in this context of "self-deception," "counterfeiter's skill," "lying to oneself," and "not wanting to see something *as* one sees it" indicates that all the relevant elements in this process are supposed to be located at the personal, conscious level. The subjects consciously believe that they are committed to certain values for their own sake. Their conscious, though unacknowledged, motivation for this belief about themselves is hatred of, and a desire for superiority over, the resented Other. Their aim, again conscious but unacknowledged, is the diminution in thought of that Other. The subjects are self-deceived in a twofold sense. They are alleged not only to deceive *themselves*, but also to deceive themselves about *their own current, conscious mental states*. The self of self-deception here is simultaneously agent (as deceiver), victim (as deceived), and topic of the deception. We can now see why Nietzsche should be so confident that this account of the origins of morality, if it can be made to work, would also provide the materials for a critique of it. For if it turns out that the motives for embracing morality are not merely psychological causes in the distant past, but that they typically continue to be constituent features of moral consciousness, and if we have reason to find these motives objectionable, then, if we accept Nietzsche's genealogy we also have reason to reject morality. Genealogy is thus a highly ambitious project. To be successful, it would have to show the following:

(1) Firstly, that, and on what grounds, the unacknowledged motives sustaining morality are objectionable. This task is clearly easier if what genealogy aims at is no more than an internal critique of specific

instances of morality, say, its Christian or Kantian versions, for these classify as *immoral* the very motives which, according to Nietzsche, generate morality – which, on his analysis, would render these forms of morality practically inconsistent. But there is reason to think that Nietzsche aims not merely at an internal critique. His hope seems to be that the diagnosis of the motives of *ressentiment* also can ground a critique which is "external" in the sense of not needing to appeal to the explicit value commitments of those criticized.[6]

(2) Secondly, genealogy would have to show that the pattern diagnosed in the context of morality's historical emergence, or at least an analogous pattern, continues to be operative at later historical stages, including modernity. Many passages (e.g. *GM*, III, 14; *TI*, "'Reason' in Philosophy," 6), indicate that Nietzsche believes that the original psychological nexus of *ressentiment* continues to be (at least) frequently present among individuals considering themselves to be motivated by the ostensibly intrinsic values of morality. In addition, he sketches a theory of a later introjection of *ressentiment* which, in conjunction with his psychology of the will to power, aims to demonstrate that actions, commitments, and "ideals" in which the agent takes herself to be motivated entirely by moral considerations, even where they do not involve outward-directed *ressentiment*, can be explained in terms of an introjected analogue to it, which takes as its object components of the agent's own empirical self (*GM*, III, 11, 15, 16). Thus it is said to be characteristic of the "ascetic ideal" that it rejects and *externalizes* the self that is motivated by affective desires as other to the real, or "higher," or "autonomous" self, or indeed as not strictly a self at all. I cannot assess the plausibility of this theory of introjected *ressentiment* here.

(3) Thirdly, Nietzsche has to show that the psychological pattern he outlines is coherent and plausible. Since this is obviously the fundamental task, I want to devote the remainder of this section to it. The central logical problem with Nietzsche's theory is easily stated. It seems to fall prey to two paradoxes often said to vitiate any literal construals of self-deception. The *ressentiment* subjects are supposed both to believe, at a certain time, that they are currently motivated by certain values for their own sake, and also to be aware, at the same time, of not being motivated thus, but rather by a negative, detractive, affect. This might be construed as generating what has been called the static paradox of self-deception: the subjects, it seems, are claimed simultaneously to believe

---

[6] See Owen 2007: 128–30, and section 3 below.

both that p and that not-p. Moreover, Nietzsche's theory also seems to give rise to a version of another, the so-called dynamic paradox: The subjects are assumed to believe that the values of morality are *intrinsic* values, ends, while also having a conscious *instrumental* motive for thinking thus, namely the aim of elevating themselves above the "immoral" Others. But how could their awareness of this aim fail to undermine, in their own minds, their avowed grounds for the adoption of those values?[7]

One approach to resolving these apparent paradoxes seems to me unpromising. It won't do to say that the offending motives or affects are "unconscious," if this means: located in some mental subsystem such that they do not normally display any typical phenomenal properties to the mind's conscious main system. They cannot be simply *inaccessible* to consciousness in the way that, for a blindsight subject, the items in the occluded part of his visual field are completely inaccessible to his phenomenal consciousness.[8] For if a subject can legitimately be said to undergo unconscious affects, or to have unconscious motives or aims, these must manifest themselves in a reasonably systematic way in the subject's behavior, judgments, and feelings in appropriate circumstances.[9] And when they do become thus manifest, their inconsistency with the subject's avowed beliefs and commitments becomes *available* to the subject's phenomenal consciousness and appraisal. A different kind of explanation is required at this point of how the subject can systematically and in a topic-specific manner *fail to notice* her own practical inconsistency. A more fruitful approach to defusing the alleged paradoxes, without abandoning Nietzsche's idea of *ressentiment* as an intentional "project," is the distinction drawn by phenomenologists like Husserl and Sartre between implicit conscious contents and the implicit attitudinal character of experiences on the one hand, and their conceptually articulated character and contents on the other. Much clearly depends on what is meant by "implicit" or "unarticulated" here. According to the phenomenological mainstream, the "implicit" in the relevant sense is neither

---

[7] On these apparent paradoxes of intentional self-deception, see Mele 1997: 91–101. For an examination of the dynamic paradox, see also Lazar 1999: 277–80.

[8] For further criticisms of the "split-mind" model, as found in its classical form in Freud, and in a contemporary version in Pears 1985 and 1991, see Johnston 1988: 83; and Lazar 1999: 272–74.

[9] For this reason, a subject who is motivated by "unconscious" affects incompatible with her professed motives cannot be said to have fully internalized the latter. One problem with Wallace's construal of *ressentiment* is that it assumes both genuine internalization of the *ressentiment* values (Wallace 2007: 119) and a continued dependence of their appeal on a persistent, unacknowledged, "unconscious" hatred incompatible with them (Wallace 2007: 131). I do not think that these characterizations are mutually consistent.

phenomenally unconscious (like the objects in blindsight) nor fully or adequately conceptually structured. To see more precisely how this might apply to the case of *ressentiment*, we need to distinguish between two respects in which one's conscious commitments might be opaque to full conceptualization. We might have a certain occurrent attitude towards a *content* which, while we are conscious of it, we do not or cannot adequately conceptualize. For example, I may feel distaste or dislike for something that is perceptually presented to me, while not being able to conceptualize what precisely it is about the object as consciously presented that motivates my dislike.[10] Or we might be consciously experiencing a certain *attitude* towards an object or state of affairs without at the time conceptually representing that attitude to ourselves. For example, I might be consciously *aiming to bring about* a certain state of affairs (as opposed to imagining it or perceiving it or regretting it) without my intention-in-action being conceptually represented as such by me at the time. In phenomenological parlance, my intention-in-action may be consciously "lived through" without being a representational object for me. There are many arguments by phenomenologically oriented philosophers purporting to show on *a priori* grounds that not all experiential characters or attitudes consciously lived through by a subject can be "presented as objects" – i.e. conceptually represented – by her at the time.[11] For present purposes it does not matter whether these arguments succeed. It suffices to accept that we can *sometimes* be aware of the experiential (noetic) character of our present mental state, our conscious occurrent attitude towards some content, without *eo ipso* having a conceptual, objectifying representation of that phenomenally conscious attitude. If we accept this, it opens the way for avoiding the so-called paradoxes of self-deception. For these require that all the elements that generate the practical inconsistency are available to the subject in a way that makes it possible for them to contribute to the content of propositions entertained by the subject, for only then can they figure in inferences by him which produce the sort of explicit inconsistencies which might become troublesome for him.

Only if the *ressentiment* subject had a conceptual representation of himself as aiming to undermine or reduce an Other in order to establish a sense of superiority over that Other could this awareness of his project undermine his self-understanding as being committed to the *ressentiment* values for their intrinsic worth. And only if the subject had a *conceptual* representation

---

[10] For a more detailed discussion of this point, see Poellner 2003: 32–57.
[11] See e.g. Sartre 2003: 6–12; Zahavi 1999: 52–62, 92–103; Moran 2001: 124–48; Poellner 2003: 45–57.

of the actual target of his aversion as, for example, another's power or social prestige or material possessions, would he be in a position, and rationally compelled, to describe his motives in a way that conflicts with his explicit self-interpretation (*GM*, I, 14) as "hating injustice."

By contrast, on the picture I am recommending, we can coherently think of the *ressentiment* subject's state of mind as literally self-deceived. The subject experiences a negative affective response to another, a "not-self." He conceptualizes this response as enjoined by normative requirements ensuing from what he believes to be his commitment to certain ostensible values, values which are violated by that Other. But this interpretation of his experience is false. The hatred is in fact directed at quite different properties of the Other, such as his power or prestige. But the subject neither knows nor believes this, for the evidence available to her as to the precise target, and thus the precise identity, of her affective state is insufficient. The target, as Sartre says in a similar context, is "not [intuitively] given or is given indistinctly."[12] It *would* presumably be given "distinctly" if the subject were confronted with a situation, either imaginatively or in actuality, where the different possible targets of her affect diverged; for example where the Other possessed power but not the disvirtues of character ostensibly objected to, or where she possessed the latter but not the former. The subject's affective response in these counterfactual situations would tend to make his actual state of mind cognitively transparent to him. In the absence of such disambiguating evidence, it is perfectly possible for a subject to believe that he disapproves of A (injustice) while in fact not doing so, but instead hating B (another's power), without this creating any cognitive conflict for him. To say that the subject may not be in a position to *know* what the object of his mental state is prior to such an imaginative or actual exercise in disambiguation does not compel us to say, as some intentional expressivists do, that as long as the cognitive disambiguation does not happen, the mental state of the self-deceived subject is no different from that of a non-self-deceived one with the same avowed commitments. On the contrary, even the non-dispositional phenomenal properties of their mental states, as given to them first-personally, will differ. The world of the self-deceived person is different from that of one who is not. Specifically, in the *ressentiment* case, the subject's consciousness will in part be characterized by an intentional *resistance* to the kind of open imaginative or actual confrontation with decisive disambiguating evidence which would render the actual content of his affective state distinct to himself. What makes

[12] Sartre 2003: 91.

possible the subject's false construal of the intentional object of his negative affect is his *expectation*, which itself may or may not be explicit, of being able to intuitively fulfill his avowed commitment to the *ressentiment* values in circumstances that would present its target distinctly and unambiguously. And what makes it legitimate to speak of *ressentiment* as a *project* is the subject's effective intention to avoid such evidence. But does the construal just given of *ressentiment* as an intentionally pursued project not still fall victim to the dynamic paradox? Is it coherent to say that someone consciously *pursues a project of avoidance* without conceptualizing it in this way, and without knowing that he is engaged in such a project – and, finally, without this knowledge undermining his preferred self-interpretation?

To circumvent the alleged paradox, we have to be able to say that an aim can be consciously pursued by the *ressentiment* subjects without their *pursuing* it being conceptually represented by them. And of course we often pursue aims in this way. When I aim to return the ball during a tennis match, it is plausible to say that I intentionally aim at a certain state of affairs, and that my experience is different from what it would be if I merely imagined that state of affairs or wished for it; I am conscious of *pursuing* an end rather than just *envisaging* it. Yet I do not, at that time, conceptually represent my actively aiming at or pursuing the respective end, even if I conceptually represent the state of affairs which is my end. If my consciousness of seeking to bring something about can be non-conceptual in this way, then what this consciousness presents to me is unavailable to me for inferences, and the dynamic paradox does not arise. Conceptualization requires attention,[13] and reflective attention to our own mental states is – and arguably must be – generally absent when we are engaged in the world.[14] The difference between ordinary unreflectiveness in immersed action and self-deception is that in the latter case this characteristic absence of reflective attention is topic-specific and *motivated*. I conclude, then, that there is no incoherence in supposing that what distinguishes the *ressentiment* subject's consciousness from a corresponding non-self-deceived consciousness is, in part, a systematic, topic-specific, motivated conscious avoidance of actual or imaginary confrontations with situations which would disambiguate the intentional content of his negative affect.

---

[13] The idea of constitutive connections between conceptual representation and conscious attention is currently being widely revived. Its classical statement can be found in Husserl (1973: §§ 13, 17, 18).

[14] For an argument attempting to show quite generally that reflective attention to oneself is incompatible with immersed activity requiring attention to the object of one's action, see O'Shaughnessy 1980, vol. II, 22–38.

While the considerations just sketched suffice to legitimize talk of *ressentiment* as involving a project of *avoiding relevant self-knowledge* (though of course not a reflective strategy), Nietzsche's analysis suggests that it includes a further element of conscious aim-directedness. Recall that the *ressentiment* values are said to be arrived at with a detractive, superiority-craving *intention*. We need not take this to mean, despite Nietzsche's occasional wording, that the slaves search for values that might best justify blaming their enemies. We may rather assume that candidates for a new, "anti-noble" evaluative framework just *occur* to them, present themselves to them by way of a mental mechanism that is neither intentional nor fortuitous. But the *appeal* of these prospective new values, their actually being espoused by the subjects is explained, Nietzsche suggests, by the subjects' desire or aim to "appear superior in *some* way" (*GM*, III, 14) relative to their opponents. This explanation is not merely causal, but is more akin – with important qualifications I shall come to presently – to explanation in terms of reasons. What can be said on behalf of this Nietzschean claim? Well, it is not too fanciful to hypothesize that those "slavish" features of actions, character, and belief which will eventually be embraced by the *ressentiment* subjects as having superior worth, are presented to them in the initial phase of their evaluative "revolt" or conversion merely as *possible* values; as, so to speak, awaiting evaluative appraisal or reappraisal. And it is perhaps also not outlandish to imagine that, in that situation, entertaining the thought that these features *do* have superior worth, trumping the values of the warrior rulers, should be a source of intense satisfaction to the oppressed slaves, and that this satisfaction should motivate their acquisition of the corresponding beliefs (e.g. the belief that being just really *is* supremely good or highly desirable, or the metabelief that the higher values are such as to demand recognition by all humans, irrespective of their actual desires). In order to make sense of Nietzsche's thesis that embracing the *ressentiment* values involves an instrumental aim – the attainment of a certain kind of power – it may be sufficient to assume that the satisfaction which motivates the slaves' explicit (albeit self-deceived) acceptance of a new evaluative standard depends on their appreciation that by this standard the resented not-selves come out as inferior. The content of this appreciation is a conceptual representation and thus in principle suited to be a *reason for* the slaves in the adoption of the new values. It is this content that explains the appeal which the new evaluative standard has for the *ressentiment* subjects and the latter explains their embracing of it. These explanations are not just causal explanations, since explicating the motivations involved requires essential reference to the subjects' grasp of certain conceptual contents. And the combination of this conceptual grasp and the nexus of motivations involved is arguably sufficient to warrant Nietzsche's description of the subjects as pursuing a conscious aim (superiority over the Other) and the *ressentiment* values being embraced because they meet that aim. Yet this account is not a full-fledged rational explanation in terms of reasons which the subjects are fully, explicitly aware of; the circumstance that the resented Others are reduced in stature and worth by the new evaluative standard is not taken by the subjects *as their* (primary) reason for espousing it. For while the appeal to them of the new evaluative framework essentially depends on their grasp that it implies a diminution of the resented Other, the subjects need not – and indeed cannot without practical inconsistency – conceptualize that appeal primarily in this way. The precise content, and hence the precise nature, of their satisfaction about the contemplated new evaluative standard need not, and cannot without raising the dynamic paradox, be reflectively identified and articulated by them. In the absence of such articulation, the subjects' efficacious motives, while conscious, are not *known* by them and are unavailable for inferences by them that would undermine their avowed commitments.

I conclude then, that Nietzsche's account of *ressentiment* as intentional self-deception is coherent and does not require a reconstruction in terms of non-intentional or subpersonal processes. The theory is arguably a powerful tool for explaining various phenomena of individual and social psychology, including many manifestations of nationalism, chauvinism, and indeed some religious psychologies. But we should be more skeptical about Nietzsche's claim, in the *Genealogy* at least (*GM*, I, 10, 13, 14), that we cannot explain the original emergence of morality without recourse to some such hypothesis. In fact, in *The Anti-Christ*, he himself effectively revokes this claim with respect to some specific virtues upheld by some variants of morality, such as humility and non-violence (*A*, 29–30). But I think that the claim is more generally problematic. To see why, recall that values are, also on Nietzsche's view, response-dependent properties of a special sort. For something to be a value is necessarily for it to be such that certain kinds of responses are appropriate to, or merited by, items that exemplify it, in virtue of exemplifying it. For Nietzsche, these responses essentially include affective experiences. Witness his remarks that "every ideal presupposes *love* and *hatred*, *admiration*, and *contempt*" (*KGW* VIII.2.10.9), and that "moralities too are only a *sign-language of the affects*" (*BGE*, 187). Grasping the concept of some specific value involves knowing what sort of conscious responses are appropriate to instances of it – responses which include actions, judgments, but also, essentially, conscious affective responses such as respect or admiration or distaste or contempt. Here the overused and limited analogy with secondary properties is helpful; to grasp the secondary-property concept of purple is to know what sort of appearance purple things present in suitable conditions, and to know this requires some conscious intuitive *acquaintance* with things which present an appearance of the right sort – things which appear, precisely, purple. The class of purple things is unified by presenting *that* sort of color appearance (to perceivers with appropriate receptivity in suitable circumstances). Somebody without any acquaintance with instances of the relevant appearance-type will lack the secondary-property concept of purple.[15]

Now cast your mind back to Nietzsche's *ressentiment* values, say, egalitarian justice. For me to grasp this *as* a value would require, on Nietzsche's general metatheory of value, that certain kinds of actual or possible institutional arrangements, actions, and attitudes are experientially unified for me in part by systematically appearing to me as distasteful and deeply unattractive in a special way; for instance the attitude of treating some people exclusively as means and never as ends, or political arrangements tending to deprive some classes of people of important material or educational goods on account of their birth. But the whole thrust of Nietzsche's argument is that the *ressentiment* subjects do *not* respond to instances of injustice in this affectively unified way – that's why they are self-deceived about their commitments. But if *that* is the case, then they have no acquaintance with justice as a value, as an evaluative property. Hence they have no adequate grasp of the concept of justice as a value (the value property concept of justice, we might say, by analogy with the secondary-property concept of purple). But then it is unclear how they could, as Nietzsche suggests, falsely attribute to themselves, in a motivated way, a commitment to this specific value, whose concept they do not adequately grasp.

Ressentiment, it seems to me, is perfectly intelligible as the response of a subject who has a genuine, even if perhaps weak, commitment to the values instrumentalized in the *ressentiment* situation, while being primarily motivated, *in that particular situation*, not by those values but by other aspects of the situation – in Nietzsche's example, by someone's being in a position of power over her. This pattern no doubt occurs frequently and Nietzsche is right and extremely insightful in highlighting its importance for ethics. It is analogous to a viewer of a painting, say Balthus's *Thérèse rêvant*, who professes to be fascinated by the painting on account of its subtle color structure, while

---

[15] The basic point made by talk of response dependence in the present context is not that values are fundamentally dispositions, but that they are *phenomenal* properties, that is, properties which need to be understood in terms of certain appearances they present when actualized. For criticisms of dispositional accounts of phenomenal properties such as secondary properties, see e.g. Johnston 1997 and Stroud 2000: 127–44.

in fact being primarily attracted by its insinuated erotic content, an attraction which he would find unacceptable and which he therefore refuses to acknowledge. This is a familiar kind of self-deception. But the more radical idea Nietzsche asks us to accept is analogous to a different scenario where the viewer of the painting, who claims to appreciate the painting on account of its intricate color pattern of shades of brown, red, green, and off-white, rather than its erotic content, is in fact partially color-blind, being unable to discriminate the specific color shades he claims to be responding to. This situation is not *prima facie* unintelligible, since the viewer has at least a generic concept of color and is acquainted with colors other than those in the painting. But assume now that color concepts were less straightforwardly perceptual, that their acquisition required a more complex process of learning and immersion in local cultural practices, and that we had first learned the concepts of those precise shades exemplified in Balthus's painting from that professed *connoisseur* who, it turns out, has in fact no acquaintance with them, being unable to discriminate them from a range of very different shades. This would be a fairly close parallel to the story Nietzsche asks us to accept in his genealogy of morality. But just as we could not possibly have learned our concepts of the specific color shades in Balthus's painting from that hypothetical viewer who is blind to them, so we could not have learned *our* moral concepts from the initiators of the slave revolt in morals as Nietzsche proposes; for on his account the original slaves could have had no experientially unified concepts of *those* values at all. What this suggests is that Nietzsche's radical genealogical claim, that at least some moral values are "created" by *ressentiment*, is implausible. *Ressentiment* seems rather to be intelligible only as a secondary or parasitic phenomenon, depending on the subject's prior internalization, however weak or tenuous, of the values he then self-deceivedly instrumentalizes in the *ressentiment* context.

3. WHAT IS WRONG WITH *RESSENTIMENT*?

I have argued that *ressentiment* cannot play the fundamental "value-creating" role Nietzsche attributes to it. Nevertheless it is a real phenomenon and Nietzsche shows great insight in diagnosing its presence in evaluative discourse and practice. But, granting that he has identified an important feature of evaluative life, let us revert to the question we started out from. What is it that is objectionable about *ressentiment*? Two answers have been prominent in the literature. The first is, broadly, consequentialist: a culture in which the "slave values" which for Nietzsche originate largely in *ressentiment* prevail is unconducive to the flourishing of individuals who would otherwise be capable of embodying the kinds of excellence Nietzsche values (and perhaps also thinks that we, or some of us, *should* value). There can be little doubt that considerations of this sort are among those that fuel his animus against morality (see e.g. *BGE*, 62, 199; *GM*, I, 11; III, 14).[16] But an interpretation focusing exclusively or primarily on these cannot account for the marked difference in Nietzsche's assessment of *ressentiment* valuation on the one hand and of the practices of Buddhism and of the founder of Christianity on the other, since similar value *contents* (such as humility and non-violence) are professed and disseminated in both cases (cf. *A*, 29–31). Yet Nietzsche's virulent distaste for *ressentiment* valuation simply bears no comparison with his peculiar ambivalence about Buddhism and indeed about the "*décadence*" of the "only Christian" ("One could, with some freedom of expression, call Jesus a 'free spirit'"; *A*, 32). The consequentialist reading cannot explain this difference.

Another influential approach sees the main problem with *ressentiment* in its essentially being a type of motivated self-misunderstanding, and in the lack of "power over oneself" or *autonomy* entailed by this.[17] But it is clear that, for Nietzsche, not all kinds of self-deception are evaluatively on a par, and that the evaluatively relevant differences between them are not primarily a matter of the depth of self-misunderstanding involved. Having just asserted the prevalence of self-deception in human affairs – "the most common lie is the lie one tells to oneself" (*A*, 55) – Nietzsche continues:

Ultimately the point is to what *end* a lie is told. That "holy" ends are lacking in Christianity is *my* objection to its means. Only bad ends: the poisoning, slandering, denying of life, contempt for the body, the denigration and self-violation of man through the concept sin – *consequently* its means too are bad. (*A*, 56)

So Nietzsche's suggestion seems to be that there may be kinds of self-deception, even about deep issues, which, while no doubt undesirable, nevertheless do not merit the contempt he thinks is called for by *ressentiment*. But if we take seriously his insistence that it is not the lie *per se* – the motivated self-misunderstanding – that is most deeply objectionable about *ressentiment*, but the "bad ends" to which the lie is told, does this not take us back to the consequentialist reading of his critique? Well, not if the bad ends of *ressentiment* are not, or not merely, a matter of the values it happens to generate in the particular context that particularly interests Nietzsche – that of the "slave revolt" – but are also intrinsic to that psychological condition: if the latter

---

[16] For a detailed reconstruction of this Nietzschean line of criticism of morality, see Leiter 2002: esp. ch. 4.
[17] For an interpretation broadly along these lines, see Ridley 2005: 170–75.

inherently involves a "poisoning, slandering, denying of life," irrespective of the professed value contents its subjects happen to end up with.

An alternative suggestion would therefore be that Nietzsche's main objection to *ressentiment* is that it is essentially characterized by an *intrinsic phenomenal disvalue*. By this I mean that it is a conscious psychological state that is *necessarily experienced as undesirable by a subject being in that state if it is presented adequately to her and if it is considered by itself*.[18] A conscious state is presented adequately just in case the subject has an explicit first-personal awareness of all its evaluatively relevant constitutive features. Since *ressentiment* is an intentional state, its adequate first-personal presentation would require, therefore, an explicit awareness by the subject of all the relevant intentional objects which co-constitute it, of the aspects under which they are presented in this state, and of the subject's conscious attitudes or responses towards them.[19] What underwrites Nietzsche's rejection of *ressentiment*, I submit, is the claim that this psychological condition is *necessarily* experienced as profoundly undesirable – as distasteful or repulsive – if it is experienced explicitly, transparently as what it is. Considered by itself, irrespective of its consequences, no one could lucidly desire to be in that state. The reason why the *ressentiment* subject is not explicitly aware of its intrinsic phenomenal disvalue, and thus can unproblematically remain in that condition, is that he avoids such lucid self-transparency by means of the dynamic of self-deception described earlier.

But, of course, *ressentiment* does not just exemplify *some* sort of phenomenal disvalue – any ordinary toothache does that. For Nietzsche, it rather

---

[18] The necessity alluded to here is stronger than nomological necessity. For more detail, see Poellner 2009. For Nietzsche, to experience something as undesirable, rather than merely thinking or believing it to be so, necessarily involves a negative affective response to it – a distaste or repulsion. Note that I am not claiming that a psychological state could have the value that it has if it *existed* in isolation, an assumption of dubious coherence associated with G. E. Moore's "method of isolation" (Moore 1903: 187). I am making a much weaker assumption: that it is possible to consider or be aware of, among the properties of a conscious state, only those that constitute it as what it, *qua* conscious state, is – in contradistinction to relational properties involving its unintended effects or consequences, or its enabling conditions. "Considering the state by itself" here is not intended to imply an objectifying stance towards it, but only the absence of considerations relating to its unintended effects or enabling conditions.

[19] It might be objected that the requirement that all the relevant constitutive components of a conscious intentional state should be *explicitly* present to the subject's awareness is inappropriate, or at least sometimes irrelevant, to determining that state's intrinsic phenomenal value. Doesn't the experienced value of intentional comportments in many cases depend precisely on their various aspects or "moments" *not* being explicitly presented in the experience itself? One might think here, for example, of the experience of "flow." These are complex issues and here I can only indicate the rudiments of a response. One need not deny that many experience-tokens we rightly consider intrinsically valuable have evaluatively relevant implicit intentional characteristics. What I need to deny for present purposes is only that these features must be *essentially* implicit for the state to be the kind of state it is.

seems to represent something uniquely distasteful – the nadir of the universe of values, as it were: a "poisoning, slandering, denying of life." We can see why it does so if we consider that *ressentiment*, as Nietzsche describes it, is intrinsically a project that, if universalized, would be tantamount to the subversion of the conditions of the possibility of valuing, of recognizing value, as such. This subversion has two main components, which we may call *radical heteronomy* and *inauthenticity*. The world-relation of the *ressentiment* subject is fundamentally shaped by a certain way of responding to some pain or suffering occasioned by another.[20] In *ressentiment*, the subject enacts a disposition in which a pain believed to have been caused by a "not-self" is a *sufficient* motive to negate that Other (to hate him, as Nietzsche puts it more bluntly). But this negation, as we have seen, takes a very distinctive form. It is interpreted by the *ressentiment* subject not as a hatred of a *particular* Other, nor of a *specific type of action*, nor of a *specific relation* between himself and that Other (e.g. an asymmetry of power), but of the *general value orientation* that makes the Other what he is – of his practical identity, we might say. In *ressentiment*, a deficiency experienced in relation to another subject is thus implicitly taken as sufficient to reject the values in terms of which that Other understands himself. And this negation provides the content of the *ressentiment* subject's own professed practical identity. He is thus heteronomous in a much more radical sense than in common or garden-variety self-deception even about important matters, in that the content of his avowed evaluative identity is here, quite literally, determined by the power of another, for he allows that content to be fixed by some contingently experienced deficiency or inferiority in relation to some equally fortuitous "not-self." And he is *inauthentic* in that he intentionally, albeit not reflectively and strategically, misconstrues what valuation is – the *form of valuation in general*. For, whatever may be required for a subject correctly to be said to value something as an end (for its own sake), it cannot be sufficient, as the *ressentiment* subject takes it to be, sincerely to ascribe to oneself some set of commitments; and it is incompatible with the purely instrumental relation to those commitments which is characteristic of *ressentiment*. A person or a culture, to the extent that it is in the grip of that condition, has intentionally rendered itself incapable of recognizing value, and it therefore is a state which, once one sees it transparently as what it is, one cannot rationally desire to be in. It is in this sense that *ressentiment* intrinsically aims at "bad ends."

---

[20] The argument that follows applies in this form only to the other-directed form of *ressentiment*, and would have to be modified appropriately for *ressentiment*'s derivative, introjected variants.

CHAPTER 7

The role of life in the Genealogy

Nadeem J. Z. Hussain

I. INTRODUCTION

Nietzsche is quite clear that at least one central purpose of *On the Genealogy of Morality* is to help us assess the value of the values, the value judgments, of morality:[1]

[U]nder what conditions did man invent the value judgments good and evil? *and what value do they themselves have?* Have they up to now obstructed or promoted human flourishing [*Gedeihen*]? Are they a sign of distress, poverty and the degeneration of life? Or, on the contrary, do they reveal the fullness, strength and will of life, its courage, its confidence, its future? (*GM*, Preface, 3)

Later in the same preface he writes:

[W]e need a *critique* of moral values, *the value of these values should itself, for once, be examined* ... People have taken the *value* of these "values" as given, as factual, as beyond all questioning; up till now, nobody has had the remotest doubt or hesitation in placing higher value on the "good man" than on "the evil," higher value in the sense of advancement, benefit and prosperity [*Gedeihlichkeit*] for man in general (and this includes man's future). What if the opposite were true? ... So that morality itself were to blame if man, as species, [*des Typus Mensch*] never reached his *highest potential power and splendour?* (*GM*, Preface, 6)

One kind of assessment being made is relatively clear. We are to assess the values of morality instrumentally: do they promote human flourishing? What is less clear is precisely what is meant by human flourishing.

---

[1] The translations used for *On the Genealogy of Morality* and *Daybreak* are the Cambridge translations. Other translations are as follows: *The Birth of Tragedy*, trans. W. Kaufmann ([1872] 1967a); *The Gay Science*, trans. W. Kaufmann ([1882–87] 1974); *Thus Spoke Zarathustra*, trans. W. Kaufmann ([1883–85] 1966b); *Beyond Good and Evil*, trans. W. Kaufmann ([1886] 1966a); *Twilight of the Idols* in *The Portable Nietzsche*, ed. and trans. W. Kaufmann ([1888] 1968d); *The Antichrist* in *The Portable Nietzsche*, ed. and trans. W. Kaufmann ([1888] 1968a); *Ecce Homo*, trans. W. Kaufmann ([1888] 1989); *The Case of Wagner*, trans. W. Kaufmann ([1888] 1967b); and *The Will to Power*, trans. W. Kaufmann and R. J. Hollingdale ([1901–11] 1968).

Obviously it has something to do with power and splendor but without further elaboration one would worry that the circle of concepts might be too tight for comfort. Flourishing also seems to be connected to something called "life" where life is being conceived of as something that can be stronger or weaker, degenerating or growing, confident or in distress. Consider the focus in *GM*, Preface, 3, on the values of morality as symptoms of the condition of life. Again, it is not obvious what to make of this.

But perhaps the most fundamental puzzle is that these apparent values of flourishing, power, or splendor are themselves never critiqued or questioned. Why would precisely the genealogy of these very values not be an obvious, and crucial, task to take up? It is not as though Nietzsche promises to carry out this task elsewhere, and it does not look as though any such critique or genealogy is carried out in *GM* itself. How could someone with Nietzsche's endless suspicions, with his fine sense for psychological blind spots, with his intense self-reflective curiosity, *not* have taken up precisely the question of where these values come from, what *their* origin is? After all we are talking of someone who wrote:

Every philosophy is a foreground philosophy – that is a hermit's judgment: "There is something arbitrary in his stopping *here* to look back and look around, in his not digging deeper *here* but laying his spade aside; there is also something suspicious about it." (*BGE*, 289)

Indeed, the very phrase, repeated in various forms by Nietzsche, "the *value* of these 'values'," cries out for the repeated application of the question.[2]

One can miss this fundamental puzzle if one focuses on the almost analytic connections between, at least, the cluster of notions surrounding "flourishing" and some central notions of "good"; the claim that it is good to promote human flourishing can sound almost tautological. But, of course, despite whatever conceptual connections may lurk here, there are crucial differences between valuing my own flourishing at the cost of others, valuing everyone's flourishing equally, and valuing the flourishing, say, of a particular type of person. Indeed, as we shall see, there is even a difference between this and valuing flourishing in the sense of valuing the creation and

---

[2] Note how Brian Leiter's suggestion that for Nietzsche it is, in some sense, merely a matter of "evaluative taste" and that Nietzsche does not think that his evaluative perspective enjoys any kind of "metaphysical or epistemic privilege over its target," morality, does not address the puzzle (Leiter 2000: 290–91). How could Nietzsche not wonder about the origin of his values, his evaluative taste? What is the value of this evaluative taste? Cf. *GS*, 335: "Your judgment, 'this is right' has a prehistory in your instincts, likes, dislikes, experiences, and lack of experiences; '*How* did it originate there?' you must ask, and then also: 'What is it that impels me to listen to it?'"

existence of exemplary persons even if at the cost of the flourishing, in some other sense, of others.[3] Nietzsche is well aware of this:

> The question: what is this or that table of values and "morals" [*Moral*] *worth*? needs to be asked from different angles; in particular, the question "value for *what*?" cannot be examined too finely. Something, for example, which obviously had value with regard to the longest possible life-span of a race (or to the improvement of its abilities to adapt to a particular climate, or to maintaining the greatest number) would not have anything like the same value if it was a question of developing a stronger type. The good of the majority and the good of the minority are conflicting moral standpoints [*Werth-Gesichtspunkte*]: we leave it to the naïvety of English biologists to view the first as higher in value as *such* [*an sich*]. (*GM*, I, 17, "Note")

As we shall see below, flourishing, and the related notions Nietzsche uses to express his evaluative standpoint, are also given fairly substantive content. This ensures that there are also other potential conflicts: for example, the conflict between having humans of a certain type and having, say, art of a certain type. All of this, again, merely highlights the puzzle: he is picking a particular evaluative standpoint and so why does it seem not to occur to him to do a critique and genealogy of his standpoint? Why is the spade laid aside?

I will argue that the answer to this puzzle lies in the special role that the notion of "life" plays in Nietzsche's account.

2. POWER

Before we can solve our puzzle, we need to have a somewhat better grasp on what flourishing for Nietzsche comes to and what the relationship is with notions such as splendor, power, life, and so on. I will begin, however, by making an important concession: I cannot provide anything like a full account of the dimensions along which Nietzsche assesses possible humans, higher men, or superhumans, in order to determine whether the values of

---

[3] The difference, that is, between defining a type first, say everyone in a particular geographical area or the possessors of some kind of native endowment, and then valuing their flourishing as opposed to taking flourishing, perhaps of humanity as a whole, to just be the emergence of a certain exemplary type of person. Valuing flourishing in the second way just is to value the emergence of a particular type of person. It is clear then what one values in valuing flourishing even if one has not, explicitly or implicitly, answered the question of whose flourishing it is. I will take Nietzsche to, in general, use flourishing in the second way – particularly in contexts of expressing the fundamental values that he uses for assessing the value of morality.

As a result, some of what I will say about Nietzsche will end up being in tension with parts of Leiter's interpretation in his *Nietzsche on Morality* which ascribes a relativized notion of flourishing, where a person's flourishing is what is prudentially good for that person (cf. 2002: 105–12). For reasons of space, I will not directly try to lay out the differences in detail.

morality are helping or hindering their emergence and flourishing.[4] Nietzsche often talks of higher men but besides the systematically positive evaluation he gives of them, there is little that identifies them substantively. Often where properties of such men are mentioned, they seem like symptoms or signs for what really makes them higher men, rather than defining characteristics of such men. However, I shall point to the kind of passages that I think do let us pick up on the fundamental dimensions of assessment that identify humans that are flourishing – passages where Nietzsche either seems to come closer to describing the essential properties of the kind of human he clearly values or the many more passages where he depicts the kind of person that morality produces, the kind of person then that is not an exemplar of the highest power and splendor possible to man. In addition to the ones we have already seen, consider the following sampling of what he regards positively. I start with *GM*:

> But from time to time grant me … a glimpse, grant me just one glimpse of something perfect, completely finished, happy, powerful, triumphant, that still leaves something to fear! (*GM*, I, 12)

Nietzsche claims that "the plant 'man' has so far grown most vigorously to a height" not in the absence of suffering but in the "opposite conditions":

> his power of invention and simulation (his "spirit") had to develop under prolonged pressure and constraint into refinement and audacity, his life-will had to be enhanced into an unconditional power-will. (*BGE*, 44)

Or here is another passage from *BGE* that, precisely because it focuses on compassion (*Mitleid*), an attitude that normally comes under withering criticism for the danger it poses to the development of humans, seems to give us insight into the kind of person that has succeeded in achieving splendor and power:

> A man who says, "I like this, I take this for my own and want to protect it and defend it against anybody"; a man who is able to manage something, to carry out a

---

[4] See Leiter 2002: 115–22, for a more ambitious attempt. I find his list a curious mixture of what seem to me to be more essential features of the kind of humans Nietzsche values and features that are more contingent in the sense that these humans have to have them, given the natural features of the world they find themselves in, for the purpose of having their essential features. Consider, for example, Leiter's claim that the "higher type is solitary" (116). This strikes me as not essential for Nietzsche but something he would regard as a frequent result of the fact that being powerful, creative, brilliant, capable of independence, and knowledgeable of what maintaining those features requires will often lead, in a world where the majority are not that way, to a certain distance, psychological and sometimes more, from others (*WP*, 885). It is a feature but not in any way even a partially definitive one. It is true though that Nietzsche's own lists seem to have this feature of being a curious mixture of what is essential to greatness and what seem to be means or symptoms.

resolution, to remain faithful to a thought, to hold a woman, to punish and prostrate one who presumed too much; a man who has his wrath and his sword and to whom the weak, the suffering, the hard pressed, and the animals, too, like to come and belong by nature [*gern zufallen und von Natur zugehören*], in short a man who is by nature a *master* – when such a man has pity, well, *this* pity has value. (*BGE*, 293)

We should also consider his condemnations of Christianity as a conspiracy "against health, beauty, whatever has turned out well, courage, spirit, *graciousness* of the soul" (*A*, 62). The "true Christian" opposes "the beautiful, the splendid, the rich, the proud, the self-reliant, the knowledgeable, the powerful – in summa, the whole of culture" (*WP*, 250).[5]

One can worry about how much of a substantive ideal emerges. After all, often the right-hand side, so to speak, moves within the same worryingly small cluster of concepts. The sustained discussions of all the ways of being that Nietzsche finds bad are perhaps more helpful. Those negative comments can raise the worry one has with "negative theology" – is there really a way of being that avoids all those criticisms? Nonetheless, I think that as long as we work hard to put aside our temptations to defang Nietzsche on the behalf of morality, we can, so to speak, go on: we can, that is, tell what Nietzsche would take to be instances of human power and splendor and, with some confidence, to rank these instances.[6] (Think of an instance, a whole character, a psychological episode, and – forgive me the joke – ask yourself, "What would Nietzsche think?")

Part of what comes through in the above passages, I suggest, is that for Nietzsche the cluster of evaluations in terms of power, vigor, self-reliance, health, creativity, intelligence, a strong will, and so on, hang together. We must understand why he thought that even if we eventually conclude that in fact they do not hang together in the way Nietzsche thinks they do. One traditional way of seeing the unity in such lists is to think of "power" as the umbrella notion. After all, health, creativity, intelligence, a strong will, and so on, can be seen as part of what it would take for a human to have power over himself and his environment. This is the kind of reading that gets support from passages such as these:

What is good? Everything that heightens the feeling of power in man, the will to power, power itself.

What is bad? Everything that is born of weakness. (*A*, 2)

---

[5] See also *D*, 201; *GM*, I, 7; *WP*, 873, 943, 936, 949.
[6] This is not, it should go without saying, to endorse the Nietzschean ranking.

Or from the *Nachlaß*:

What is the objective measure of value? Solely the quantum of enhanced and organized power. (*WP*, 674)[7]

Without countervailing arguments that draw on other textual material, these claims can be read as pointing to what the central good-making feature in the world is: it is in virtue of power, or the lack thereof, that things are better or worse, good or bad.[8] That power is the fundamental value or standard that Nietzsche uses for the purposes of assessing the values of morality has been a widely held view.[9]

However, even if we are confident that this is the best way to express his evaluative standpoint, the puzzle remains as to why Nietzsche thinks this is the appropriate standard for assessing the value of moral value judgments of good and evil. And why this value is not itself apparently being subjected to a genealogy.

Once the fundamental measure is put in terms of power, however, it is tempting to think that some argument lurks in claims like the following:

There is nothing to life that has value, except the degree of power – assuming that life itself is the will to power. (*WP*, 55)

Nietzsche, furthermore, does at least at times accept this assumption. Indeed, he seems to commit himself to an even stronger doctrine of the will to power:

Physiologists should think before putting down the instinct of self-preservation as the cardinal instinct of an organic being. A living thing seeks above all to *discharge* its strength – life itself is *will to power;* self-preservation is only one of the indirect and most frequent *results.* (*BGE*, 13)

Or, most dramatically:

This world is the will to power – and nothing besides! (*WP*, 1067)[10]

---

[7] See also *WP*, 858.
[8] In contrast to a more metaethical reading that would like to read these as property identifications. See Leiter 2000 and Hussain 2007 for further discussion.
[9] "Power, then, is the standard of value which Nietzsche affirms with all the eloquence at his command" (Morgan [1941] 1965: 118). The "quantitative degree of power is the measure of value" (Kaufmann 1974: 200). There is "one standard about which Nietzsche does not take a relativist position. He evaluates the worth of persons on the basis of a single standard: the degree to which they have attained what he calls power" (Hunt 1991: 131). "Nietzsche's advice: maximize power" (Richardson 1996: 148). See also Wilcox 1974: 194–96, Schacht 1983: 349, 398, and May 1999: 15.
[10] Cf. *BGE*, 22, 36.

All of life, or perhaps everything, is always striving for power. Once power appears as the central evaluative *and* ontological term, then it can hardly appear to be a coincidence that everything aims at power and that power also turns out to be what is good.[11] Surely, the thought goes, Nietzsche thinks power is valuable in part because everything aims at power. The hard part is figuring out what precisely Nietzsche thought the connection here might be.

3. LEITER'S MILLIAN MODEL

Brian Leiter, noting the widespread ascription of such an evaluative standard to Nietzsche, asks: "But what exactly is the *argument* here? When pressed, commentators are never able to say" (Leiter 2002: 138). He suggests an interpretation of the argument on the behalf of commentators attracted to this line of interpretation before proceeding to criticize this interpretation both for the quality of the argument it ascribes to Nietzsche and the textual evidence to which it appeals. A careful look at these criticisms, however, shows, as I will argue below, that there is a related interpretation that can quite plausibly be ascribed to Nietzsche even if, as I shall grant, the arguments ascribed to Nietzsche are not ones that we might philosophically endorse.

Leiter claims that what he calls the "Millian Model seems the most charitable reconstruction of what the commentators do say, and of Nietzsche's few scattered remarks on the subject" (2000: 282 n. 19). The Millian model derives its name from John Stuart Mill's "proof" for the principle of utility. On Leiter's reconstruction, this proof rests on a crucial pattern of inference:

to show that something is desirable (i.e., valuable), show that it is desired. (2000: 282)[12]

Into this schema we then, on the behalf of Nietzsche, "plug in ... the doctrine, roughly, that all persons intrinsically 'desire' only power" (282). If this form of argument is generally valid, we could then conclude that power is valuable. We would have our bridge from the premise that everything aims at power to the conclusion that power is valuable, that power is what is good.

[11] Cf. May 1999: 16.
[12] "No reason can be given why the general happiness is desirable, except that each person, so far as he believes it to be attainable, desires his own happiness" (Mill 2003: 210).

The fundamental philosophical problem with such an argument, as Leiter points out, is that "from the fact that only happiness *is* desired, nothing at all follows about what *ought* to be desired" (Leiter 2002: 139). The version that replaces happiness with power seems to suffer from the same problem.

Leiter considers a version of the argument that appeals to an "Internalist Constraint":

(IC) Something cannot be valuable for a person unless the person is capable of caring about (desiring) it. (Leiter 2000: 283)

Assuming nihilism is false, then, if "it is only power that persons ever aim for or desire" (284), we can conclude that power, and only power, is valuable.

Leiter grants that such an argument would be valid, but thinks that it is clear that Nietzsche did not accept the descriptive doctrine of the will to power in the strong form required for it – the form in which power is the *only* thing desired.[13] He provides evidence of varying degrees of strength. After putting aside some of his evidence that seems to me of less significance, I focus on the more interesting evidence that does indeed, I will agree, mitigate against ascribing the above strong form of the doctrine of will to power to Nietzsche.

Leiter points to passages where Nietzsche talks of the will to power "declining" (*A*, 17) or being undermined (*TI*, "Skirmishes of an Untimely Man," 38) (Leiter 2002: 141). These passages could be read as merely suggesting that the strength of the motivation towards power decreases. Such passages are, by themselves, consistent with the claim that power is still the only thing desired or aimed for. The more interesting passages are therefore those in which the will to power is placed alongside, and apparently at the same level as, what seem to be other motivational elements (Leiter 2002: 142). Thus in *EH*, "Why I Am a Destiny," 4, Nietzsche writes: "In the great economy of the whole, the terrible aspects of reality (in affects, in desires, in the will to power) are to an incalculable degree more necessary than that form of happiness which people call 'goodness'." This passage, read alongside perhaps the many others that ascribe all kinds of desires to people besides a desire for power, does indeed suggest that some particular motivational, psychological state in favor of power is not somehow always at the bottom of every instance of desiring. This in turn makes ascribing a strong form of the descriptive will to power thesis in terms of a desire for

---

[13] He is willing to grant for the purposes of argument that Nietzsche accepts IC, since if with it we could ascribe to Nietzsche an argument that led from the premise that everything strives for power to the conclusion that power is a fundamental standard of value, then we would *ipso facto* have good reason to ascribe it to Nietzsche (Leiter 2000: 284).

power – the one needed by Leiter's reconstruction of the will to power argument – quite difficult.

Perhaps even more importantly, Leiter writes:

> Indeed, if, as the defenders of the strong doctrine of will to power believe, "his fundamental principle is the '*will to power*'" (Jaspers 1965: 287), then it is hard to understand why he says almost nothing about will to power – and nothing at all to suggest it is his "fundamental principle" – in the two major self-reflective moments in the Nietzschean corpus: his last major work, *Ecce Homo*, where he reviews and assesses his life and writings, including specifically all his prior books [*EH*, "Why I Write Such Good Books"]; and the series of new prefaces he wrote for *The Birth of Tragedy, Human, All-too-Human, Daybreak*, and *The Gay Science* in 1886, in which he revisits his major themes. (Leiter 2002: 142; see the bibliography for Jaspers 1965)

It does seem important that neither the explicit monistic descriptive claim (everything, or even every living thing, is a will to power and nothing else) nor the explicit monistic evaluative claim (being better is a matter of more power) play the kind of central role in these writings that one would expect them to. It is true that *The Antichrist*, where the value monism gets its above strong expression, is from after the time when these prefaces were written, but the point about *Ecce Homo* remains. This evidence does then militate against ascribing to Nietzsche some commitment to a fundamental evaluative claim expressed in terms of the will to power or to the claim that the only thing people care about or desire is power. Ascribing to him the argument for the value of power that goes through IC then does seem implausible.

4. LIFE

I do think, though, that there is a version, or close relative, of the traditional will to power interpretive line that avoids the textual problems Leiter highlights. Indeed, this alternative interpretation is suggested by one of the main targets of Leiter's above criticisms, Richard Schacht. Schacht writes that Nietzsche "takes 'life' in this world to be the sole locus of value, and its preservation, flourishing, and above all its enhancement to be ultimately decisive for determinations of value" (Schacht 1983: 359). "In the last analysis, value can only be 'value for life', and can only be understood in terms of what life essentially involves" (367). Of course, for Schacht, "Life, as [Nietzsche] construes it, *is* 'will to power' in various forms – an array of processes all of which are 'developments and ramifications' of this basic tendency" (367).[14]

---

[14] Cf. Schacht 1983: 396.

The heart of this alternative interpretation rests on taking the notion of "life" as central to Nietzsche's revaluative project. This should come as no particular surprise since, as we saw above, the notion of "life" seems to stand in some special relationship to the question of the value of value judgments of good and evil in *GM*. And not only in *GM*:

> In the . . . sphere of so-called moral values one cannot find a greater contrast than that between a *master* morality and the morality of *Christian* value concepts: the latter developed on soil that was morbid through and through . . ., master morality ("Roman," "pagan," "classical," "Renaissance") is, conversely, the sign language of what has turned out well, of *ascending* life, of the will to power as the principle of life. (*CW*, Epilogue)[15]

I am going to accept that it does not make sense to ascribe to Nietzsche a view on which there is always some particular mental state, a desire or a caring, that has power as its aim. However, to grant this is not yet to grant the implausibility of ascribing a more amorphous version of the will to power doctrine. As Nietzsche says, "life itself" is "the instinct for growth, for durability, for an accumulation of forces, for *power*" (*A*, 6). Or as he puts it in the *Genealogy*:

> The democratic idiosyncrasy of being against everything that dominates and wants to dominate . . . has already become master of the whole of physiology and biology, to their detriment, naturally, by spiriting away their basic concept, that of actual *activity*. On the other hand, the pressure of this idiosyncrasy forces "adaptation" into the foreground, which is a second-rate activity, just a reactivity, indeed life itself has been defined as an increasingly efficient inner adaptation to external circumstances (Herbert Spencer). But this is to misunderstand the essence of life, its *will to power*, we overlook the prime importance that the spontaneous, aggressive, expansive, re-interpreting, re-directing and formative forces have, which "adaptation" follows only when they have had their effect; in the organism itself, the dominant role of these highest functionaries, in whom the life-will is active and manifests itself, is denied. (*GM*, II, 12)

What is crucial to see here is that the goal of power is not being ascribed to some particular psychological state. Rather talk of the will to power is clearly meant as shorthand, as a statement of the fundamental tendency, a tendency that is essential to life, towards expansion, domination, growth, accumulation of force, and power.[16]

---

[15] Though, not surprisingly, he points back to *GM*: "The opposition between '*noble* morality' and 'Christian morality' was first explained in my *Genealogy of Morals*" (*CW*, Epilogue, "Note").

[16] Cf. "Every animal . . . instinctively strives for an optimum of favourable conditions in which to fully release his power and achieve his maximum of power-sensation; every animal abhors equally

The contrast being drawn in this passage is with some form of a theory of evolution being ascribed to Spencer that gives "adaptation" a central role. But perhaps for us the contrast would be better drawn with contemporary evolutionary theories. Consider the following unexceptional quote from a contemporary textbook:

> "Life" is difficult to define at the border of the nonliving. (In isolation from their hosts, for example, viruses lack many of the features of more "typical" life forms.) Undoubtedly the salient feature of living things is their ability to replicate themselves, thereby increasing in number and producing copies of variant forms. (Futuyma 1998: 166)

Of course, the author does not mean by "ability" merely that it is *possible* for living things to replicate themselves. Rather what he means is that living things are the kind of things that *do* replicate themselves. That is their fundamental tendency. In individual cases they will fail to do so. And of course someone could easily be tempted to make stronger claims: life is a tendency to replicate in ways that ensure the copies will survive and spread. Neither this immodest version nor the modest alternative requires ascribing to the creature a particular motivational state with replication as part of its content.

The same holds for Nietzsche, I suggest, though in his case the fundamental tendency that defines, or is at least essential to, life is a tendency towards expansion, domination, growth, overcoming resistances, increasing strength – in shorthand: power. Again, no particular individual mental state needs to be ascribed to the organism. This comes out very clearly in an 1888, thus relatively late, note from the *Nachlaß* (here the contrast is drawn with hedonism rather than adaptationism):

> Der Wille zur Macht als *Leben*
> Der Mensch sucht *nicht* die Lust and vermeidet *nicht* die Unlust: man versteht, welchem berühmten Vorurtheile ich hiermit widerspreche. Lust und Unlust sind bloße Folge, bloße Begleiterscheinung, – was der Mensch will, was jeder kleinste Theil eines lebendes Organismus will, das ist ein plus von Macht. Im Streben danach folgt sowohl Lust als Unlust . . . Nehmen wir den einfachsten Fall, den der

instinctively . . . any kind of disturbance and hindrance that blocks or could block his path to the optimum (– it is *not* his path to 'happiness' I am talking about, but the path to power, action, the mightiest deeds, and in most cases, actually, his path to misery)" (*GM*, III, 7). "[W]hat was at stake in all philosophizing hitherto was not at all 'truth' but something else – let us say, health, future, growth, power, life" (*GS*, Preface, 2). Cf. *BGE*, 259: "life itself is *essentially* appropriation, injury, overpowering of what is alien and weaker; suppression, hardness, imposition of one's own forms, incorporation and at least, at its mildest, exploitation . . . life simply *is* will to power. . . . 'Exploitation' . . . belongs to the *essence* of what lives, as a basic organic function; it is a consequence of the will to power, which is after all the will of life."

primitiven Ernährung: das Protoplasma streckt seine Pseudopodien aus, um nach etwas zu suchen, was ihm widersteht – nicht aus Hunger, sondern aus Willen zur Macht. Darauf macht es den Versuch, dasselbe zu überwinden, sich anzueignen, sich einzuverleiben: – das, was man "Ernährung" nennt, ist bloß eine Folge-Erscheinung, eine Nutzanwendung jenes ursprünglichen Willens, *stärker* zu werden. (*KSA*, 13:14[174])

We cannot sensibly ascribe to Nietzsche the view that even an amoeba has a psychological state like a desire aimed at power. Again, the view is clearly that the tendency towards power is a disposition or tendency of the creature as a living thing. At least part of what it is for it to be alive is for it to be so disposed.

The real will to power doctrine, I propose therefore, is actually a doctrine about what is essential to life. To be alive is, in part, at least, to have a tendency towards expansion, growth, domination, overcoming of resistances, increasing strength, and so on. Talking of a will to power is a shorthand for this just as talking of a will to replicate would be a shorthand for a more contemporary, more plausible (but still no doubt inaccurate) understanding of what is essential to life. It is this picture of life – and some crucially related evaluative notions I will come to in a moment – that is of central importance to Nietzsche. And it is this picture of life, I suggest, that is present even where Nietzsche does not use the reductive-sounding locution of the will to power.[17]

Once we shift to focusing on the role that the notion of "life" plays, while remembering how talk of the tendency to the accumulation of power is a shorthand for a tendency to expand, grow, dominate, and so on, then we see that Leiter's claim that "it is hard to understand why [Nietzsche] says almost nothing about will to power" in his *Ecce Homo* or in the series of new prefaces of 1886 seems no longer to have the force that it did against interpretations that did take explicit talk of the will to power to be essential to stating Nietzsche's position. When we turn to *Ecce Homo* and those prefaces, "life" does play the role one would expect of a fundamental evaluative standard.[18]

---

[17] I suggest that the passages from the *Nachlaß* and *BGE* that are often quoted to ascribe to Nietzsche a very strong form of the will to power doctrine should be interpreted as signs that Nietzsche was indeed occasionally tempted to a more reductive and extreme doctrine. The use, though, of the notion of life as involving some fundamental tendency towards growth, exploitation, domination, increase of strength, is far more widespread, as the rest of the passages quoted throughout this chapter show.

[18] Cf. *TI*, "Skirmishes of an Untimely Man," 33.

Let us start with *Ecce Homo*. After a long discussion of various qualities, experiences, and so on, that he possesses in the sections entitled "Why I Am So Wise" and "Why I Am So Clever," Nietzsche notes:

One will ask me why on earth I've been relating all these small things which are generally considered matters of complete indifference: I only harm myself, the more so if I am destined to represent great tasks. Answer: these small things – nutrition, place, climate, recreation, the whole casuistry of selfishness – are inconceivably more important than everything one has taken to be important so far. Precisely here one must begin to *relearn*. What mankind has so far considered seriously have not even been realities but mere imaginings – more strictly speaking, *lies* prompted by the bad instincts of sick natures ... All the problems of politics, of social organization, and of education have been falsified through and through because one mistook the most harmful men for great men – because one learned to despise "little" things, which means the basic concerns of life. (*EH*, "Why I Am So Clever," 10)

When he turns to his assessment of his own books, the centrality of the evaluative standard of life comes out clearly. He claims that one of the two "decisive innovations" of *The Birth of Tragedy* is

the understanding of Socratism: Socrates is recognized for the first time as an instrument of Greek disintegration, as a typical decadent. "Rationality" *against* instinct. "Rationality" at any price as a dangerous force that undermines life. (*EH*, "The Birth of Tragedy," 1)[19]

The other decisive innovation has to do with the recognition of "the Dionysian phenomenon" as involving "the ultimate limit of affirmation" – an affirmation of life:

Saying Yes to life even in its strangest and hardest problems; the will to life rejoicing over its own inexhaustibility even in the sacrifice of its highest types – that is what I called Dionysian. (*EH*, "The Birth of Tragedy," 3)[20]

The fundamental question of whether in individuals or cultures there are instincts that are undermining life, turning against it, leading to lives that are less powerful, or whether there is an affirmation and rejoicing of life – and thus a sign that the tendency to growth and domination is strong and successful – is the question that Nietzsche takes himself to have been the first to highlight:

---

[19] "Every kind of contempt for sex ... is the crime *par excellence* against life – is the real sin against the holy spirit of life" (*EH*, "Why I Write Such Good Books," 5).
[20] He is quoting himself from *TI*.

I was the first to see the real opposition: the degenerating instinct that turns against life with subterranean vengefulness (Christianity, the philosophy of Schopenhauer, in a certain sense already the philosophy of Plato, and all of idealism . . .) versus a formula for the highest affirmation, born of fullness, of overfullness. (*EH*, "The Birth of Tragedy," 2)

These passages bring to the fore the centrality of the notion of "decadence" and "degeneration." "Decadence" I suggest is closely connected to the notion of "life" Nietzsche is deploying: decadence is a matter of declining life. And thus mentions of decadence, and the assignment of a negative value to it, are also a deployment of a fundamental evaluative standard having to do with "life." And it is precisely the task of assessing morality, taken up in detail in the *Genealogy*, in relation to the question of decadence – to its role in turning against life – that Nietzsche claims in *Ecce Homo* is his singular innovation:

seeing morality itself as a symptom of decadence is an innovation and singularity of the first rank in the history of knowledge. (*EH*, "The Birth of Tragedy," 2)

Nietzsche claims that the ultimate task, namely that of revaluing our values so that the morality of good and evil is undermined and new values are created that now serve life rather than undermine it, was already foreshadowed in *BT*:

A tremendous hope speaks out of this essay. . . . let us suppose that my attempt to assassinate two millennia of antinature and desecration of man were to succeed. That new party of life which would tackle the greatest of all tasks, the attempt to raise humanity higher, including the relentless destruction of everything that was degenerating and parasitical, would again make possible that excess of life on earth from which the Dionysian state, too, would have to awaken again. (*EH*, "The Birth of Tragedy," 4)

The fundamental task of revaluing the values of morality for the sake of life gets repeated again and again through the rest of *Ecce Homo*. Of *Dawn*, he writes, "[w]ith this book my campaign against morality begins." He seeks new "dawns" in "a *revaluation of all values*" (*EH*, "Dawn," 1). Thus: "The question concerning the origin of moral values is for me a question of the very first rank because it is crucial for the future of humanity" (*EH*, "Dawn," 2). The role of the priest in this story – the story that gets much elaboration, obviously, in the *Genealogy* – shows clearly the standard Nietzsche is using to assess morality:

But the priest desires precisely the degeneration of the whole, of humanity: for that reason he *conserves* what degenerates – at this price he rules. When seriousness is deflected from the self-preservation and the enhancement of the strength of the body – *that is, of life* – when anemia is construed as an ideal, and contempt for the body as "salvation of the soul" – what else is this if not a *recipe* for decadence? (*EH*, "Dawn," 2; emphasis in original)

The centrality of "life" as the standard for the revaluation of values reaches a crescendo in the final section of *Ecce Homo*, "Why I Am a Destiny." As he emphasizes: "*Revaluation of all values:* that is my formula for an act of supreme self-examination on the part of humanity":

Blindness to Christianity is the crime *par excellence* – the crime against life. . . . Christian morality . . . that which *corrupted* humanity . . . it is the utterly gruesome fact that *antinature* itself received the highest honors as morality . . . To blunder to such an extent, not as individuals, not as a people, but as humanity! – That one taught men to despise the very first instincts of life . . . What? Is humanity itself decadent? Was it always? – What is certain is that it has been *taught* only decadence values as supreme values. The morality that would un-self man is the morality of decadence *par excellence* – the fact "I am declining," transposed into the imperative, "all of you *ought* to decline" – and not only into the imperative. – This the only morality that has been taught so far . . . reveals a will to the end; fundamentally, it negates life. (*EH*, "Why I Am a Destiny," 7)

As Nietzsche emphasizes, this is compatible with what he claims is his particular insight, namely, that it is not humanity that is "degenerating" but rather only a particular type of man exemplified by the priest which found "in Christian morality the means to come to *power*." These individuals were "decadents: *hence* the revaluation of all values into hostility to life, *hence* morality – *Definition of morality:* Morality – the idiosyncrasy of decadents, with the ulterior motive of revenging oneself against life – successfully" (*EH*, "Why I Am a Destiny," 7):

Finally – this is what is most terrible of all – the concept of the *good* man signifies that one sides with all that is weak, sick, failure, suffering of itself – all that ought to perish: the principle of selection is crossed – an ideal is fabricated from the contradiction against the proud and well-turned-out human being who says Yes . . . and he is now called *evil*. (*EH*, "Why I Am a Destiny," 8)

And Nietzsche then ends *Ecce Homo*: "Have I been understood? – *Dionysus versus the Crucified.* –" (*EH*, "Why I Am a Destiny," 8).

In other words, the fundamental contrast is between those who side with what is weak, sick, and so on, and those who side with, who affirm, what is essential to life: the tendency to strength, health, domination, and so on. As these passages make clear, in *Ecce Homo*, Nietzsche does have a fundamental standard: it is the standard of life. Life itself strives towards growth, domination, expansion, strength – in short power. To affirm life is to affirm this fundamental tendency. The fundamental task is to assess evaluative systems according to whether they help the fundamental instincts of life or hinder them. Nietzsche takes one of his fundamental insights to be that morality is a product of life that is declining in strength. The result is a set of values that reject and condemn the fundamental tendencies of life to strength, domination, growth, and power and instead support weakness of all kinds. The institution of these values actually succeeds in weakening life, in weakening the tendency to growth and domination. The "decadents" thus revenge themselves "against life – successfully" (*EH*, "Why I Am a Destiny," 7). Nietzsche, on the other hand, is going to side with the "new party of life," with Dionysus against the Crucified.

When we turn to the above-mentioned prefaces of 1886, the concept of "life" plays the same central role. The preface to *BT* claims that this book tackles the following problem for the first time: *"to look at science in the perspective* [unter der Optik] *of the artist, but at art in that of life"* (*BT*, Preface, 2). And to the "whole cluster of grave questions with which this book burdened itself" he "add[s] the gravest question of all. What, seen in the perspective of *life* [*unter der Optik des* Lebens], is the significance of morality?" (*BT*, Preface, 4). Again he emphasizes how he sensed behind morality a *"hostility to life"*: "life *must* continually and inevitably be in the wrong, because life *is* something essentially amoral ... might not morality be 'a will to negate life' ... the beginning of the end? Hence, the danger of dangers?" (*BT*, Preface, 5). One could continue with quotations from the remaining prefaces mentioned, but the same themes of the proposed interpretation get sounded again and again.[21]

The above discussion succeeds in showing that the textual evidence deployed against a strong form of the will to power doctrine does not work against the interpretation that takes the notion of "life" as essential to articulating Nietzsche's fundamental evaluative standard and as expressing a fundamental descriptive claim about, at least, a central part of reality. Life itself is a tendency to grow, dominate, accumulate strength, in short, increase power. But it also provides Nietzsche's standard for evaluating value systems: we have to ask whether evaluative systems help growth, domination, and the accumulation of strength or whether they undermine it.[22]

---

[21] Cf. *HAH*, Preface, 1, 6; *GS*, Preface, 2. The way in which the preface of *Daybreak* fits with my interpretation will become clearer, I hope, once the rest of it is laid out below.

[22] Let me deal briefly with two objections. First, the interpretation that takes life as fundamentally a tendency to power should not be read as ascribing the kind of teleological view to Nietzsche that he would disapprove of. Indeed, he clearly contrasts precisely this view with a teleological view. He

5. THE BENTHAMITE MODEL

As I said analogously about the interpretation that focuses on articulating Nietzsche's position in terms of the will to power, it is hard to think that there is no connection between the descriptive claims about what is essential to life and the use of life as a fundamental standard for evaluating values. And Nietzsche's texts certainly seem to claim the existence of some connection:

Every naturalism in morality – that is, every healthy morality – is dominated by an instinct of life; some commandment of life is fulfilled by a determinate canon of "shalt" and "shalt not"; some inhibition and hostile element on the path of life is thus removed. *Anti-natural* morality – that is, almost every morality which has so far been taught, revered, and preached – turns, conversely, *against* the instincts of life: it is *condemnation* of these instincts, now secret, now outspoken and impudent. (*TI*, "Morality as Anti-Nature," 4)

A naturalist morality is one that goes along with life's fundamental tendency to dominate. It affirms this tendency and looks for "shalts" and "shalt nots" that help life achieve these goals. Unlike the anti-natural morality it does not fight, it does not revolt against, the fundamental instincts of life by condemning them. Nietzsche continues:

Once one has comprehended the outrage of such a revolt against life as has become almost sacrosanct in Christian morality, one has, fortunately, also comprehended something else: the futility, apparentness, absurdity, and *mendaciousness* of such a revolt. A condemnation of life by the living remains in the end a mere symptom of a certain kind of life: the question whether it is justified or unjustified is not even raised thereby. One would require a position *outside* of life, and yet have to know it as well as one, as many, as all who have lived it, in order to be permitted even to touch the problem of the *value* of life: reasons enough to comprehend that this problem is for us an unapproachable problem. When we speak of values, we speak with the inspiration, with the way of looking at things, which is part of life [*unter*

writes: "[L]ife itself is *will to power;* self-preservation is only one of the indirect and most frequent *results*. In short, here as everywhere else, let us beware of *superfluous* teleological principles – one of which is the instinct of self-preservation ... Thus method, which must be essentially economy of principles, demands it" (*BGE*, 13). There are two ways of making sense of Nietzsche's view here. One is to interpret him as thinking of the claim that life is the will to power as teleological but not as a *superfluous* teleological claim. The second option, the one I prefer, is to ascribe to him the view that a general tendency to growth, domination, expansion, increase of strength, and so on, is simply too diffuse to count as having a *telos* in the relevant sense. Compare, again, the kind of claim about life that a contemporary biologist might make.

The second objection involves *BGE*, 9, where Nietzsche mocks the Stoics for the imperative "live according to life." As Nietzsche says, "how could you *not* do that? Why make a principle of what you yourselves are and must be?" As I hope my discussion of the Benthamite model below will show, this in fact can be read as supportive of my eventual interpretation rather than undermining it.

der Optik des Lebens]: life itself forces us to posit values; life itself values through us when we posit values. From this it follows that even that anti-natural morality which conceives of God as the counter-concept and condemnation of life is only a value judgment of life – but of what life? of what kind of life? I have already given the answer: of declining, weakened, weary, condemned life. (*TI*, "Morality as Anti-nature," 5)

I suggest that implicit in these Nietzschean texts is a kind of naturalism about values that was quite widespread among late nineteenth-century thinkers working in the wake of, as Nietzsche would put it, the "death of God." Mill is an example, but only one example. And perhaps Mill is not as good an example as Bentham. The Benthamite model, as I am tempted to call it, focuses on the *inescapability* of certain fundamental tendencies or dispositions. Once we really see ourselves as natural creatures – once, to use Nietzsche's language, we "translate man back into nature" (*BGE*, 230) – then we have to look for direction from nature. Where else could one look? And nature has constituted us, so the understandable thought goes, in certain ways. One would have reason to act against our natural constitution only on the basis of some set of commands or injunctions from beyond nature and that is precisely what we give up in our attempts not to place God at the center of things. Instead we affirm, rather than deny, what is essential to life.

Bentham writes:

Nature has placed mankind under the governance of two sovereign masters, *pain* and *pleasure*. It is for them alone to point out what we ought to do, as well as to determine what we shall do. On the one hand the standard of right and wrong, on the other the chain of causes and effects, are fastened to their throne. They govern us in all we do, in all we say, in all we think: every effort we can make to throw off our subjection, will serve but to demonstrate and confirm it. In words a man may pretend to abjure their empire: but in reality he will remain subject to it all the while. The *principle of utility* recognises this subjection. (Bentham 2003: 17)

Now one can try, as one can try with Mill, to find a valid argument here. Certainly for using the relevant stretches of Bentham or Mill for purely philosophical purposes one would have to determine whether or not there was a valid argument. However, for the purposes of the history of philosophy – for the purpose of figuring out the probability that an interpretation reflects what the philosopher was thinking – what is more important, at least here, is the widespread tendency to think along such lines.

In addition to Mill and Bentham, I would classify Marx as another example:

The theoretical conclusions of the Communists are in no way based on ideas or principles that have been invented, or discovered, by this or that would-be universal reformer.

They merely express, in general terms, actual relations springing from an existing class struggle, from a historical movement going on under our very eyes. The abolition of existing property relations is not at all a distinctive feature of Communism. (Marx [1848] 1978c: 484)

Communism is for us not a *state of affairs* which is to be established, an *ideal* to which reality [will] have to adjust itself. We call communism the *real* movement which abolishes the present state of things. The conditions of this movement result from the premises now in existence. (Marx [1845–46] 1978b: 162)

The working class . . . have no ready-made utopias to introduce *par décret du peuple*. They know that in order to work out their own emancipation, and along with it that higher form to which present society is irresistibly tending by its own economical agencies, they will have to pass through long struggles, through a series of historic processes, transforming circumstances and men. They have no ideals to realise, but to set free the elements of the new society with which old collapsing bourgeois society itself is pregnant. (Marx [1871] 1978a: 635–36)

Such quotes can be multiplied without end and the point comes across even more strongly in Engels' writings. The thrust is that somehow fundamental historical tendencies settle, or make irrelevant, certain fundamental evaluative questions. And reading the evaluative off of these natural tendencies is precisely what one does when one rejects the traditional non-scientific, metaphysical, religious groundings for morality. There were neo-Kantians who worried about precisely this kind of materialism in Marx and others, but there were also defenders of what came to be regarded as the orthodox Marxist line. Karl Kautsky, "the embodiment of Marxist orthodoxy" as Kolakowski put it, responded to the neo-Kantian worries as one might expect:[23]

[If] the sceptic aimed to be correctly informed about marxist ethics, he would recognise . . . that ethics are not a matter of convention, nor something which the individual chooses at will, but are determined by powers which are stronger than the individual, which stand over him. How can scepticism arise out of the recognition of necessity?[24]

[It is] the materialist conception of history which has first completely deposed the moral ideal as the directing factor of social evolution, and has taught us to deduce our social aims solely from the knowledge of the material foundations.[25]

---

[23] The quoted phrase about Kautsky is from Kolakowski 1978: II, 31.
[24] Quoted in Lukes 1985: 16–17.   [25] Quoted in Lukes 1985: 18.

This line, famously, was picked up by Lenin and Trotsky. As Trotsky wrote, the "morality of the proletariat ... deduces a rule of conduct from the laws of development of society, thus primarily from the class struggle, this law of all laws."[26]

Much of the appeal of the various different strands in social Darwinism, whether more individualistic or not, also clearly lay in a similar line of thought: nature, rather than something outside of nature, must give us direction. The nineteenth century is thus replete with this line of thought. Indeed, the intuition that something like this has to be right lies behind many contemporary forms of naturalism – those that focus, in one way or another, on articulating what we "really" want – and, I would suggest, contemporary "constitutivist" theories that attempt to deduce how we ought to behave from the rules that we already supposedly inevitably follow, at some level, when we act.[27]

The point is not at all that such arguments work. Indeed, I have argued that even the arguments by the most sophisticated of contemporary defenders of such views do not work.[28] The point is rather that the temptation towards some such view, that people find some such line of thought intuitive, is understandable even if the various attempts to work out the details turn out to fail. In all these cases, cases that share a rejection of the non-natural, the metaphysical in some pejorative sense, it makes sense to ascribe to the philosopher a strongly held belief or intuition to the effect that what we are naturally disposed to go for in our lives at the most fundamental level somehow settles what we should go for – or, at least, makes that question somehow irrelevant.

Leiter, recall, used Schacht as the example of someone committed to a strong form of the doctrine of will to power and suggested that the "Millian Model seems the most charitable reconstruction of what the commentators do say, and of Nietzsche's few scattered remarks on the subjection" (2000: 282 n. 19); however, I suggest, the above interpretation fits what Schacht does say much better. Here is Schacht ascribing what should now look like a very similar argument to Nietzsche:

---

[26] Quoted in Lukes 1985: 24.

[27] For naturalisms of the former kind, see the work of Peter Railton. For prominent contemporary forms of constitutivist views see the work of Christine Korsgaard and J. David Velleman. For an attempt to provide a detailed, philosophically defensible interpretation of Nietzsche along contemporary constitutivist lines, see Katsafanas 2011a. Cf. Schacht 1983: 367: "As a constitutive principle [will to power] is the ultimate basis of all value."

[28] Hussain 2004 and 2008.

Human life, for Nietzsche, is ultimately a part of a kind of a vast game in which reality generally consists, the basic rules of which allow of innumerable variations but are unalterable in their general outlines. It is so to speak, the only game in town. Once its nature is discerned, and the impossibility of getting outside of it is recognized, its affirmation presents itself as the only alternative to a rejection leading nowhere but to nihilism. ... The nature of the game, he holds, establishes a standard for the evaluation of everything falling within its compass. (Schacht 1983: 398)

Some such thought of inescapability, I suggest, lies behind the connection Nietzsche clearly sees between the fact that life is essentially a tendency to grow, dominate, and so on, and the use of life as a standard by which to assess values, to assess whether they promote growth, domination, and power or undermine it. We should read these passages as involving implicitly the above line of thought that was widespread among turn-of-the-century materialists – or naturalists in some broad sense. Life is a tendency towards domination, growth, expansion, overcoming resistances, and so on – power, in short. This is, to use Bentham's phrase, our "subjection." To reject this subjection, to question the value of pursuing domination, growth, and so on – to question the value of life – is fundamentally pointless. It inevitably involves a commitment to something beyond nature. "For a philosopher to see a problem in the value of life is thus an objection to him, a question mark concerning his wisdom, an un-wisdom" (*TI*, "The Problem of Socrates," 2).[29]

Again none of this is to claim that I have a reconstruction of a valid argument that we can ascribe to Nietzsche – an argument that would show how the fact that life does have this fundamental tendency towards power does indeed entail either that we should value power or, at least, that it does not make sense for us to ask whether or not we should go along with our

---

[29] I am willing to grant that it is not exactly clear what Nietzsche's complaint is, either here or in some other passages we will consider below. But this reflects the problems of the general strategy. I think it is quite unclear in all the cases we considered – Bentham, Mill, Marx, Darwinism, contemporary naturalists and constitutivists – why a certain kind of normative question is supposed to be closed off. Nietzsche has company – whether one takes it as good or bad company is another matter.

See also *WP*, 675: "To have purposes, aims, intentions, *willing* in general, is the same thing as willing to be stronger, willing to grow – and, in addition, willing the means to do this. The most universal and basic instinct in all doing and willing has for precisely this reason remained the least known and most hidden, because *in praxi* we always follow its commandments, because we *are* this commandment –. All valuations are only consequences and narrow perspectives in the service of this one will: valuation itself is only this will to power. A critique of being from the point of view of any one of these values is something absurd and erroneous. Even supposing that a process of decline begins in this way, this process still stands in the service of this will. To appraise being itself! But this appraisal itself is still this being! – and if we say no, we still do what we *are*. One must comprehend the absurdity of this posture of judging existence, and then try to understand what is really involved in it. It is symptomatic." See also *WP*, 706; *CW*, Epilogue.

tendency to pursue power. But given the historical context of the nine-teenth century – indeed, given contemporary tendencies in those who reject non-naturalism – philosophical charity does not force us to avoid the ascription of the above Benthamite argument. The text, as I hope to have shown, warrants just such an ascription.

I have ignored so far one passage that Leiter appeals to in rejecting some strong form of the will to power doctrine. The question is whether the passage also provides evidence against the interpretation of Nietzsche in terms of the notion of "life" that I have been defending. I will argue that it does not but that seeing why will eventually show us why and how *On the Genealogy of Morality* is absolutely essential to Nietzsche's overall project.

Leiter quotes the following passage from *The Antichrist*:

Life itself is to my mind the instinct for growth, for durability, for an accumulation of forces, for *power:* where the will to power is lacking there is decline. It is my contention that all the supreme values of mankind *lack* this will. (*A*, 6)

Leiter focuses on the claim that the "will to power is lacking" as textual evidence that undermines the strong form of the will to power doctrine. As he puts it, "But if all actions manifested this *will*, then this *will* could never be found lacking" (Leiter 2002: 141). Now, so far, there is an obvious response to be made. It is, recall, the "values" that "*lack* this will" and it seems perfectly fine to read this as just the claim that the values are values that reject power, that condemn power. For my purposes what is crucial is that it does not follow, yet, that life itself isn't a tendency to power and growth. Indeed, since Nietzsche explicitly claims, right here, that "[l]ife itself is ... the instinct for growth, for durability, for an accumulation of forces, for *power*," he would apparently be contradicting himself in the space of the same sentence if he granted that there could be life that doesn't involve a tendency for growth and power. On pain of ascribing this contra-diction, we need to see Nietzsche as claiming that *values* can be lacking the will to power – I suggest in the sense of condemning power – but that life always involves striving for power.

This does, however, raise a puzzle: Why would living creatures that, *qua* living, embody a fundamental tendency to dominate and grow come none-theless to have values that do not assign positive value to domination, growth, power, and so on? The answer that Nietzsche almost has to give, and that has been suggested in many of the passages we have already considered, is that it is the fundamental tendency to dominate and grow that *itself* generates value judgments that are hostile to life. This is precisely the kind of claim Nietzsche needs to make in order to use what I have called the Benthamite model of inescapability or subjection. Thus its repeated presence in the texts we have considered is further evidence that he is committed to the Benthamite model.[30]

6. THE GENEALOGY OF MORALITY

However, if this interpretation is right, then we should see Nietzsche defending this claim. After all, it is one thing to assert this and another to provide evidence. Here is where we come to see the centrality of *On the Genealogy of Morality* in Nietzsche's overall project. One of the crucial tasks that the *Genealogy* carries out is precisely such a defense. What it shows is that even the occurrence of value judgments that condemn life, that condemn life precisely by condemning tendencies to dominate, sub- jugate, grow, and so on, is to be explained by appealing to the fundamental tendency that is life, to grow, to dominate, and so on. The *Genealogy* is an extended study of how this essential tendency of life, when it is in life forms that are relatively weak, that cannot directly dominate their environments, that are declining in strength – in short, to use one of Nietzsche's favorite words from later in the passage, in cases of decadence – this tendency of life itself generates value judgments according to which striving for power, dominating, expanding, and so on, are condemned. The *Genealogy* thus shows that the tendency towards power is, even in these extreme cases, inescapable. At the same time it shows that the values of morality serve the relatively weak, declining forms of life.

A brief tour of the *Genealogy* should suffice to make this point. In *GM*, I, 7, Nietzsche claims that part of the aristocracy was a "*priestly* caste." A caste that was, at least relative to the warrior knights, powerless. The suggestion seems to be that this is in part because of a fundamental unhealthiness among this group (*GM*, I, 6).[31] "Out of their powerlessness their hate grows into something enormous and uncanny" (*GM*, I, 6). The only way for them to gain power over the natural ruling classes is through "an act of *spiritual revenge*" which involves "a radical revaluation of their values."

It was the Jews who in opposition to the aristrocratic value equation (good = noble = powerful = beautiful = happy = beloved of God) dared its inversion, . . . namely: "the miserable alone are the good; the poor, powerless, lowly alone are the good . . .

---

[30] Consider again *TI*, "Morality as Anti-Nature," 5. Or *WP*, 675 again.
[31] I take the appeal of Nietzsche to contingent, but, as far he seems to think, common occurrences to be part of his denial that his arguments appeal to any fundamental teleological conception of reality.

whereas you, you noble and powerful ones . . . you will eternally be the wretched, accursed, and damned!" (*GM*, I, 7)

What is crucial for Nietzsche is that this "*slave revolt in morality* . . . has been victorious" (*GM*, I, 7). In other words, the strategy of insisting on this inversion, "with fear-inspiring consistency, and held . . . fast with teeth of the most unfathomable hate (the hate of powerlessness)," has indeed been successful in replacing the traditional aristocratic value equation and succeeded in giving those who were powerless a way to increase their power in society. But what this has allowed is the continued existence, indeed dominance, of "mediocre and uninspiring" creatures. The reversal of values prevents the emergence of more powerful humans, of those who are "completely formed, happy, powerful, triumphant, in which there is still something to fear!" (*GM*, I, 12). The tendency to accumulate power has thus driven those who were relatively powerless to invent morality, a set of values that condemns this basic tendency to domination and power that is life. In turn the widespread acceptance of morality has undermined, so far, the emergence of even more powerful individuals. It prevents the development of a "stronger type" (*GM*, I, 17).[32]

The second essay focuses on the emergence of guilt and bad conscience, both essential to the functioning of morality.[33] They give the values of morality their bite, their sting, and thus get individuals not to consciously pursue their own growth and development. The story of the emergence of guilt and bad conscience is again a story in which it is the fundamental tendency to dominate, overpower, and expand that explains their emergence. A "race of conquerors and lords . . . lays its terrible paws on a population enormously superior in number perhaps, but still formless, still roaming about" (*GM*, II, 17). These lords are the "state" that "as a

---

[32] How could the powerful lose out against the relatively powerless? Doesn't this just show that they aren't relatively more powerful? There is no denying that there are deep tensions in Nietzsche's view here – tensions that are actually reflected in analogous tensions in the other forms of naturalism and constitutivism I pointed to earlier. For reasons of space, I cannot say much about this here. We would need to work through a plausible range of different senses of power and address questions of the power of collectives of individuals. Consider simply physical power and some everyday notion of intelligence. Imagine the practically brilliant warrior who is both smarter and more physically powerful than I am in general. I contend that it would be acceptable shorthand to say that this person is just more powerful than I am. I could still succeed in managing to outwit him on some particular occasion for contingent reasons that do not count against the general claim that he is smarter and more physically powerful than I am. I just happen to know that this stream I am leading him to is contaminated. Or, now the point about groups, I gang up on him with others. Our everyday notions allow us to say, apparently sensibly, that the weak can defeat the powerful. Cf. *A*, 58.

[33] For my purposes here, and for reasons of space, I am going to ignore the many complexities surrounding the relations between conscience, bad conscience, and guilt.

terrible tyranny, as a crushing and ruthless machinery . . . continued to work until finally such a raw material of people and half-animals was not only thoroughly kneaded and pliable but also *formed*" (*GM*, II, 17). They enclose this population "once and for all within the sway of society and peace" (*GM*, II, 16). In turn:

> Those terrible bulwarks with which the organization of the state protects itself against the old instincts of freedom . . . brought it about that all those instincts of the wild free roaming human turned themselves backwards *against man himself*. . . . *that* is the origin of "bad conscience." (*GM*, II, 16)

As Nietzsche emphasizes:

> Fundamentally, it is the same active force as the one that is at work on a grand scale in those artists of violence and organizers, and that builds states, which here, internally, and on a smaller, pettier scale, turned backwards, in the "labyrinth of the breast" . . . creates bad conscience for itself, and builds negative ideals, it is that very *instinct for freedom* (put into my language: the will to power). (*GM*, II, 17)

The full story here is inevitably more complicated, and for reasons of space I cannot do it justice, but this suffices to show that again it is life, the tendency to power itself, that lies behind the emergence of morality and its condemnation of life.[34]

The third essay makes the same kind of argument though here it is the emergence of the ascetic ideal that is being explained. The ascetic ideal is "anti-nature" (*GM*, III, 3) in the sense that it rejects the fundamental tendencies of life, rejects this life in favor of a supposed "other existence" (*GM*, III, 11).[35] Even this dramatic rejection of life is to be explained by the fundamental tendency that is life, namely, the will to power. And again it is the priest that plays a crucial role: the "ascetic priest has not only his faith in that ideal but also his will, his power, his interest." The ascetic priest "does not belong to any single race; he flourishes everywhere; he grows forth from every social rank" (*GM*, III, 11): "It must be a necessity of the first rank that makes this species that is *hostile to life* grow and prosper again and again – it must be in the *interest of life itself* that this type of self-contradiction not die out" (*GM*, III, 11).

Nietzsche is clear about what this necessity is:

[34] Part of what is crucial to the story is the role of the priest (*GM*, III, 20).
[35] "One knows the three great pomp words of the ascetic ideal: poverty, humility, chastity" (*GM*, III, 8). For a forceful statement of the ways in which the ascetic ideal is anti-life see the very end of *GM*, III, 28. There is a kind of asceticism that Nietzsche clearly approves of, but I will not attempt to untangle those knots here (cf. *A*, 57).

the ascetic ideal springs from the protective and healing instincts of a degenerating life that seeks with every means to hold its ground and is fighting for its existence; it points to a partial physiological hindrance and tiredness against which the deepest instincts of life, which have remained intact, fight incessantly with new means and inventions. (*GM*, III, 13)

The ways in which, according to Nietzsche, the ascetic ideal, in the hands of the priest, succeeds as such a means are quite complicated and we do not need to rehearse them here.[36] What is crucial for my purposes is the fact that Nietzsche goes to such lengths to show how the emergence of even the most extreme form of an ideal that is hostile to life is to be explained by appealing to the fundamental tendencies that constitute life.

The *Genealogy* thus plays an essential role in defending in detail the crucial premise of the Benthamite model, namely, that these are the fundamental tendencies of life to which we are inescapably subjected.

The final twist to the story emerges when we ask ourselves how Nietzsche's own attempt to revalue values is to be explained. If indeed life needs morality – needs values that reject life – then what chance does Nietzsche's attempt at a revaluation have? If indeed we are all degenerate in the way Nietzsche supposes, then how can we give up the hostility to life expressed by the ascetic ideal? Here is where the discussion of science and philosophy in the third essay plays a central role.

After describing in some detail how the ascetic ideal "has ruined the health of the soul" (*GM*, III, 22), Nietzsche asks "*where* is the opposing will in which an *opposing ideal* expresses itself?" (*GM*, III, 23). Most of science he thinks does not at all provide such opposition. There are some rare cases though where science and philosophy do involve "passion, love, ardor, *suffering*" (*GM*, III, 23); however, such exceptions do not present an alternative, rather – and this is Nietzsche's crucial move – they are the ascetic ideal's "*most recent and noblest form*" (*GM*, III, 23) because "*they still believe in truth*" (*GM*, III, 24): "What *compels* one to this, however, this unconditional will to truth, is the *belief in the ascetic ideal itself*... it is the belief in a *metaphysical value*" (*GM*, III, 24). But this final, purest form of the ascetic ideal, this will to truth and truthfulness, finally "forbids itself the *lie involved in belief in God*." Indeed this will to truth finally leads to the self-destruction of morality and the ascetic ideal: "In this manner Christianity *as dogma* perished of its own morality; in this manner Christianity *as morality* must now also perish" (*GM*, III, 27).

But this perishing creates a tremendous opportunity, indeed a necessity:

---

[36] See Leiter 2002: 260–63, for one interpretation.

If one disregards the ascetic ideal: man, the *animal* man, has until now had no meaning. His existence on earth contained no goal; "to what end man at all?" – was a question without answer . . . behind every great human destiny a still greater "for nothing!" resounded as refrain. Precisely *this* is what the ascetic ideal means: . . . an enormous *void* surrounded man – he did not know how to justify, to explain, to affirm himself; he *suffered* from the problem of his meaning. (*GM*, III, 28)

If the ascetic ideal destroys itself, then life itself will now generate a new ideal. Once it gives up the "concept of the 'beyond', the 'true world' invented in order to devaluate the only world there is" (*EH*, "Why I Am a Destiny," 8), then it will have to affirm this world and that is to affirm life itself, the tendency, the will, to power. This is why the immoralists, those on the side of life, do stand a chance of revaluing values for the sake of life. The "economy in the law of life . . . finds an advantage even in the disgusting species of . . . the priests. *What* advantage? But we ourselves, we immoralists, are the answer" (*TI*, "Morality as Anti-Nature," 5).[37]

7. CONCLUSION

We began with certain puzzles about Nietzsche's *On the Genealogy of Morality*. Why did Nietzsche assume that morality was to be assessed in terms of its ability to help or hinder man from reaching his "*highest potential power and splendour*" (*GM*, Preface, 6)? We also wondered why there seemed to be a close connection between this standard and the emphasis on either the degeneration or increasing strength of "life." Why is it so crucial, as he puts it elsewhere, to assess the "significance of morality" from "the perspective of life" (*BT*, Preface, 4)? Finally, we wondered why the value of the values of *morality* were to be assessed in the light of a genealogy of these values, but no similar task seemed to be taken up for the standards, the apparent values, that Nietzsche *himself* was clearly using to assess the values of morality? Why was not the value of these in turn to be questioned?

With the above, extended discussion in place, we can finally sum up the answer to these puzzles. Life itself essentially involves a tendency to expansion, growth, domination, power, and splendor. We are always under the "subjection" of this tendency. The natural, Benthamite thought to have is that once one has rejected any appeal to anything other-worldly, anything non-natural, anything beyond this life, then nothing makes sense but to affirm this "subjection." As I granted, I do not think we can philosophically defend this inference, but its widespread appeal prevents the principle of

---

[37] Cf. *GS*, 1.

charity from undermining the ascription of this inference to Nietzsche. The puzzle, then, is why we do ever value anything else. As we have just seen, one crucial role of the *Genealogy* is to show that even when our values are hostile to life, these very valuations emerge from the fundamental tendency to power and domination that is life. The *Genealogy* shows that even in such cases this tendency is inescapable. The *Genealogy* itself shows that there is no similar genealogy to be done for this fundamental tendency. It is simply essential to what it is to be a living creature.

Or, if you prefer, the *Genealogy* is a genealogy of both the tendency towards power, and Nietzsche's affirmation of it. The genealogy gives us vivid evidence of how the tendency to dominate, to grow, and so on, is there even in the cases in which it might seem clear that it is not, for example, in the ascetic ideal. Finally, it is this ascetic ideal itself that is leading to its own destruction. And, as Nietzsche hints above, the fundamental tendency to grow and expand that is life must find another solution to the problem of the meaning of human life. Since "man has become a fantastic animal that has to fulfill one more condition of existence than any other animal" (*GS*, 1), that needs a justification of life, a purpose for life. The solution is to affirm this life rather than hopelessly look outside of this life. And this life is in essence a tendency to dominate, to expand, to exploit, in short to accumulate power. Affirming this life is affirming this pursuit of power. Life itself needs this affirmation. Life itself needs the immoralist. As Nietzsche writes:

Consequently –. Consequently. Consequently. O, do you understand me, my brothers? Do you understand this new law of ebb and flood? There is time for us too! (*GS*, 1)

CHAPTER 8

The relevance of history for moral philosophy: a study of Nietzsche's Genealogy

Paul Katsafanas

The fact is that conversions are difficult because the world reflects back upon us a choice which is confirmed through this world which it has fashioned.

Simone de Beauvoir, *The Ethics of Ambiguity* (1976)

Nietzsche's *On the Genealogy of Morality* occupies an unstable position in philosophical thought: it oscillates between seeming damning and irrelevant. The text's central argument is that our most cherished evaluative beliefs have a revolting history: our moral beliefs are the product of a *ressentiment*-inspired revolt carried out by a lackluster, vengeful underclass approximately two thousand years ago. But what is the import of this conclusion? On the one hand, the reader is tempted to agree with Charles Taylor, who writes, "no one can fail to recognize that, if true, Nietzsche's genealogies are devastating" (Taylor 1989: 72). On the other, one soon finds oneself wondering why, exactly, a recounting of events that took place two millennia ago should have any bearing on one's acceptance of modern morality. One finds oneself torn between wanting to insist that the history of our moral evaluations must be relevant, while at the same time failing to see how the history could so much as aspire to relevance.

These reactions are heightened by Nietzsche's own seemingly ambivalent stance toward history's relevance for moral philosophy. Nietzsche tells us that the *Genealogy* comprises "three crucial preparatory works for a revaluation of all values," thereby suggesting that the *Genealogy* constitutes a critique of morality (*EH*, "The Genealogy of Morality").[1] Yet he also insists that "the inquiry into the *origin of our evaluations* and tables of the good is in absolutely no way identical with a critique of them, as is so often believed,"

---

[1] When quoting from Nietzsche, I use the translations published by Cambridge University Press. I have sometimes made minor modifications.

thereby seeming to reject the idea that the *Genealogy* could serve a critical function (*WP*, 254).

For these reasons, Nietzsche's *Genealogy* generates vexing interpretive questions. How could a recounting of morality's history have any critical function? Moreover, why does Nietzsche write a historical critique, given his seeming disavowal of history's relevance? Any adequate interpretation of the *Genealogy* must answer these questions. More precisely, any adequate interpretation must meet two criteria:

The critical criterion: the interpretation must explain why the *Genealogy* constitutes (or enables) a critique of modern morality.

The historical criterion: the interpretation must explain why the *Genealogy*'s argument takes a historical form.

This chapter develops an interpretation that meets these conditions. I argue that Nietzsche's aim in the *Genealogy* is to show that modern morality has systematically (and deliberately) broken the connection between *perceptions* of increased power, and *actual* increases in power. In particular, modern morality leads agents to perceive actual reductions in power as increases in power.[2] It thereby strongly disposes agents to reduce their own power. This is Nietzsche's primary objection to modern morality: it configures our affects and presuppositions about agency in such a way that it systematically undermines the will to power. Accordingly, when Nietzsche begins the *Genealogy* by asking whether morality might undermine the *"highest potential power and splendour"* of human beings (*GM*, Preface, 6), the text shows that and why the answer is yes.

The structure of this chapter is as follows. Section 1 introduces the currently dominant interpretation of the *Genealogy*, which treats the text as establishing that modern morality undermines flourishing. I argue that this interpretation faces two problems. First, it has difficulty meeting the critical criterion, because it does not offer a satisfactory explanation of why flourishing is normatively relevant. Second, it fails to meet the historical criterion, because it is committed to treating the history as adventitious rather than a necessary component of Nietzsche's critique. Section 2 begins developing a new interpretation of the *Genealogy*, by offering a characterization of flourishing that explains why flourishing is normatively relevant. In particular, I argue that flourishing is defined in terms of will to power, and that Nietzsche has arguments establishing the will to power's normative authority. Section 3 considers an objection to this reading: as a normative

---

[2] This is a central point in David Owen's extremely insightful analysis of the *Genealogy* (Owen 2007). Section 7 discusses how my interpretation diverges from Owen's.

principle, will to power seems vacuous, failing to generate any substantive normative conclusions. In section 4, I show that the will to power thesis actually does generate substantive results when it is applied to *evaluative orientations*, rather than discrete, context-free moral judgments. Section 5 shows that this is exactly what Nietzsche does in the *Genealogy*. Sections 6 through 8 explicate this point, showing how, in light of the above facts, the *Genealogy* constitutes a will-to-power-based critique of modern morality. Finally, Section 9 explains why, according to this interpretation, the historical form of the *Genealogy* is necessary rather than adventitious.

I. INTERPRETING THE *GENEALOGY*'S CENTRAL ARGUMENT

How exactly might Nietzsche's *Genealogy* serve as a critique of modern morality? In the preface, Nietzsche writes,

> What if a regressive trait lurked in "the good man," likewise a danger, an enticement, a poison, a narcotic, so that the present *lived at the expense of the future?* ... So that morality itself were to blame if man, as species, never reached his *highest potential power and splendour?* So that morality itself was the danger of dangers? (*GM*, Preface, 6)

Here, Nietzsche asks a straightforward question about morality: does it undermine flourishing? Perhaps the most natural way of reading the *Genealogy*, then, is as an attempt to establish that modern morality does indeed undermine flourishing.[3]

On this reading, the *Genealogy* plays an evidential role: it provides evidence that Judeo-Christian morality has deleterious effects. It does so by contrasting the ways of life prior to and after the adoption of this moral system. Prior to the adoption of Judeo-Christian morality, certain agents flourished, serving as paradigms of health, power, and self-affirmation. After the adoption of this moral system, agents in general experienced a decline in flourishing. If this is correct, it serves as strong evidence that Judeo-Christian morality was responsible for a decline in flourishing.

Christopher Janaway and Brian Leiter have recently argued for this view. As Janaway puts it, the *Genealogy* "strongly suggests that genealogy ... is

---

[3] This is, of course, a common theme in Nietzsche's work. To choose just a few examples: he writes, "well-being as you understand it – that is no goal; it looks to us like an *end*! – a condition that immediately renders people ridiculous and despicable" (*BGE*, 225). What "has been called morality" will "deprive existence of its *great* character" (*EH*, "Why I Am a Destiny," 4). And he warns that "our weak, unmanly social concepts of good and evil and their tremendous ascendancy over body and soul have finally weakened all bodies and souls and snapped the self-reliant, independent, unprejudiced men, the pillars of a *strong* civilization" (*D*, 163; cf. *BGE*, 62, and *A*, 5).

distinct from, and instrumental towards, the critique or revaluation of values that Nietzsche hopes will take place. Genealogy does not itself complete the process of revaluation, but is a necessary start on the way to it" (Janaway 2007: 10). Leiter concurs, writing that "the genealogy of morality ... is but *one* instrument for arriving at a particular end, namely a critique of morality. This should alert us to the possibility that the critique of morality does not *depend* on the genealogy of morality, though the genealogy may help us arrive at it" (Leiter 2002: 177). He continues, "the point of origin of a morality has special *evidential* status as to the *effects* (or causal powers) of that morality, for example, as to whether morality obstructs or promotes human flourishing" (Leiter 2002: 177).[4]

Might this interpretation succeed? It is at least incomplete, for notice that the reading as described thus far does not meet the critical criterion. Suppose it is true that modern morality has undermined flourishing. In order for this fact to serve as an indictment of modern morality, we must accept a normative principle of the following kind:

If X undermines flourishing, then X is to be rejected.

To be sure, this principle has considerable appeal to a certain class of modern readers. But it is not uncontroversial. After all, the ascetic priest will reject the above principle, given that Nietzsche presents ascetic priests as explicitly valuing the *reduction* of flourishing (*GM*, III).[5] More generally, it is important to recognize – as Nietzsche himself does – that a consistent Christian will reject the above principle. For, as Nietzsche is at pains to emphasize, the Christian is committed to denying that the aim of life is flourishing.

This point is often not appreciated, so it will be helpful to quote at length from an especially lucid analysis of the phenomenon. Charles Taylor has recently argued that we can mark the distinction between secular and religious world views in terms of their answer to the following question:

Does the highest, the best life involve our seeking, or acknowledging, or serving, a good which is beyond, in the sense of independent of human flourishing? (Taylor 2007: 16)

---

[4] In particular, Leiter suggests that "persons adopt moralities for self-interested reasons," so, by understanding *who* promulgated Judeo-Christian morality, we understand whose interests it promotes: those of the weak (Leiter 2002: 177–78).
[5] One example: "The idea that we are fighting over here is the *valuation* of our lives by the ascetic priest: he juxtaposes it ... with a quite different mode of existence which is opposed to it and excludes it *unless* it should turn against itself and *deny itself*... The ascetic treats life as a wrong path ..." (*GM*, III, 11). Here, as elsewhere in the third essay, Nietzsche explicitly states that the ascetic priest views flourishing as disvaluable and the reduction of flourishing as valuable.

He continues:

> It's clear that in the Judeo-Christian religious tradition the answer to this question is affirmative. Loving, worshipping God is the ultimate end ... The injunction "Thy will be done" isn't equivalent to "Let humans flourish" ... (Taylor 2007: 16–17)

So too with other religions. For example, according to Buddhism, "the way to Nirvana involves renouncing, or at least going beyond, all forms of recognizable human flourishing" (Taylor 2007: 17). Thus, Taylor writes,

> In both Buddhism and Christianity, there is something similar ... This is that the believer or devout person is called on to make a profound inner break with the goals of flourishing in their own case; they are called on, that is, to detach themselves from their own flourishing, to the point of the extinction of the self in one case, or to that of renunciation of human fulfillment to serve God in the other. (Taylor 2007: 17)

In sum, the dominant religions teach that flourishing is *not* normatively authoritative. The fact that serving the poor, mortifying the flesh, renouncing sexuality, and so forth, conflict with flourishing is not an *objection* to these practices; it is *their point*.

But if this is correct, then Nietzsche cannot simply be assuming that flourishing is normatively authoritative. He needs some argument for that idea. Absent such an argument, the mere fact that morality undermines flourishing is not a critique of morality. Again, notice that Nietzsche emphasizes *exactly* this point in the third treatise of the *Genealogy*, arguing that the ascetic ideal – the ideal that has, at its core, the rejection of the claim that flourishing is normatively relevant – has hitherto been the *only* accepted ideal. This is tantamount to claiming that hitherto, flourishing has not been accepted as normatively relevant.

Put simply: saying to a consistent proponent of the ascetic ideal, "you should reject *X*, because *X* undermines flourishing" is exactly analogous to saying to a Nietzschean, "you should reject *X*, because Judeo-Christian morality says that *X* is bad." In both cases, the proponent will view the objection as utterly missing the point.

So the evidential reading faces a problem: insofar as the *Genealogy* is aimed to shake (e.g.) Christians out of their acceptance of modern morality, it will fail. For the above normative principle will be rejected by a consistent Christian. Thus, if the evidential reading is to meet the critical criterion, it will need to explain why flourishing is normatively relevant.

Moreover, a complaint can be lodged against the way in which the evidential interpretation treats the relevance of history for Nietzsche's critique. Leiter and Janaway suggest that the history is not necessary for showing that morality has undermined flourishing. They do allow history to play a derivative role in the argument: history is a source of evidence for the claim that morality undermines flourishing. However, history, as such, is unimportant; one might just as well gather this evidence in an ahistorical fashion. This is not obviously wrong; Nietzsche may think that history has only a derivative role. However, I submit that the evidential reading would be strengthened if we could show why, exactly, the history might be playing a deeper role, a role in which the history is *essential* rather than just a *perspicuous means* to the critique.

In sum, although the evidential interpretation seems attractive in certain respects, it faces two problems: it needs to explain why flourishing is normatively relevant, and it offers a rather reductive view of history's role. The following sections develop a new interpretation, which overcomes these problems.

2. FLOURISHING IS DEFINED IN TERMS OF WILL TO POWER

Let's begin by addressing the first problem: a successful interpretation needs to explain why flourishing should be considered normatively relevant. This necessitates a more determinate characterization of what flourishing is. I suggest that Nietzsche defines flourishing in terms of *will to power*. Consider again the quotation from the preface:

> What if a regressive trait lurked in "the good man," likewise a danger, an entice-ment, a poison, a narcotic, so that the present *lived at the expense of the future?* . . . So that morality itself were to blame if man, as species, never reached his *highest potential power and splendour?* So that morality itself was the danger of dangers? (*GM*, Preface, 6)

Notice that Nietzsche asks whether morality might undermine the highest *power* and splendor of human beings. In other texts, Nietzsche places a similar emphasis upon the will to power: he not only speaks of "a world whose essence is will to power" (*BGE*, 186), but asserts that "the will to power" is "the will of life" (*BGE*, 259). He claims that "there is nothing in life that has value, except the degree of power – assuming that life itself is the will to power" (*WP*, 55). Echoing this claim in *The Antichrist*, he writes, "What is good? – All that heightens the feeling of power, the will to power, power itself in man . . ." (*A*, 2). To return to the *Genealogy* itself, he writes,

> Every animal . . . instinctively strives for an optimum of favourable conditions in which to fully release his power and achieve his maximum of power-sensation;

every animal abhors equally instinctively . . . any kind of disturbance or hindrance that blocks or could block his path to the optimum (– it is *not* his path to "happiness" I am talking about, but the path to power, to action, the most powerful activity . . .) (*GM*, III, 7)

More generally, references to will to power – both explicit and implicit – are ubiquitous in the *Genealogy*. After all, as Janaway points out, we might fairly summarize the *Genealogy* as arguing that "morality's various phenomena are explained as ways in which human beings, like all animals, strive to discharge their power and maximize their feelings of power under the exigencies of their own characters and externally imposed constraints" (Janaway 2007: 145).

For these reasons, it seems plausible to interpret flourishing in terms of will to power. But what, exactly, is will to power? As Bernard Reginster has persuasively argued, Nietzsche identifies willing power with perpetually *seeking* and *overcoming* resistances to one's ends (Reginster 2006: 127). For example, an agent wills power in the pursuit of knowledge by striving to encounter and overcome intellectual problems in her pursuit of knowledge; or, an ascetic wills power by willing to encounter and overcome his body's own resistances to self-inflicted suffering. As Nietzsche puts it, "the will to power can manifest itself only against resistances; therefore it seeks out that which resists it" (*WP*, 656).[6]

So willing power is seeking to encounter and overcome resistance. Given that flourishing is characterized in terms of will to power, an agent flourishes to the extent that she encounters and overcomes resistances. For example, an agent who seeks only minimal resistance, or who fails to overcome modest resistances, is not flourishing. By contrast, an agent who sets herself great resistances and manages to overcome them is flourishing. This is why Nietzsche's ethical exemplars are individuals such as Goethe, Napoleon, and Beethoven: these are individuals who devote themselves to immensely challenging ends, and nonetheless manage to achieve them.

With this in mind, let's return to our overriding problem: explaining why flourishing is normatively authoritative. Above, I pointed out that the consistent proponent of modern morality would reject the claim that flourishing is normatively authoritative. If the *Genealogy* is a critique of modern morality, Nietzsche will need some argument to establish that, despite modern morality's insistence on the contrary point, values and courses of action that undermine flourishing should be rejected.

---

[6] For discussions of this idea, see Reginster (2006) and Katsafanas (2011a).

To make the problem vivid, suppose we discover that some cherished value, such as compassion, conflicts with power. Why should that fact constitute an objection to our valuation of compassion? Why not instead view it as an indictment of power? Or why not simply live with the fact that the world is inhospitable to the joint realization of these two values, and strike some sort of compromise, trading a reduction in power for an increase in compassion?

The answer is that power has a privileged normative status – Nietzsche argues that power is the one value to which we are inescapably committed. His argument for this claim is complex, and I lack the space to reconstruct it here. Let me simply summarize the view I have defended elsewhere. Nietzsche argues that we are committed to valuing power precisely because, in aiming at any end at all, we also aim at power. He takes this ineluctable fact about our aim to establish that we must, on pain of contradiction, accept power as a standard of success for action. So power's privileged normative status is established by its connection to agency. If this is correct, then the fact that a given value conflicts with power is a decisive reason to reject the value.[7]

Thus, Nietzsche is not simply stipulating that flourishing is normatively relevant. Rather, he offers a subtle argument for this claim.

3. A POTENTIAL PROBLEM: IS THE WILL TO POWER THESIS DEVOID OF CONTENT?

If the above reading is correct, then Nietzsche can establish that power has a privileged normative status, and therefore serves as an appropriate standard for revaluation. However, the view faces a problem, which might seem insuperable. To say that we will power is to say that we aim at encountering and overcoming resistances in the course of pursuing other, more determinate ends. So, if we treat will to power as a normative standard, it enjoins us to pursue those ends that generate resistances and obstacles. But this standard seems too vague, too formal, to generate any substantive conclusions.

To see this, consider a pair of opposed, discrete evaluative judgments such as "murder is wrong" and "murder is not wrong." Which of these judgments would maximize the encountering and overcoming of resistance? There seems to be no satisfactory way of answering this question. Certainly, attempting to murder another person would typically be quite difficult, so perhaps the principle "murder is not wrong" promotes more resistance. On

---

[7] For the details, see Katsafanas (2011a).

the other hand, part of the reason why murder is so difficult in our society is that it is strongly disvalued. Thus, one might argue that the valuation "murder is wrong" promotes more resistance for those tempted to murder. A determinate verdict seems unachievable here.

I have chosen a rather simplistic example, in order clearly to illustrate the difficulties with using will to power to assess discrete and context-free evaluative judgments. Of course, most of Nietzsche's examples are far more complex. Take asceticism. If one simply examines a claim such as "asceticism is good," neither it nor its opposite can be assessed simply *as* an independent, context-free judgment. For both it and its opposite can be dialectically justified in terms of power. In particular, Nietzsche makes it clear that in certain historical circumstances and in certain respects, asceticism is power-maximizing; after all, self-mortification is enormously difficult. It's just that in our time, it has outlived its usefulness and now is power-reducing. However, even these characterizations are insufficiently nuanced: Nietzsche is at pains to point out that certain manifestations of asceticism, such as those present in various philosophers, are actually power-maximizing (*GM*, III, 7–9). So again, it is difficult to see how the injunction to maximize power yields any determinate content.

Simon May draws attention to a deeper version of this difficulty, writing,

the problem of defining and measuring "power" would be very great even if it referred simply to efficient force or political control or, in general, stateable "outcomes." But this problem seems insuperable if all human behaviour in its inexhaustible variety, including such activities as knowing and self-discipline, is to be explained in terms of power. ... Although Nietzsche speaks of value as directly correlated to a "scale of force" (*WP*, 710), it is hard to see what such a common scale of force might be. (May 1999: 27)

According to May, the notion of power is simply too vague and indeterminate to play the role that Nietzsche assigns it.

May's objection appears decisive. He is certainly correct that there is no real way of placing different episodes of willing on a scale of power. As he notes, this would be hard enough if we localize our inquiry to one type of activity: who pursues and overcomes more resistance in writing, Goethe or Melville? That question is baffling, but, as May goes on to note, the question grows even more intractable when applied to activities belonging to different types. The pursuit of great literature, the pursuit of knowledge, the pursuit of athletic prowess, and the pursuit of political power are all difficult, but in quite different ways. They may be incomparable. Who pursues and overcomes more resistance: Gabriel García Márquez or

Stephen Hawking or Lance Armstrong or Barack Obama? It is not clear how one could even begin to answer this question. Consequently, one must concede May's point: we cannot array all actions on a scale, and simply pick the one that overcomes the most resistance.

For all of these reasons, the will to power thesis can seem utterly devoid of content and consequently incapable of generating any determinate normative conclusions. If this is so, then the reading I have advanced is hopeless.

Fortunately, I believe these objections to the will to power thesis can be answered. The *Genealogy* itself shows how. In the following sections, I argue that the *Genealogy* provides us with a way of seeing that although May is perfectly correct that actions cannot be arrayed on a scale of resistance overcome, the will to power standard nonetheless generates determinate conclusions about which values to embrace and which actions to perform.[8] Moreover, I will argue that by understanding how the will to power standard functions, we will understand why the *Genealogy* takes its historical form.

4. SOLUTION: THE WILL TO POWER THESIS GENERATES DETERMINATE RESULTS WHEN APPLIED TO EVALUATIVE ORIENTATIONS RATHER THAN DISCRETE JUDGMENTS

The above examples indicate that if will to power is to serve as a normative principle, it cannot be brought to bear on discrete, context-free evaluative judgments. But nowhere in the texts does Nietzsche do *that*. On the contrary, he applies the will to power thesis to whole systems of moral judgments, coupled with their associated classes of affects and perceptions. (I will use the term "evaluative orientation" to refer to these systems of judgments, affects, and perceptions.)

Nietzsche constantly reminds us that it is a mistake to think that we can simply isolate particular moral judgments and assess them in a context-free fashion. He writes,

We should admit to ourselves with all due severity exactly *what* will be necessary for a long time to come and *what* is provisionally correct, namely: collecting material, formulating concepts, and putting into order the tremendous realm of tender value feelings and value distinctions [*Werthgefühle und Werthunterschiede*] that live, grow,

---

[8] May agrees with a version of this point, arguing that if the will to power thesis is supplemented in certain ways (by Nietzsche's notions of sublimation and form-creation), then it can generate determinate results.

reproduce, and are destroyed – and, perhaps, attempting to illustrate the recurring and more frequent shapes of this living crystallization, – all of which would be a preparation for a *typology* of morals. Of course, people have not generally been this modest. Philosophers have demanded (with ridiculously stubborn seriousness) something much more exalted, ambitious, and solemn as soon as they took up morality as a science: they wanted to furnish the *rational ground* of morality ... What a distance between this sort of crass pride and that supposedly modest little descriptive project, left in rot and ruin, even though the subtlest hands and senses could hardly be subtle enough for it. (*BGE*, 186)

The task of the moral philosopher is not the examination of discrete moral judgments. It is, instead, the scrutiny of complex systems of affects, distinctions, and tacit moral beliefs. This is evident in Nietzsche's own work. He does not simply present us with a list of direct consequences of his will to power thesis; he does not suggest that one can simply derive various values or their negations from the will to power thesis.[9] Instead, we must carefully prepare *typologies* of moralities. What would this involve?

Nietzsche sometimes describes this process by claiming that philosophers must apply "a vivisecting knife directly to the chest of the *virtues of the age*" (*BGE*, 212). The image of vivisection, which occurs several times in Nietzsche's works, suggests that real ethical inquiry does not consist merely in examining the surface content of morality; we don't simply assess the discrete moral judgments preached by the common man, judgments such as "murder is wrong" or "you should help others." Instead, we *cut through* these surface judgments, trying to find the deeper motives, implicit principles, defunct ideals, conceptions of agency, and so forth, that underlie them. We try to understand how these values causally impact our affects and the ways of classifying and distinguishing actions that seem natural to us.

So, part of Nietzsche's point is that morality is not merely present in explicit moral *judgments*. For the particular moral system that the agent embraces will influence not just his explicit thoughts about what is right and wrong, good and bad, but his very perceptions of the world. This is why Nietzsche writes that there "are no experiences other than moral ones, not even in the realm of sense-perception" (*GS*, 114). It is these complex perceptions and evaluative orientations that must be dissected and examined. We go astray, then, in trying to evaluate discrete, context-free actions and moral judgments in terms of will to power.

---

[9] On this point, see Katsafanas (2011a).

5. ONE INSTANCE OF THIS APPROACH: HOW PERCEPTIONS OF POWER CAN DIVERGE FROM FACTS ABOUT POWER

Nietzsche's claim that moral critique proceeds by vivisection of evaluative orientations is exceedingly difficult and complex, and I will not attempt anything like a systematic analysis of it here. Instead, I focus on just one aspect: Nietzsche's claim that values influence *our perceptions of our own power*. This is a key element of Nietzsche's attack on the Judeo-Christian moral system: he argues that it systematically obfuscates the connection between perceptions of power and actual power, and thereby undermines actual power. Over the next few sections, I explain and develop this interpretation.

Nietzsche distinguishes *perceptions* or *feelings* of increased power from actual increases in power.[10] David Owen has recently drawn attention to this point. Owen notes that the perception of power can be distorting: one can experience an actual reduction in power as an increase in power, and conversely. In other words, feelings or perceptions of power need not track actual power. As Owen puts it,

(*the degree of*) *the feeling of power* that human beings experience need have no necessary connection to the (*degree of*) *power* expressed. Nietzsche's point is this: because human beings are self-conscious creatures, the feeling of power to which their doings give rise is necessarily mediated by the perspective in terms of which they understand (or misunderstand) themselves as agents and the moral evaluation and ranking of types of action expressed within that perspective. Consequently, an expansion (or diminution) of the feeling of power can be an effect of a change of perspective rather than of an actual increase (or decrease) of the power expressed. (Owen 2007: 34)

In short: the degree to which we experience an act as expressing power depends on our perspective, and in particular on our evaluations.

Consider a homely example. Suppose that I am incapable of defending myself against an aggressive agent. Ordinarily, I would perceive myself as lacking in power. However, suppose I convince myself that submitting to abuse is valuable or meritorious. Then, quite straightforwardly, I provide myself with a way of heightening my sense of power: I can tell myself that I don't refrain from action due to lack of power; I refrain from action precisely because refraining is a greater expression of power.

---

[10] This is explicitly and succinctly stated in *The Antichrist*, where Nietzsche writes, "what is good? Everything that enhances people's feeling of power, will to power, power itself" (*A*, 2).

Nietzsche draws attention to this point in *GM*, I, 13. There, he asks us to consider what happens "when the oppressed, the downtrodden, the violated say to each other with the vindictive cunning of powerlessness: 'Let us be different from evil people, let us be good'." In particular, he imagines weak agents who condemn strength, which expresses itself as "a desire to overcome, crush, become master, to be a thirst for enemies, resistance and triumphs." He writes that in such condemnation, weakness has,

> thanks to the counterfeiting and self-deception of powerlessness, clothed itself in the finery of self-denying, quiet, patient virtue; as though the weakness of the weak were itself – I mean its *essence*, its effect, its whole unique, unavoidable, irredeemable reality – a voluntary achievement, something wanted, chosen, a *deed*, an *accomplishment* ... [This] facilitated that sublime self-deception whereby the majority of mortals, the weak and the oppressed of every kind could construe weakness itself as freedom, and their particular mode of existence as an *accomplishment*. (*GM*, I, 13)

In this passage, Nietzsche suggests that weak agents come to reinterpret their own weakness such that their weakness appears, to them, as strength.[11]

There are a number of perfectly ordinary examples of this phenomenon. A person of below-average intellect can't become a professor, so he rails against education as liberal effeteness. Or, a person of diminished physical abilities can't participate in competitive athletic endeavors, so he tells himself that only people of impoverished intellect are attracted to sports. I take it that this phenomenon is familiar.

6. HOW JUDEO-CHRISTIAN MORALITY SYSTEMATICALLY (AND, INITIALLY, DELIBERATELY) BREAKS THE CONNECTION BETWEEN FEELING OF POWER AND ACTUAL POWER

So there is a distinction between perceived power and actual power, and the agent's values impact the extent to which the former tracks the latter. In this section, I argue that the *Genealogy* reveals ways in which the Judeo-Christian evaluative orientation systematically distorts perceptions of power, inclining us to perceive actual increases in power as reductions in power, and actual decreases in power as increases in power.

Nietzsche singles out three particular ways in which the Judeo-Christian moral system breaks the connection between feeling of power and actual

---

[11] As Aaron Ridley puts it, "the slave has brought a certain kind and amount of suffering under a self-empowering interpretation" (Ridley 1998a: 42).

power. First, the values proposed by the Judeo-Christian system valorize weakness and demonize power. Second, the Judeo-Christian system associates negative emotions with manifestations of actual power and positive emotions with manifestations of actual weakness. Third, it employs a conception of agency that enables the weak to see their weakness as chosen, and hence as strength. I will explain these points in turn.

Start with the first point: the Judeo-Christian moral system operates with a conception of value that valorizes expressions of weakness. Nietzsche catalogues a number of examples:

> Weakness is being lied into something *meritorious* ... impotence which doesn't retaliate is being turned into "goodness"; timid baseness is being turned into "humility"; submission to people one hates is being turned into "obedience" ... The inoffensiveness of the weakling, the very cowardice with which he is richly endowed, his standing-by-the-door, his inevitable position of having to wait, are all given good names such as "patience," also known as *the* virtue; not-being-able-to-take-revenge is called not-wanting-to-take-revenge, it might even be forgiveness ... (*GM*, I, 14)

Actual manifestations of weakness are here reinterpreted as valuable.[12] In attaching positive valuations to states of affairs and events that actually constitute reductions in power, the Judeo-Christian interpretation inclines agents to pursue reductions in power (though not under that description). If the agent accepts these evaluations, the agent can view his manifestations of actual weakness as chosen, and hence as an expression of power.

This brings us to the second point: the Judeo-Christian interpretation associates negative emotions (such as feelings of guilt) with actual expressions of power, thereby discouraging agents from pursuing them. Nietzsche frequently draws attention to this phenomenon, writing that "for too long, man has viewed his natural inclinations with an 'evil eye', so that they finally come to be intertwined with the 'bad conscience' in him" (*GM*, II, 24), and decrying the "sickly mollycoddling and sermonizing, by means of which the animal 'man' is finally taught to be ashamed of all his instincts" (*GM*, II, 7). If expressions of actual power can in these ways be associated with the painful affect of guilt, then agents will be disinclined to pursue the courses of action that constitute increases in actual power.

---

[12] Consider a few additional examples. The nobles "designate themselves simply by their superiority in power" (*GM*, I, 5), for the typical character traits of the noble are "a powerful physicality, a flourishing, abundant, even overflowing health" (*GM*, I, 7). The noble "conceives the basic concept 'good' by himself, in advance and spontaneously, and only then creates a notion of 'bad' ..." (*GM*, I, 11). By contrast, "slave morality from the outset says No ..." (*GM*, I, 10), to the noble traits, valuing instead their opposites.

The final way in which the Judeo-Christian system distorts the connection between actual power and perceptions of power is by employing a distinctive conception of agency. This requires some explanation. Nietzsche writes,

The reason the subject (or, as we more colloquially say, *the soul*) has been, until now, the best doctrine on earth, is perhaps because it facilitated that sublime self-deception whereby the majority of mortals, the weak and oppressed of every kind could construe weakness itself as freedom, and their particular mode of existence as an *accomplishment*. (*GM*, I, 13)

Here, Nietzsche emphasizes that embracing a particular conception of the subject enables the weak to see their weakness as chosen or meritorious. What is this conception of the subject? Nietzsche explains:

Just as the common people separates lightning from its flash and takes the latter to be a *deed*, something performed by a subject, which is called lightning, popular morality separates strength from the manifestations of strength, as though there were an indifferent substratum behind the strong person which had the *freedom* to manifest strength or not. But there is no such substratum; there is no "being" behind the deed, its effect and what becomes of it; "the doer" is invented as an afterthought, – the doing is everything. (*GM*, I, 13)

Consider an alternative: an agent is weak if he performs actions that an observer would characterize as weak. This is a natural conception of agency, a conception that identifies the agent's character with the character of the agent's actions. The Judeo-Christian system severs this connection between the agent's character and the character of the agent's actions, by treating the agent as something separable from and essentially distinct from its deed. If the subject is a characterless will, free to choose as it deems appropriate, then *any* action whatsoever can be interpreted as being chosen out of strength. Even the most craven acts, such as giving up at the first sign of resistance or difficulty, can be seen as not impacting the agent's character: like the gambler who claims that he is not essentially a gambler because he is always free to choose not to gamble, the craven agent can claim that he is not essentially craven, despite performing nothing but (overtly) cowardly actions.[13]

Nietzsche's primary concern is not whether any particular philosopher has overtly embraced this conception of agency. Rather, he is interested in the tacit acceptance of this view by ordinary individuals. If an individual has

---

[13] I have in mind Sartre's discussion of the gambler (Sartre 1993: 69–72).

internalized such a view, he will tend to experience his choices and actions in a certain way. In particular, he will tend to experience his actions in a way that breaks the connection between *actual* increases in power and *perceptions* or *feelings* of increased power. For *any* choice whatsoever – the choice to flee from an enemy, the choice to be meek, the choice to reject difficulties – can be interpreted as an expression of power.

In sum, the Judeo-Christian moral system obfuscates the connection between actual power and perceived power in three ways:

(i) The Judeo-Christian moral system labels as good character traits that tend either to reduce power, or to be typical of those lacking power; similarly, the moral system labels as good those actions that tend to constitute reductions in power. Conversely, the moral system labels as bad character traits that tend to increase power, or to be typical of those possessing power; and it labels as bad those actions that tend to constitute increases in power.

(ii) The Judeo-Christian system associates negative emotions (such as guilt) with actual expressions of power, hence discouraging agents from pursuing them. Conversely, it associates positive emotions (such as pride) with actual reductions in power, hence encouraging agents to pursue them.

(iii) Judeo-Christian morality employs a particular conception of agency that enables weak agents to interpret their weakness as freely chosen.

Thus, Judeo-Christian morality comprises a picture of agency, a set of values, and an associated class of emotions that, when taken together, have two effects. First, they lead agents to interpret expressions of *reduced power* as expressions of *increased power*. Second, they incline agents to experience negative affects of *reduced feelings of power* when expressing *actual increases of power*, and positive affects of *increased feelings of power* when expressing *actual reductions in power*. In this sense, the Judeo-Christian morality systematically breaks the connection between perceptions of increased power and actual increases in power.

Additionally, although this will not be essential to our story, in the *Genealogy* Nietzsche claims that this reversal is initially deliberate. The ascetic priests have an intense craving for positions of dominance. Systematically thwarted from achieving dominance by their set of values, they revalue values, such that their own traits are labeled as good (and hence entitle them to dominance) while the traits of the ruling class are labeled as evil (and hence entail that the current rulers should not rule).

7. WHY DO THESE FACTS CONSTITUTE AN OBJECTION TO JUDEO-CHRISTIAN MORALITY?

Suppose this is right: Judeo-Christian morality systematically breaks the connection between perceptions of increased power and actual increases in power. Why should this matter? Why should this be an objection to Judeo-Christian morality?

Above, I mentioned that David Owen has recently emphasized the crucial distinction between feelings of power and actual power. Owen suggests that this distinction plays a foundational role in Nietzsche's evaluation of moral systems:

The criterion of evaluation that Nietzsche proposes is whether the feeling of power expresses and tracks power, where this criterion can be taken to be well grounded just in so far as the principle of will to power provides a compelling explanation of human behavior . . . Hence the crucial question is this: under what conditions does the feeling of power *necessarily* express and track power? (Owen 2007: 35–36)

In other words, Owen interprets Nietzsche as basing his critique on the following principle:

If X falsifies the connection between perceptions of power and actual power, then X is to be rejected.

Or, perhaps, more generally:

If X falsifies our perceptions, X is to be rejected.

As Owen notes, the *Genealogy* demonstrates that Judeo-Christian morality fails this test: it does not accurately represent the connection between feeling of power and power. It is thus to be rejected.

For all its insight, Owen's interpretation cannot be correct in claiming that Nietzsche's critique rests on the above principle; the problem cannot simply be one of truth. After all, if modern morality is dear to us, then it is hard to see why the mere fact that it distorts our perception of our own power should be a decisive objection to it. One imagines a contemporary moral philosopher responding to Owen's Nietzsche: "I care far more about such virtues as egalitarianism, compassion, and justice than I care about whether I accurately perceive the extent of my own power." Moreover, Nietzsche himself does not often take the falseness of a perception as a decisive indictment of it; witness his claim that "we do not consider the falsity of a judgment as itself an objection to a judgment" (*BGE*, 4).

However, notice that there is a deeper problem than mere inaccuracy with the misrepresentation of power. The Judeo-Christian system not only misrepresents degrees of power; it also, in part by that very misrepresentation, strongly disposes us to *decrease* our own power. By associating feelings of increased power with actual reductions in power, it inclines agents to seek out actual reductions in power. Conversely, by associating guilt and other negative emotions with actual increases in power, it strongly disposes agents *not* to seek actual increases in power. Thus, the Judeo-Christian interpretation has the result of reducing actual power.

This is Nietzsche's real objection to modern morality. The problem is not merely that modern morality is inaccurate; the problem is that it is inaccurate in a way that systematically undermines the will to power.

Thus, to recover the context of the quote above: "we do not consider the falsity of a judgment as itself an objection to a judgment . . . The question is how far the judgment promotes and preserves life" (*BGE*, 4). As Nietzsche emphasizes here (and elsewhere), veridicality is not the primary problem. The primary problem is whether a particular judgment – especially an evaluative judgment – undermines life. And "the essence of life," Nietzsche tells us, is simply "its *will to power*" (*GM*, II, 12).

8. TAKING STOCK

Although Nietzsche's argument is long and complex, we are now in a position to summarize its core quite briefly:

(1) The Judeo-Christian moral system comprises a set of values, associated emotions, and a conception of agency that jointly incline the agent to perceive reductions in power as increases in power, and increases in power as reductions in power.

(2) In virtue of the facts cited in (1), Judeo-Christian morality strongly disposes agents to pursue reductions in their own power.

(3) By (2), Judeo-Christian morality undermines our commitment to power.

(4) If X undermines our commitment to power, X is to be rejected.

(5) Therefore, Judeo-Christian morality is to be rejected.

Or, even more briefly: Judeo-Christian morality is to be rejected because it undermines the will to power.

With this in mind, consider again the objection raised in section 3: will to power cannot be Nietzsche's standard of evaluation, for it does not yield determinate rankings of actions or values. I promised that my reading of the *Genealogy* would explain how this objection could be answered. We can now see why: although the will to power thesis does not enable us to evaluate discrete actions or values, it does allow us to evaluate more general patterns of behavior and systems of value. Although we cannot rank Melville and Goethe, we can rank a system of values that disposes agents to become Melvilles and Goethes, and a system that disposes them to become the "last man." That is, we can distinguish between systems of values encouraging and valorizing actual expressions of power, and systems of values discouraging and demonizing the same. This is, after all, what Nietzsche's texts display. He shows immense concern with the broad patterns of behavior induced by particular moral systems, and devotes far less time to the examination of discrete moral judgments such as "lying is wrong" or "promises should be kept."

9. WHY NIETZSCHE'S ARGUMENT MUST BE HISTORICAL

Suppose I am correct in arguing that one of the main roles of the *Genealogy* is to show that Judeo-Christian morality systematically distorts the connection between perceptions of power and actual power, and thereby inclines agents to pursue reductions in their own power. This would explain the critical force of the *Genealogy*: the text reveals that modern morality does, indeed, undermine "the highest power and splendor" of mankind, by inclining us to pursue ends that reduce power (while appearing to increase power). Thus, the interpretation fulfills the critical criterion. However, I argued above that an adequate account of the *Genealogy* must also meet the historical criterion, by explaining why Nietzsche's critique takes a historical form. In this section, I show how my reading meets this criterion.

There are two reasons for the text's historical form. First, Judeo-Christian morality's transformation of our drives and affects was gradual and aggregative. Charting these transformations requires examining long stretches of history. Second, in order to display the ways in which Judeo-Christian morality falsifies perceptions of power, Nietzsche needs to employ competing perspectives on manifestations of power.

Let's start with the first point. Nietzsche frequently emphasizes that affects and drives cannot be altered by direct, immediate conscious decisions. Rather, transforming these psychic states takes time:

Drives transformed by moral judgments. – The same drive evolves into a painful feeling of *cowardice* under the impress of the reproach custom has imposed upon this drive: or into the pleasant feeling of *humility* if it happens that a custom such as the Christian has taken it to its heart and called it *good*. That is to say, it is attended by either a good or a bad conscience! In itself it has, *like every drive*, neither this moral character nor any moral character at all, nor even a definite attendant sensation of pleasure or displeasure: it acquires all this, as its second nature, only when it enters into relations with drives already baptized good or evil or is noted as a quality of beings the people has already evaluated and determined in a moral sense. (*D*, 38)

In this passage, Nietzsche contrasts the ways in which ancient and modern moralities evaluated a particular drive, and he insists that *by evaluating drives in particular ways, moralities gradually transform these drives* (cf. *D*, 35). The selfsame drive, Nietzsche tells us, can manifest itself as humility in one evaluative framework and cowardice in another. Presumably, Nietzsche has in mind a drive to avoid confronting or challenging other agents. In the ancient Greeks, this drive manifested itself as the aversive conscious emotion of cowardice; in us, it manifests itself as the attractive conscious emotion of humility. The former emotion would tend to cause perceptions of reduced power and to disincline agents toward the act in question; the latter, increased power and a propensity toward the act.

One cannot simply turn these affective associations on and off, like a light switch. To see this, consider a more familiar example. Suppose an agent, under the pressure of a religious interpretation, regards manifestations of his sex drive as sinful. When he experiences or acts on sexual urges, he feels guilt, shame, and so forth. However, later in his life this individual consciously rejects his religious upbringing: he becomes a committed atheist. Although the agent consciously pronounces his sex drive perfectly good, and rejects completely the concept of sinfulness, it is natural to assume that he will experience lingering traces of the old evaluation. We can imagine that, without being able to justify it, he still experiences residual shame and negative affects when sexual urges manifest themselves. Such a situation might persist for decades, indeed for his entire life. Ridding oneself of the old evaluations does not immediately transform the emotions associated with the drive. Thus, to understand why the drive manifests itself in a particular way during the individual's atheistic adult life, we will also need to understand his theistic childhood. As Nietzsche puts it, "in the mental realm there is no annihilation" (*KSA*, 12:7[53]).

Or take another example of values gradually transforming affects. Marrying one's first cousin was quite common in the ancient world, and is still widely practiced in certain parts of the Middle East and sub-Saharan Africa. However, most individuals in the United States and Europe view cousin marriage as disgusting or even repellent. We tend to concoct justifications for this emotion. For example, we tell ourselves that cousins who marry are more likely to have children with birth defects. However, this is demonstrably false; cousins are no more likely to have genetically defective children than non-cousins (Prinz 2007: 240). I suspect that even upon appreciating the falsity of this belief, most individuals in Western societies will continue to view cousin marriage as disturbing or even disgusting. This provides an example of the way in which an evaluative belief – that marrying one's cousin is wrong – gradually generates a variety of affects (disgust, revulsion, etc.), which are resistant to transformation, persisting even in the absence of evidence for the belief.[14]

These examples indicate that a change in evaluative judgments does not by itself generate an immediate transformation in affects. Nonetheless, gradual transformations do occur. What causes them?

Presumably, changes in affects arise when the new evaluations are coupled with habituation into new forms of life. This would include the acceptance of new interpretations of what one's affects mean (e.g. interpreting the affect of bad conscience as guilt), new inducements to certain forms of activity (e.g. via religion and custom), and new conceptions of agency and responsibility (e.g. viewing the self as distinct from the deed). These factors, when coupled with the change in evaluative judgments, would gradually reconfigure our affects and drives. And these factors are precisely the ones whose influence Nietzsche's history is designed to uncover: the history both charts the subtle transformations induced in our drives and affects by this complex of factors, and shows that Judeo-Christian morality was responsible for the emergence of these factors. This is the first reason for the text's historical form.

But there is also a second reason. The way in which Judeo-Christian morality undermines power is invisible until we step outside that evaluative framework. When evaluated in its own terms, Judeo-Christian morality appears not to reduce power. After all, this evaluative system tells us to aim at meekness, humility, and the like. Insofar as acting in accordance with one's values is taken to be an exemplary expression of will to power, the adherents of Judeo-Christian morality will not detect any problems with their evaluative system. Analogously, insofar as acting in accordance with one's perceptions of power is taken to be a manifestation of will to power, all will appear to be well.

---

[14] The reader is invited to try this experiment in a class: ask students whether marrying one's first cousin is wrong. Students almost inevitably say that it is. When asked *why* cousin marriage is wrong, students typically respond by citing the alleged potential for genetic defects. When told that this belief is false, students tend not to revise their moral judgment. Instead, they resort to saying that cousin marriage is revolting or disturbing. Here we have exactly the process that Nietzsche describes: a moral evaluation – based on any superstition, custom, or false belief – generates a strong affect; the affect is then taken to justify the moral evaluation that caused it.

However, history reveals that this perspective is not inevitable. It supplanted a prior perspective, which Nietzsche is at some pains to present as more accurate.[15] Rather than taking Judeo-Christian morality's interpretation of itself as authoritative, then, the history invites us to adopt a more nuanced and potentially more accurate stance.

Thus, there are (at least) two reasons for the text's historical form: Nietzsche needs to chart gradual transformations in drives and affects, and he needs to reveal competing perspectives on manifestations of power.

10. CONCLUSION

According to the reading that I have advanced, the story that Nietzsche tells in the *Genealogy* constitutes a historically grounded critique of modern morality. The history reveals that acceptance of modern morality was causally responsible for producing a dramatic change in our affects, drives, and perceptions. This change caused us to perceive actual increases in power as reductions in power, and actual decreases in power as increases in power. Moreover, it led us to experience negative emotions when engaging in activities that constitute greater manifestations of power, and positive emotions when engaging in activities that reduce power. For these reasons, modern morality strongly disposes us to reduce our own power. Given Nietzsche's argument that power is normatively authoritative, this fact entails that we have decisive reason to reject modern morality.

This interpretation meets the historical and critical criteria: it explains both why the *Genealogy* constitutes a critique of modern morality, and why the history plays an essential role in that critique. The reading also helps us to understand exactly how Nietzsche's normative principle of will to power is to be applied: while the principle is incapable of generating any substantive results when applied to discrete, context-free moral judgments, it does yield results when applied to whole systems of moral evaluations, which are bound up with affective orientations, configurations of perceptions, and so forth.

This is a point with more general applicability. Instead of worrying about whether we can justify claims such as "lying is wrong," "promises should be kept," and the like, Nietzsche enjoins us to concern ourselves with broad features of moral systems – features that manifest themselves only over long

---

[15] Nietzsche frequently emphasizes the falsification inherent in modern morality. For two examples, see *GM*, I, 10, and I, 13. Of course, these remarks introduce another difficult topic, which is beyond the scope of this paper: how we determine whether one perspective is more accurate than another.

stretches of historical time. These features are completely missed by those who examine merely discrete, particular moral judgments. For, in treating these judgments in isolation from their historical context and ignoring the complex interactions between moral concepts, affects, and perceptions, these thinkers "accept concepts as a gift ... as if they were a wonderful dowry from some sort of wonderland," rather than recognizing that they are "the inheritance from our most remote, most foolish, as well as most intelligent ancestors," and therefore stand in need of "an absolute skepticism" (*WP*, 409/*KSA*, 11:34[195]). These concepts gradually alter the manner in which we experience and affectively respond to the world, in ways that are invisible until we trace the shifting of affects and evaluations over historical time. For, as Beauvoir puts it in the epigraph to this essay, the world reflects back to us the view that we impose on it. Or, as Nietzsche would add, it does so until, with the help of history, we impose on it a *new* view, and thereby see the contingency of our current evaluative orientation.

CHAPTER 9

Why would master morality surrender its power?

Lawrence J. Hatab

The fundamental question underlying the *Genealogy* is: Can there be meaning and value in natural life following the death of God?[1] The eclipse of the supernatural in modern thought is a presumed turn to nature, but Nietzsche insists that this turn is in fact a looping reliance on the theological tradition,[2] and that the eclipse of God forces a more radical naturalistic challenge: If the Western tradition in one way or another is beholden to a nature-transcending or life-averse condition, then the loss of this condition's divine warrant undermines traditional sources of meaning and value, to the point where the West faces the choice between nihilism and a new, affirmative philosophy of nature.[3]

The *Genealogy* is a historical study that fills out the details of the above scenario by trying to show how and why the tradition has been life-averse and cannot be sustained in the wake of modern developments. The genealogical history unfolding in the book is meant to simultaneously clarify and critique the counter-natural drives in European culture, no less in its supposed departures from supernatural beliefs. Nietzsche wants this historical narrative to shock us out of complacency, which hides troubling questions that a genealogical treatment may reveal and that Nietzsche is more than willing to launch: Can our intellectual and moral convictions actually stem from life-negating or live-averse conditions?

A main element in Nietzsche's critique in *GM* is the historical picture he paints about slave morality coming to supplant master morality, wherein weaker, life-averse values replaced an earlier and stronger set of values

---

[1] Passages from *The Gay Science* in this essay are taken from the Walter Kaufmann translation (1974); those from *Beyond Good and Evil* are also taken from Kaufmann's translation, in *Basic Writings of Nietzsche* (1968b).
[2] See *GS*, 108, 125; and *TI*, "Skirmishes of an Untimely Man," 5.   [3] See *GS*, 346.

marked by worldly power and success.[4] If we grant some degree of historical validity to this picture – especially in terms of the ascendancy of Christianity over pagan antiquity – then the fact that such a course has indeed happened still leaves open the question of why it happened. Why would presumably healthier and more capacious forms of life give way to counter-values marked by the denigration of natural life instincts? Is such an outcome simply a regressive story of degeneration that is irreversible, or reversible only by a retrieval of master values that can cure the West of its slavish infirmities?

In sum: Given Nietzsche's apparent disdain for the life-negating effects of slave morality, and given the original position of social power enjoyed by master types, it seems surprising that master morality would give way to slave values in European history. In *GM*, Nietzsche does not really give an extensive and pointed treatment of this question. In the third essay he does identify the genius of slave morality in fostering guilt not only in the sick but in powerful and happy types as well (*GM*, III, 14). Yet it is not exactly clear why the latter types would be susceptible to guilt in the first place. I think that there are implicit elements in *GM* and other texts that can help us gather Nietzsche's answer to this question. Possible explanations for the eclipse of master morality include: effects of the growing domestication of culture, an exhaustion of externalized forms of power, and the novel attractions of internalized forms of power, one example of which is Socratic dialectic.

Yet the question at hand also bears on how to read Nietzsche's overall aims in *GM*. Beyond the explanations mentioned above, it seems that the turn from master to slave morality initiated a terrible decline for life in Nietzsche's view, making the turn not only surprising but lamentable. However, Nietzsche's analyses in *GM* show so many ambiguities that we should read the turn as both an endangerment and an enhancement of cultural life, the latter because the original brute power of master types could be refined into higher cultural production when modified by the slave mentality.

In this chapter I will attempt to flesh out these questions, organized around the following discussions: (1) the master–slave distinction in Nietzsche's analysis; (2) the domestication of culture and the attractions

---

[4] In my discussions I will deploy the master–slave distinction even though in *GM* Nietzsche uses the term "noble morality" rather than the term "master morality" that was used in *BGE*. The master–slave distinction has become a term of art in treatments of Nietzsche, and I do not see any significant difference between "master" and "noble." Nietzsche does mention the term "master" in *GM*, II, 5; and in the epilogue to *CW*, "master" and "noble" morality seem to be interchangeable terms.

of slave morality; (3) the role of Socrates in Nietzsche's historical picture; and (4) the ambiguities in Nietzsche's account of master and slave morality.

MASTER AND SLAVE MORALITY

Nietzsche's genealogical treatment of traditional moral ideals aims to disturb the pretense of moral purity and the presumption of moral foundations by suggesting a different look at the historical context out of which these moral values arose. Ideals such as neighbor-love, peacefulness, and humility were not derived from some transcendent source, but from the interests and needs of particular types of human beings, weaker peoples suffering at the hands of stronger types. Hierarchical domination was the ruling condition of early human societies (*BGE*, 257). What has been exclusively called "morality" was originally only a particular kind of morality, one quite different from another kind of morality that reflected the interests of stronger types:

There are *master morality* and *slave morality* . . . The moral discrimination of values has originated either among a ruling group whose consciousness of its difference from the ruled group was accompanied by delight – or among the ruled, the slaves and dependents of every degree. (*BGE*, 260)[5]

In *GM*, I, 10–11, master and slave morality are distinguished by Nietzsche according to two sets of estimation: good and bad in master morality, and good and evil in slave morality. Master types discover what is good out of their own condition of strength; they experience pleasure and exaltation in their victories and their distance from the powerless. Characteristics such as courage, conquest, aggression, and command that produce feelings of power are deemed "good," while traits of weaker types such as cowardice, passivity, humility, and dependence are deemed "bad." What is important for Nietzsche here is that good and bad are not absolutes. What is good is good only for the master; what is bad in the slave arouses embarrassment and contempt in the master, but not condemnation or denial. In fact the existence of the slave is essential for maintaining the master's sense of distance, rank, and thus "goodness." The condition of the slave is not esteemed but at the same time it is not annulled, since it provides the master with psychological (and material) benefits. In sum, what is good for the master is something active, immediate, and spontaneous, arising

---

[5] Note the added phrase "and dependents of every degree," which tells us that "slavery" should be read as rhetorical shorthand for various kinds of submission.

directly out of the master's accomplishment; what is bad is a *secondary* judgment in contrast to an antecedent experience of self-worth.

In relation to master morality, slave morality is constituted by a number of reversals. What the master calls "bad" is deemed good by the slave, and what is good for the master is called "evil" by the slave. The difference between "bad" and "evil" is essential for Nietzsche's analysis. What is evil is absolutely negative and must be annulled if the good is to endure. Nietzsche traces this different kind of judgment to the existential situation of the slave: The *immediate* condition of the slave is one of powerlessness and subservience; the master is a threat to the very existence and well-being of the slave; in effect the slave lacks agency and so the initial evaluation is a negative one: the "evil" of the master is in the foreground, while what is "good," the features of the slave's submission, is a reactive, secondary judgment. Moreover, because of its immediate powerlessness, the slave's power for revenge cannot be actualized except in an *imaginary* realm of divine punishment (*GM*, I, 10).

According to slave morality, anything that opposes, destroys, or conquers is evil and should be eliminated from human relations. In master morality, however, strife, opposition, and danger are essential to the feelings of power and accomplishment that spawn a sense of goodness (one thinks of the warrior ideals in Homer's *Iliad*). Harmlessness and security, which are good for the slave, are an embarrassment and encumbrance for the master (*GM*, I, 11). Slave morality reverses master morality and recommends humility, selflessness, and kindness as the measure for *all* human beings, but only out of a condition of weakness and as a strategy for self-protection and self-enhancement. Slave morality seeks the simultaneous exaltation of the weak and incapacitation of the strong; but in doing so, slave types find enhancement not through their own agency but through the debilitation of others.

Slave morality is Nietzsche's redescription of Judeo-Christian ideals. The stories and exemplars embodying this moral outlook have promoted the ideal of supplanting worldly power with "justice" and "love." In the context of cultural history, however, Nietzsche sees in this ideal a disguised form of power, in that it is meant to protect and preserve a certain type of life; even more, the images depicting divine punishment of the wicked suggest to Nietzsche that the slave type has simply *deferred* its own interest in conquest (*GM*, I, 15). Both master and slave moralities, therefore, are expressions of will to power. A current distinction in the literature draws from Nietzsche's differentiation of *aktive* and *reaktive* attitudes (*GM*, II, 11) and stipulates that the master expresses active will to power, while the slave expresses reactive will to power. The slave has no genuine agency and therefore can compensate only by reacting to an external threat and attempting to annul it. For Nietzsche, slave morality is not immediately an affirmation of a good, but a denial of something dangerous and fearful, and he grounds this evaluation-by-negation in the psychological category of *ressentiment*.

> The slave revolt in morality begins when *ressentiment* itself turns creative and gives birth to values: the *ressentiment* of those beings who, denied the proper response of action, compensate for it only with an imaginary revenge. Whereas all noble morality grows out of a triumphant Yes-saying to itself, slave morality from the outset says No to what is "outside," what is "different," what is "not itself"; and *this* No is its creative deed. This reversal of the value-positing eye – this *necessary* orientation to the outside instead of back onto itself – is a basic feature of *ressentiment*: in order to come about, slave morality always first needs an opposing, external world; it needs, physiologically speaking, external stimuli in order to act at all – its action is fundamentally reaction. (*GM*, I, 10)

For Nietzsche, it should be said, the difference between active and reactive will to power, between affirmation and *ressentiment*, is a fundamental issue that bears on *all* intellectual and cultural topics. The general question is the ability or inability to affirm a finite world of limits, losses, conflicts, and dangers.[6] His analysis of the social arena in the *Genealogy* targets the concrete soil out of which grew a host of intellectual movements. Nietzsche is trying to subvert long-standing social values that are animated by notions of universality, equality, harmony, comfort, protection, and the like – seemingly positive notions that Nietzsche insists are connivances of negative attitudes: fear of danger and difference, hatred of suffering, resentment and revenge against excellence, superiority, and domination.

In *GM*, I, 13, Nietzsche reiterates the historical discussion of master and slave conceptions of goodness. To illustrate the difference he presents an image of birds of prey victimizing lambs. In such a natural setting it is no surprise that the lamb resents the bird of prey, but this is no reason to blame the bird for carrying off the lamb. Nietzsche says that actually there should be no objection to the lamb judging the bird as evil, except that the bird would see things differently. The bird will simply view the lamb-ideal with derision and bear no grudge against it – indeed the bird loves (to eat) the lamb.

At this point Nietzsche engages a fundamental position that occurs again and again in his writings: a critique of free agency. From a natural standpoint the power of the bird cannot be blameworthy, because it cannot help but express itself. The resentful judgment of the lamb presumes that the

[6] See *Z*, II, 20, "On Redemption," and *TI*, "The Problem of Socrates," 1.

bird could refrain from its violent actions. Here Nietzsche is targeting a long-standing assumption in Western moral philosophy and ethical sensibilities: that moral blame must presuppose the possibility to act otherwise and thus the freedom to choose whether or not to act in a certain way. Yet Nietzsche claims that the force of the bird's action is its very nature; it could not act otherwise. He notes "the seduction of language" that tempts us to distinguish an agent from its deeds by way of the grammatical difference between nouns and verbs ("the eagle killed the lamb"). Nietzsche believes that the very notion of agency is a fiction born from such linguistic constructions. For Nietzsche, activity itself is primal; it is not "caused" by an "agent." But moral judgment relies on just such a fiction of agency.

... popular morality separates strength from the manifestations of strength, as though there were an indifferent substratum behind the strong person which had the *freedom* to manifest strength or not. But there is no such substratum; there is no "being" behind the deed, its effect and what becomes of it; "the doer" is invented as an afterthought – the doing is everything. (*GM*, I, 13)

Nietzsche tells us that emotions of revenge *require* a belief in free agency, since otherwise moral blame and responsibility would be futile exercises. For those driven by moral revenge, nothing is defended more vigorously "than that *the strong are free* to be weak, and the birds of prey are free to be lambs – in this way they gain the right to make the birds of prey *responsible* for being birds of prey" (ibid.). It is only the weak lamb that requires concepts of freedom and responsibility in order to rectify its powerlessness and suffering. Now the strong are deemed "free" to renounce their power, and weakness (not exhibiting power) is converted into an "accomplishment," something chosen, desired, and thus something virtuous and praiseworthy. Nietzsche says that the concept of a "subject" – which is "free" to choose its course (of exercising or not exercising power) – has been crucial for the self-preservation and self-affirmation of the downtrodden, in that it has given natural weakness its meaning, its simultaneous judgment of the strong and valorization of the lowly. *GM*, I, 14, catalogues how various incapacities of the weak are converted by slave morality into admirable virtues that are an "accomplishment" as something chosen. Impotence now becomes a primary measure of "goodness" (e.g. timidity is now the virtue of "humility"). Such values represent, for Nietzsche, a kind of alchemy that makes a virtue out of necessity. With external subordination to the master, slave morality fashions an "internal" sphere that judges master values as inferior to slave virtues, and this internalized sphere is even promoted as a recipe for happiness.

THE ATTRACTIONS OF SLAVE MORALITY

In the third essay of *GM*, Nietzsche addresses a fundamental question: Assuming that nature is the only reality, how could anti-natural forces have emerged and prospered in life? In sections 11 and 13, Nietzsche organizes anti-natural forces around the ascetic priest and the ascetic ideal. He stipulates his opposition to the ascetic ideal as well as an admission that the ascetic priest is a formidable adversary. He also says, somewhat oddly, that the priest is not the best defender of his ideal, and that we (opponents) must "help him ... to defend himself well against us." This gesture is not easy to understand. Surely it cannot be a defense of asceticism's metaphysical project (a transcendent reality). Rather, I think it advances a naturalistic account of how and why such an ideal would succeed in natural life – because, as Nietzsche insists, the ascetic ideal is far from a historical "exception and curiosity," it is a historical *reality*, indeed "one of the most widespread and long-enduring facts there are"(*GM*, III, 11). The ascetic priest's hostility to life has continually "grown and prospered" *in* life. Consequently Nietzsche's life-philosophy cannot rest with an utter rejection of its importance or an overconfident critique of its truth. The prosperity of the ascetic ideal must stem from "a necessity of the first rank." Despite the fact that "an ascetic life is a self-contradiction," its "necessity" must be found in its being a form of *life*. Indeed, Nietzsche concludes that "*life itself must have an interest* that such a self-contradictory type not die out" (*GM*, III, 11). In section 13, he says that the "self-contradiction" of an ascetic "life *against* life" is only an apparent contradiction, only a provisional expression and interpretation, indeed a "psychological misunderstanding" of the *reality* of the situation, which is presented as follows: Even though the ascetic ideal may perceive itself as against life (this would be its metaphysical vision), from a naturalistic standpoint he claims that this ideal "*springs from the protective and healing instincts of a degenerating life*, which uses every means to maintain itself and struggles for its existence" (*GM*, III, 13). In other words, when some forms of life are degenerating, are losing a more original natural vitality, life itself will engender different strategies (of power) to prevent an utter abnegation of life (suicidal despair, for instance).

Since anti-natural forces are genuine life forces, we are in a better position to understand and take seriously the different ways in which slave morality took hold in life. How could such a revised measure of virtue and happiness gain traction and attraction in worldly circumstances of deprivation? Early on, the images of a promised life of bliss after death provided incentive and motivation. But such rewards come only in the future in another life, and so the slave type can only "in the meantime" present *earthly* life as a preparation for bliss and as a *continuation* of servile characteristics now converted into estimable virtues. In the context of Christian morality, Nietzsche says that the slave's life on earth can only be one of "faith" in salvation, "hope" for its rewards, and "love" expressed toward all the abusive conditions of earthly life (*GM*, I, 14).

In *GM*, I, 15, Nietzsche turns a merciless look at the twofold character of the Last Judgment in Christian morality: eternal rewards for the righteous and eternal punishments for the wicked. Here Nietzsche is highlighting his contention that slave morality is not only the rectification and elevation of weak values, but also a deferred expression of a desire for power *over* the master (which cannot be actualized in natural conditions). But Nietzsche's analysis reaches further than simply the understandable notion that "our abusers will get their just deserts some day." He plumbs the psychology of *ressentiment* that has a current *need* for experiencing the satisfaction and delight that turning the tables on the master would provide.

As evidence for his psychological diagnosis, Nietzsche offers two documents from the Christian theological tradition. First he cites Aquinas, who says that the bliss of paradise is *enhanced* by the *enjoyment* of witnessing the torments of the damned (one wonders why simply *knowing* of these torments would not suffice for bliss, why *seeing* the torments is required). Then Nietzsche cites the remarkable passage from Tertullian, which goes Aquinas one better with a detailed picture of such a spectacle. In one respect the passage is a full condemnation of the pagan world, but it does this by outbidding the *attractions* of that world with the greater joys in the world to come, where all pagan types will be visited with terrible punishments.

In any case, Nietzsche's interest in the retributive vision of Christianity does not really concern its specific content, which from his standpoint is sheer fiction. What matters to Nietzsche is how such a fiction is symptomatic of a certain form of *life* that came to contest and succeed master morality, how a "supernatural" vision had natural *effects* in promoting the self-overcoming of more natural expressions of power. In particular, the link between slave morality and a morally responsible free will was a prime example of a powerful effect on life that changed human history. One way to put this point is as follows: We could imagine a version of slave morality that simply counseled passive subjugation to the master with only the prospect of future salvation as the focus of interest. But for Nietzsche it is unsurprising that this was not the case, because his naturalism dictates that immanent life-effects are the only "real" issue, and the history of slave morality bears this out in the sense that salvation was not enough. The doctrine of free will and responsibility showed that slave morality was not satisfied simply with other-worldly rectification; it wanted to *convert* master morality to the slave perspective, so that the strong would *willingly* renounce their worldly forms of power and way of life.

In *GM*, III, 14, Nietzsche stipulates that "sickliness" has become the human norm in history. Yet now the analysis shifts from the powers engendered by this illness to its "danger for the healthy." Since sickness is the norm, then cases of health – "spiritual-corporeal powerfulness" (*seelisch-leiblichen Mächtigkeit*) – are rare and a matter of luck for humanity. Without the possibility of some kind of life-affirming health in human culture, Nietzsche warns against a looming "will to nothingness" that can grow out of two correlated dispositions: *compassion* for human suffering, and *nausea* at human existence. The danger, as Nietzsche sees it, is that compassion and nausea "might some day mate," which would magnify the danger of asceticism into a full-force depletion of life energies and a deadening of the human spirit.

The rest of section 14 and section 15 offer a recapitulation of Nietzsche's psychological critique of slave morality and the ascetic ideal: a layout of the rancorous and vengeful dispositions that weak types launch against the strong to valorize their own impotence and incapacitate the powerful. Section 15 repeats how the ascetic priest persuades the sick to find the source of their *suffering* in themselves, in an internalized guilt. Yet section 14 targets the different problem of the effect of ascetic power on healthy types, where they develop guilt about their *happiness*. Nietzsche singles out the "ultimate, finest, most sublime triumph of revenge," which reaches its peak when people who by nature are happy, successful, and "powerful in body and soul" become infected by bad conscience and "begin to doubt *their right to happiness*."

It is this second problem that is not fully fleshed out in *GM*. Nietzsche has presented a naturalistic explanation for why life-denying values could take hold in life *for* the sick and powerless. Yet such values have also achieved forms of worldly power. Indeed, Nietzsche finds the effects of ascetic illness "almost everywhere in Europe," in all its cultural spheres (*GM*, III, 14). But why would such norms succeed in displacing master morality on the world stage? How could values such as responsibility and guilt have become attractive enough to *strong* types so that erstwhile forms of worldly power could be converted or renounced? A central explanation would have to involve not immediate change by choice but changing external circumstances that could make conversion possible. Implicit in *GM* is a notion expressed in another text (*BGE*, 262): Aristocratic values originally stem from conditions of danger, war, and conflict. When cultures become more settled, successful, and peaceful, aristocratic values wither for lack of stimulus. Then different values can become attractive or needful. In *Daybreak*, 42 (which is included in references cited in *GM*, II, 6), Nietzsche discusses how active types can become contemplative types, when outlets for action diminish and aggressive instincts turn into critical judgments in thought. With conditions of diminished vitality, something like the Christian doctrine could become appealing. The inwardness of belief and promises of deliverance from death came to supplant mainstream pagan religion in the Roman era, a conversion that Nietzsche attributes to the genius of Paul (*A*, 58). Christian martyrs were also effective in attracting interest; their willingness to passively endure terrible deaths for their beliefs seduced non-believers to their cause (*A*, 53).

Also pertinent to this story is a figure who does not explicitly make an appearance in *GM*, yet who can be seen as a significant player in Nietzsche's historical analysis, namely Socrates.

SOCRATES

The *Genealogy* examines more than simply the moral and religious aspects of anti-natural forces in Western history; the focal term for such forces, the ascetic ideal, is also associated with philosophy and science, particularly with respect to a belief in truth (developed in the third essay). Accordingly, the same question would arise concerning the conversion of original aristocratic powers toward new standards of rationality. Why would something like philosophy and science become attractive enough to displace more vital sensibilities in early culture? Although this question is not examined explicitly in *GM*, in other texts Nietzsche does address it by naming Socrates as the key figure in the emergence of scientific rationality. In *The Birth of Tragedy*, Socrates is called a decisive turning point in history for overturning tragedy by force of the spirit of science.[7] The task here is to explore how Socrates could be woven into the *Genealogy*'s account of cultural transformation.[8]

---

[7] We should note that the German word *Wissenschaft* can refer to any rationally organized sphere of knowledge, including history and philosophy (cf. the distinction between *Naturwissenschaft* and *Geisteswissenschaft*). In *GM*, III, Nietzsche intends the wider sense, although he also focuses significantly on natural science (*GM*, III, 25). We should also note that Nietzsche calls *The Birth of Tragedy* "my first revaluation of all values" and the "soil" for his later teachings (*TI*, "What I Owe to the Ancients," 5).

[8] On this question see helpful essays by Migotti (2006) and Acampora (2002).

Socrates is typically identified as the primary figure in the birth of philosophy. In the *Genealogy*, Nietzsche clearly connects philosophy with the ascetic ideal. In *GM*, III, 8, he catalogues various dispositions of intellectual life that by nature run against normal goods. The development of intellectual powers (*Geistigkeit*) has required a "desert" of freedom from sensuality and common practices, a psychic desert that renounces most of what the world values in order to think differently and deeply. The next section summarizes Nietzsche's discussion by saying that "a certain asceticism" is both a precondition for, and a consequence of, the "highest spirituality [*Geistigkeit*]." The link between philosophy and the ascetic ideal has been so close and strong that he concludes: "it was only by the *leading-strings* of this ideal that philosophy ever learned to take its first little steps on earth" (*GM*, III, 9). This is so because the drives and virtues of philosophers – doubt, analysis, research, investigation, risk, non-partisanship – began as violations of primary and prevailing modes of morality and conscience. Measured against the morality of custom, philosophy was a kind of outlaw phenomenon, and philosophers themselves sensed their heretical status.

In this manner Nietzsche establishes a historical relation between philosophers and religious ascetics. Although philosophers were not identical to ascetic priests, the posture against normal life in both types had similar or analogous features. That is why Nietzsche says that philosophers had to pattern themselves on previously established religious types in order to get their bearings or appear in an already familiar form. Since philosophy *is* a struggle against normal modes of life, it took its cues, or found its inspiration, from the life-denying disposition of ascetics.

The extent to which Socrates can plausibly be linked to the ascetic ideal might emerge by bringing in Plato's philosophy and its historical background. Asceticism cannot be called a Christian invention, because throughout the ancient era, from the seventh century BC to the fifth century AD, there were a number of pagan mystery cults that promoted ascetic practices, a denial of the value of natural life, and a belief in another world after death that promised immortality and moral rectification.[9] Such cults were mainly of Asian origin and adherents were drawn mostly from lower, common strata of society. Ascetic traditions were not in the mainstream of pagan religions, and yet early Christianity was able to draw on these movements in the formation of its world view and practices. With the ascent of Christianity, ascetic religious tendencies became more mainstream

[9] See Burkert 1987.

in cultural life. Indeed, Nietzsche claims that through the influence of Paul, Christianity was able to both "sum up" and "outbid" ancient pagan mystery cults (*A*, 58).

Although Plato's philosophy differed in many ways from Christianity, its apparent dualism of soul and body and its transcendent aim beyond time to a sphere of eternity show some common elements, especially when Socrates counsels against grief over his death, since the very practice of philosophy has been a preparation for the soul's release from the body, and thus has been "the practice of death" to the physical world (*Phaedo* 80e–81a). The dialogues also tell stories of punishment of the wicked in the afterlife (*Republic* 615e ff. and *Gorgias* 525c). Such elements in Plato were influenced by Orphic and Pythagorean ascetic traditions in the Greek world.[10] Perhaps it is the link between Plato, asceticism, and Christianity that prompted Nietzsche to call Christianity "Platonism for 'the people'" (*BGE*, Preface). And despite the relative absence of Socrates and Plato in the *Genealogy*, in the third essay Nietzsche gathers the problem of life-denial subverting noble vitality around the phrase "Plato *versus* Homer" (*GM*, III, 25).

Against this background, the question of how something like Socratic reason could have converted master morality can now be addressed. Nietzsche maintains that original strong types measured value simply in terms of outward action and success. They were spontaneous and not given to much reflection before or after their deeds. They were, according to Nietzsche, governed by unconscious instincts (*GM*, I, 10). Slave types, on the other hand, because of their precarious condition and passivity, were more reflective and thus more clever than noble types (ibid.). When society became more settled and peaceful, the conditions demanding unconscious, instinctive behavior diminished and the master types now "were reduced to relying on thinking, inference, calculation, and the connecting of cause with effect, that is, to relying on their 'consciousness' ..." (*GM*, II, 16).

Such conditions spawning reflection opened space for slave morality's insistence that moral behavior be grounded in free agency, that strong types could have acted otherwise and thus could be persuaded to act differently. Long before the rise of Christianity in the ancient world, Socrates had provided a sophisticated method for exacting just this kind of measure to guide action, and Nietzsche stresses the parallel in some of his other writings. The Socratic revolution was dialectic, a method that challenged the instinctive spontaneity of noble Athenians by calling for reflection on, and justification for, their actions. The guiding principle of Socratic

---

[10] See Dodds 1968: 140–56 and ch. 5. Orphism is mentioned favorably in *Republic* 365a.

dialectic was that immoral action was a function of ignorance, that rational inquiry could lead away from instinct toward forms of knowledge that would subsequently revise behavior for the good. As Nietzsche puts it, "Reason = virtue = happiness only means: you have to imitate Socrates and establish a permanent state of *daylight* against all dark desires – the daylight of reason" (*TI*, "The Problem of Socrates," 10).

Nietzsche tells us that Greek nobility was guided more by instinct than reflection, indeed that pressing people for reasons was considered in bad taste (*BGE*, 191; *TI*, "The Problem of Socrates," 5). Yet the authority of the old aristocracy was declining as Athens became more settled and cultivated (*TI*, "The Problem of Socrates," 9), and the old instincts became fatigued (*BGE*, 212). Democratic Athens not only posed a formal challenge to aristocratic rule, the habits of public debate and persuasion only furthered the call for reason-giving. Socratic dialectic drew on these new forces, but introduced something unique. Socrates' method not only asked for conscious attention to the reasons supporting beliefs and action; he insisted on unprecedented criteria for argumentative success. One's reasons had to be based on clear and precise definitions, and such definitions could not involve mere general terms illustrated with specific examples (e.g. "justice" is given in *x*, *y*, or *z*), they had to involve unified, universal principles that *governed* particulars, such that any example has to be traced to a single form *not* fulfilled by any particular example. Consequently, any particular statement that could not accord with other statements on common ground would bring the charge of inconsistency and self-contradiction. Socrates' interlocutors were frustrated not because they were entirely inept but because they often did not even understand the *point* of asking for universals in this manner.[11]

Nevertheless, Socratic dialectic was consonant enough with new developments in Athenian culture that it could register as interesting and impressive, especially because Socrates was so successful at exposing deficiencies and defeating opponents. It is in this respect that Nietzsche suggests how it was that Socratic dialectic became alluring: it fit in with the competitive spirit of Athenian culture. In an early unpublished essay, "Homer's Contest,"[12] Nietzsche extolled the prevalence of the *agōn*, or contest for excellence, that was exhibited in all elements of Greek culture. Nietzsche claims that in the dialectic, Socrates "discovered a new type of *agōn* . . . He fascinated by appealing to the agonistic drive of the Greeks – he introduced

[11] See *Laches* 192a and *Hippias Major* 287d–e.
[12] A translation is included in the Cambridge edition of the *Genealogy*, pp. 174–81.

a variation into wrestling matches between young men and youths" (*TI*, "The Problem of Socrates," 8). With verbal competition becoming more and more a factor in Athens, Socratic debate could attract noble attention as a new arena for competition, victory, and defeat, even if now transformed into a battle of beliefs. Nietzsche also points out that Socrates was "a great *erotic*" (ibid.). His personal appeal was a complex set of seductions and powers that both enticed and vexed the elite of his day. A perfect example of such ambivalence is the figure of Alcibiades portrayed at the end of the *Symposium*. He confesses that only Socrates can make him feel shame, because he cannot defeat Socrates' argument for an unconditional good; he therefore has to give honor to Socrates' moral standard, but he cannot live up to it.[13]

Nietzsche not only highlights the challenge of Socrates to noble values, he goes further in his genealogical account by attributing slavish qualities to Socrates. He claims that "Socrates was descended from the lowest segment of society: Socrates was plebeian" (*TI*, "The Problem of Socrates," 3). He suggests that dialectic stemmed from *ressentiment* and revenge (*TI*, "The Problem of Socrates," 7). This seems a stretch. We do not know enough about Socrates' early life, but it appears unlikely that he was low born. And the bearing of Socrates does not seem to match slavish weakness. It should be pointed out, however, that slave morality in Nietzsche's analysis did not simply follow from the subordinate condition of weak types; it was not an expression of the masses, so to speak. Within slave ranks there were *creative* types who fashioned the world view that was able to give meaning to slavish existence and reverse master morality. This is the function of the "ascetic priest" in the *Genealogy*, the creative type who forms the voice of slave morality. Indeed, Nietzsche describes such creativity as coming from an "*active* bad conscience" (*GM*, II, 18), which is different, therefore, from the reactive, passive condition of the weak. And the ascetic priest exhibits a form of *power* that alters and serves life in certain ways (*GM*, III, 11), something also exhibited by the philosopher (*GM*, III, 8–10). We could insert Socrates into this framework quite easily, as an active, creative individual who serves the inversion and conversion of noble values.

I have also noted how Socratic–Platonic philosophy bears enough common ground with later Christian developments to make plausible Nietzsche's interpretive linkage. In an important sense, Socratic dialectic

---

[13] See Migotti 2006: 115. What was most vexing about dialectic was that Socrates only worked with the positions advanced by his interlocutors. If those positions ran into trouble, it could only be taken as a self-inflicted wound.

was an *agōn* that could not be contested with any measures from natural life. The Platonic Forms that serve as the standard for dialectical critique cannot be located in any physical or worldly phenomena, which by their very nature cannot measure up to pure universality and permanence.[14] This is why Platonic knowledge implies the existence of a soul that cannot reach fulfillment in the natural world, but only upon death and the separation from the body. It is in this respect that Nietzsche can with some justification include Socrates in the classification of ascetic life-denial (*TI*, "The Problem of Socrates," 1–2).

THE MASTER–SLAVE DISTINCTION REVISITED

This last section of my essay will take up a different question than preceding discussions, one that touches on how we should read Nietzsche's overall genealogical analysis. No longer simply a matter of historical explanations for why slave morality took shape and why master morality could succumb to it – now the question bears on the status of this conversion in Nietzsche's eyes. The *Genealogy* is sometimes read as a delineation of two radically different human types, master and slave, strong and weak, where the displacement of master morality was an unqualified degeneration of life that must in turn be replaced by something akin to master morality if life is to avoid a collapse into nihilism. One of the hidden implications of the discussions in this essay, however, is that the typology of master and slave, strong and weak, is essentially ambiguous, that the boundaries between these tropes are more porous than we might expect – which if true would make the "conversion" of master morality less mysterious. The ambiguities in Nietzsche's account, in fact, are consistent with his primary concept of will to power, which is counterposed to a "metaphysical" faith in opposite values (*BGE*, 2), where concepts like being and becoming are exclusive of each other and fight a zero-sum game of conflict. Will to power, on the other hand, as an ongoing structural *relation* of resistance and overcoming, can never settle into exclusive opposition. Natural phenomena, therefore, are always ambiguous, measured against metaphysical suppositions, because the very nature of things is caught up in resistance from "otherness."[15] Accordingly, the question at hand here concerns the essential ambiguity of

---

[14] See the *Phaedo* 74–75. This is why Acampora can claim that from a Nietzschean perspective, Socratic dialectic differs from other instances of Greek *agōn* in its implication of total victory over opponents, who cannot hope to win on Socrates' terms (Acampora 2002: 29–33).

[15] "Above all, one should not want to divest existence of its *rich ambiguity*" (*GS*, 373).

Nietzsche's typology, which bears on the supposed story of essential decline in the movement from master morality to slave morality and the ascetic ideal.

I believe that Nietzsche's genealogical analysis is not meant to reject or even regret the slave/herd mentality, as much as to redescribe the environment of such moral values in naturalistic terms. In doing so Nietzsche aims to disarm the high-minded pretense of the moral tradition by contextualizing it and showing it to be no less interested in power and control than is aristocraticism (*BGE*, 51; *GM*, I, 15). Moreover, for Nietzsche, slave morality is no less *creative* than master morality; it is the *motive* behind creative forming that differentiates master and slave (*GM*, I, 10).

A careful reading of Nietzsche does not support the thesis that his genealogy is exclusively a defense of crude physical power or overt social control. Throughout his writings, the meaning of weakness, strength, and power is polymorphous and far from clear. For instance, Nietzsche calls the values he criticizes necessary for life. Morality has been essential for human development in its contest with nature and natural drives (*WP*, 403), and for this it deserves gratitude (*WP*, 404). The exceptional individual is not the only object of honor for Nietzsche; conditions of the rule are equally important for the species (*GS*, 55). The "weak" herd turns out to have a practical advantage, since it has prevailed over the strong, owing to being in the majority and more intelligent (*TI*, "Skirmishes of an Untimely Man," 14). Indeed, the higher types of creative individuals that Nietzsche favors are more vulnerable and perish more easily, because of their complexity, in contrast to the simplified order of herd conditions (*BGE*, 62).[16]

There cannot be rigid delineations between master, slave, and creative types in Nietzsche's overall analysis. The powers of the original master type are restricted to the more natural domain of overt action and physical prowess. The internalization of power in slave morality, while problematic, opens up the capacities of imagination and thus the more refined forms of culture creation that Nietzsche himself celebrates. Therefore, slavish tendencies are not only life-enhancing for weaker types, they are also not altogether regrettable when mixed with creative power. And since Nietzsche claims that such creative power emerges not through the slavish masses but through special individuals (the ascetic priest and its offshoots), then here we notice a possible blending of slavish passivity and masterly

---

[16] See also *WP*, 949 and 951. The precariousness of creativity provides another angle on why higher types might convert to the consolations of slave morality.

activity, of the withdrawing effect of weaker types and the productive effect of stronger types. It seems that higher *culture*, for Nietzsche, would not be possible apart from the creative redirection of power made possible by *natural* weakness.

We should conclude, therefore, that the kind of artistic, cultural, and intellectual creativity championed by Nietzsche was made possible by the slave mentality. Outwardly thwarted and powerless, the slave turned to the inner realm of imagination. Cultural creativity is the internalization or spiritualization of more overt and brute manifestations of power (the condition of the original master). This greatly expands the possibilities of innovation (since it is not completely bound by external conditions) and so cultural invention is set loose as a contest with existing conditions (*GM*, III, 4). Accordingly, cultural creators, like the original master, will be perceived as threats, as destroyers, as evil. In this light, the genealogy of morals is a complex code for understanding the dialectics and dynamics of cultural development.

Will to power is connected with creativity, with "spontaneous, aggressive, expansive, form-giving forces that give new interpretations and directions" (*GM*, II, 12). The slave can exercise will to power only in the inner domain of imagination.

All instincts that do not discharge themselves outwardly *turn inward* – this is what I call the *internalization* [Verinnerlichung] of man: thus it was that man first developed what was later called his "soul." The entire inner world, originally as thin as if it were stretched between two membranes, expanded and extended itself, acquired depth, breadth, and height, in the same measure as outward discharge was inhibited. (*GM*, II, 16)

Nietzsche tells us that the slave mentality is the prerequisite for spiritual cultivation (*BGE*, 188); the "weak" represent a positive power of spirit (*TI*, "Skirmishes of an Untimely Man," 14) because their resentment of the strong opens up the possibilities of a higher culture, which is based on *der Vergeistigung und Vertiefung der Grausamkeit*, "the spiritualization and deepening of cruelty" (*BGE*, 229). Such a turn begins to make mankind "an interesting animal," because the most ancient cultural concepts were "incredibly uncouth, coarse, external, narrow, straightforward, and altogether *unsymbolical* in meaning" (*GM*, I, 6). Now higher culture is possible, since "human history would be altogether too stupid a thing without the spirit that the impotent have introduced into it" (*GM*, I, 7).

So the master–slave distinction may have clear delineations at first, but it begins to get complicated in the context of cultural creativity and

Nietzsche's brand of higher types, who should be understood as an "inter-penetration" of master and slave characteristics combined in a "single soul" (*BGE*, 260). We noted that only certain individuals carry slave instincts in a higher direction: The priest type, though weak in a worldly sense, is strong in will to power by *creating* values that promote the sick and castigate the healthy (*GM*, III, 15). Nietzsche tells us that the *conflict* between master and slave forces is the most decisive mark of a higher, more spiritual nature (*GM*, I, 16). As a result, the "evil" that designated the destructive threat of the master is now recapitulated in creative disruptions of established conditions.

The strongest and most evil spirits have so far done the most to advance humanity: again and again they relumed the passions that were going to sleep – and they reawakened again and again the sense of comparison, of contradiction, of the pleasure of what is new, daring, untried; they compelled men to pit opinion against opinion, model against model. Usually by force of arms, by toppling boundary markers, by violating pieties – *but also by means of new religions and moralities* [my emphasis]. In every teacher and preacher of what is *new* we encounter the same "wickedness" that makes conquerors notorious, even if its expression is subtler and it does not immediately set the muscles in motion, and therefore also does not make one that notorious. What is new, however, is always *evil*, being that which wants to conquer and overthrow the old boundary markers and the old pieties. (*GS*, 4)

Innovators are the new object of hatred and resentment (*Z*, III, 12, "On Old and New Tablets," 26), they are the new "criminals" (*TI*, "Skirmishes of an Untimely Man," 45), the new "cruel ones" (*BGE*, 230), the new perpetrators of "war" (*GS*, 283).

In sum, cultural creativity is made possible by a dialectic of master and slave characteristics, so that not everything in the latter is "slavish" and not everything in the former is "noble." In the end, therefore, the creator–herd distinction is *not* equivalent to the master–slave distinction; there are over-laps, but the crude domination found in the original condition of the master cannot be considered the primary focus of Nietzsche's analysis of creative types.

In addition to recognizing the preserving strength of herd factors, Nietzsche at times talks about creativity as a form of "degeneracy" as mea-sured against social norms (which adds a complicating element to Nietzsche's critical charge of degeneracy leveled against modern social forces). In *HAH*, I, 224 (a section titled "Ennoblement through Degeneration"), Nietzsche discusses the preserving "strength" of social custom counterposed against "morally weaker individuals" who cannot or will not fit in with social norms and capacities. Yet such individuals, precisely because they do not fit in, can discover new pathways and effect "spiritual progress." Nietzsche is playing on the fact that the *possibility* of innovation stems from misfits, who from the perspective of social cohesion *must* be perceived as weak or degenerate. So Nietzsche can analyze weakness and strength from various perspectives and show their shifting virtues and tensions. In this passage Nietzsche highlights the intrinsic tension of necessary forces in human life that promote both stability and novelty. The cohesion of "strong communities" faces the danger of a "gradually increasing inherited stupidity such as haunts all stability like its shadow." Individuals who are weak by social standards *may* bring forth new horizons, but it is also true that "countless numbers of this type perish on account of their weakness without producing any very visible effect." Yet when such types can discover something new, their "social degeneracy" corrects for the stupidity of "social strength."

Degenerate natures are of the highest significance wherever progress is to be effected. Every progress of the whole has to be preceded by a partial weakening. The strongest natures *preserve* the type, the weaker help it to *evolve* ... The more sickly man, for example, will if he belongs to a war-like and restless race perhaps have more inducement to stay by himself and thereby acquire more repose and wisdom ... To this extent the celebrated struggle for existence does not seem to me to be the only theory by which the progress or strengthening of a man or a race can be explained. Two things, rather, must come together: first the augmentation of the stabilizing force through the union of minds in belief and communal feeling; then the possibility of the attainment of higher goals through the occurrence of degenerate natures, and, as a consequence of them, partial weakenings and injurings of the stabilizing force; it is precisely the weaker nature, as the tenderer and more refined, that makes any progress possible at all. (*HAH*, I, 224)

Material such as this must be kept in mind when considering Nietzsche's complicated and ambiguous analysis of weakness and strength. In the *Genealogy*, the analysis of weakness and strength is not limited to the debilitating capacity of social norms in slave morality measured against the natural strength and vitality of master morality. It can be said that "weakness" can exhibit productive strength, but it matters whether this strength is understood from the perspective of social regulation or social transgression. Regulation is a cohesive strength, for which transgression is a weakness. Yet transgression (whether in master morality or innovative movement) is a life-advancing strength, for which cohesion is a weakness. The *Genealogy* exhibits much of this perspectival ambiguity, which must be recognized if the course of Nietzsche's text is to be fathomed well.

Similar complications arise in Nietzsche's account of the link between philosophy and the ascetic ideal. *GM*, III, 10, echoes the idea of the "degeneracy" of creative types when measured by established codes.

Nietzsche tells us that reflective contemplation was originally so different from an active, warlike world that it had to arouse a certain fear of its deviancy in both the community and contemplatives themselves. Philosophers in the beginning had to struggle against their own *resistance* to their posture against existing ways of life. In other words, philosophical thinking was both an internal and external struggle; it was a fight against the outside world, but it had to fight *for* its deviant power within the living psyches of philosophers. They had to use terrible means of self-castigating cruelty against the forces of custom and tradition in their own selves, so that "they could *believe* in their own innovations" as something worthy and achievable.

Such is the historical relation between philosophers and religious ascetics, as previously noted. Philosophers found established religious dispositions of life-denial useful for giving sense and meaning to their alienated posture. Nietzsche seems to be claiming that philosophy would not have been historically possible without the precedence of the ascetic ideal. Why? Because philosophy developed and had to sustain itself in "conditions of crisis" that needed something like the ascetic ideal to shape and valorize its radical bearing. At the same time, Nietzsche is at pains in this section of the text to differentiate the philosopher from religious asceticism. The historical function of the ascetic ideal in philosophy's development is called by Nietzsche an outward appearance, a mask, even philosophy's own self-misconception. Although philosophy always bears a certain struggle of natural life against itself (thus showing some resemblance to the ascetic ideal), Nietzsche nonetheless wants to keep open the possibility of a liberation of philosophy from the ascetic ideal – despite the fact that this ideal "has been maintained until most recently" as the guiding spirit of philosophy. Even though the ascetic priest had been the prevailing model for philosophers in the past, he asks: "have things *really* changed" in our "more enlightened world"? He wonders:

Is there enough pride, daring, courage, self-confidence, will of spirit, will to take responsibility, *freedom of will*, for "the philosopher" on earth to be really – *possible*? . . . (*GM*, III, 10)

In *GM*, III, 11, Nietzsche makes it clear how the ascetic priest's power differs from other forms of will to power. The will to power of asceticism "wants to be master, not over something in life, but over life itself and its deepest, strongest, most profound conditions." The ascetic priest turns against the beauties and joys of carnal life, and yet a *new* kind of satisfaction unfolds: "pleasure is *looked for* and found in failure, decay, pain, misfortune, ugliness, voluntary deprivation, self-destruction, self-flagellation, and self-sacrifice." From the standpoint of nature, this amounts to "a conflict that *wills* itself to be conflicting," that exalts in itself proportionate to the degree in which its *natural* life capacities are *diminished*.

Despite the ambiguity in the discussion of asceticism, creativity, and philosophy, the danger in the ascetic ideal is a looming nihilism that haunts modern life. In *GM*, II, 24, Nietzsche hopes for the possibility, not of a return to master morality, but a new kind of cultural creativity that can turn against the nature-denying spirit of culture heretofore. What is needed is a "creative spirit" who renounces anything outside or beyond natural life, who is thoroughly "immersed" in this life (Nietzsche actually uses the term "reality" here), who can "redeem it from the curse put on it by the former ideal." Nietzsche concludes by echoing the crisis that follows the death of God:

This man of the future will redeem us, not just from the former ideal, but also from what *had to arise from it*, from the great nausea, from the will to nothingness, from nihilism . . .

Such a human of the future will give back to the earth its "goal" and to humankind its "hope." Nietzsche exhorts that "this antichrist and anti-nihilist, who has overcome both God and nothingness – *he must come one day* . . ."

I hope I have been able to establish that what Nietzsche hopes for in overcoming the tradition's life-averse character is not a return to master morality, but the *self*-overcoming of the tradition,[17] a *cultural* renovation that is possible only by way of the tradition's overcoming of original master morality.[18]

---

[17] See *GM*, III, 27. [18] Portions of this chapter were drawn from Hatab 2008.

CHAPTER 10

"Genealogy" and the Genealogy

P. J. E. Kail

I. INTRODUCTION

Among the rich veins of gold running through *On the Genealogy of Morality* is supposedly the methodologically distinct one of "genealogy" itself. Genealogy as a method is associated with Michel Foucault (2001) and, more recently, the work of Bernard Williams (2002).[1] But how Nietzsche himself understood "genealogy" and its import is a contested matter. Some take genealogy to be quite a weighty notion. According to David Hoy genealogy "is for Nietzsche a way of doing philosophy that shows not only the inadequacy of traditional metaphysics or 'first philosophy' but also the prospects for non-metaphysical philosophy" (Hoy 1994: 251), an "immanent critique" (268 n.) with which Nietzsche intends "to come up with a definite valuation of . . . traditional morality" (252). Others are less sure that there is anything distinctive or novel here. For example, Raymond Geuss writes that genealogy is "not some particular kind of method or special approach, rather it 'simply *is* history, correctly practiced'" (2001: 336)[2] and that the "purpose and effect of a genealogy can't be to criticize values or valuations directly" (338). Indeed Nietzsche explicitly says that a "history of origins [of moral judgments] . . . is something quite different from a critique" (*GS*, 345). So *if* genealogy is just a history of origins, it is not itself a critique, be it immanent or otherwise.

My aim in what follows is to give a general articulation of what a "genealogy" might be. I argue that it is primarily an explanatory account of the emergence of some distinctive set of beliefs, practices, and associated phenomena, involving situating agents with a particular psychology in a social-cum-environmental situation to which that psychology is responsive. I support this claim by examining what is common between Nietzsche and

---

[1] All English translations cited here are published by Cambridge University Press, except for *The Will to Power*, trans. W. Kaufmann and R. J. Hollingdale (1968).
[2] Geuss is quoting Alexander Nehamas 1985: 46. We shall return to this issue.

the "English psychologists," rather than by discussing twentieth- and twenty-first-century conceptions of genealogy that are themselves based predominantly on readings of Nietzsche's work. This allows us some distance from Nietzsche's own work and helps us to see that some claims about what genealogy *is* extrapolate too much from *Nietzsche's* own version of it.

Having got straight on what genealogy *is*, I discuss some of its consequences. I shall say something about its being a naturalistic, but non-reductive, form of understanding but show that that no genealogy has *normative* consequences simply in virtue of its being a genealogy. The normative consequences (if any) of a given genealogy depend on the particular *kind* of genealogical account offered. I then discuss and reject the idea that Nietzsche's particular genealogy constitutes an "internal" or "immanent" critique of morality or a "revaluation of values." Instead, I shall argue Nietzsche's genealogy has the normative consequence of *destabilizing* the moral beliefs it explains, namely by motivating the requirement to seek some further justification for those beliefs. I then briefly explain the role of destabilization in Nietszche's wider project of the "revaluation of values." I conclude by discussing some issues regarding genealogy as "real history."

2. GENEALOGY AND PSYCHOLOGICAL EXPLANATION

Our immediate question is: What is a "genealogy" of morality (or of anything else)? But how are we to answer this question? How, in other words, are we to distinguish between a genealogy of morality *per se* and those features peculiar to Nietzsche's own genealogy? Nietzsche does not claim to be the first to offer a genealogy of morality[3] (a striking fact, given Nietzsche's fondness for claiming firsts for himself). Instead he situates himself against the "English psychologists," whom he recognizes as offering genealogies. He thinks their genealogies "are no good" (*GM*, II, 4), "don't amount to much" (*GS*, 345), and are "back-to-front and perverse" (*GM*, Preface, 4), and we shall come to his disagreements with them presently. Of course, the term "English" can mislead. For one thing, one of *GM*'s most immediate springboards is the work of Nietzsche's erstwhile German friend, Paul Rée. Referring to Rée's *The Origin of Moral Sensations*, Nietzsche tells us that he "may never have read anything to which I said [so emphatically] 'no'" (*GM*, Preface, 4), and Christopher Janaway has recently shown in detail how the view described and criticized in *GM* is Rée's own (see Janaway 2007). Second, Nietzsche consulted Lecky's *History of European Morals*

---

[3] Cf. Owen 2007: 144.

(1869),[4] and many of the psychologists therein, like Hume or Mill, are Scottish. "English" refers not to a nationality but to a faulty genealogy. But Nietzsche does categorize their authors as "genealogists." This affords the opportunity of comparing and contrasting their approaches to distinguish genealogy *per se* from features peculiar to the genealogy offered by Nietzsche.

Nietzsche and the "English" share in common an attempt to give a naturalistic account of the "origins" of moral phenomena. Nietzsche talks repeatedly in *GM* both about "origins" (and in other relevant texts e.g. *GS*, 345; *WP*, 254), and his "hypotheses" concerning them from his earlier discussions in *D* and *HAH* right up to *GM* (Preface, 4). So *GM* and, say, Hume's *Treatise of Human Nature* share in an attempt at a "naturalistic" explanation of the emergence of certain moral beliefs and practices. The details, assumptions, and scope of these hypotheses obviously vary from thinker to thinker, but the explanatory aspiration is common. Second, the term "psychologist" – quite a compliment coming from Nietzsche – marks a further commonality. Moral thought is explained by appealing to a relatively independently intelligible type-psychology, which in turn renders moral thought more tractable and less mysterious. Third, to a greater (Hume) or lesser (Hutcheson) extent, the relevant explanation involves not merely the postulation of a particular psychology but conjectures about the kinds of *situations* in which human beings find themselves with such a psychology, and how the two interact. So Hume explains the emergence of the practice of justice, construed as property rights, by a combination of limited benevolence, self-interest, and our capacity to learn the benefits of mutual cooperation in our experience of family life, under conditions of great scarcity. These motivate the establishment of conventions, whose normative force derives first from self-interest, but which subsequently become "moralized" (i.e. conceived of as binding on agents independently of their own interest) and figure in the motivational set of the agent. One can then see how the emergence of a certain form of behavior which can be described as justice could emerge, given *that* psychology in *that* situation.

So what marks Nietzsche's out from the others? Nietzsche's psychology differs markedly from others, but that is a difference, first, in "input" rather than methodology. Second, he accuses his predecessors of being historically insensitive, an issue to which we shall return. Third, he takes his

---

[4] For a discussion see Thatcher 1989, and on Nietzsche's knowledge of English-language philosophy more generally, Brobjer 2008.

predecessors to approach morality with insufficient *suspicion.* He notices – and applauds – in them a glimmer of it, not believing them to be "cold, boring frogs" but crediting them with "suspicion" and "mistrust," and a "certain subterranean animosity and *rancune* toward Christianity (and Plato)," willing to face "plain, bitter, ugly, foul, unchristian, immoral truth" (*GM*, I, 1).[5] Why, though, would *more* suspicion be better? In barest outlines, the problem with the "English" psychologists is that they are biased by their own pro-attitude to the central tenets of morality and so "unsuspectingly stand under the command of a particular morality, and without knowing it, serve as its shield-bearers and followers . . ." (*GS*, 345). Their lack of suspicion renders them blind to morality's real origin.[6] Fourth, and something else to which we shall (briefly) return, in *GM*, II, 12, Nietzsche criticizes his predecessors for taking the present purpose of some practice as that which is causally responsible for its emergence (e.g. inferring from the fact that punishment has a deterrence function to the thought that it was invented to deter).[7] Still, none of this means Nietzsche's account is not itself a situated psychological explanation like those "English" psychologists offer, though he thinks his is methodologically more sophisticated.

Two things might seem to tell against this claim. First, "English" explanations are typically conjectural and not situated in any determinate historical context, but Nietszche's claim to "real history" might suggest that his genealogy avoids such speculation. Nietzsche complains about "English hypothesis-mongering" (*GM*, Preface, 6), that the "English" stare "into the blue," and his is a "better" "grey" direction involving that which "can be documented, which can be actually confirmed and has actually existed" (*GM*, Preface, 6), and, to put it Foucault's way, shouldn't genealogy be "grey, meticulous, and patiently documentary" (2001: 341)? But, to put it bluntly, although Nietzsche does makes some historical claims in *GM*, the contents of that work are anything *but* "grey, meticulous, and patiently documented."[8] As Janaway puts it, *GM* is to "a large extent psychological," inasmuch as it seeks to explain by appeal to a generic psychology (2007: 11),

---

[5] Compare *GS*, 345, where the terms "cold" and "frogs" are connected to an "impersonal" approach to morality.
[6] Here I am merely skating on the surface of some complex issues about objectivity in Nietzsche. For a fuller account (from which I have greatly benefited), see Janaway 2007: 40–50.
[7] It is not true, however, that all the "English" psychologists do make such an inference. Hume, for example, takes government to maintain justice but its emergence owes itself to the need to repel external threats. There is little evidence however that Nietzsche read much Hume, beyond his *Dialogues Concerning Natural Religion* that Nietzsche owned in translation. See Brobjer 2008: 53–58.
[8] It is true of course of Foucault's own detailed historical studies, but not, I submit, of *GM*.

one, furthermore, "not properly localized to times, places or individuals" (2007: 11). A good many of the explananda – such as the emergence of bad conscience – lie in prehistory, beyond the reach of any "grey documentation." Nietzsche of course thinks that aspects of his explanation are sensitive to documented movements of history in a way that the English ones are not (in particular the triumph of a certain pattern of "slave evaluation" over an earlier "noble one") but none of this makes it any less a psychological explanation, nor indeed different from some earlier British genealogies of religious belief. Hume's 1757 *Natural History of Religion*, for example, offers a psychological explanation of the emergence and some transmutations of religious belief that makes use of a good deal of historical and anthropological data to corroborate its claims. Nietzsche's complaint is that "English" genealogies don't pay enough attention to such non-psychological context and data in their accounts; he thinks his account is methodologically more sophisticated and so better represents the actual history of the emergence of morality. He is not claiming that his genealogy is different in *kind*.

Second, though I have stated that genealogy is an explanation of the "origins" of morality – which indeed Nietzsche claims to be seeking – Foucault has written, influentially, that genealogy "opposes itself to the search for 'origins'" (2001: 342). But this is easily handled by distinguishing (as Foucault does) between "origins" as *Herkunft* and "origins" as *Entstehung*. *Herkunft* one can translate as "pedigree" or "provenance," "stock," etc., and is redolent of a pattern of descent bestowing positive value. Nietzsche clearly offers no such account of origins in that sense, and it is in this spirit that Geuss says genealogy "for Nietzsche is the exact reverse of what we might call 'tracing a pedigree'" (2001: 322). But this is consistent with "origins" as *Entstehung*, or "emergence." Hence the question of *GM*, Preface, 3, namely "under what conditions did man invent the value judgments 'good and evil'?" is on all fours with the project of the "English" psychologists.

What does *GM* purport to explain? The true but uninformative answer is the origins of "morality." But as Nietzsche (see e.g. *BGE*, 186) recognizes *many* moralities, *GM*'s object is a *particular* evaluative orientation – "our value judgments 'good and evil'" – that we shall call, following Brian Leiter's useful shorthand "morality in the pejorative sense" (MPS).[9] Its characteristic normative content centers on the "three great pomp words" (*drei grossen Prunkworte*) of asceticism – "poverty, chastity and humility" (*GM*, III, 8) – which serve as placeholders for three clusters of norms, all associated

---

[9] Leiter 2002: 74. My use of the phrase doesn't mean that I accept Leiter's exact characterization of it.

with selflessness. These concern the negative evaluation of material well-being (poverty), sensual pleasure, its gratification and bodily conduct (chastity) and self-interest and self-aggrandizement (humility). One sense in which MPS is "anti-life" is its negative appraisal of what are in fact strong and intelligible impulses towards natural goods (morality would not be difficult, as it were, if we were not drawn towards riches, sensory indulgence, and self-aggrandizement). MPS's norms are further embedded in a conception of agency involving a substantive self and deserts free will[10] involving the principle of alternate possibilities (*GM*, I, 13; II, 4) and the reactive attitude of guilt, all of which furthermore interlock with the notion of bad conscience.

Nietzsche's explanation of MPS involves a complex interplay of the three – superficially separable – essays comprising *GM*.[11] The first describes the slave revolt, the emergence of a pattern of evaluation marked by its reactive negation of the pattern of evaluation structured around the *gut/schlecht* contrast. This inversion is the result of the psychologically intolerable situation in which slave types find themselves, which triggers the reactive attitude of *ressentiment*, which in turn is sublimated by the "invention" of the slave values. The second essay concerns the emergence of bad conscience and guilt, phenomena emerging from the internalization of cruelty and the creditor–debtor relationship as man is "imprisoned by the state" (*GM*, II, 17). Both of the slave revolt and the phenomena of bad conscience and guilt are exploited by the ascetic priest to form an interpretation that gives meaning to the nihilistic withdrawal (*GM*, III).

Given this characterization of MPS, how is it embodied in human life? I shall take it that MPS's presence is a matter of the existence of evaluative *concepts*, which figure in evaluative *beliefs*, which explain behavior.[12] The *GM* explains more than beliefs of course. The phenomenon of evaluative self-awareness or conscience is a central explanandum, and though beliefs about it emerge, the central phenomenon is not itself a belief. Nevertheless, a significant part of what Nietzsche seeks to explain is evaluative belief. Recent literature has hotly debated what metaethical presuppositions guide

---

[10] This terminology comes from Ken Gemes – see e.g. his 2009.

[11] As Nietzsche tells us in a postcard to Franz Overbeck dated 4 January 1888 – see Risse 2001: 55. We should add that Nietzsche's other works – in particular *Daybreak* and *Beyond Good and Evil* – also contribute to the overall explanation, as Nietzsche himself indicates both in *GM* and the postcard.

[12] I am here concentrating on the cognitive status of the narrow class of evaluation, namely MPS. Matters regarding the cognitive states of evaluation more generally in Nietzsche are more complex where there is scope to read Nietzsche as assuming something other than an error-theory.

Nietzsche's thought, and though I cannot defend my view fully here,[13] there is plenty to suggest that he treats moral commitments as beliefs. Thus, for example, he writes that "what moral and religious judgments have in common is the belief in things that are not real" (*TI*, "Improving Humanity," 1). The central aim of *GM*'s first essay is to explain a "conceptual transformation" (*Begriffs-Verwandlung*) and hence the presence of the evaluative concepts of MPS. The slave revolt issues falsification (*Fälschung*) (*GM*, I, 10), including the false belief (*Glauben*) in the neutral subject of free choice (*GM*, I, 13). Some might object that calling such commitments "beliefs" makes matters too "rationalistic." But that MPS, and Nietzsche's explanation of its emergence, centrally concerns belief does not mean that a thinker's possession of such states is determined by some rational process or some appreciation of rational considerations in their favor. The states involve claims about how things stand in the world, but their fixation is not a matter of responsiveness to epistemic norms.

So when, for example, Nietzsche says "morality is a sign-language for the affects" (*BGE*, 187) we should read him as meaning that the relevant beliefs are held because of the affects held by the believer. And it is in these terms that we can understand Nietzsche's claim that "morality is just an interpretation of certain phenomena, or (more accurately) a *mis*interpretation" (*TI*, "Improving Humanity," 1). Morality is a matter of imposing a certain set of beliefs, including metaphysical and evaluative beliefs, onto natural facts and behavioral dispositions. The practice of withdrawal, for example, has superimposed on it beliefs about the value of worldly goods and the existence of a world beyond this one. *GM* involves unpicking these interpretations, showing how different meanings (*Sinne*) become attached to behavioral dispositions and practices (*Brauche*). These meanings form a synthesis, which is one reason why "definitions" are ultimately unimportant since they at best yield only a snapshot of a particular stage in different interpretations. *GM* provides an account of how these different interpretations converge at a given historical moment, but does not take there to be any "unity" or necessary progressiveness in these interpretations. It is this aspect of Nietzsche's *GM* that occasions Geuss to write that giving "a genealogy is to provide a historical dissolution of self-evident identities" (2002: 212),[14] which is the "exact opposite of giving a pedigree": in denying a

---

[13] See e.g. Hussain 2007 and Clark and Dudrick 2007.

[14] Cf. Saars 2002. Geuss's emphasis on interpretation might also explain why he says that "Nietzsche says he is trying to answer two questions" (2001: 336), one regarding the value of morality, the second regarding the meaning of the ascetic ideals, thus entirely and curiously omitting Nietzsche's

pedigree one denies a unitary descent, exposing the supposed thoroughbred to be a mongrel. But if what we have said so far is on track, this is Nietzsche's *form* of genealogy but not essential to genealogy *per se*. It is a form of explanation contingent on Nietzsche's own psychology, and in particular the will to power (*GM*, II, 12), but when the psychologies and topics change, the interpretive element may well disappear.

3. GENEALOGY, CRITIQUE, AND REVALUATION

Like the English psychologists – whom we "have to thank for the only attempts so far to produce a history of the genesis of morality" (*GM*, I, 1) – Nietzsche's account is "naturalistic." It constitutes a form of self-understanding by offering not a reduction of our evaluative concepts, but an explanation. But Nietzsche says that, besides issues surrounding "hypotheses, mine or anyone else's, on the origin of morality," there is the more important question of the "value of morality" (*GM*, Preface, 5). The next section tells of the need to give "voice to this *new demand*; we need a *critique* of moral values, *the value of these values should itself, for once, be examined.*" But it is a mistake to view Nietzsche as offering a *sustained* critique – an examination of the value of values – within the pages of *GM* and a profound mistake to think there is some peculiarly *genealogical* critique. If a genealogy is a situated psychological account of the origins of moral beliefs, then merely being a genealogy cannot by itself constitute a critique. As Nietzsche says, "the history of origins [of moral judgments] . . . is something quite different from a critique" and a "morality could even have grown *out of* an error, and the realization of this fact would not as much as touch the problem of its value" (*GS*, 345).

But Nietzsche's *particular* genealogy evidently does have *some* connection with the project of revaluation. In meeting the "new demand" we need "to know about the conditions and circumstances under which the values [of MPS] grew up, developed and changed . . ." (*GM*, Preface, 6). A genealogy contributes *to* the possibility of the project of revaluation, rather than *constituting* it: or as Nietzsche puts it, the *GM* constitutes "a psychologist's three crucial *preparatory* works for a revaluation of all values" (*EH*, "Why I Write Such Good Books"). I shall explain just how presently, but we first consider and reject readings which interpret genealogy as critique.

explanatory interest in the emergence of ascetic morality. It seems that Geuss is guided by what is a central and perhaps essential aspect of *Nietzsche's* version of genealogy rather than what a wider notion of it might be.

3.1 Genealogy as immanent critique

Let us first distinguish (a) criticisms of MPS made within *GM* from (b) normative consequences for MPS linked essentially to its genesis. There are criticisms of MPS in *GM* – e.g. that the priestly interpretation of suffering actually increases suffering and so is at odds with itself – whose force does not depend in any interesting way on its psychological genesis. Nietzsche's explanation might assist in putting us in a position to *appreciate* the criticism, but that makes genealogy preparatory for a moral critique, not a form of it. Put another way, the priestly interpretation has bad consequences but that is a fact about the *product* that does not derive from the *process* that produces it. So, for example, David Owen (2007) argues that *GM* shows that MPS obscures the correct view of agency and so is harmful in that respect. I agree that this is a criticism raised in *GM* but any normative force possessed by that criticism is not a function of the genetic story told within its pages. The genetic account explains how we got into the mess – but the causal origins are not what *make* it a mess.

So-called "internal-" or "immanent-"critique readings argue that the *GM* shows that the values of MPS are at odds with their causal bases, so forging the link between the genetic and the critical. Walter Kaufmann, for example, suggests that *GM* both reveals the motives of morality and demonstrates that they are condemned by its own standards. *GM* shows that "our morality is, *by its own standards*, poisonously immoral: that Christian love is the mimicry of impotent hatred; that most unselfishness is but a particularly vicious form of selfishness; and that *ressentiment* is at the core of our morals" (1974: 113; emphasis in the original).[15] This suggestion is flawed in a number of ways. First, it works – if it does at all – only on the assumption that the psychological states and processes that originally produced the values of MPS continue to be operative in the psychology of the moral agents of today. But there is little evidence that Nietzsche is committed to this assumption. *Some* judgments made by *some* agents may now be so motivated (and indeed part of the plausibility of the whole story rests on our recognizing the possibility of such psychological processes) but that plausible idea is miles away from crediting all present moral agents with a whole package of serious self-deception. Nietzsche, furthermore, seems not to think we are systematically self-deceived.[16] Thus

---

[15] Compare Geuss 1981: 44.
[16] It's true that this passage comes from a work earlier than *GM*, but in the absence of any evidence that Nietzsche changed his mind, it remains decisive.

"To deny morality" – this can mean *first*: to deny that the moral motives which men *claim* have inspired their actions really have done so – it is thus the assertion that morality consists of words and is among the coarser or more subtle deceptions (especially self-deceptions) which men practice . . . *Then* it can mean: to deny moral judgments are based on truths. Here it is admitted that they really are motives of action, but in this way that it is *errors* that, as the basis of all moral judgment, impel men to their moral actions. This is *my* point of view. (*D*, 103; emphasis in the original)

Nietzsche goes on to make the point made above regarding the existence of some moral hypocrites, but note he here denies precisely what Kaufmann seems to require of him.[17]

Second one might then switch to the claim that the *originating* cause of the values which are *now* embodied in beliefs sustained by morally respectable motives, are themselves something which morality condemns. But this will run aground on the genetic fallacy, a fallacy of which Nietzsche is acutely aware.[18] Third, even if we grant everything Kaufmann claims, the exposure of universal hypocrisy doesn't tell us anything about the status of the *values* of MPS at all: it would confirm, as a rather dour Christian might suspect, that human beings are thoroughly immoral. It provides no grounds to reject the values themselves.[19]

A different take on the "self-undermining character" of morality is quasi-Hegelian (see e.g. Guay 2006). The genetic account Nietzsche gives is not a mere unnecessary appendage to making the point that the will to truth, itself the last expression of the ascetic ideal, reveals truths inconsistent with

[17] Here I agree with Leiter (2002: 174). Leiter also points out that maintaining that the motivations exist now would also seem to violate Nietzsche's injunction to avoid inferring origins from present practice.

[18] See e.g. *BGE*, 2. One might take the intent rhetorically, so that the reader becomes distanced from the values by seeing their shameful origins. That would chime well with a superficial impression left by the tone of Nietzsche's language. But a mere rhetorical attack is in itself weak. That is not to say it won't have that effect on some readers, and Nietzsche may indeed have intended that (see Leiter 2002: 176, for this idea). But I don't think it's the whole story, and if, as I suggest below, Nietzsche has his fellow naturalists in his sights, then assuming they are not so prone to the genetic fallacy, they would be doubly unimpressed by a rhetorical invitation to it. *Some* philosophers, however, might take the denial of a "pedigree" to have serious normative consequences. Thus in *BGE*, 2, the genetic fallacy is discussed under the aegis of "the prejudices of philosophers," and those whose position on causation is dominated by an eminence model (such as Plato) hold that only good can cause good. On Nietzsche's rhetorical strategies in *GM*, see Owen 2007, chapter 3.

[19] This problem attends David Owen's recent reading (see Owen 2003 and 2007). Owen argues interestingly and convincingly that Nietzsche moves to genealogy because the project begun in *Daybreak* could not be furthered. This is because Nietzsche had (a) underestimated the tenacity of MPS in those who had accepted the death of God, (b) accepted without question the authority of scientific knowledge and (c) failed to give any basis from which to revalue values other than Nietzsche's own preferred values. Still, Owen goes for elements of an immanent critique, writing that *GM* is designed to "promote a cognitive problematization of . . . "morality" in terms of its own constituent commitment to the "immorality" of *ressentiment*, cruelty and partiality" (2007: 71).

morality. The falsity of the presuppositions of morality could be demon-strated without such apparatus. Instead the explanation is required because it shows, somehow, that it is *inevitable* that this occurs, because of the "purposiveness" of morality.[20] On the assumption that the function of morality is to "make sense of existence," the ascetic ideal's attempt to do so produces the will to truth, which in turn shows the ultimate failure of that aim.[21] But it is unclear whether this *is* inevitable, and its inevitability is crucial to the success of this reading. It is true that the will to truth is the last – i.e. the most *recent* – expression of the ascetic ideal and, furthermore, the will to truth means that unsustainable metaphysical commitments – namely Christianity and the metaphysics of free will – fall away.[22] Furthermore, we "seekers after knowledge" become aware that the source of our commitment to "truth at any price" is the highest sublimation of the ascetic ideal (*GM*, III, 27). *GM* explains the source of the value placed on truth which he describes as "the will to truth's becoming-conscious-of itself." So the naturalist now knows that the source of his counter-ideal to Christianity – the will to truth – is the last expression of it. But this does not show that *any* ascetic ideal is impossible, since in *BGE*, Part I, Nietzsche allows that the "falsity of a judgement is no objection." We could realize that there is falsity through and through in MPS but, on reflection, remain untroubled by it. At this stage, knowledge of the sources of our commit-ment to truth provides a reason to question it (see below), but does not imply that *reflective* endorsement of asceticism is impossible as a counter-weight to nihilism. Our commitment to truth shows the falsity of certain assumptions about asceticism and its sources, so *those assumptions* are undermined (its Christian interpretation). It is being fully reflective about

[20] The will to power eats itself, as Alec Hinshelwood nicely put it to me.

[21] One worry here is the quasi-Hegelian tone, which seems at odds with Nietzsche's general orientation (cf. Geuss 1999: 183). Guay (2006: 366–67) tries to support this Hegelian reading, but some of the texts he uses to support the claim about "self-contradiction" do not seem to bear out his claims. Thus he appeals to the phrase "self-overcoming of morality" in *BGE*, 32, but the main point in that section is the rather more prosaic idea that the centrality of intention in morality is something we have come to realize to be false.

[22] Geuss suggests *GM* is relevant to Christianity because Christianity must involve beliefs regarding the origins of morality and a commitment to truth, and the latter undermines the former. Since it is "a peculiar and idiosyncratic problem of Christianity that it cultivates truthfulness ... and is a form of evaluation which requires its devotees to make claims and have beliefs [about those origins] that won't stand up ... to scrutiny ... [so Christianity] dissolves itself" (2001: 339). I think Nietzsche does believe this, but that, as it were, is what is *reported* in *GM* (e.g. III, 27), and not something that Nietzsche's explanatory account itself brings about. *GM itself* won't persuade the Christian, unless they accept the premises and, as I shall suggest below, it is implausible to think a Christian would.

the sources of value that *puts us in a position* to critique all values, a critique which Nietzsche thinks in fact will destroy MPS. As Nietzsche writes,

The inquiry into the *origin* of our evaluations ... is in no way identical with a critique of them ... even though the insight into some *pudenda origo* certainly brings with it a *feeling* of a diminution in value of the thing that originated thus and prepares the way to a critical mood and attitude to it. (*WP*, 254)

3.2 Genealogy and non-naturalism

One might take *GM* to be a critique of MPS's non-naturalistic assumptions and/or any non-naturalistic interpretations of it. One thing *GM* does is explain morality without the materials peculiar to a Christian world view. Thus in *GM*, Preface, 3, Nietzsche recounts his shift from his adolescent question – concerning the origin of concepts of our good and evil – to his mature, genealogical, reframing of it as the investigation of the conditions under which humans *invented* these concepts. His earlier "theological" answer invoked God, the latter "psychological" approach does not (cf. *EH*, "Why I Write Such Good Books" – conscience is not "the voice of God in man"). One might, therefore, be tempted to infer from this that Nietzsche's *GM* is intended as a critique of the Christian account of the origins of morality. But this is exceedingly unlikely for a number of reasons.

First, Nietzsche is interested in calling into question the values of MPS themselves and not (merely) a Christian account of their origin. There may be *some* connection between the values themselves and accounts of their etiology, but merely denying a "Christian origin" doesn't call those values into question. Second, Christians need not accept the presumption of naturalism, and so it is unlikely that Nietzsche took committed Christian believers to be the intended audience of *GM*.[23] A fundamentalist would part company with Nietzsche at *GM*, Preface, 3, and take our beliefs as God-given. Historical evidence of different patterns of evaluation might be accommodated in a way parallel to Calvin's accommodation of widespread polytheism with our innate monotheistic *sensus divinus*. Our innate mono-theistic sense is liable to corruption, and the religious practice in Greco-Roman times is a manifestation of our natural liability to corruption.[24] Analogously, our innate ascetic morality is liable to corruption by the immoral nobles. A Christian of a different stripe might accept that a naturalistic account of morality is required, but see it as constrained by

---

[23] Cf. Janaway 2007: 7–8. A wavering Christian might of course be affected by *GM*.
[24] See e.g. *Institutes of the Christian Religion*, Book I, chapter 3.

the idea that a condition on the correctness of any account is that it is not inconsistent with Christian belief. That Nietzsche's account is *inconsistent* with Christianity is very different from saying that the Christian has a reason to accept it. In any case, the people he names as targets in *GM* are all atheists: Paul Rée (*GM*, Preface, 4), Schopenhauer (*GM*, Preface, 5), and the English psychologists (*GM*, I, 1). Now, I don't mean to suggest that the cumulative effect of a general naturalizing program might not eventually undermine the belief in God. But it seems that Nietzsche has already assumed the truth of atheism for the purposes of *GM* and so its targets lie elsewhere.

Another, more interesting, sense of "naturalism" in Nietzsche is the sense that his explanations advert to what Williams (1994) calls his "minimalist moral psychology." That is to say, the psychological states and processes to which he appeals – *ressentiment*, the introjection of cruelty – do not, as Williams puts it, have "excess moral content" but can be understood independently, relatively speaking, of the concepts and beliefs which those states are invoked to explain. We don't need to invoke distinct moral properties in order to explain the presence of what are admittedly distinct moral concepts. The promise of an explanation allows us to avoid a crude reduction and reject the claim that the concepts cannot be understood in naturalistic terms.

That such concepts and their associated practices can be so explained also suggests a contingency in them that might not otherwise be evident. One might then claim a demonstration of contingency is itself a critique, because morality presents itself as anything but contingent. But again things are not straightforward, since it is not clear that the values themselves have this modality built into them, rather instead having a modality imposed upon them from philosophical or theological interpretations. Nietzsche complains that in the "science of morals" morality "itself . . . was thought to be 'given'" (*BGE*, 186). But these "intuitions" – the "data" for the theory – are privileged only because "moral philosophers had only a crude knowledge of moral *facta*, selected arbitrarily and abbreviated at random" (*BGE*, 186). Kant's claim that "we have drawn our concept of duty from the ordinary use of our practical reason" (*Groundwork*, Kant 2005: 70) is, for Nietzsche, a moral phenomenology with only a local specificity which does not question that phenomenology or try to "get behind it" and turns this local specificity into a universal and necessary characterization of morality *per se*. It proclaims "I am morality itself and nothing else is moral!" (*BGE*, 202). A genealogy can serve to (a) remove the phenomenology of "givenness" from moral intuitions and (b) the idea that only the sets of "intuitions" within that framework count as moral (and hence "authoritative") and (c) show how such concepts relate to human interests, and are thus contingent upon them. It is certainly plausible to think that *GM* does figure in a criticism of non-naturalistic interpretations such as Kant's. After all, Nietzsche tells us that *GM* is "appended to the recently published *Beyond Good and Evil* as a supplement and clarification," and the explanatory project of *GM* relates to *BGE*, Part V, "On the Natural History of Morals," which discusses what we have just touched upon. The materials of *GM* will be relevant to Kantian conceptions of morality that seek to distance moral judgment from the contingency of interest by building into the notion of moral authority a modality that is independent of those interests.[25] This is not, however, what I see as Nietzsche's central target or central weapon.

3.3 Destabilization and the naturalists

Nietzsche is saying "no" to Rée, Schopenhauer, and the English psychologists. So if Nietzsche's genealogy is calling into question the evaluations shared by that group, there must be something further to be said, since they have little sympathy with non-naturalistic interpretations of morality. Nietzsche recognizes, after all, that some of the "English" are critical of aspects of morality Kant prizes, especially the "myth of free will." But they still fail to "have criticized morality itself" (*GS*, 345).

What they do not question is its central normative component, with its emphasis on altruism and selflessness. They are among those who "have taken the *value* of these 'values' as given, as factual, as beyond all questioning" (*GM*, Preface, 6). "Nobody," he continues, "has had the remotest doubt or hesitation in placing higher value on the 'good man' than on the 'evil'" (*GM*, Preface, 6). Moral reasoning and justification works within a framework structured by these central normative claims, which are the touchstones of MPS. As such, they are relatively impervious to direct confrontation with Nietzsche's alternative set of values. If one is convinced of the central normative authority of selflessness and altruism, objections stemming from alternative evaluative perspectives may simply fail to touch those central evaluative concerns, or may be written off as a non-moral value which is to be trumped by morality. MPS *requires* self-sacrifice, it *demands* it: pointing out that morality is very demanding and may, for example, stifle creativity or bring "higher types" down, need not dent its pretensions. To

---

[25] For a reading of *GM* situating it against Kant's ethics, see Hill 2003.

avoid a mere stand-off between competing conceptions of morality (broadly conceived), *GM* must dislodge the privileged status of these central normative beliefs (and not merely non-naturalistic interpretations of them). Its role, then, in the project of revaluation, is to break the closed circle of moral evaluation by preventing his interlocutors from helping themselves to the central beliefs that frame their normative thinking, and so effect the possibility of a genuine revaluation.

Hence *GM* constitutes "a psychologist's three crucial *preparatory* works for a revaluation of all values" (*EH*, "Why I Write Such Good Books"). Guay, however, writes that it is mistaken to read genealogy as "merely preparatory" (2006: 354). One of the reasons behind this is the assumption that in "preparatory readings" the "influence that genealogy exerts is purely causal, rather than epistemic or normative: genealogy happens to lead us away from defective beliefs" (ibid.). But Nietzsche's explanatory account does have normative consequences. To see why, let us divide genealogies into three general categories, bearing in mind that in giving a successful genealogy one thereby becomes *aware* of the causes of the relevant phenomena. Awareness can be *vindicatory* where knowledge of the causes provides a *reason* to endorse that which is thereby explained. Suppose I find myself with the belief that 1997 was a poor vintage in Bordeaux, and can't remember from whence I got that belief. Looking in my notes I come to learn that I acquired it from Michael Broadbent, a leading authority. The awareness of how I acquired the belief serves to vindicate it. A *neutral* cause is one such that my awareness of it tells me nothing about the belief. A *destabilizing* account involves an awareness of causes of the belief that motivates a requirement to provide further justification for that belief. Suppose I acquired the belief that Michael Atherton played cricket for Lancashire from Fred, but I then come to learn that Fred is a pathological liar who delights in misleading people. In the absence of some other reason in favor of the belief, such knowledge will undermine my confidence in the belief and motivate me to secure some justification for that belief. But the undermining of my confidence is not a merely psychological effect: it is produced by my grasp of the epistemic unreliability of the source.

GM's account is destabilizing.[26] Typically (but not exclusively) the emergence of the beliefs in *GM* involves a good deal of self-deception. Most conspicuous is the falsification effected by the slave revolt, whereby the slaves acquire a set of beliefs about the "rank order of values" which involves a falsification of the prior rank order, and whose intelligibility rests

[26] For similar thoughts see Sinhababu 2007.

on the recognition of the slave's occupying the bottom rank of that order.[27] The creation of deserts free will rests not on any appreciation of epistemic grounds for it, but is rather the upshot of an unconscious strategy to maintain this inversion ("that sublime self-deception [*Selbstbetrügerei*] of . . . [interpreting] weakness itself as freedom" [*GM*, I, 13]). The valorization of the withdrawal patterns of the priest of course requires a good deal of false belief in order for them to gain currency. Now, prescinding from what are admittedly complex issues, what the mechanisms that Nietzsche identifies as productive of the beliefs distinctive of MPS have in common with one another is that they are not sensitive to features relevant to the truth of the belief thus explained, but emerge because they serve the psychological well-being of the believer. The belief that altruism is good, for example, emerges not through an appreciation of evidence in its favor, but because acquiring that belief palliates the discomfort engendered by *ressentiment*. The appeal of a world beyond this one to the ascetic priest is again not a matter of a disinterested appreciation of evidence in its favor, but rather arises because it provides an evaluative rationalization of the "suicidal nihilism" (*GM*, III, 28) of the priest. Knowing that beliefs have such sources destabilizes the beliefs not merely, or indeed, primarily because their explanation is consistent with their falsity but because they emerge regardless of any evidence in their favor, or indeed in the case of *ressentiment*'s operation in the slave revolt, *despite* the presence of what should be evidence to the contrary.

If this is on the right track, then Nietzsche's account of the emergence of the beliefs distinctive of MPS destabilizes the beliefs by uncovering the fact that the mechanisms productive of the beliefs are epistemically unreliable. Knowledge of this fact provides a reason to treat such beliefs with suspicion unless and until some further justification for them is forthcoming. It should be emphasized that it is not at all necessary that the psychological, and epistemically unreliable, mechanisms from which the distinctive evaluative concepts originally emerged, need operate *today*. We acquire the values through immersion in culture and the mechanisms that fix the beliefs that embody them can be epistemically impeccable. In that "evaluative world" there can be reasoning and deliberation that is rationally governed by the norms that are constitutive of the evaluative concepts of MPS. Furthermore, as Nietzsche is fully aware, there can be philosophical

---

[27] Self-deception is vital to the relative success of the slave revolt. Merely consciously pretending that one's status is morally better than the masters' will not have the psychologically comforting effects that *believing* it to be so will have. For a pertinent discussion, see Wallace 2007.

attempts to justify morality. However, what the practices share in common is an assumption of the normative authority of central beliefs such as the moral wrongness of selfishness or the goodness of altruism. These are taken to be "givens" or "data" around which the "science of morals" (*BGE*, 186) is shaped, and so all discussion takes place within that evaluative perspective. Now, even though I acquire this belief without any self-deceptive mechanism, the sins of the ultimate source rebound on me. Suppose I acquire a belief that *p* from Fred, and Fred is no liar, but Fred got it from Mabel, who is. Assuming that Fred merely transmits the beliefs (and doesn't add any justification) I am in just as bad a situation as if Mabel had told me. The beliefs become institutionalized and passed on, but knowledge of their originating causes requires me to justify them rather than just accept them. Dialectically speaking, it cannot therefore be assumed by Nietzsche's naturalistic opponents that, say, selflessness is obviously or unproblematically a value. Nor, given that its emergence depends on a subset of human beings, can it be assumed to be universal in its scope. Given this, MPS's values lose their special authority and grip and become a further set of values to be compared with others in Nietzsche's project of revaluation. They become not moral phenomena, but yet another interpretation of them. This leaves the question of *what* value they have wide open of course: as Nietzsche says, a "morality could even have grown *out of* an error, and the realization of this fact would not as much as touch the problem of its value" (*GS*, 345). But showing such an error invalidates the confidence his fellow naturalists have in the "popular superstition of Christian Europe, which people keep repeating so naively to this day, that what is characteristic of morality is selflessness, self-denial, self-sacrifice, or sympathy and compassion" (*GS*, 345).

4. HISTORY OR FICTION?

As noted, some commentators echo Nehamas's claim that genealogy "simply *is* history correctly practiced." But Nehamas does not expand on what "history correctly practiced" means or whether he intends what *he* understands by correct practice or what *Nietzsche* understood by it. The latter at least involves a critical attitude to the object of inquiry, an attitude he thinks Rée fails to have had, and this opens up Nietzsche's discussion of history in his "Uses and Disadvantages of History for Life." But we also noted that although a historical context and some philological corroboration is sometimes given for some of the claims made in *GM*, the explanation is largely a matter of situating a generic psychology in a plausible social environment from which a new evaluative commitment or phenomena can be seen to emerge. Nietzsche's explanations are constrained and corroborated by what can be ascertained from history – and most conspicuously the difference between the earlier "master" morality and the subsequent rise of "slave" or "Christian" morality – but the main work of *GM* is done by the psychological explanation. As such, *GM* does not offer "history correctly practiced," if by that we understand the methodology of academic history.

The more interesting question is whether Nietzsche understands *wirkliche Historie* as the real or actual account of the emergence of morality – as the German words suggest. Is Nietzsche telling us that this is what really happened? One ground for concern might be the old idea that Nietzsche holds there is no such thing as empirical truth, and, on that ground, we must read *GM* as some kind of "mythology." But this once prominent view of Nietzsche as such a "truth-skeptic" has been decisively refuted and we can leave it behind. Instead we could take *GM*'s "actual history of morality" as an inference to the best explanation. Of course that leaves everything open regarding what kinds of epistemic constraints and criteria govern such explanations. That Nietzsche tells us little on this score, however, doesn't warrant any inference that he intended his explanation to be something other than an attempted best explanation of the emergence of MPS. Hume's explanation of the emergence of religious belief in his 1757 *Natural History of Religion* exhibits many of the features of *GM*. Hume's account is just as Janaway describes *GM*, namely it is to "a large extent psychological," and "not properly localized to times, places or individuals" (2007: 11) and concerns the prehistoric emergence of religious belief for which no firm date can be given. And, as an early foray into naturalistic accounts of religious belief the account is wanting in discussions of the epistemic constraints that must govern such explanations. For all that, Hume transparently thinks his account is *true*.[28]

However, Bernard Williams's recent work of genealogy[29] suggests an alternative concept of genealogy as something that can be explicitly fictional in nature. For him, genealogy is a fictional developmental story which "represents a new reason for action as being developed in a simplified situation as a function of motives, reactions, psychological processes which we have reason to acknowledge already" (2000: 156). This fictional

---

[28] For a discussion see my 2007, and in connection with Nietzsche see Craig 2007 and my 2009.

[29] Williams 2000 and 2002. For good discussions, both of which I am indebted to, see Owen 2007: 138–44, and Craig 2007. Williams also allows that there are historical or non-fictional genealogies too (Williams 2002: 20).

account then shows how such a seemingly distinct area of thought can be made "intelligible" (2002: 36) in terms of those other states. Then the question is whether we "could, if we knew such a story to be true, go on giving the derived value the respect we do" (2000: 160). A vindicatory genealogy would allow us to do so, a debunking genealogy would presumably prevent us. That is to say, the emergence story is one that is either compatible with our continued faith in the value, or incompatible with it.

Williams's views, though independently interesting, are nevertheless puzzling when placed in the context of Nietzsche's account. One key source of puzzlement is the fact that Williams also uses the term "state of nature" in this connection, of which Hobbes is the paradigmatic exponent. Hobbes's attempt to legitimate the state does seem to exhibit something like Williams's idea. Hobbes's account has the force it does because the story dramatizes what life would be like without the sovereign, and through this it renders salient to the reader normative considerations, based on the supposition that they have certain motives. The connection between those motives and the present regime, and in particular the way that the latter can intelligibly be seen to serve the former, gives a reason to obey the sovereign. So it can reinforce one's faith in allegiance to the state by showing the function that value serves. Williams views Hume's account of justice (which does attract the term "genealogy") in this light, and I remain unconvinced that Williams is right about Hume. But whatever the truth might be on that score, it is very implausible with respect to Nietzsche. One reason to be skeptical is that the explanations Nietzsche offers do not have as unproblematic a reason-giving relationship as do those of Hobbes. The relation between the states of mind and the conditions that produce the slave revolt is not simply a matter of showing that it is practically rational for the slaves to do such and such, given such and such circumstances. That is because what is done by the slaves is an unconscious invention of a set of evaluative beliefs which *falsify* their objects (*GM*, I, 10). The revenge is an imaginary one inasmuch as the psychological discomfort is relieved via a comforting set of false beliefs about the evaluative order. Now, quite how this trick is supposed to be pulled is a matter of some delicacy but, as I said, first, its relation to means–end reasoning is hardly perspicuous. Second, what results is not "a new reason for action" but a set of values which constitute the framework within which moral reasons function. Third, other features of Nietzsche's account – such as the forced internalization of cruelty – seem impossible to conceive of in Williams's way. Williams is aware of some of the ways in which Nietzsche's account in *GM* differs from his official characterization of genealogy (see e.g. Williams 2002: 35–38). He acknowledges that

Nietzsche's own genealogy is intended as partly historical, and further, that the psychological process identified by Nietzsche must be unconscious, and that those within that pattern of evaluation will be resistant to acknowledging the explanation Nietzsche advances. He also holds that Nietzsche's account is intended to serve some critical ends. But on the face of it, this last point makes it very difficult to see Nietzsche's genealogy as anything other than that which he represents it to be, namely the real history of morality. For, in order to have any critical impact that extends beyond the rhetorical or dramatic, there must be something more than a mere fictional account of how such valuations *could* have arisen. It is open to the agent to say that morality could serve those ends, but, in fact, it doesn't, and find nothing disturbing in the story. It has to be at least a genuine possibility that this was in fact how morality emerged, or, stronger, that this is really how morality did emerge. For while Hobbes's story does serve to render salient, or indeed provide, a reason for allegiance to the state by showing how that institution *is* fit to serve the ends the agent has, Nietzsche's account taken as fictional does nothing to shift the idea that morality is anything other than it seems to be – it merely says that it *could* serve other ends. I suspect what is really doing the work for Williams is that once we acknowledge that we *do* have the psychological states that figure in Nietzsche's explanation – which I take it is what Williams intends by "motives, reactions, psychological processes which we have reason to acknowledge already" (2000: 156) – there is now a real or live possibility that in *fact* this was indeed what produced the emergence of morality. If this is correct, then I think the term "fictional" is unhelpful. Instead, I think *conjectural* might be better here, since it carries with it connotations of the possibility of a *genuinely* correct explanation which the notion of "fiction" does not.[30,31]

---

[30] See also Owen 2007: 138–44.

[31] Some of the ideas herein were tried out at Oxford, Cambridge, Southampton, and Chicago. Particular thanks to Simon May, Chris Janaway, David Owen, Simon Robertson, Manuel Dries, Brian Leiter, Guy Elgat, Vid Simoniti, Alec Hinshelwood, Jakob Reckhenrich, and Claire Kirwin. Other thanks to S. M. S. Pearsall and E. M. P. Kail.

The promising animal: the art of reading On the Genealogy of Morality *as testimony*

Stephen Mulhall

(1) GETTING UNDERWAY

We are unknown to ourselves, we knowers, we ourselves, to ourselves, and there is a good reason for this. We have never looked for ourselves – so how are we ever supposed to *find* ourselves? How right is the saying: "Where your treasure is, there will your heart be also"; *our* treasure is where the hives of our knowledge are. As born winged-insects and intellectual honey-gatherers we are constantly underway towards them, concerned at heart with only one thing – to "bring something home" . . .

We remain necessarily strangers to ourselves, we do not understand ourselves, we *must* confusedly mistake who we are, the motto "everyone is furthest from himself" applies to us forever – we are not "knowers" when it comes to ourselves . . . (*GM*, Preface, 1)[1]

Why are we knowers not only unknown to ourselves (as Nietzsche begins by claiming) but necessarily so self-estranged (as he finds himself insisting by the end of this opening section of his preface)? Why *must* we be confused or mistaken over who we are? If the problem were just that we have never hitherto looked for ourselves, then it would be easily solved: we could simply start looking, and thereby overcome our ignorance of ourselves. But how would born intellectual honey-gatherers go about such a task? They would think of it – as they think of all knowledge – as something that is to be gathered or collected, something to be brought home. But then seeking to know ourselves would require us to regard ourselves as essentially capable of being brought home, hence as presently (and perhaps forever) not-at-home to ourselves; to gather knowledge of ourselves, we must first be willing to conceive of ourselves as necessarily self-estranged or self-distanced.

---

[1] *On the Genealogy of Morality*, trans. C. Diethe (1994) – hereafter *GM*: translation modified on occasion. I have also used *Thus Spoke Zarathustra*, trans. R. J. Hollingdale (1969).

So if Nietzsche thinks that we knowers are condemned to misunderstand ourselves, that must be because he thinks we are condemned to resist any understanding of ourselves as in need of gathering or collection, hence as dispersed or disseminated or internally differentiated, call it non-self-identical. What makes it impossible for us to achieve self-knowledge is thus the depth of our commitment to a conception of ourselves as always already at-home to ourselves – as self-identical, hence essentially transparent to ourselves (both from moment to moment – no sooner thinking something than knowing that we do – and with respect to our essence, which is of course thinking). We are essentially unknown to ourselves because we persist in regarding ourselves as essentially known; we will never look for ourselves because we think we have always already found ourselves, and have done so without ever really having to look. For when all is said and done, what there is to know about ourselves – the full depth and extent of our nature – is that we are knowers, essentially cognitive creatures, born collectors.

And yet the very conditions of our lives as intellectual honey-gatherers declare the underlying truth of our condition to be otherwise – to be in fact exactly as our conception of (self-)knowledge as gatherable would expect. For as such gatherers, we are constantly making towards the hives of our knowledge, hence always returning from journeying away from those homes, and so never actually residing in them: we are, in short, always on the way to or from home but never at home – always not-at-home. And if knowledge is a phenomenon of the hive, to which we make one essential contribution (even if not the one Nietzsche's words attribute to us, since what foraging bees gather is not honey but pollen, honey's raw material), then the honey of knowledge is not merely essentially collectable, its emergence or creation is also essentially collective – an achievement of the group and its dynamic hierarchies and divisions of labor. And the point of this shared enterprise is not the piling up of treasure as an end in itself, but the production of something useful to the survival and reproduction of the group. So if our treasure really is where our heart is, and our heart is with the hive, then our heart is itself dispersed or disseminated, residing essentially outside ourselves, something in relation to which we are always either no longer or not yet there.

One might, however, ask whether the hearts of such intellectual honey-gatherers really can be in the hive; more precisely, one might ask exactly what it is that such honey-gatherers really treasure. Is it the knowledge, or the gathering of it, that they value most – the collection or the collecting? If these winged creatures of cognition really treasured the collection above the collecting, why would they never stay with the collection but rather dedicate themselves to the unending task of enhancing it, which inevitably means maintaining their distance from it in order to look for (more of) it? Such a creature is either mistaking the means for the end, and so mislocating her treasure and her heart; or else she truly prefers seeking knowledge to having it, and so treasures being under way above being home. More exactly, her form of life suggests that her true home is to be found, is indeed a matter of her being, underway – that her creaturely essence lies in seeking or voyaging. She is, after all, a winged thing.

This does not exactly mean that we are wrong to think of ourselves as knowers (since the term captures the process of collecting as naturally as it does the product). Perhaps one should rather say that it reveals us as not really understanding what it means to say this of ourselves – that the true significance of that self-description is not something we have as yet brought home to ourselves, or allowed ourselves to be struck by, something we have not yet properly experienced. And indeed, in the portion of the first section of his preface that we have so far passed over (the sentences connecting the two paragraphs I began by quoting), Nietzsche connects our confusion about knowing to a certain estrangement from our own experiences:

> As far as the rest of life is concerned, the so-called "experiences" – who of us ever has enough seriousness for them? or enough time? I fear we have never really been "with it" in such matters, our heart is simply not in it – and not even our ear! On the contrary, like somebody divinely absent-minded and sunk in his own thoughts who, the twelve strokes of midday having just boomed into his ears, wakes with a start and wonders "What hour struck?," sometimes we, too, *afterwards* rub our ears and ask, astonished, taken aback, "What did we actually experience then?" or even "Who *are* we, in fact?" and afterwards, as I said, we count all twelve reverberating strokes of our experience, of our life, of our being – oh! And lose count . . . (*GM*, Preface, 1)

It is the human being immersed in his own thoughts, apparently at one with his mind, who is in truth absent-minded, because he is in fact lost to his experiences, incapable of being struck by them even when they boom into his ear. If one is seriously to experience each reverberating stroke of the world's impact, one must count them or rather recount them – think of this as taking the time to provide a recounting. So being present to my experiences is a matter of first suffering their impress, and then offering an account of them: the fulfillment of any impression lies in its expression, and thus requires a capacity and willingness on my part to make that impression other to me, to actively distance myself from it in time and thereby allow it to re-verberate – that is, to re-appear in verbal form, to find words for it for which I am willing to be accountable, and thereby to take responsibility for my own experiences, in the absence of which my experiences, and so my life and my being, will remain absent or lost to me, something in which I am simply immersed or sunk.

Properly recounting our conception of "experience" thus reveals two things about ourselves as beings possessed of an inner world or interior life as well as a place in nature, call it genuine subjectivity: we are necessarily capable of distancing ourselves from ourselves – call it taking a perspective on our experience; and this capacity is inseparable from a capacity to articulate our experiences – which means both finding words for them and taking responsibility for doing so in the sight (or rather the hearing) of others, call it contributing to the collectivity of speech. It follows that properly to know ourselves as knowers – no longer being simply immersed or sunk in my being as a knower but genuinely experiencing what it means to be a man or woman of knowledge – will involve distancing ourselves from that state, getting underway on a journey or transition from it to whatever state lying beyond it allows us to gain perspective on it by providing a recounting of it. Only those who no longer wholly inhabit that mode of being can properly bring it home to themselves as it really is, or rather was.

Those who are (still, presently) knowers cannot, therefore, seriously understand themselves as such – they cannot mean or take responsibility for describing themselves as "knowers" (since they are confused about what it means to do so); and they would also (equally mistakenly) reject any description of themselves as knowers who are unknown to themselves. Conversely, anyone who is in a position not only to say but to mean (to be genuinely accountable for saying) that she is a knower who is unknown to herself will not say so, for she must no longer be (purely or simply or wholly) a knower, and hence would, in so describing herself, misdescribe her current self in terms appropriate to her past self, the self from which she has departed.

From what perspective, then, could anyone advance the claim that "We are unknown to ourselves, we knowers . . ."? The problem here is one of time, or say tense: using the present tense seriously in such a self-description appears to be either beyond us or behind us, depending on whether we truly remain self-unknown knowers or have gone beyond that state or condition. Or one might say that it is a problem of pronouns or persons: someone who is no longer a self-ignorant knower might coherently describe those who remain so in such terms, but then the third-person or the second-person would be the appropriate mode of address – and yet this speaker talks not of "they" or "you" but of "we" (that is, him and us, the author and his readers) being knowers who are unknown to ourselves. But if either he or we really were unknown knowers, then he would not say so – because he would regard it as either false, or a point not worth making (since anyone to whom it applied would reject it, as if it were mere booming in their ears).

Suppose, however, that our author has therapeutic designs on us; then it might be essential to his purpose to speak as if from an impossible perspective or subject position. For what he says presupposes that we are simultaneously both self-ignorant knowers, and beings who no longer inhabit that mode of being; and that presupposition would in a sense be valid if we were underway from the former state to the latter – that is, inherently between states, transitional, becoming, but also inherently between just those two states, beings whose aspiration to go beyond the condition of self-ignorant knowing was engendered and oriented by some aspect of that condition. If that were the case, then we would be in (an internal relation to) both states: we would be moving away from the first and towards the second, and the latter precisely because of the former. And what, after all, is more calculated to stimulate a knower's energies than the insinuation that her knowledge is not only somehow deficient, but is so with respect to the one domain of her knowledge that she has hitherto assumed to be beyond doubt – her knowledge of herself?

The real point of saying something to us whose apparent point presupposes that we are simultaneously both self-ignorant and becoming otherwise is thus not that Nietzsche thinks that that presupposition currently holds true of us, his readers; it is that he hopes thereby to encourage us to *make* it true. For if our commitment to knowing does drive us to figure out this presupposition of Nietzsche's address, then in so doing we will come to realize not only that he apparently believes that our relation to ourselves might be other than it currently is, but also that only someone who was already underway in just that sense – already effecting this transformation in his own case – could have attained the perspective from which to offer such encouragement. If Nietzsche can do it, and if, having done it, he addresses us in a way which identifies himself with us, quite as if – as far as he can see – he is essentially indistinguishable from us in the relevant respects, then why can't we? And then we might find ourselves realizing that simply to be so encouraged is in fact already to go beyond our initial condition of self-ignorant knowing, because it involves at least imagining things to be otherwise than they appear to be, realizing that what seems necessary may not in fact be so. And we might further appreciate that the willingness to offer such encouragement constitutes one way in which another might take responsibility for their own experience of self-overcoming, by finding words for it which he can give to those most in need of them – his fellow intellectual honey-gatherers whose winged nature is currently unknown but nevertheless essentially knowable to them, if they can only find the time and the seriousness properly to bring their current mode of being home to themselves.

(2) THE KINGFISHER AND THE FISHER KING

As if to confirm his claim to be underway or transitional, the remainder of Nietzsche's preface presents a select autobiography of his writing life as first on the way to knowing, and then on the way beyond it – strokes of the pen recounting strokes of the clock. The two most distant markers of this process are his adolescent suspicions of God's relation to evil, and his adult interrogations of Schopenhauer's nihilistic morality of compassion (begun at least by the time of *Untimely Meditations*, and renewed in every text thereafter, but still apparently in need of reenactment). It is perhaps particularly worth noting the ways in which Nietzsche takes the first of these ventures as prophetic with respect to his current one, as having sounded notes to which his later ear simply becomes more thoroughly attuned. For his thirteen-year-old self was concerned with the origin of evil, and "gave God the credit for it, making him the *father* of evil" (*GM*, Preface, 3). And that last phrase not only assigns to God one of the traditional titles of the Devil; it also puts into play the fateful image of God as creditor to which the second essay will return, as well as (via the idea of metaphysical paternity) giving a material or literal inflection to the notion of genealogical descent to which all three of his present essays give a cultural and historical inflection, just as they transpose his ontological query about evil into a linguistic or etymological one (about the origin of "evil"). The implication seems clear: a deeper understanding of what is at stake in these issues requires no shift of focus, but rather a transfiguration of method – from the material mode to that of language and form of life, the medium in which (as the first section of the preface suggests) the distinctively human animal fundamentally finds itself, and loses itself.

Two other such signposts are, however, both more proximate and more immediately significant. The first is the 1878 edition of *Human, All Too Human*, which coincided with Nietzsche's brief perception of Paul Rée's work on *The Origin of Moral Sentiments* as that of a companion free spirit (a member of the company to which *HAH* dedicates itself in its subtitle). Some commentators have been skeptical of Nietzsche's claim that, even then, his views and Rée's were significantly divergent; and one could certainly have hoped to see a more nuanced presentation of Rée's book than as straightforwardly "contradictory and antithetical" to Nietzsche's own 1878 text (cf. *GM*, Preface, 4). But as I have argued elsewhere,[2] *Human, All Too Human* is itself far less straightforward an endorsement of the merits of scientific naturalism than many commentators assume; so Nietzsche's claim that the essays of the *Genealogy* ought to be viewed as expressing "mainly the same thoughts" as *Human, All Too Human*, only "riper, brighter, stronger and more perfect" (*GM*, Preface, 2), posits a degree of continuity between these two stages of his career that is worth taking seriously.

Doing so need involve no discounting of the weight Nietzsche also assigns to the degree of discontinuity – most clearly when he talks of "a *fundamental will* to knowledge deep inside me which took control, speaking more and more clearly and making ever clearer demands" (*GM*, Preface, 2). This description of himself as a man of knowledge, so swiftly after identifying such men as his current target of critical evaluation, hardly suggests an unwillingness for self-criticism. So when he takes Rée to task for being an English genealogist, it is worth remembering that he also presents the process of saying "no" to each of Rée's propositions as not only internal to the composition of *Human, All Too Human*, but also as his way of "bringing to the light of day those hypotheses on descent to which these essays are devoted" (*GM*, Preface, 4); in this sense, Rée's apparently absolute otherness was and is internal to Nietzsche's own progress, a way of being a man of knowledge which Nietzsche insists upon rejecting precisely because remaining within it was a live option for him. Perhaps this is why, whereas in *Human, All Too Human* the wandering free spirit is figured in conclusion as suspended between the tenth and twelfth strokes of the midday clock, the critic of knowledge is envisaged at the outset of his labors as being properly awake to all twelve strokes. Each is listening to the same clock at the onset of midday (and thus is to be distinguished from the likes of Justice Shallow, whose recollection of the chimes at midnight expresses a nostalgia for gaiety long lost); but the genealogist is – shall we say – fractionally more advanced or untimely, being in a position to recount additional strokes of time's passage through the forenoon.

The second, even more proximate, signpost appears only in the final section of the preface, when Nietzsche is attempting to account for the difficulty of understanding his present book.

---

[2] "Fetters, Shadows and Circles: Freedom and Form in *Human, All too Human*," unpublished.

With regard to my *Zarathustra*, for example, I do not acknowledge anyone as an expert on it if he has not, at some time, been both profoundly wounded and profoundly delighted by it, for only then may he enjoy the privilege of sharing, with due reverence, the halcyon element from which the book was born and its sunny brightness, spaciousness, breadth and certainty. In other cases, the aphoristic form causes difficulty: this is because this form is *not taken seriously enough these days*. An aphorism properly stamped and moulded [coined and cast], has not been "deciphered" just because it has been read through; on the contrary, this is just the beginning of its proper *interpretation*, and for this, an art of interpretation is needed. In the third essay of this book I have given an example of what I mean by "interpretation" in such a case: – this treatise is a commentary on the aphorism that precedes it. I admit that you need one thing above all in order to practise the requisite *art* of reading, a thing which today people have been so good at forgetting – and so it will be some time before my writings are "readable" –, you almost need to be a cow for this one thing and certainly *not* a "modern man": it is *rumination* . . . (*GM*, Preface, 8)

Although Nietzsche here appears to distinguish the case of *Thus Spoke Zarathustra* (completed two years earlier) from those "other cases" in which the aphoristic form of his writing is the source of its difficulty, he also conjoins the two, by choosing as his epigraph to the third essay a sentence from *Zarathustra* which is not only aphoristic in form but derives from a section of that book that (like most of its other transcriptions of Zarathustra's discourses) is composed almost wholly of aphorisms, and furthermore is entitled "Of Reading and Writing":

Carefree, scornful, outrageous – that is how wisdom wants us to be; she is a woman, and never loves anyone but a warrior. (*Z*, I, 7, p. 68)

No doubt in part because of this conjunction, many commentators have tended to assume that this epigraph is the preceding aphorism upon which the third essay is a commentary. More recently, it has been argued that the relevant aphorism is rather to be found in (or consists of) the first section of that essay, which was in fact added to the essay at the last moment, at which point Nietzsche also added to his preface the final section that explicitly adverts to it:

What do ascetic ideals mean? – With artists, nothing or too many different things; with philosophers and scholars, something like a nose and sense for the most favourable conditions of higher intellectuality; with women, at most, one *more* seductive charm, a little *morbidezza* on fair flesh, the angelic expression on a pretty, plump animal; with physiological causalities and the disgruntled (with the *majority* of mortals), an attempt to see themselves as "too good" for this world, a saintly form of debauchery, their chief weapon in the battle against long-drawn-out pain and boredom; with priests, the actual priestly faith, their best instrument of power; with saints, an excuse to hibernate at last, their *novissima gloriae cupido*, their rest in nothingness ("God"), their form of madness. *That* the ascetic ideal has meant so much to man reveals a basic fact of human will, its *horror vacui*; *it needs an aim –*, and it prefers to will *nothingness* rather than *not* will. – Do I make myself understood? . . . Have I made myself understood? . . . "*Absolutely not, sir*" – So let us start at the beginning. (*GM*, III, 1)

Christopher Janaway (2007) has made perhaps the most extensive and convincing case for taking the climactic remark that we "prefer to will nothingness rather than not will" as the aphorism Nietzsche really had in mind, with the preceding list of domains in which the ascetic ideal shows up functioning as, in effect, a contents list for the long and involved essay that follows, with each item on that list being ruminated upon – chewed over long and hard, swallowed and multiply digested – by some specific subsequent section or sequence of sections.[3] And he is careful to point out that accepting his hypothesis need not prevent us from cleaving to the thought that relating the epigraph to the essay remains relevant to the business of the latter's proper interpretation: "It is conventional for such epigraphs to be pregnant and oracular, putting the reader temporarily off balance, gesturing away from the work they preface, creating a tension within it, or providing an indefinitely large space for associations" (2007: 177–78). More specifically, for instance, Janaway points out that the epigraph lies immediately adjacent to the concluding gesture of the second essay, which silences its own invocation of a man to come who might redeem us from the ascetic ideal, on the grounds that it risks appropriating to itself something "to which *Zarathustra* alone is entitled" (*GM*, II, 25). Such connections can be recognized and exploited, Janaway suggests, "without forcing the [essay] into the uncomfortable mould of 'commentary' upon it" (2007: 180).

My concern is to exploit the associative field between epigraph and essay by relating both to the specific ways in which the final section of the preface first invokes Zarathustra. So doing will not bring this reading into conflict with Janaway's general interpretive claims: indeed, it will allow us to identify certain important tensions between epigraph and essay that become more rather than less apparent if we accept Janaway's picture of its first section as listing the essay's forthcoming sequence of particular cases.

We are told in the preface that only someone who has been profoundly wounded and profoundly delighted by *Zarathustra* can share the halcyon element from which the book was born, and thereby claim expertise in relation to it. "Halcyon" is originally a name for the kingfisher, a bird said by

---

[3] See chapter 10.

the ancients to breed in a nest floating on the sea around the time of the winter solstice, and to charm the wind and waves so that the sea was calm for this purpose: hence, by extension, the phrase "halcyon days" refers to a period of calm weather, idyllic happiness, or prosperity. This already gives us good reason to prefer Hollingdale's translation of the epigraph's third specification of how wisdom wants us to be as "outrageous" rather than (as, say, Diethe has it) "violent." More importantly, it entails that Nietzsche's reference to *Zarathustra* as having been born is no accident: the halcyon element is that of breeding and birth, and more specifically (given its affinity for the winter solstice, and its capacity to calm the waves) of a birth that amounts to an alternative incarnation of divinity.

If the kingfisher represents Christ, then the Fisher King is not far away – the last in the mythological line of guardians of the Holy Grail, the ruler whose wounded groin not only immobilizes him but figures the decline of his realm into sterility, until both he and it are healed by one of Arthur's knights, Sir Percival, and the grail recovered. Little wonder, then, that Nietzsche's discussion of the ascetic ideal in art focuses on Wagner's late opera *Parsifal*, which recounts exactly this Christian story, but in accents of utter seriousness that lead Nietzsche to wish that its creator meant it to be a parody of tragic religiosity, rather than an exemplary incarnation of the ascetic wasteland in which Nietzsche himself now wanders, fishing for vitality and finding only ruination, seeking a warrior to heal life's pervasive woundedness, a kingfisher for the true descendant of the Fisher King.

This intimate contestation of the example of *Parsifal* confirms what the preface already declares – namely that on Nietzsche's understanding of this redemptive matter, the cure for woundedness lies in woundedness. More specifically, just as the Fisher King's recovery of a world in which enjoyment might once again be taken is effected by a spear's insertion into the wound it aspires to heal, so rebirth from the wound of asceticism involves suffering a more profound wounding from which comes the taking of a more profound delight – undergoing the enjoyable injury of Zarathustra's words. If Zarathustra's readers are thus Fisher Kings to his Sir Percival, then Nietzsche's citation of Zarathustra's words on reading and writing as at once displacing and propelling his own (as a mode of utterance to which the second essay reaches out only for the third essay to reach beyond) suggests that he has internalized their thrust. His current writing appears as the outcome of his reading even his most proximate earlier writing as if it had been composed by another, thereby becoming the Sir Percival to his own Fisher King – once again taking his bearings from his prior state or condition. Revitalizing this wasteland will thus involve overcoming the wasteland in oneself by going through it, intensifying the wound in order that it might fructify, transcending asceticism by means of asceticism. The first step in so doing is coming to see that one's current circumstances really have been laid waste by such asceticism – in fields and in ways that one might never have suspected of harboring such sterility; and the second is to admit the extent to which that sterility is constitutive of one's own present state.

This is why Nietzsche stresses in the first section of the third essay that the ascetic ideal has "meant so much to man": by this he certainly means that its meaning has gone deep with us, but he equally certainly means that it has taken on so many different guises and inflections – not only in religion and ethics, but in art, in science, and in philosophy. The ascetic ideal is most clearly recognizable as a morality of compassion and pity, of self-sacrifice and self-denial, of life-denial and self-hatred; but it turns out to be not so much an ethics as an ethos – a mode of evaluation that is equally capable of structuring one's impressions and articulations of art and the artist (as in Wagner's late, decadent turn towards Christianity), of science (with its practitioners' willingness to sacrifice themselves to the pursuit of the under-lying truth about reality, and thereby to the diremption of the world of appearance, perception, and affect from that of a reality comprehensible only by means of the timeless categories of mathematics), and of philosophy (with its association of knowledge with virtue, its commitment to the ultimate intelligibility of the real, its preference for Being over Becoming, and its own version of our all-consuming love for truth). To understand the will to truth as an expression of the ascetic ideal is to understand that morality is never just a matter of moral evaluation: there is no corner of human culture whose form and content cannot incarnate an ethical stance and system of values. Morality is thus not so much a sector of human life as a dimension of it. The Enlightenment vision of the autonomy of morality from religion, politics, science, and art in fact functions as a way of occlud-ing the moral dimension of art and science, and thus of overlooking the true reach of the religious values it aspired to transcend.

More specifically, however, acknowledging the ascetic roots of the will to truth means recognizing the ascetic dimension of philosophy; it means recognizing the extent to which that wound is carried even by one who aspires to wage war against it – precisely because the banner under which that war is waged is the desire to discover the truth about morality, and so about its offshoot the will to truth. Nietzsche incarnates the will to truth's ultimate perversion – its turning upon itself; the truth about truth includes acknowledging that men and women of knowledge are ignorant of the extent to which their own enterprise, and hence their own identity, is marked by the ascetic ideal itself. Fully to diagnose the problem involves seeing that the diagnosticians constitute part of that problem; any serious polemic against asceticism must accordingly become a form of self-criticism – it must commit one to suffering an intensification of one's woundedness, by making that woundedness into the instrument of its own deepening. It is not just a matter of becoming the Sir Percival to one's own Fisher King; it is also a matter of recognizing this Sir Percival as the Fisher King's progeny, as another mask or manifestation of the king himself.

What, however, of the delight that is supposed to go together with this woundedness? It can only derive from the hope that the self-wounding turn of our inner woundedness will take us beyond that mode of self-injury. But the term "delight" turns a particular facet of its meaning towards the light, in the context in which Nietzsche here sets it – a context in which the preface's halcyon element symbolizes birth, the epigraph of the third essay specifies a warrior's way of satisfying wisdom's womanly desires, and the first section of the third essay talks of the seductive charm of fair female flesh. The deeper organizing idea here is that of "woman," and so of "delight" understood as female "delectation, allure, charm." One should certainly not take Nietzsche's detection of a "little *morbidezza*" on that fair flesh to be expressive solely of scornfulness or contempt: as a term of art, *morbidezza* originally referred to ways of painting human flesh so as to capture its lifelike delicacy, before it acquired connotations of sickliness and decay; and we have anyway already established that healing and new life are to be found in injury, in the vulnerability of living flesh, if they are to be found at all. What is rather more striking is the way in which these prefatory and epigraphic registrations of Zarathustra's inwardness with femaleness highlight the presence of "woman" in the third essay's initial list of contents; for in truth, that item is the only one of the seven types that Janaway distinguishes to receive next to no detailed, ruminative analysis in the essay itself. Janaway refers us to section 14, alone among the subsequent twenty-seven sections, as having any bearing on that type; but that section contains just two sentences in which women are invoked – more precisely, two sentences in which the sick woman is presented as a tyrannical extreme version of another general type, that of modern human weakness or debility. Since every other type or category announced in the first section receives extended and elaborate consideration, why is that of "woman" barely registered?

My intuition is that "woman" is nowhere to be found in the essay because she is everywhere in it; but such omnipresence might be realized in two different ways. The first possibility is that the category of "woman" is given no specific analysis because every category that is so analyzed can be regarded as an inflection of it. The implication of Nietzsche's omission would then be that the ascetic formations of morality, religion, art, science, scholarship, and philosophy are individual variations on the angelic expression that the plump, well-fed human animal likes to adopt for itself, each one way of giving vulnerable, bovine, self-interested flesh a tint of delicacy, a species of seductive charm, and ultimately the possibility of overcoming the perversity it incarnates through a certain, generative radicalization of that very perversity. But there is also a second possibility: that the category of "woman" is given no specific analysis because every specific analysis in that essay is conducted from a female point of view – from the viewpoint of a self-aware wisdom who actively encourages the outrageousness of the warrior she recognizes as her intimate other, her twin self, desirous above all of the impulse to exceed oneself, to go beyond, to be extravagant in the way that the word "outrage" connotes (and that Zarathustra's imaginative inhabitation of a perspective in which he can "see myself under myself" [Z, I, 7, "Of Reading and Writing," p. 69] prophesies).

Such intercourse between male and female allows wisdom to combine woundedness with delight in a manner that promises to bear new fruit, of a kind that might charm waves into placidity and infuse the wasteland with bright, breeding light. This would (in turns of phrase at work in Zarathustra's discourse "Of Reading and Writing") be the divine birth of a writer who writes in blood (say, out of, and about, genealogy), and whose relation to his readers goes beyond merely knowing them, to embodying the desire to stimulate their desire to exalt themselves (as wisdom seeks to stimulate her warrior self). He does so by declaring that, although he is currently looking down at them, in so doing he sees himself under himself; in other words, their current lack of exaltation is one he previously shared, and he attained his current exaltation solely by a process of self-mastery or self-overcoming – first aspiring to something higher, and then ascending to it on the stepping stone(s) of his earlier self, through a self-abasement that disclosed and emancipated a divine, dancing wisdom that was always already within him.

(3) GIVING NAMES AND MAKING WORDS

If the structure of the third essay is explicitly declared to exemplify the correct, ruminative way to read a Nietzschean aphoristic text, it might be worth taking seriously the possibility that the other two essays that make up the *Genealogy* exemplify the same structure, and hence aspire to suffer the same interpretive practice, the same art of reading. If so, we should expect to find each to begin with (if not an aphoristic remark then) a claim that initially poses some kind of challenge to the understanding, and the remainder of the essay to constitute an elaborate unfolding of the signifi-cance it incarnates. And insofar as each preceding essay contributes to our understanding of the nature of the wound that the ascetic ideal has delivered to the human animal, then each thereby enhances our understanding of what it means for Nietzsche to identify all knowers, and hence himself, as animals whose essence derives from their ways of bearing that wound.

Suppose we approach the first essay, "Good and Evil, Good and Bad," on the basis of that assumption. Then we find ourselves presented in its first section with not so much an aphorism as a riddle in human form:

– These English psychologists, who have to be thanked for having made the only attempts so far to write a history of the emergence of morality – provide us with a small riddle in the form of themselves; in fact, I admit that as living riddles they have a significant advantage over their books – *they are actually interesting!* These English psychologists – just what do they want? You always find them at the same task, whether they want to or not, pushing the *partie honteuse* of our inner world to the foreground, and looking for what is really effective, guiding and decisive for our development where man's intellectual pride would least wish to find it (for example, in the *vis inertia* of habit, or in forgetfulness, or in a blind and random coupling of ideas, or in something purely passive, automatic, reflexive, molecular and thoroughly stupid) – what is it that actually drives these psychologists in precisely *this* direction all the time? (*GM*, I, 1)

Nietzsche canvasses two possible solutions to his riddle: either these psychologists manifest some combination of malicious anti-humanism, disillusioned idealism, anti-Christianity, and a lewd need for the thrill of self-debasement, or they manifest the bravery of "generous and proud animals, who know how to control their own pleasure and pain and have been taught to sacrifice desirability to truth . . . even a plain, bitter, ugly, foul, unchristian, immoral truth . . . Because there are such truths. –" (*GM*, I, 1). Nietzsche declares that, although he has been told that they are, in reality, "old, cold, boring frogs" who have transformed the inner life of man into a swamp simply because that is the element in which they are most at home, he is not only resistant to hearing this, he refuses to believe it: "if it is permissible to wish where it is impossible to know, I sincerely hope that the reverse is true" (*GM*, I, 1). In other words, he wants to respect these analysts holding a microscope to the human soul, by thinking of them as possessed of a presiding good spirit – the spirit of scientific endeavor.

Even if we aren't yet in a position to recognize that good spirit as the will to truth, and thus as an extreme expression of the ascetic ideal, the related ironies at work in this passage are hard to miss. To begin with, the first solution to his riddle assigns to the English psychologists exactly the range of predicates which his own, coming genealogical analysis will invite from its initially resistant readers; so by presenting himself as rejecting that first solution in favor of interpreting these English psychologists in the apparently more flattering terms offered by the second (terms that he will later claim for his own work), Nietzsche enacts a certain kind of identification with the riddling object of his interest. They are, he hopes, no more frogs than he is; they are, he would like to believe, animals as brave, generous, and proud as he takes himself to be: this is why such hoping is also the fulfillment of a wish. But if it is barely permissible to have these hopes for others (whose real motivation is presented as somehow beyond his knowledge, presumably because the riddle their existence poses finds no expression in their essentially uninteresting texts), is it more or less permissible to hope as much for one's own project? Is it a realistic hope, or mere wish-fulfillment? And is it in the end permissible to substitute hoping and wishing for knowing – quite as if pure or mere cognition articulates itself on ground to which the claims of desire and the projections of hope also stake a claim (so that truth is entangled with goodness, and the present with the future, and the former pair with the latter)?

We will have to return to this last question; but the earlier ones are here more pressing. One might at first think that knowing one's own motives and attitudes cannot be a challenge (at least not in the way that knowing the motives of another may be), and so conclude that such hopes are rather better grounded in one's own case – except that the preface has just told us that knowers are unknown to themselves, and Nietzsche is articulating these displaced hopes at the very outset of his project, when it is (surely?) impossible to know its fruits (whether immediate or ultimate), and hence its nature.

One might, accordingly, conclude that, when Nietzsche asks "What do these English psychologists want?," he is also asking (and so inviting us to ask) "What do I want?" (thereby reinforcing, for those of his current readers familiar with Freud's analogous and [in]famous question, the idea of his identification with the female perspective). He is expressing an anxiety about what will turn out to be the correct solution to the riddle posed by his own existence; and in so doing, he declares at once an indebtedness to the English psychologists and a desire to resist a possible fate or threat that they also embody. He thereby presents his own project as one in which a certain mode of knowing aspires to overcome itself from within, to find a way of inheriting its current realization otherwise; and the first step in that process appears to be a willingness to think the best of that current realization – to make an effort to find cheer and inspiration in what might otherwise represent the expiration of heat, vitality, and interest.

Such a conclusion is not undermined, but rather underlined, by recalling the role played by that (ironically) exemplary English psychologist, Paul Rée, in the preface to the *Genealogy* – about whose book, *The Origin of Moral Sentiments*, Nietzsche there has the following to say: "I have, perhaps, never read anything to which I said 'no', sentence by sentence and deduction by deduction, as I did to this book: but completely without annoyance or impatience" (*GM*, Preface, 4). This mood of calmness and patience is enough on its own to qualify this gesture of negation; but even Nietzsche's way of articulating that gesture takes on a rather different cast when recounted together with the way he shapes the contrast between masters and slaves in a later section of this first essay:

Whereas all noble morality grows out of a triumphant saying "yes" to itself, slave morality says "no" on principle to everything that is "outside," "other," "non-self": and *this* "no" is its creative deed. This reversal of the evaluating glance – this *inevitable* orientation to the outside instead of back onto itself – is a feature of *ressentiment*: in order to come about, slave morality first has to have an opposing, external world, it needs, physiologically speaking, external stimuli in order to act at all – its action is basically a reaction. The opposite is the case with the noble method of evaluation: this acts and grows spontaneously, seeking out its opposite only so that it can say "yes" to itself even more thankfully and exultantly, – its negative concept "low," "common," "bad," is only a pale contrast created after the event compared to its positive basic concept, saturated with life and passion, "We the noble, the good, the beautiful and the happy!" (*GM*, I, 10)

Against the background of this account, Nietzsche's prefatory dramatization of his relation to Rée as that of systematic nay-saying to an author whose way of putting things was "back-to-front and perverse" (*GM*, Preface, 4) in relation to his own – this portrait of Rée as his absolute other or non-self – would amount to an indictment of Nietzsche himself as belonging to the party of the slaves. Little wonder, then, that the beginning of the first essay not only manifests real uncertainty about the border between the English psychologists and himself, but also looks for a way of making this internal relatedness to that which he most deeply resists somehow productive or vital rather than cause for self-hatred and despair.

And sure enough, in the second section of the essay, some cause for overcoming that despair is indeed found, even if it lurks only in parenthesis.

For at this point, Nietzsche declares his difference from the English psychologists as one in which he maintains their presiding spirit while infusing it with an essentially historical philosophical practice – one which overcomes the "idiocy" of their moral genealogies by contesting their essentially unhistorical assumption that unegoistic acts have always and everywhere been called "good."

> Now for me, it is obvious that the real breeding-ground for the concept "good" has been sought and located in the wrong place by this theory: the judgement "good" does *not* emanate from those to whom goodness is shown! Instead, it has been "the good" themselves, meaning the noble, the mighty, the high-placed and the high-minded, who saw and judged themselves and their actions as good, I mean first-rate, in contrast to everything lowly, low-minded, common and plebeian. It was from this *pathos of distance* that they first claimed the right to create values and give these values names ... (The seigneurial privilege of giving names even allows us to conceive of the origin of language itself as a manifestation of the power of the rulers: they say "this is so-and-so," they set their seal on everything and every occurrence with a sound and thereby take possession of it, as it were) ... It is only with a *decline* of aristocratic value-judgements that this whole antithesis between "egoistic" and "unegoistic" forces itself more and more on man's conscience, – it is, to use my language, the *herd instinct* which, with that, finally gets its word in (and makes *words*). (*GM*, I, 2)

On the one hand, Nietzsche commits himself not only to the claim that master morality precedes slave morality, but also to the hypothesis that the first expression of master morality is also the origin of language as such – a seigneurial privilege indeed; he thereby reconceives evaluative judgment as not merely one domain of language use but rather as its originating medium, so that language as such, in all its more specific formations and deformations, must be conceived of as inherently possessed of an evaluative dimension (a point upon which the third essay will fatefully elaborate). On the other hand, there is something unsettlingly biblical or Judaic about the terms in which Nietzsche presents this vision of the masterly origin of language. His masters' first words declare the goodness of their actions and their consequences (and so their own goodness), just like God's first words in response to His acts of creation *ex nihilo* (according to the book of Genesis); and Nietzsche's account further assumes that language begins with acts of naming that are also expressions of power or mastery – thereby following the basic structure of the Genesis narrative of language's primordial human use (in which Adam is invited to take up his stewardship of creation by assigning names to all its creatures). Perhaps Nietzsche would regard this predecessor narrative as one further, unwitting philological trace of the moral reality that preceded the form of life that Genesis aspires to underwrite; but I can't be the only reader to recall here that the same trace is activated when Wittgenstein opens his later investigation of language by citing Augustine's memories of his own acquisition of language, according to which "grown-ups name some object and at the same time turned towards it . . . [indicating] the affections of the soul when it desires or clings to, or rejects or recoils from, something."[4] And this conjunction of naming with the expression of a desire for possession (or dispossession – call it owning or disowning) is isolated for particular exploration by Wittgenstein, in important part by contrasting it with an imagined shopping trip in which words appear more variously equipped and desire more domesticated or at-home in the world, so that speaking remains internally related to desire without desire as such necessarily being expressive of setting one's personal seal on creation, as if to be human were to be desirous of mastering the universe as such, making ourselves its center.

The extent of Nietzsche's uncritical commitment to such a vision of language is, however, put in question by the partly parenthetical remark which concludes the passage I cited: "it is, to use my language, the *herd instinct* which, with that, finally gets its word in (and makes *words*)." The thought that slave morality sets its seal on our thinking and living by enforcing the connection between goodness and altruism is familiar; what is less familiar is Nietzsche's association of slave morality's forging of this particular linguistic connection with the making of words as such – quite as if whatever the masters had achieved by their initial, powerful, evaluative naming of things, these names were not (not yet, not quite) *words*, not until the slaves got their word in. Why not?

A world in which creatures do nothing but apply "names" to things in accordance with their settled attraction or aversion to them is one in which utterances are closer to sound than to speech, because insofar as these acts of possessing the world are purely expressive of their utterers' unchanging character and its spontaneous, undeviating manifestations, they will be purely repetitive – utterly invariant, hence essentially unchanging and essentially unresponsive to any change in their environments. "Words" which are essentially incapable of such responsiveness – call it projection into new circumstances which elicit new possibilities of sense – are not really words at all, any more than a parrot's acquisition of a small menu of sounds keyed to a small menu of phenomena amounts to the mastery of a vocabulary, a set of ways of saying something. Words must be capable of iteration;

---

[4] Cf. Wittgenstein 2009: section 1.

but words that are never used in anything other than the elemental or original ways in which they were first used are not capable of constituting a language, and so are not capable of constituting their users as users of language.

Slave morality's getting its word in amounts to making words out of the masters' "words" because the slaves' use of them involves, and so introduces (in the terms of section 10), reversal, opposition, and reaction against the static iterations of the masters' essentially self-involved and self-reinforcing self-expressions. They initiate an "orientation [of language and its users] to the outside instead of back onto itself" (*GM*, I, 10) which introduces the possibility of a genuine reaction to the external world, because it involves the capacity to recognize stimuli as genuinely external, hence not absolutely within the utterer's possession but other to him (as the master is other to him). The connection that slave morality makes between goodness and altruism may be resentful, but it is genuinely original – it remakes the world, together with everyone in it; and even if it amounts to the expression of a herd instinct, it thereby at least acknowledges the collective nature of genuine speech.

Insofar, then, as Nietzsche's gestures (in the preface, and in the first section of the first essay) put into play the possibility of a certain identification with the English psychologists specifically and the ascetic ideal more generally, they align him *with* rather than against those who first embody a genuine use of language (as he acknowledges when he describes his making of the point about slave morality making words as something he does in *his* language, language that is genuinely his own – just as his recognition that the collective nature of language is inherently vulnerable to failures of individuality finds expression in his coining a new phrase for that failure – "herd instinct" – thereby enacting the other possibility that words, collectively owned, open up). Finding his own way with words does not mean jettisoning the idea that words as such express evaluations (that concepts are expressions of our interests) and so register desire; but it does mean acknowledging that creativity here and now, in the aftermath of the slave revolt, will mean tapping into the creativity of that revolt, and so will require a reflexive employment of the capacity of words to invert, reverse and oppose – a turning or conversion of the key concepts of our form of life against themselves, in the name of a hoped-for future.

* * *

Towards the end of the first essay of the *Genealogy*, Nietzsche invents Mr. Rash and Curious, in order to act as an explorer of the underground workshop within which morality is cobbled together. There is much of significance in this scene and its immediate contexts, and I have tried to articulate some of it in Mulhall (2009); but I haven't the space to do so here. For present purposes, however, three elements of that more detailed discussion are worth at least identifying, since they might all be viewed as illustrating the conversion process I just described – in which Nietzsche aspires to turn the words of Christianity against themselves.

First, although Mr. Rash and Curious testifies that the true meaning of "faith," "hope," and "love" in the mouths of Christians is "vengeance" and "hatred," he does so just after we have heard those very words in Nietzsche's own mouth – when he prays for a glimpse of a man "who makes up for and redeems man, and enables us to retain our *faith in mankind!*" in the light of what he sees as the threat of losing "our love for him, our hope in him, and even our will to be man" (*GM*, I, 12).

Second, one incarnation of the redemptive figure for whom Nietzsche prays is here identified as Napoleon; but his value resides in his nature as a synthesis of the monstrous and the more-than-human, which in Nietzsche's language means a synthesis of Judaea and Rome (rather than embodying a late triumph of noble Rome over the Judeo-Christian edifice of slave morality). So understood, Napoleon exemplifies the internalization and overcoming of the contradiction that has hitherto dominated our history.

This denial of any simple denial of Judaea is linked to the third element I want to stress: the suggestion I claim to find in this portion of Nietzsche's text that his vision of the human future involves overcoming the opposition between masters and slaves by internalizing it in such a way as to achieve self-mastery in the form of self-denial, where self-denial means not so much the once-for-all denial of self and life as such, but rather the denial of every attained or actualized (call it mastered) state of the self in the name of another, unattained but attainable state of that self – an aspiration to the realization of which one willingly enslaves oneself, in the knowledge that, once attained, each such state will reveal another, unattained but attainable state that neighbors it.

(4) THE PROMISE OF KNOWLEDGE: GIVING, TAKING, AND TURNING ONE'S WORD

If the third essay interprets an aphorism, and the first solves a riddle, the second essay confronts a paradox:

To breed an animal *which is able to make promises* – is that not precisely the paradoxical task which nature has set herself with regard to humankind? Is it not the real problem *of* humankind? . . . (*GM*, II, 1)

The problem, in other words, is that of the origins of moral responsibility: the ability to make promises is exemplary of rendering oneself accountable for one's actions, which involves the construction or development of what philosophers would call freedom of the will – the elaboration and maintenance of whatever is needed "so that a world of strange new things, circumstances and even acts of will may be placed quite safely in between the original 'I will', 'I shall do' and the actual discharge of the will, its *act*, without breaking this long chain" (*GM*, II, 1). But the ability to make promises is also, and equally, exemplary of the more general ability to give one's word:

The "free" man, the possessor of a durable, unbreakable will . . . will necessarily respect his peers, the strong and the reliable (those *with the right* to give their word) . . . [and] gives his word as something which can be relied on, because he is strong enough to remain upright in the face of mishap or even "in the face of fate" . . . (*GM*, II, 2)

In short, to contemplate our acquisition of the right to make promises is to contemplate our accession to the realm of language as such, the domain in which one gives and takes words from one's fellow language users, the sharers of the form of animal life that is informed by the circulation of words; it is our accession to humanity, the becoming human of the human. And to present the making of promises as exemplary of that distinctively human capacity is to imply that there is no use of language that is not possessed of a distinctively ethical dimension; it invites us to think of any and all acts of speech as exercises of personal responsibility – as ways in which we commit ourselves, laying ourselves open to evaluation.

What is paradoxical about the emergence of the ability under question here is precisely that it emerges from nature: the domain of causal law and determination manages to engender a creature capable of achieving freedom from such determination.[5] If the reality of that capacity is not to constitute an irrefutable argument for supernaturalism, and so for the very religious conception of humanity that Nietzsche is concerned to criticize, he must take the responsibility for providing a wholly natural accounting of it – call it a genealogy. And it turns out that the key elements of that genealogy will emerge from the very mechanisms and processes upon which the English

---

[5] A point made by Stanley Cavell, in a paper entitled "On Nietzschean Perfectionism" (2008), delivered to the American Philosophical Association meeting in Philadelphia, December 2008: this section of my essay is pervasively indebted to the way Cavell there aligns Nietzsche and Austin with respect to their ways of aligning promises and claims to knowledge.

psychologists lay such emphasis: the business of memory and forgetting, and its companion pair of habit and novelty.

Nietzsche's first essay reported that, according to these psychologists, although the original connection between "goodness" and altruism was forged in recognition of the usefulness of such acts to their recipients, this connection became so routine and repetitive that its real origin was forgotten, and altruism began thereby to appear intrinsically good. In his second essay, he turns these explanatory concepts against their employers by turning them against themselves: he argues that forgetfulness is not a passive but an active phenomenon, and that habit or routine is not an alternative to creativity or originality but rather a precondition for it.

On Nietzsche's account, forgetfulness is a strength rather than a weakness or a malfunction, because it is an activity essential to life – "like a doorkeeper or guardian of mental order, rest and etiquette" (*GM*, II, 1); without it, every single thing that a creature lives through or experiences, together with every phase of the process of internal absorption to which it is then subject, would be routed through its consciousness, and it simply could not cope with the overwhelming, chaotic immensity of what was going on around and inside it. In short, "there could be no happiness, cheerfulness, hope, pride, *immediacy* without forgetfulness ... that apparatus of suppression" (*GM*, II, 1). Forgetfulness is thus the default position, the starting point of any healthy animal; but for the human animal, a counter-device is needed to that repression mechanism; for if promises are to be made, remembering must be possible. But this kind of memory is no passive inability to be rid of an impression; it, too, must be understood as active and engaged, as "an active *desire* not to let go, a desiring to keep on desiring what has been, on some occasion, desired, really it is the *will's memory*" (*GM*, II, 1). To remember is thus an achievement rather than an automatic effect of experience; more precisely, it is a counter-achievement, a form of self-overcoming, the creation within the self of a continuity (between past and present) that is also a discontinuity (between the merely actual and the previously envisaged or desired or willed present) – a resistance to what is in itself an achievement of robust animal health. An animal with the right to give its word is thus an animal that must overcome its animality, transcending it from within in order to fulfill its unnatural nature.

And what are the conditions for the possibility of such self-overcoming?

In order to have that degree of control over the future, man must first have learnt to distinguish between what happens by accident and what by design, to think causally, to view the future as the present and anticipate it, to grasp with certainty what is end and what is means, in all, to be able to calculate, compute – and before he can do this, man himself will really have to become *reliable, regular, automatic,* even in his own self-image, so that he, as someone making a promise is, is answerable for his own future! (*GM*, II, 1)

It is vital to note that regularity or habituation, which finds its cultural expression in what Nietzsche calls "the morality of custom," is not the end of nature's project but rather one of its most demanding and time-consuming preconditions: the ultimate point of making man truly predictable is to engender the sovereign individual, an autonomous creature like only to himself, the one not only able to make a promise but possessed of the right to do so, because possessed of the individuality without which the word he gives to others cannot truly be regarded as his own to give. But it is equally vital to note what is involved in establishing the automaticity or herd-identity from which such self-sovereignty can alone grow: for Nietzsche's list of preconditions amounts to a synthesis of two types of category – those internal to understanding action as that for which the agent is responsible, and those comprising the armature or skeleton of human cognition. The former type includes the distinction between accident and design, and the idea of ends as opposed to means (call this the field of practical reason), and more specifically the preconditions for excusing or otherwise accounting for one's deeds; the latter type includes the notion of causal relations, predictions of the future on the basis of the past (induction), and the practice of computation or calculation (epitomized by the certainty attainable by logical calculi, whether propositional or predicate) – call this the field of theoretical reason.

From the outset, therefore, Nietzsche's account of responsibility presents pure cognition as something whose primary function is to make possible the creation of the genuinely creative human being: theoretical reason is not just internally related to the domain of practical reason (as the blending of types of category in the cited list already implies), but is a human organ whose basic structure can facilitate the emergence of the sovereign individual. In other words, properly evaluated, knowledge subserves the ability to give one's word: cognition is not to be understood as an abstraction from practical, moral, and existential concerns but rather as always already imprinted or informed by exactly such values.

Two possibilities immediately arise. The first is engendered by the fact that pure cognition is a precondition for enforcing the predictability of human beings, rather than directly facilitating their creativity or originality. For that lack of immediacy raises the possibility that its essentially instrumental function will become detached from the end which accounts for it, and instead be regarded as (and so become) an end in itself (just as, according to the preface, we knowers come to value collecting over what is collected). In such circumstances, men and women of knowledge will constitute an obstacle to the creation of fully human beings, rather than a means towards their emergence; the plurality and indirectness of these processes of becoming human – call it the fluidity of their form and meaning (*GM*, II, 12) – threatens to loosen our grip on the distinction between end and means. The second possibility depends upon taking seriously the fact that knowledge itself finds expression in language – knowledge is something claimed, hence given, taken, and contested in acts of speech. But if, as Nietzsche thinks, the use of language as such can be epitomized in the speech act of promising, he thereby invites us to consider claims to knowledge as a (perhaps radical) variation on that way of giving one's word. It would then follow that claims to knowledge are not only to be understood as speech acts, but as possessing an ineliminable moral dimension; knowing is not an alternative to, but a particular way of, taking a stand in the distinctively linguistic space of cares and commitments. Accordingly, Nietzsche's ensuing account of the conditions for the possibility of giving one's word ought to be regarded not as an account of promising (and so morality) as opposed to knowing, but rather as an account of the root from which both ways of becoming humanly accountable grow, each in its own way.

The story Nietzsche goes on to tell has three main stages. First, the counter-achievement of memory is established and maintained by the infliction of pain deployed as a mnemonic technique. Forgetfulness is overcome by branding what must be remembered onto the physiology of the not-yet-human animal – by systems of bloodletting, torments, sacrifices, and forfeits; and these systems are primarily designed to impress upon their recipients a range of their most important presocial responsibilities – their answerability to those with whom they stand in primitive relationships of credit and debt (barter, buying and selling, and trading more generally). Punishment for reneging on a debt establishes an equivalence between the value of the debt and the pleasure the creditor can take in the infliction of suffering on the debtor; it amounts to an extension of economic thinking from objects to experiences, and thereby to the subjects of experience. Indeed, Nietzsche goes further:

Fixing prices, setting values, working out equivalents, exchanging – this preoccupied man's first thoughts to such a degree that in a certain sense it *constitutes* thought: the most primitive kind of cunning was bred here ... man designated himself as the being who measures values, who values and measures, as "the calculating animal as such." (*GM*, II, 8)

If, as we have seen, the calculating animal is the knowing animal, then knowing as such carries traces of specifically economic evaluation: its categories carry with them a conception of things and persons as elements in a system of exchange value, access to which requires a willingness to regard one's own suffering (as well as that of others), together with the pleasure to be derived from either, as further elements in that system. This is a vision of economics and thought (and so the capacity for speech they depend upon and help constitute) as sadomasochism.

The second stage of the story concerns the transition from presocial and prehistorical practices to collective or genuinely communal life. On the one hand, the demands of shared existence compel us to moderate the techniques of punishment, so that wrongdoing can be entirely paid off and so the doer separated from the deed: once the debt is settled, the one in debt can slough off the imputation of being a debtor, and thereby maintain a sense of his punishment as akin to a visitation of fate or a natural disaster, rather than the external sign of intrinsic personal failure. On the other hand, even moderate versions of these penal practices encourage those subject to them to moderate their desires, thus exemplifying the ways in which social life forces the repression of one's instincts and impulses, and thus the internalization of punishment:

All instincts which are not discharged outwardly *turn inwards* – this is what I call the *internalization* of man: with it there now evolves in man what will later be called his "soul." The whole inner world, originally stretched thinly as though between two layers of skin, was expanded and extended itself and gained depth, breadth and height in proportion to the degree that the external discharge of man's instincts was *obstructed*. (*GM*, II, 16)

This process amounts to the systematic infliction of cruelty by the individual on the individual, and so to a form of self-hatred or self-abuse; but without that internalization of punishment, there could be nothing resembling an individual in the first place, since the idea of human individuality presupposes the idea of a distinction or division between the interior world of the self and the external world it inhabits. What Nietzsche's account makes clear is that the existence of that division is inseparable from the enforcement of a division within the self: if an interior impulse fails to find expression in action, that can be so only if another aspect of the self opposes that impulse. Individuality and self-division thus come into being together (call it selfhood as non-self-identity). And this double creation is also the creation of the human being as an interesting animal:

[T]he prospect of an animal soul turning against itself, taking a part against itself, was something so new, profound, unheard-of, puzzling, contradictory and *momentous* on earth that the whole character of the world changed in an essential way . . . Since that time, man . . . arouses interest, tension, hope, almost certainty for himself, as though something were being announced through him, were being prepared, as though man were not an end but just a path, an episode, a bridge, a great promise . . . (*GM*, II, 16)

This is the creation of conscience in the form of bad conscience: but this kind of bad conscience is also good – in part because from this desire "to give form to oneself as a piece of difficult, resisting, suffering matter . . . a wealth of novel, disconcerting beauty [comes] to light" (nothing less than all the creativeness and originality of Western culture); but most importantly because the creation of such bad conscience is the creation of the human, of the animal capable of giving his word. And here, being an animal with the right to make a promise is explicitly equated with being a promising animal – an animal whose existence takes the form of being promising. To make a promise is to anticipate the future, and to take responsibility for how it will be; to be promising is to be more or other than one presently is, to relate to oneself as being not-yet-realized, constantly open to the future, and taking one's bearings for that future state of oneself from the state one currently instantiates.

But promises can be broken as well as fulfilled; and a promising animal can have its anticipatory relation to the future foreclosed by its relation to the past. The third stage of Nietzsche's narrative tells the tale of how this happened – when the relationship between creditor and debtor, having first been extended to the community's relationship to its forebears, is then absolutized by the substitution of God for the tribe's actual and mythological ancestors. For how, in the first place, can we be sure that we have properly repaid our debt to our actual forefathers? How much sacrifice is enough to satisfy an ever-increasing body of those without whom we would not exist at all? But when our ultimate father is God, then our debt becomes crushingly beyond measurement; and when God's Son gratuitously takes the burden of that debt upon himself, He only intensifies the burden. The religious narrative of original sinfulness and its overcoming thus intensifies the sadomasochism of bad conscience to the point at which human existence appears cursed rather than promising, essentially incapable of escaping its past and hence essentially closed to the future. The human promise becomes not so much unfulfillable as invisible; the morality of custom becomes an end in itself rather than a means to sovereign individuality.

What remains importantly unclear (even deliberately unsettled) in this narrative is the structure of its second stage. We are never sure whether the interiorization of man is established solely by the demands of social life and the natural amelioration of presocial punishment regimes, and so by shifts that need not be tainted by specifically ascetic or priestly motives; or whether the self's decisive turning upon itself is necessarily cruel and self-lacerating in the ways distinctive of slave morality (dependent, for instance, upon practices of confession, with their disciplines of interior scrutiny and scouring). The problem is encapsulated in Nietzsche's ambivalence about the priests, whom he describes from the outset as both a branch of the nobility and the prime movers of the slave revolt; does their revolution construct a counter-civilization to that of the masters, or does it rather create the conditions for the possibility of civilization as such? Would masters who had already turned their natural cruelty upon themselves (and thereby given themselves the interior room for dissembling, reflection, and cleverness) still be masters, or would they rather be suffering the onset of the revaluation of values that their priestly brothers have encouraged (or even be beginning to become priests themselves)? Perhaps this ambivalence is one more way in which Nietzsche acknowledges his awareness that recovery from the ascetic ideal will involve finding the necessary resources for that emancipatory transformation within our currently unredeemed condition.

Regardless of whether we judge the ascetic revaluation process to begin at the second or the third stage of this narrative, however, the outcome seems clear. The interlinked enterprises of cultivating a will to remember and a willingness to become predictable have been (re)shaped in such a way as to occlude the possibility for which they could be preconditions. Instead of functioning as the background of regularity or routinization against which the sovereign individual becomes a single, coherent being of the kind who might achieve freedom, they come to figure as ends in themselves, in the form of a morality of custom or conformity that is constitutionally averse to individuality, in which everyone does only and always what everyone else does (*GM*, II, 24). Instead of allowing painful self-discipline to open up the possibility of taking pleasure in the endless reachievement of self-mastery, our culture prefers us to take pleasure in the infliction of pain upon ourselves as an end in itself, thereby closing ourselves off within a vicious circle of reiterated, endlessly intensifying cruelty. And insofar as this evis-ceration of our right to make promises exemplifies our current nature as language users, it is figured by our willingness to use words as if their rates of exchange (both with one another and with whatever they represent) were fixed, as if fated to reiteration – to the repetition of inherently impersonal patterns of use inherited from our ancestors and passed on to our descendants, without ever realizing their potential to make something new of our experience of the world, and thereby to renew both their own intelligibility and that of their users.

In effect, then, the current realization of our (birth)right to make promises is the interiorized inflection of a regime in which pleasure is taken from the infliction of pain, and in which evaluation is a matter of seeking equivalence rather than celebrating singularity – call them the customary morality and economics of speech, hence of humanity and selfhood. Since there cannot be genuine individuality without some version of these preconditions, its achievement must involve their being inflected otherwise – perhaps by suffering the world's capacity (or that of another within it) to inflict pleasure on us (call it a willingness to be delighted by what wounds us), perhaps by seeing the equality of all in each human being's capacity for singularity. After all, when Nietzsche asks: "What is more deeply offensive to others and separates us most profoundly from them than allowing them to realize something of the severity and high-mindedness with which we treat ourselves?" (*GM*, II, 24), he need not simply be indicting his others for lacking something he possesses; he may rather be pointing out that realizing that his way of living exemplifies such self-mastery may inspire them to realize it in their own cases, which would mean genuinely realizing their own individuality – something which would require that they be repelled rather than attracted by him, since it could hardly avoid enforcing their separateness from their examplar.

Recalling Nietzsche's invitation to see the making of promises as exemplary of speech as such, we might accordingly take particular aversive, emancipatory delight in the way Nietzsche's tentative visions of human redemption are saturated in economic terms – credit and debt, interest, exchange value, contracts, even redemption itself (figured as the self's indebtedness to itself, taken together with its willingness to credit the possibility of a future of its own) – that have been reversed, inverted, turned against themselves. In this way, our culture's apparently inveterate tendency to conceive things in terms of evaluative equivalence has been turned back on itself; its evaluative terms have been redeemed by being spiritualized and interiorized.

What, then, of knowledge? Its nature is such that it helps at once to compose a picture of the world as essentially predictable (necessarily subject to causal determination, and to inductive and deductive calculation), and to

occlude the self altogether (insofar as the will to truth is an offshoot of the
ascetic ideal, and so is a mode of self-denial that is also a mode of self-
ignorance). One might say that it aspires to abolish the openness of the
future, to discredit the idea of novelty in the world and our experience of it.
And in so doing, it resonates with the broader cultural world whose group
portrait Nietzsche paints in his third essay – one whose apparently various
and vital inhabitants ultimately appear to be mere instantiations of a single,
life-occluding and self-denying ethos, with each reflecting the others' orientation, and thereby reinforcing its hegemony to the point at which even
the possibility of original thought, speech, and experience goes missing.

At the same time, however, this mode in which knowledge currently
manifests itself actually occludes its own nature as an aspect of the distinctively human, talking form of life: for claiming to know something is before
all else a speech act, hence one way in which the promising animal gives its
word – a way in which one speaker gives others his authority for believing
that things are as he says they are, which means authorizing them too to
claim that things are that way. In short, when a speaker gives his word in this
way, others may take it, and then give it to others in their turn – putting that
claim into circulation. One might say that the one who claims to know
places others in his debt, but only insofar as they credit what he says, which
means accepting his credentials as an authority on the matter at hand. In
short, knowledge takes on the aspect of testimony – this is, after all, the
burden of Nietzsche's creation of Mr. Rash and Curious at the end of the
first essay, the emissary who bears witness to the reality of our world's
construction, and so functions both as Nietzsche's proxy or servant and
(insofar as his final testimonial outrages even his author) his master or over-
masterer. Claiming to know is a way of inviting others to credit assertions
that rightly aspire to objectivity, but are nonetheless rooted in evaluations of
the credibility of the one who claims knowledge (of whether he is really in a
position to know, whether it is within his cognizance).[6]

And what, finally, of the one who claims to know about knowledge – to
know of its indebtedness to the ascetic ideal, and so to know that we knowers
are unknown to ourselves, hence unaware of our specific position in the
world, hence to that extent not properly authorized to make any claims to
know, that is to say, uncomprehendingly suffering an injury to our cognitive
status (not so much philosophical kingfishers as Fisher Kings)? What exactly
is the basis of his claims to know these things about knowledge, and about us
knowers; how should we go about evaluating his testimony?

[6] Cf. J. L. Austin 1979.

To do so, we must recall that the one advancing these claims explicitly includes himself within their range of application (if, as his prefatory remarks declare, "we" are unknown to ourselves, then so too is he – he is one of us, and so what he says of us declares how things stand, or partly stand, or used to stand, with him: he is baring his own soul). We should also recollect that (at the beginning of his first essay, when resisting commonly accepted claims about the character of the English psychologists) he all but explicitly identifies the terrain his cognitive claims occupy as equally open to the demands of desire and the aspirations of hope. If we further assume Nietzsche's continued willingness to turn the terms of religion against themselves, we might conclude that this amounts to saying that Nietzschean knowledge claims are at once modes of confession and modes of prophecy.

This places them fully in the stream of time: what might otherwise appear solely to aim at the representation of what is the case now appears to look at once backwards (identifying wounding errors that inform the present) and forwards (calling for a future that will look otherwise than the present from which it emerges). For taken seriously, confession and prophecy do not ignore the present in favor of attending exclusively to the past and the future respectively; Augustine's radical and scathing confession of his past errors is something he takes to be required of him in order to re-ground and re-orient himself at the moment of confession, just as the biblical prophets do not claim divinely underwritten knowledge of what is yet to come so much as invite us to make something of our unwritten future by acknowledging their radical and scathing critiques of the present to be divinely underwritten. Nietzsche's use of Zarathustra to bridge his second and third essays certainly implies a sense on his part that the furthest reaches of his current thinking go beyond what his not very much earlier self could have managed; but after all, Zarathustra himself was always only the overman's prophet, so to get further than Zarathustra need only involve attaining a better critical perspective on the present, and so a clearer prophetic vision of the possibility and necessity of that overman. It certainly need carry no claim to have attained that status, except insofar as such an exercise in self-overcoming amounts to an instance of the generic human capacity for existing in, and as, a transition – for being underway.

What, then, should be our criteria for evaluating the credibility of words offered to us as knowledge claims that are both confessional and prophetic? According to Nietzsche himself, we should ask ourselves how far those claims wound and delight us, and delight us because they wound us; and we should further ask what the relation between pain and pleasure here really is – which means asking how far they contribute to the vicious circle of delighting in self-inflicted pain (pain inflicted by another knower), and how far they break that circle by envisioning and internalizing a way of achieving self-mastery, and so self-abasement, that leaves room for hope for the human future. This would mean achieving a certain kind of self-knowledge about our experience of this book, these words in these orderings. Can we credit ourselves with the capacity to achieve this?

CHAPTER 12

Nietzsche and the "aesthetics of character"

Edward Harcourt

On the Genealogy of Morality calls for a "critique of moral values" (*GM*, Preface, 6), a critique which has no ambition to be value-neutral: "the value of these values should itself . . . be examined."[1] At least if the object of the critique is morality as a whole, the values invoked cannot themselves be moral, on pain of making the critique self-defeating. So the question arises what these values – in particular, what Nietzsche's ideals of and for humanity – might be. It has been proposed, citing evidence as much from the *Genealogy* as elsewhere, that the values in question are "aesthetic" (Foot 2002a: 147).[2] Indeed Nietzsche's ethical thought seems to act as a kind of flypaper to the word "aesthetic," which sticks to it in a variety of more and less appropriate meanings. However, given the availability of the distinction between the moral and the ethical, which marks out morality – in ways indebted of course to Nietzsche himself – as a "particular development of the ethical" (Williams 1985: 6),[3] we do not need the term "aesthetic" in order to label a set of ideals simply insofar as they do not belong to morality: if the "aesthetic" label is to justify itself, it needs to do more work than that. And to understand what work it is capable of doing, we need to understand better what it is for an ideal – an ideal of character or of human living, that is, rather than an ideal of the appearance of art objects – to be aesthetic. The aim of this chapter is to do that, with a view to establishing that, tempting as it is to reach for the phrase "aesthetic" in connection with Nietzsche, it is poorly motivated as a description of what is distinctive about his ideals of character.

The direction I shall take is as follows. First I suggest that "(merely) aesthetic" is the way *any* non-moral ideal of character might be expected to

---

[1] I deliberately sought out the Cambridge University Press translations, so all the quotations are from these.

[2] See also Ridley 1998b, Janaway 2007, and, in a rather special sense, Nehamas 1985 and 1998.

[3] Cf. Mackie's distinction between "morality in the narrow sense" and "morality in the broad sense" (Mackie 1977: 106).

look from within the perspective of morality, narrowly understood (section 1). But since we can't understand anything about Nietzsche's ideals of character without including his critique of morality in the story, if we want to describe how Nietzsche saw his own ideals of character, we will have every reason *not* to describe them as aesthetic in this sense. And, to the extent that we are ourselves impressed by Nietzsche's critique of morality, we will also have reason not to describe ideals of character as aesthetic in this sense *in propria voce*.

Next (section 2) I distinguish another use of "aesthetic" in connection with ideals of character, in which it labels either a kind of conception of character Nietzsche did not have, or is simply synonymous with "ideals" of no distinctively aesthetic variety. Then in section 3, I outline a phenomenon – though not the only one – that's quite properly labeled by the phrase "having an aesthetic ideal of character." Roughly, it's the phenomenon of a person's life being dominated, in a certain way, by a model of how to live that is derived from narrative art. (It could thus be derived from cinema or opera or epic poetry, but in this chapter I keep to literature.) However, whether one subscribes to a narrow conception of morality or not, for a person's life to be dominated in this way is a character defect. It doesn't of course follow from this fact that Nietzsche didn't have an aesthetic ideal of character in this sense, but it ought to make us think twice before interpreting him this way.

With these various understandings before our minds, it should be easier to ask (as I do in sections 4–5) if there's any real work left for the notion of an aesthetics of character to do: that is, whether there are ideals of character which remain discernible from outside the narrow perspective of morality, which are genuine ideals (i.e. not defects), and which there is some point in picking out as distinctively aesthetic. My conclusion is that there are not.

1. It's always hard to keep Aristotle out of the discussion when human excellences and defects are at issue, and a brief mention here too will be helpful to focus ideas. For the "aesthetic" label has been attached to Aristotle's conceptions of human excellence as well as to Nietzsche's, and with the perspective of (narrow) morality behind it. Indeed it was noticing that this (as it strikes me) mistake is made about Aristotle that suggested to me the possibility that the same mistake may in part account for the temptation to flourish the term "aesthetic" in connection with Nietzsche.

Distinguishing between the way the noble (*to kalon*) functions as an end of action in the *Rhetoric* (*R*) and in the *Nicomachean Ethics* (*NE*), Roger Crisp comments that in the former work, beneficial actions are said to be noble and thereby worth doing, whereas in *NE*, "virtuous action is solely for the sake of the noble" (Crisp 2003). So, Crisp says, in the *NE* Aristotle gives as the ground-level reason for acting virtuously not the possibly non-eudaimonistic reason of the interests of others – possibly non-eudaimonistic because one's own eudaimonia and the interests of others might conflict – but the eudaimonistic reason of the good to oneself of acting nobly. Whereas in *R*, acts are worth doing because they're noble and noble because they're beneficial to others, in the *NE* acts are worth doing because they're noble and their nobility makes them worth doing because nobility is, fundamentally, good *for the agent.*

Whether this is correct as an interpretation of Aristotle is not of interest here – all I'm interested in is the contrast between the two conceptions of nobility.[4] For Crisp then immediately goes on:

> The "aesthetic" aspect of nobility [in *NE*] of course makes this charge all the easier. The agent [in *NE*] is being encouraged to attend to the beauty of his character, rather than the interests of others. . . . Aristotle converts nobility [in *R*] from a morally loaded notion capable of providing its own reasons resting on the interests of others to an aesthetic feature of the agent's own character, the significance of which rests not so much on the interests of others but on the contribution a beautiful character can make to the agent's own happiness. (2003: 78)

However, would anything have been lost, in the expression of his view, had Crisp said simply "encouraged to attend *to his own character*," rather than specifically to its beauty? I think not. In a slightly later passage, Crisp goes on to say that Aristotle's portraits of virtuous people in Books II–V of *NE* "can be seen as a further development of an aesthetics of character consisting in descriptions of the attractions of the noble life, and the unattractiveness of the shameful" (2003: 78) – no explicit mention of beauty here. What's driving the application of the label "aesthetic" to nobility as an ideal, then, seems not to be specifically the *beauty* of a noble character (as might be the case if nobility were then explained as involving some formal feature of character such as harmony among the faculties or among one's ends) but the less specific notion of nobility's *attractiveness to its possessor.* That is to say, where the goodness of virtue is fundamentally explained by reference to the good of its intended beneficiaries, we have a *moral* ideal; by contrast it's enough in Crisp's parlance to label an ideal of character "aesthetic" that the goodness of virtue is fundamentally explained by reference to the good of its possessor.

---

[4] On the interpretive issue, I follow Irwin (2009: 607–9), who traces to Sidgwick the erroneous thought that Aristotle "does not distinguish moral from aesthetic judgments" *because* Aristotelian virtuous agents, in acting for the sake of the *kalon*, act egoistically.

With this understanding of Crisp's use of the "aesthetic" tag in mind – which, by the way, was not developed with the intention of offering any reflection on Nietzsche – now consider the following remarks of Christopher Janaway's. Nietzsche's targets in the *Genealogy* are Rée and Schopenhauer, Janaway says, who assume that the essence of morality is *das Unegoistische*; Nietzsche's is "a critique of value conceived as selflessness" (Janaway 2007: 9). His revaluation, meanwhile, consists in "assigning positive value to character-istics of human behaviour that have been decried as 'egoistic', and negative value to those that have been lauded as 'unegoistic' or 'selfless'" (2007: 13). The dividing line between Rée and Schopenhauer on the one hand and Nietzsche on the other would seem to fall, then, exactly at the point which divides the "moral" Aristotle of the *Rhetoric* (on Crisp's interpretation) from the "aesthetic" Aristotle of the *Nicomachean Ethics*. Nonetheless, is there yet a good reason for describing Nietzsche's ideals of character as aesthetic? I would say not. For one thing, the "aesthetic" label is rather wasted if what attracts it is only the non-specific feature of goodness to the possessor, since there seem to be non-moral ideals that are *not* illuminatingly described as aesthetic – being a good husband or a good friend, for example. More importantly, to apply the label to Nietzsche's ideals of character for the reason Crisp applies it to Aristotle's in the *NE* would be precisely to affirm, though as it were from the other side, the centrality of the distinction between "egoistic" and "self-less" that Crisp insists on. But it's evident that once "this whole antithesis between 'egoistic' and 'unegoistic' [had] forced itself more and more on man's conscience" (*GM*, I, 2), something had gone wrong, so I take it that though Nietzsche indeed wants to bring some characteristics "[formerly] decried as 'egoistic'" into the fold of human excellences, he wants to do so not by affirming the distinction and as it were reversing the signs but by moving beyond the distinction altogether. From a point of view "beyond good and evil," it will be easy to recognize some characteristics formerly decried as egoistic *and* some not so decried as human excellences, because the good to oneself/good to others distinction will have become unimportant. But with that distinction, out too goes the justification for describing excellences of character as "aesthetic" simply on the grounds that they are attractive to their possessor.

Crisp's mention of "beauty" of character recalls an even weaker justifi-cation for the "aesthetic" label as applied to ideals of character, namely that an excellence of character is an aesthetic excellence if its possessor takes pleasure in the thought of having it. This is distinct from Crisp's Sidgwickian justification just dismissed, since the thought of having a given excellence may be pleasing to its possessor even if what fundamentally *explains* its status as an excellence – and what earns it the "aesthetic" label on the Sidgwickian justification – is something other than its goodness to its possessor (its goodness to others, for example). This weaker justification could be passed over altogether were it not that one trips over the thought that excellences of character are "beauties" of character in all sorts of places, perhaps as a residue of a more fully fleshed out eighteenth-century conception of a "beautiful soul"[5] (scoffed at, incidentally, by Nietzsche in *Ecce Homo*[6]). Consider for example the following passages from the early nineteenth-century theologian J. F. Fries:[7]

It is only by reference to the ideals of sublimity and beauty that man can be truly pleasing or displeasing to himself. The only thing which duty commands . . . is the beauty of the life of man. (Fries 1982: 15)

I wish and will, in the depths of my heart, one thing alone – that my life should correspond to . . . moral ideals, that I should raise myself, in accordance with those ideals, to nobility and beauty of soul. (Fries 1982: 31)

The passages show just how empty aesthetic vocabulary can be in connection with character. For when one looks at how "duty" is explained, it turns out that its "primary requirements" are "honour and justice"; the "moral ideals" in the second passage are "the requirements of virtue." Now the inference from "pleasing to its possessor" to "aesthetic" is weak enough, since the class of pleasing things – Greek vases, rest, hot toast – seems to include many things which are not aesthetically pleasing. But just suppose we agree to use the word "aesthetic" in connection with traits of character so that any excellence which pleases its possessor (or perhaps anyone else) counts as an aesthetic excellence. The trouble is that *any* excellence will count as aesthetic, since it's possible to enjoy the thought of one's possessing any trait of character that one regards as good. In particular, narrowly moral ideals – including, presumably, meeting the "requirements of virtue" as Fries conceives them, though the point does not seem worth pursuing in detail – will count as aesthetic ideals. Hence "aesthetic" as so defined will be

---

[5] For the career of the "beautiful soul" idea in the eighteenth century, see Norton 1995. The afterlife of the conception is prolonged still further in Colin McGinn's "aesthetic theory of virtue" (McGinn 1997). (I am indebted to McGinn for the reference to Norton.) Unless much more is said, McGinn's view seems simply to expand the category of the beautiful to include both aesthetic beauty and the "particular *kind* of beauty proper to the soul that virtue consists in" (1997: 95). In old money, therefore, excellences of character are precisely *not* aesthetic. For a little more on the more fully fleshed-out conception, see section 4 below.

[6] "[T]o demand that everyone should become 'good', herd animals, blue-eyed, benevolent 'beautiful souls' . . . would mean robbing existence of its *great* character" (*EH*, "Why I Am a Destiny," 4).

[7] The work in question originally appeared under the title *Julius und Evagoras*.

hopeless as a way of capturing the contrast between Nietzsche's own ideals, whatever they were, and those he rejected.

2. Just the same problem besets a second possible kind of understanding of the notion of an aesthetics of character, which I'll introduce gradually. "The most crucial flaw that [Nietzsche] finds in the interpretation that produces moral values," Nehamas writes, is the presupposition that "everyone should live according to a single code of conduct" (Nehamas 1985: 209), though "the avowed aim to be . . . universal and to apply equally to all human beings on the basis of reasons provided by some features in which we all essentially share" may, he argues, also be shared by "codes of conduct that [are not] moral in the specific sense discussed in the *Genealogy*" (1985: 224). But if this flaw may be common both to moral and to non-moral codes of conduct, how is Nietzsche to respond? According to Nehamas, his escape route was "to create an artwork out of himself," since this effort "is . . . also his effort to offer a positive view [of how to live] without falling back into the dogmatic tradition he so distrusted" (1985: 8). The ideal character instantiated but not described by Nietzsche's work "constitutes an implicit commendation of that character, and at the same time constitutes an obstacle to its being a general model . . . that could be followed by others" (1985: 230). Once again I'm not going to comment on Nehamas's very demanding conception of Nietzsche's "aestheticism" (1985: 7; 1998: 10), except to say that if Nietzsche really does not describe his ideal character, how can we make sense of the idea that he "produces a perfect instance of it" (1985: 230)? The concept of an instance is the concept of a relation between a particular and a type, and "no description" sounds as if it implies "no type." But surely Nietzsche does describe, partially at least, his ideal character – so we have a type, and thus something others can seek to exemplify (or not).

Does that mean Nietzsche himself is, self-defeatingly, a dogmatist, maintaining that "everyone should live according to a single code of conduct"? No. There's a gap, first of all, between a "universalizing" theory and the very strong claim that "everyone should live according to a single code of conduct": the latter is a case of the former, but not the only case. Thus a theory that says that the way one should live is determined by one's status is a universalizing theory, because it prescribes a way of life to anyone with a given status, but – at least if there is such a thing as difference of status – not a theory that prescribes the same code of conduct to everyone. So if all Nietzsche wanted to reject was the very strong claim, there would be plenty of room for him to prescribe ways of life to others: "fashioning himself into a literary character" is not the only way out of claiming that "a single mode of life . . . [is] best for all" (Nehamas 1998: 13).

But besides universalizing but status-adjusted prescriptions, there is another gradation on the scale of answers to "how should one live?" in between the very strong claim and literary self-fashioning. This is the thought that, even for people of equal status, there is a plurality of good ways of living. It's this thought that Philippa Foot seems to have partly in mind when she says that Nietzsche "affirm[s] a special kind of aestheticism":

> For an artist, rules would indeed be beside the point: the goodness of what he or she makes cannot be the same as the goodness of another artist's work, as if there could be a manual for producing what's good [in art]. (Foot 2002a: 147)

What justifies the "aesthetic" label here is that, since Nietzsche sets out to describe what's good about a particular character or way of living in such a way as not to make any claim on others to live that way, the goodness in question must be aesthetic, or else such a claim *would* be being made. This justification, however, falls apart under scrutiny. Here it's instructive to compare Irwin on Kierkegaard's "aesthetic" agent (Irwin 2009: 292), who pursues certain ends "without any conviction that they matter, but simply because they appeal" to him. Of course the aesthetic agent's long-term ends must matter more than various short-term ends that may jostle with them at this or that point of decision, otherwise it's hard to conceive of the "aesthetic" agent as a rational agent at all. The point is that it doesn't matter to him that he has the long-term ends he has, rather than some others. The description of the "aesthetic agent" certainly gives us an interpretation of a non-prescriptive conception of how to live. But it's too weak: if it really doesn't matter to one that one has this or that set of long-term ends, it's doubtful that there is room for one to think of these ends as good, since to think of them as good in some way would surely be for them to start mattering. And it doesn't fit Nietzsche at all: it seems to matter to him deeply how one lives – or, perhaps in order not to prejudice questions about his "universalism," at least how *he* lives.[8] On the other hand there seems to be plenty of room to hold an ideal – a conception of how to live such that one can say what's good about it – without any implication that other

---

[8] But surely Nietzsche did not only care about how *he* lived; otherwise it would be hard to make sense of the pervasive presence, in the *Genealogy* and elsewhere, of type expressions, most notably "man" and its cognates. For example: "man, as species" (*GM*, Preface, 6); "faith in mankind" (*GM*, I, 12); "the animal 'man' is finally taught to be ashamed of all his instincts" (*GM*, II, 7); "one single *stronger* species of man" (*GM*, II, 12); "this man of the future" (*GM*, II, 24); and cf. "how far the judgment promotes and preserves life, how well it preserves, and perhaps even cultivates, the type" (*BGE*, 4); "a higher type of man" (*BGE*, 30); "keeping the type 'man' on a lower level" (*BGE*, 62). What Nietzsche wanted was for the greatest possibilities *of human nature* to be realized, though this is far from saying that everyone is required or can even aspire to live in the same way.

people are required to live according to it. Indeed one might think this is what an ideal *is*: a conception of how to live well that goes beyond what is required of one. So if the point is that Nietzsche thinks there's "no manual" for living well, we do not need to claim his ideals of life are distinctively aesthetic in order to make it. This is not to say that any ideal would be acceptable to Nietzsche, just on the grounds that it doesn't specify ways in which one *has* to act. But if the term "aesthetic ideal" is just code for "ideal," once again the concept won't help us to identify what's distinctive about the ideals he did *not* reject.[9]

3. I turn now to the third principal meaning of "aesthetic" I want to distinguish in relation to ideals of character, a sense in which it labels a character defect. The novel has been picking over the remains of its own victims almost since the genre began, and one of its abiding themes has been the various ways in which a person's life can be taken over, and for the worse, by literary models: again and again we find characters in novels who want their own lives to be novel-like, and who are thus constantly on the lookout for representative moments, emblems, turning points, resolutions, as evidences that the unscripted muddle of real living is after all unfolding like a book. A well-known and light-hearted example is Austen's treatment of Catherine Morland in *Northanger Abbey*. Since her expectations of Northanger are molded by fiction, the real abbey with its windows "so large, so clear, so light," can hardly fail to disappoint: "To an imagination which had hoped for the smallest divisions [*sc.* windowpanes], and the heaviest stone-work, for painted glass, dirt, and cobwebs, the difference was very distressing" (Austen 1980: 128). Any number of other novels share this general theme: *Emma, Madame Bovary, Don Quixote*.

I'm going to focus, however, on a portrait of a defect closely analogous to Catherine's but painted in more somber tones, namely the character of Lord Jim in Conrad's novel of that title. Jim's career at sea begins when "after a

---

[9] We find the same apparently groundless use of "aesthetic" in connection with ideals of life in a remark of Foucault's: "In Greek ethics . . . ethics was not related to any social – or at least to any legal – institutional system. . . . What they were worried about, their theme, was to constitute a kind of ethics which was an aesthetics of existence. . . . I wonder if our problem nowadays is not, in a way, similar to this one, since most of us no longer believe that ethics is founded in religion, nor do we want a legal system to intervene in our moral, personal, private life" (Foucault 1991: 343). The thought seems to be that since "private life" is not regulated by religion or by law, it is an area in which the way we live is not *required* of us – so the norms that govern it are aesthetic. But why equate the whole of the ethical with the required, in such a way that any norms that fall short of requiring us to follow them default to the category of the aesthetic? One might diagnose the subterranean working of the "morality system," were it not that even the "morality system" doesn't make that equation, since (on some constructions at least) it leaves room, for example, for self-sacrifice, that is, something both "unegoistic" and supererogatory.

course of light holiday literature his vocation ... had declared itself"
(Conrad 1900: 4). Aboard his training ship, he would

> live in his mind the sea-life of light literature. He saw himself saving people from
> sinking ships, cutting away masts in a hurricane, swimming through a surf with a
> line; or as a lonely castaway, barefooted and half naked, walking on uncovered reefs
> in search of shellfish to stave off starvation. He confronted savages on tropical
> shores, quelled mutinies on the high seas, and in a small boat upon the ocean kept
> up the hearts of despairing men – always an example of devotion to duty, and as
> unflinching as a hero in a book. (1900: 5)

As first mate on the *Patna* carrying eight hundred sleeping pilgrims, his
thoughts once again were

> full of valorous deeds: he loved these dreams and the success of his imaginary
> achievements. (1900: 13)

But when a few moments later the *Patna* strikes a reef, Jim like all the other
crew members jumps ship while the pilgrims are still asleep, leaving them
(for all he knows) to drown. He spends the rest of his life hiding from others'
knowledge of the episode in more and more remote corners of the world,
eventually establishing a satisfactory life for himself as the unofficial gover-
nor of an island. However, raiders arrive and though Jim guarantees the
safety of the local head man's son, the son is killed. So, despite his mistress's
pleading, Jim gives himself up to the headman, and is shot by him: as the
narrator says,

> Not in the wildest days of his boyish visions could he have seen the alluring shape of
> such an extraordinary success! ... But we can see him, an obscure conqueror of
> fame, tearing himself out of the arms of a jealous love at the sign, at the call of his
> exalted egoism. He goes away from a living woman to celebrate his pitiless wedding
> with a shadowy ideal of conduct. (1900: 253)

The book has received an edifying reading (Weston 1975), according to
which Jim feels *shame* for his early *cowardice*, but *redeems* himself in his own
eyes in the end by acting with *integrity* – he does after all *say* he stakes his life
on the safety of the headman's son – in just the way he had failed to do
before. But this reading overlooks Conrad's insistence on the role of fiction
in Jim's thinking. This is not to say that people can't be straightforwardly
inspired to exemplary moral conduct by reading fiction – no doubt they
can. Nor is it to say that Jim doesn't feel shame for his conduct on the *Patna*,
and indeed feels it because his conduct was cowardly. Nonetheless – at least
if to have an ideal isn't *per se* a character defect, for all that the content of the
ideal might make it into one – the fictional models that dominate Jim's

thought are not properly thought of as his ideals, because to be dominated in that way by a fictional model, no matter what its content, *is* a defect of character. So what is the difference? The question deserves a systematic treatment but here I can only provide a sketch of an answer. For one thing, there's a difference with respect to truth: possessors both of ideals and of fictional models want to believe that they are true of them, but with fictional models – until reality presses itself so insistently that it's no longer effective – wishful thinking is a typical mechanism for satisfying this want, whereas this is not so with ideals. This connects with a second point, about self-criticism: ideals give rise to self-criticism of a kind that can be both continuous and realistic, whereas fictional models on the whole militate against realistic self-assessment, only to allow it in as a last resort in a form that is both total and damning. Thirdly and relatedly, Jim's cowardice bears an oddly oblique relation to his shame: his shame does not, for example, express itself in thoughts about his potential victims. Indeed Jim is barely capable of acknowledging that he *did* jump ship, so reluctant is he to acknowledge the gap between himself and the flattering picture of himself borrowed from fiction. The primary object of his shame is not his cowardice in jumping ship, but the mismatch between the flattering picture and reality. As to "redeeming himself," by the end of the novel the *Patna* episode is years behind him and only the fact that he is "romantic" – Conrad's word for subjection to models of conduct derived from fiction – freezes his attention on that episode and obscures the fact that the most important issue he now faces is quite a different one. A less "romantic" character – and one therefore whose thoughts were better at tracking the contours of his own changing reality – would not have needed to parade his integrity to himself, because he would have had a greater sense of the solidity of his life as it then was (the "living woman" whom he trades for a "shadowy ideal of conduct"), of his then life as a going concern.

Before we go on, we need a term for the defect of character I have been trying to outline. Conrad's "romantic" of course suggests one, but it is already fully booked so I opt for a well-established alternative – though it has to stay in italics – in memory of one of the defect's most famous exemplars: *bovarysme*.[10] To head off the suggestion that *bovarysme* is a defect

---

[10] *Le Petit Robert* records a philosopher's (Jules de Gaultier's) definition, "le pouvoir départi à l'homme de se concevoir autre qu'il n'est" – useless, because it fits more or less any imaginative exercise involving oneself. The word is found in English in, for example, Eliot 1934: 40. Though Eliot defers partially to Gaultier's definition (but only partially: "the human *will* to see things as they are not"), he also describes Othello – whose *bovarysme* is in question – as taking "an *aesthetic* rather than a moral attitude [to himself], dramatizing himself against his environment."

that only besets fictional characters, I want to look at one more case of it, admittedly a case evidenced in a piece of written work and a work of some considerable literary merit at that, but not a piece of fiction – a piece of autobiography. Peter Fuller's memoir *Marches Past* (Fuller 1986) is partly a self-conscious record of the author's struggle with his *bovarysme*, and therefore partly resembles *Lord Jim* insofar as it is a literary representation of someone with that affliction (though in Fuller's case a really existing someone). But insofar as Fuller's struggle is unsuccessful – Fuller displays his self-fictionalizing tendency in his very effort to describe how he "breaks out" of it to "real human relations" – the book is also simply evidence of his *bovarysme*, not a representation of it. Fuller, that is, appears to have suffered from what Conrad in *Lord Jim* only represented.

Fuller had for many years, he tells us, a pet axolotl, which as he explains is

the embryonic state of the Mexican salamander . . . [It] need never metamorphose and may even breed in its larval form.

That is to say, he had in a tank in his room a symbol of emotional stuntedness (forever the embryo) and cut-offness from other people (the tank's glass sides). In the course of the memoir Fuller comes to hate the axolotl ("it infuriated me because it refused to grow up"; 1986: 60) and is glad when it dies because, he says, "I have reached the other side of the window-pane . . . My assassination of it was an act of self-realization" (1986: 63). One senses, however, that his "assassination" – an overstatement in any case: the creature in fact seems to die either of illness or of an accidental overdose of axolotl medicine – isn't an act of self-realization, but only the symbol of one. Self-realization occurs in the narrative of his life that Fuller constructs with the animal as a prop, but whether real life catches up is less clear. And he knows it: when at the end of the book Fuller describes the birth of his daughter, he tells us "This was real: not a watery, wordy or painted birth" (1986: 181). (The "watery" birth is the symbolic birth into a salamander which the axolotl would have undergone if Fuller had smashed its tank.) But even this real birth, though of course it really happened, is ready to hand for Fuller as a symbol of "breaking out" to "real relations with others" – after all there is no necessity to end the book's narrative when his daughter is born. Indeed nothing could be more conveniently symbolic than a real rather than a symbolic birth, and even as Fuller weaves real events into the narrative web he compulsively casts over his own life as it unfolds, as if hoping thereby to stabilize them, events get the better of him: a postscript to the book owns up that

Just as I was beginning to break out of the citadel of the past and myself, and beginning to be able to enjoy my relationship with [his wife] . . . she left. (1986: 181)

Despite the instability of his own narrative construction, his imprisonment in it is guaranteed by his incapacity – of which he's painfully aware – not to convert everything he comes across into a literary symbol. "Damn! Damn!" he says. "As I read back what I have written, I realize how living itself becomes all 'set up'" (1986: 136); seemingly overwhelmed by the symbolic possibilities of a plate of oysters, he longs for "an oyster which is an oyster which is an oyster."

I have dwelt at length on *bovarysme* partly because of the intrinsic interest of differentiating the bad from the (presumably possible) good ways in which one can be inspired or guided in one's life by fiction. But there's also of course a connection with Nietzsche. Because of their debt to an art form, a perfectly good word for the relation to fictional models characteristic of *bovarysme* could be "having aesthetic ideals."[11] And though the thought is not to the fore in the *Genealogy*, Nietzsche famously claimed that the "great and rare art" of "'giv[ing] style' to one's character" "is practised by those who survey all the strengths and weaknesses that their nature has to offer and then fit them into an artistic plan" (*GS*, 290); we "want to be poets of our lives" (*GS*, 299). Setting on one side the highly specialized claim that Nietzsche's literary output itself constitutes the practice of this "art" (Nehamas 1985, 1998), it's at least not a foolish interpretation of Nietzsche to read him as holding an "aesthetics of character" precisely insofar as he urges us self-consciously to shape our lives in such a way that they have a plot.[12] But that is *bovarysme*: aesthetic ideals in this sense are false ideals. It does not of course follow from this that Nietzsche didn't have them, and I return to the question in section 5 below. For the time being it is enough to have fixed a sense of "aesthetic ideals" in which they are something to be avoided.

4. So far I have set up three models of what an aesthetics of character might be. The first was any ideal of character which comes out on the wrong side of the self-regarding/other-regarding divide which is central to morality's taxonomy of character traits: this clearly picks out ideals as aesthetic

---

[11] As Eliot saw: see previous footnote.
[12] If Nietzsche *were* in some sense his own literary creation ("a character whose 'biography' [his work] turns out to be"; Nehamas 1985: 199), would it follow that Nietzsche himself was a victim of *bovarysme*? As Nehamas says, whether or not Nietzsche succeeded in applying "the image of life contained in his writings" to himself is a biographical matter, not a philosophical one, so examining the work won't tell us (Nehamas 1998: 8). The most we can say is that, in the light of Fuller's experience, if he *did* apply that model to himself, it's not clear how much of a "success" that would be.

on account of their content. The second and third, by contrast, were content-neutral: any conception of how to live that is presented as worth-while but not mandatory – that is, any ideal; and *bovarysme* (which is a way of relating to an ideal that makes it a false ideal, whatever its content). If these three exhaust the possibilities for the "aesthetics of character," perhaps there's good reason to give up using the term in connection with Nietzsche – and indeed altogether. But do they? Janaway maintains that one aspect of Nietzsche's positive ideal of individuality or self-love is

aesthetic or quasi-aesthetic self-satisfaction, the shaping of one's character so that every part of it contributes to a meaningful whole in the manner of a work of art. (Janaway 2007: 254)

The idea here differs from the empty idea of a "beautiful soul" I dismissed in section 1, in that a reason is offered for calling the self-satisfaction in question distinctively aesthetic, namely that its object is not just any feature of one's character that one regards as good, but (to put it vaguely) its shape. So if the notion of a character's shape can be given a sense that's sufficiently close to (say) the shape of a vase – a property which is uncontroversially apt to elicit aesthetic appreciation – the reason offered will be a good one.[13] Meanwhile Aaron Ridley notes that "art," in certain crucial passages in the *Genealogy*, "refers to the imposition of form on raw material" (1998b: 136).[14] Since the characteristic that draws Nietzsche's admiration above all in the *Genealogy* is, Ridley argues, the capacity to impose form, his "admiration for the master-interpreters he describes, and for their master-interpretations" constitutes an "aesthetic" (1998b: 137). Ridley's point is clearly related to Janaway's, because among the things on which Nietzsche says humanity's form-giving is practiced is humanity itself, and this includes (though it's not restricted to) the form-giver's own character. If the giver and the receiver of form are one and the same, then, crediting Nietzsche with an aesthetics of character apparently has a double justification.[15]

---

[13] Cf. Nehamas 1985: 192: "Nietzsche believes that the evaluation of people and lives must appeal to a *formal* factor in addition to the content of our actions."

[14] E.g. *GM*, II, 12; II, 17; cf. *BGE*, 213.

[15] Aesthetic vocabulary for the appraisal of character and its double justification are anticipated to a remarkable extent, it would seem, by Shaftesbury: "The Beautiful, the Fair, the Comely, were never in the Matter, but in the Art and Design; never in Body itself, but in the Form or Forming Power. . . . [Hence] the only instance of 'true' beauty . . . [is] a mind that has trained its formative powers *on itself*, that has made *itself* the object of its power to impose order and harmony on external matter. . . . [T]hat which fashions even minds themselves, contains in itself all the Beauties fashioned by those Minds," from Shaftesbury's *Characteristics* 2: 407–8, cited by Norton 1995: 35–36. As Norton points out, it is unclear whether "that which fashions minds themselves" is a reference to human self-fashioning, which would make the presumptive Nietzschean parallel very close indeed, or to God.

To take the components of the double justification in turn, let's begin with the notion of a character's "shape." The notion needs to be handled with care. According to Nehamas, Nietzsche holds that

an admirable self consists in a large number of powerful and conflicting tendencies that are controlled and harmonized. . . . Style . . . involves controlled multiplicity and resolved conflict. (1985: 7)

But this doesn't seem quite right. Nietzsche writes:

In an age of disintegration . . . a person will have the legacy of multiple lineages in his body, which means conflicting (and often not merely conflicting) drives and value standards that fight each other and rarely leave each other alone. . . . [I]f conflict and war affect such a nature as one *more* stimulus and goad to life – , and if genuine proficiency and finesse in waging war with himself (which is to say: the ability to control and outwit himself) are inherited and cultivated along with his most powerful and irreconcilable drives, then what emerge are those amazing, incomprehensible, and unthinkable ones, those human riddles destined for victory and seduction; Alcibiades and Caesar are the most exquisite expressions of this type. (*BGE*, 200)[16]

Evidently Alcibiades and Caesar are cited as paragons. So Nehamas is right that Nietzsche prized "self-control" (Nehamas: "controlled multiplicity"), but wrong to identify it with harmony (Nehamas: "controlled *and harmonized*"). The kind of control in question is, on the contrary, that which consists in tolerating *dis*harmony ("conflict and war") – being such that conflicting tendencies can coexist in oneself *without* one's succumbing to the temptation either to disown one or more of them, or to harmonize them. The point is confirmed by a passage in *Ecce Homo* in which Nietzsche credits himself with this quality:

The task of *revaluing all values* might have required more abilities than have ever been combined in any one individual, and in particular contradictory abilities that could not be allowed to disturb or destroy one another. . . . not mixing anything, not "reconciling" anything; an incredible multiplicity that is nonetheless the converse of chaos. (*EH*, "Why I Am So Clever," 9)

However, as long as we take to heart the injunction "to 'reconcile' nothing," and so remember that "the opposite of chaos" isn't "harmony," but simply

---

[16] Cf. *GM*, I, 16: "there is, today, perhaps no more distinguishing feature of the '*higher nature*', the intellectual nature, than to be divided in this sense [i.e. between the "*opposing* values 'good and bad', 'good and evil'"] and really and truly a battleground for these opposites"; "Where the plant 'man' shows himself strongest one finds instincts that conflict powerfully . . . but are controlled" (*KGW* VII-2: 289), and Nietzsche's idealization of Goethe who "bore all the conflicting tendencies of his century within him" (*KGW* VI-3: 145).

"form,"[17] the point that the shape of a character – the way its parts relate to one another – is an ideal for Nietzsche is in order.

However, to get from this to the conclusion that Nietzsche's ideal of shape constitutes an *aesthetics* of character, it's not enough that the shape of a vase is an aesthetic property and that there's *some* sense of "shape" on which Nietzsche values character for its shape: the question is whether *that* sense of "shape" is sufficiently close to the unarguably aesthetic one. Nor is it enough to show that a character could be admirable on account of its shape but bad in some other way. This is not to ask whether Nietzsche would admire someone on account of their character's shape despite their being consistently and thoroughgoingly wicked: the question seems irrelevant since "shape" in the sense in which Nietzsche admires it has little or nothing to do with consistency. But it does seem possible that he could admire someone for the shape of their character who had both (and unreconciled) good and bad character traits, and I don't think we have to confine this thought experiment to the case where the bad traits are just bad from the perspective of morality narrowly conceived – they can be bad on any sane evaluative outlook. Now picking out the shape of a character as an independently admirable trait leaves room for judgments of the form "(some) bad parts, good whole," and indeed it should: we *can* surely admire somebody, independently of the value of their individual traits, for the fact that they live with them without self-deceiving attempts to tidy themselves up. But it doesn't follow that "shape" is an aesthetic notion. For since "shape" doesn't mean "harmony," what it means is well enough captured by the thought that conflicting drives or experiences or parts of oneself should not be *disowned* or *denied* or *repressed*. And this ideal sounds at least as much like an ideal of psychic (or personal) *health* as it does like a distinctively aesthetic one. Did Nietzsche himself think "shape" was an aesthetic ideal? Of course there is evidence that he did: the famous "giving style" passage already quoted from *The Gay Science* goes on that those who practice this art go on "until . . . even weaknesses delight the eye" (*GS*, 290). However, there is also some evidence that he thought of it as an ideal of health:

A strong and well-formed man digests his experiences (including deeds and misdeeds) as he digests his meals, even when he has hard lumps to swallow. (*GM*, III, 16)[18]

---

[17] Cf. "compelling one's chaos to become form" (*WP*, 842).
[18] Cf. *BGE*, 257. In *GM*, I, 10, the "forming" and "health" vocabularies are mixed: "to be unable to take his enemies, his misfortunes, and even his *misdeeds* seriously for long – that is the sign of strong, rounded natures with a superabundance of a power which is flexible, formative, healing and can make one forget." The vocabulary of sickness and health features prominently in Nietzsche's vocabulary of appraisal generally, as at e.g. *GM*, I, 7; III, 15.

If I am right, the latter way of classifying the shape ideal is better motivated than the former, and the case for crediting Nietzsche with an aesthetics of character has not yet been made out.

5. I turn now to the second component of the double justification, the fact that Nietzsche admires not only characters which *have* shape or form, in the sense explained, but also the capacity for *form-giving* itself. I don't mean to suggest that this is Nietzsche's *only* ideal of character, but since it has been said to be specially closely related to the aesthetic, it is worth focusing on. The term *virtù* will do as a shorthand for it, and indeed Nietzsche uses it himself:

> What is happiness? – The feeling that power is *growing*, that some resistance has been overcome. . . . *Not* virtue, but prowess (virtue in the style of the Renaissance style, *virtù*). (*A*, 2; cf. *EH*, "Why I Am So Clever," 1)

Read back into Nietzsche's remarks about the fashioning of one's own character, it fits his idea that we constitute a "difficult, resisting . . . matter" (*GM*, II, 18): self-fashioning would then exemplify *virtù*, because the "difficulty" of the material is a measure of the *virtù* of the artist.[19] But though *virtù* is evidently a Nietzschean ideal, is it an aesthetic ideal?

Well, isn't it just obviously an aesthetic ideal, because in Nietzsche's view it's the quality quintessentially required in artists? But that would be too quick, since one might argue on just the same basis that in its core manifestations at least – i.e. as displayed in the production of works of art – *virtù* isn't an ideal of character at all, but a skill. The two concepts are distinct (Foot 2002b: 8), because one can show off one's skill as a sculptor all the better by deliberately getting the proportions of the statue wrong, but one cannot display one's courage by deliberate acts of cowardice. Why does this difference make a difference? Because virtues of character "engage the will" (ibid.), including one's choice of ends, in a way skills don't. In reply, however, there are virtues of character – notably courage – which are not directly to do with one's choice of ends. Thus it's my honesty that's displayed in my decision to tell the truth in a room full of people who don't want to hear it, but this can *also* display courage. So *virtù* could after all be a virtue of character, but an "executive" virtue. Moreover it's not just lack of practice that interferes with *virtù* – so do lack of spontaneity, timidity, excessive deference to others, as well as more complex psychological

---

[19] For *virtù* and *difficultà* (difficulty), see Shearman 1967: 21: "Lorenzo de'Medici, in a Commentary upon his own sonnets, argued that this verse-form is the equal of any other because of its *difficultà* – because *virtù*, according to the philosophers, consists in (the conquest of) difficulty. . . . Painters and sculptors each argued the superiority of their art over the other because it was more difficult."

blockages, and these seem to "engage the will," as is evident from what's involved in trying to overcome them. But if they are traits of character, so is *virtù*.

A more worrying objection to the claim that *virtù* is an aesthetic ideal parallels the worry about shape. The thought that *virtù* is an aesthetic ideal draws its strength from the claim that it's the form-giver's virtue, and things that are thus given form are objects of aesthetic appraisal. But if in connection with one's own character, "shape" is better understood as an ideal of health than as an aesthetic ideal, this justification for treating *virtù* as an aesthetic ideal falls by the wayside.[20]

On the back of this objection comes another. Even if "shape" as an ideal of character were enough like an aesthetic property to justify the claim that in giving form to one's character one would be displaying *virtù*, is shape really something one *gives* one's character? The thought seems highly doubtful: the part played by the voluntary in the formation or re-formation of one's character, including any process by which one's conflicting traits together achieve "shape" or "form," seem to be – as Nietzsche himself has in part taught us to see – both oblique and patchy. So if Nietzsche thought of his ideals as an aesthetics of character because of the opportunities for displaying *virtù* in relation to oneself, that would have been a bad reason. But in any case, it has been argued (Leiter 1998; see also May 1999: 189) that notwithstanding the "giving style" passage and others, it's problematic to ascribe to Nietzsche the thought that one stands to one's own character as an artist to his material: certainly the last thing he thinks is that "becoming what one is" involves making one's life conform to a preconceived plan. ("Becoming what you are presupposes that you do not have the slightest idea *what* you are"; *EH*, "Why I Am So Clever," 9.) This, indeed, is why it would be wrong to say Nietzsche advocated the twisted relation to narrative models characteristic of *bovarysme* under the guise of a genuine ideal.

Before we write off *virtù* as an ideal of character in Nietzsche, however, let's not forget that there are many things *besides* oneself that Nietzsche thinks admirable people give form to – including, most notably, other people. Indeed in the *Genealogy*, the theme of giving form to others (as e.g. *GM*, II, 17, "the shaping of a population, which had up to now been

---

[20] I don't see why "shape" couldn't be an aesthetic property of character even if it were merely an instance of natural beauty. Thus, if I understand him correctly, I differ from Ridley who holds that shape is an aesthetic property of character *just* because it's a property it receives as a result of form-giving activity by the person whose character it is: "Beauty is a state of the soul: it is the result of going to work on oneself, of interpreting oneself, of exercising upon oneself that artist's violence to which Nietzsche is so attached" (Ridley 1998b: 140).

unrestrained and shapeless, into a fixed form"; cf. also *GM*, II, 12) is at least as prominent as that of forming oneself. In this context, the previous objections to *virtù* as an ideal of character in Nietzsche do not apply. But now the question arises whether Nietzsche's prizing of *virtù* serves to mark Nietzsche's own ideals off from those he rejects, and in particular from the ideals of character that belong to morality. It might appear that the answer has to be "no," for two reasons. First, the form-givers in the *Genealogy* include the priests (both the "priestly caste" of the nobles [*GM*, I, 7] and the Jews and Christians); "the 'unegoistic' as a *moral* value" too was the product of "artist's cruelty" (*GM*, II, 18). Second, as May has argued (1999: 81ff.), asceticism according to Nietzsche is not life-denying *per se* but only when it "wants to be master, not over something in life but over life itself" (*GM*, III, 11). Indeed asceticism plays a leading part in Nietzsche's specification of his own ideals, as for example in the description of any anti-moralist ("for whom conquest, adventure, danger, and even pain have actually become a necessity; . . . acclimatized to thinner air higher up, to winter treks, ice and mountains in every sense") who might dare to "intertwin[e] . . . bad conscience with . . . all the ideals which up to now have been hostile to life" (*GM*, II, 24). So there's no form-giving/ascetic polarity which we might appeal to in order to divide *virtù* from the ideals Nietzsche rejects. However, it doesn't follow from this that *virtù* is not a distinctively Nietzschean ideal. For it doesn't follow from the fact that the creators of morality *exemplified virtù* that it is an ideal *of theirs*, and indeed I take it to be one of the peculiarities of morality's asceticism (as distinct from the broader ascetic "conceptual form"; May 1999: 81) that it cannot find room in its own catalogue of virtues for this virtue, and thus cannot recognize one of its own driving forces: "'life *against* life' is . . . simply nonsense. It can only be *apparent*; it has to be a sort of provisional expression, . . . a psychological misunderstanding of something, the real nature of which was far from being understood" (*GM*, III, 13). But something can hardly function as an ideal for someone if it is not even acknowledged: the task of distinguishing Nietzsche's ideals from those he opposes is precisely a matter of specifying rival *catalogues* of excellences of character, so there can be a sharp contrast at this level even if adherents to the rival catalogues may have fundamental psychological features in common. The fact that "priests" too are form-givers is no reason, then, not to treat *virtù* as a distinctively Nietzschean ideal.

So, finally, is treating *virtù* as an ideal of character to have an *aesthetics* of character? If modesty is a (narrowly) moral virtue, I take it that its contrary and that which it is designed to guard against – boastfulness – is a narrowly moral vice. So a good way to try to place *virtù* in relation to other human excellences is to think again of the things that militate against it – for example timidity, lack of self-discipline, self-deception, all of which Nietzsche reviles. Though these are not the exclusive preserve of morality in the narrow sense, and indeed even if (improbably) none of them belong to it at all, they are very familiar defects of character, and no purpose is served by classifying them as distinctively aesthetic. Consequently, central as *virtù* may be to Nietzsche's ideals, I cannot see that it is illuminating to classify an ideal of human living that makes room for it as an "aesthetics of character."

On all the interpretations of "aesthetic" as applied to ideals of character that I have examined, then, the term turns out either to be well motivated but not to mark out a genuine ideal; or else poorly motivated, either as a way of marking out an ideal of a distinctive type or as a way of marking out what is special about Nietzsche's own ideals, or both. If we are to capture what, if anything, is special about Nietzsche's ideals of character, therefore, we are unlikely to help ourselves if we continue to reach for the "aesthetic" label.

6. The sense remains nonetheless that I have barely begun to describe the entanglement of the ethical with the aesthetic in Nietzsche's work, so let me say in conclusion a little about the direction in which further investigation might go. In his *Morality: An Introduction to Ethics*, Bernard Williams points out the dangers for the would-be amoralist of "thinking of himself as being in character really rather splendid" (1976: 20). Though Williams's imagined figure also compares himself with the "craven multitude," there's no evidence Williams had Nietzschean models in mind. But the thought Williams's amoralist needs not to have is very like a thought Foot ascribes to Nietzsche: his ideal for humanity, she says in discussing his "shift from moral to aesthetic valuation," is "a splendid human being" (Foot 2002a: 148). And "splendor" is, I take it, a term of aesthetic appraisal.

Now the thought the amoralist needs not to have is not a thought Nietzsche's nobles were in danger of having about themselves, for all their consciousness of social superiority, for aesthetic notions are notably absent from their evaluative repertoire. Their "good"–"bad" contrast expresses class difference and the traits that supposedly went with that, and even where the trait is a character trait (truthfulness rather than, say, wealth), Nietzsche emphasizes that this was originally *merely* a way of marking class difference and not a value judgment of any kind, and so *a fortiori* not an aesthetic judgment (*GM*, I, 4; I, 5). Nietzsche also mentions "reverence for age and origins" as the basis for justice (*BGE*, 260): plausible in a tribal society, but it expresses no aesthetic valuation. Other defining features of noble morality flow from the "good"–"bad" distinction: they have duties of "extended gratitude and vengefulness" to members of their own group, while it doesn't really matter how they behave towards the "bad" ("to creatures of a lower rank ... people may act as they see fit"; *BGE*, 260). Again no trace of aesthetic norms: towards the in-group it's traditional duty, towards the out-group it's whatever they feel like doing.

However, "splendor" *is* a word in Nietzsche's own evaluative vocabulary ("[man's] highest potential power and splendour"; *GM*, Preface, 6), and all I've said so far is consistent with the claim that Nietzsche himself *did* think the nobles were "really rather splendid." Perhaps that is part of what Foot had in mind. However, it seems wrong to describe this Nietzschean judgment on the nobles as evidence of an aesthetic *ideal* of character on Nietzsche's part. For one thing, the psychology of Nietzsche's "higher nature" of today (*GM*, I, 16) is vastly more complex than the psychology Nietzsche ascribes to the nobles, thanks to the whole (speculative) history of morality that lies between them and us. So however splendid Nietzsche thought the nobles (together with their non-aesthetic ideals), their way of life and their ideals cannot be ideals *for us*, or for Nietzsche, or for anyone starting off from where he was, or we are.

The judgment does, however, amount to what we might call aestheti-*cism*, a sensibility which includes the capacity to suppress moral evaluation in favor of the appreciation of properties such as splendor, magnificence, excitement, massiveness of scale – not to mention thoughtlessness and violence. It is tempting to say it is an attitude to life that is akin to typical attitudes to the representation of life in art. But it's not clear that the suspension of moral evaluation is invited by artistic representation as such. Nor is it clear that this attitude only makes an appearance in relation to ways of living which are – like that of Nietzsche's nobles – too remote to serve as models for us, though it may be more appropriate here than elsewhere: after all, if one can paint a stirring scene in which the eye is drawn away from morally problematic features, one can paint oneself into it too. This brings me back to *bovarysme*: not, admittedly, the "strategic" *bovarysme* of trying to live one's whole life according to a narrative plan, but the more "tactical" *bovarysme* of Eliot's "dramatizing oneself against one's environment" (1934: 40). But if Nietzsche does exemplify this sensibility – and I have hardly argued for that here – he is surely only one of a great many to have done so. Accordingly the proper investigation of this sensibility and its relevance to moral philosophy I leave to another occasion.

CHAPTER 13

Nietzsche and the virtues of mature egoism

Christine Swanton

(i) INTRODUCTION

A major obstacle to reading Nietzsche as a philosopher who has something to offer substantive moral theory is his self-ascriptions as both an immoralist and an egoist.[1] I overcome this obstacle by understanding Nietzsche's conception of virtues of character as those of the "*mature* egoist." I focus the discussion on the virtues of mature egoism (and correlative vices) as portrayed in *GM*, but Nietzsche's conception of the mature egoist underlies all his central works in ethics. Indeed the core ideas of mature egoism are introduced in works other than *GM*.

Much has been written about the sense in which Nietzsche is an immoralist, and its compatibility with a kind of morality, albeit a revisionary one.[2] However, an uneasy feeling remains that the sense in which he is a moralist is distinctly unattractive to modern moral sensibilities for, according to Nietzsche, the "true morality" is a form of egoism:

... we shall restore to men their goodwill towards the actions decried as egoistic and restore to these actions their *value – we shall deprive them of their bad conscience!* (*D*, 148)

I shall not dispute that Nietzsche's ethics is a kind of egoism. What I shall dispute, particularly in relation to *GM*, is that the kind of egoism he espouses is unattractive. Due to the focus on *GM*, I cannot in this chapter deal with all salient passages apparently confirming the interpretation of

---

[1] I use the Cambridge (Diethe 1994) translation of *GM* (with page references), though I very occasionally refer to the Smith translation (see below). Other translations are as follows: *The Antichrist*, trans. Walter Kaufmann (1976a); *Twilight of the Idols*, trans. Walter Kaufman (1976b); *Daybreak*, trans. R. J. Hollingdale (1982b); *Untimely Meditations*, trans. R. J. Hollingdale (1983), Essay II, "On the Uses and Disadvantages of History for Life"; *Human, All Too Human*, trans. Marion Faber with Stephen Lehmann (1984); *Beyond Good and Evil: Prelude to a Philosophy of the Future*, trans. R. J. Hollingdale (1990a); and *On the Genealogy of Morals*, trans. Douglas Smith (1996).
[2] For what might be called explicitly compatibilist readings see, for example, Bergman 1988: 29–45, Solomon 1973: 202–25, and Schacht 1973: 58–82 and 1983: 466–75.

Nietzsche's ethics as unattractive: passages such as those apparently endorsing cruelty and exploitation in *BGE* and *A*.[3]

My argument has the following general structure. What is needed is a proper understanding of the kind of egoism endorsed by Nietzsche. In particular, I claim, his kind of egoism is what he calls a "mature" egoism, to be contrasted with a number of forms of immaturity: the immature egoism of instant gratification, an unsocialized egoism, and the kind of altruism in which the self "wilts away" (*TI*, "Skirmishes of an Untimely Man," 36). I do not argue that what is to moral sensibilities unattractive should (counterintuitively) be regarded as attractive, necessitating a wholesale revision of our moral intuitions. Rather I show that Nietzsche's sophisticated psychologically insightful account of various virtues and vices is compelling, even though on a superficial understanding he apparently endorses what we would regard as an immoral form of egoism.

The central features of a mature egoist are to be found in a passage headed "The Three Phases of Morality until Now" in *HAH*, I:

The first sign that an animal has become human is that his behavior is no longer directed to his momentary comfort, but rather to his enduring comfort, that is when man becomes useful, *expedient*: then for the first time the free rule of reason bursts forth. A still higher state is reached when man acts according to the principle of *honor*, by means of which he finds his place in society, submitting to commonly held feelings; that raises him high above the phase in which he is guided only by personal usefulness. Now he shows – and wants to be shown – respect; that is he understands his advantage as dependent on his opinion of others and their opinion of him. Finally, at the highest stage of morality *until now* he acts according to his standard of things and men; he himself determines for himself and others what is honorable, what is profitable. He has become the lawgiver of opinions, in accordance with the ever more refined concept of usefulness and honor … He lives and acts as a collective individual. ("On the History of the Moral Sensations," 94)

However, though the mature individual lives in some sense as a collective individual, recognizing the need to respect and be respected in a suitably "refined" sense, he is not an impersonal self-sacrificing individual submersing himself in the collective. For as is made clearer in the subsequent passage titled "Morality of the Mature Individual," we need to cultivate what is

---

[3] I discuss the genealogical context of Part 9 of *BGE* in Swanton 2006. Here Nietzsche describes what is good *qua* aristocracy and aristocratic morality: he is not endorsing such a morality as the highest to which we can aspire, but he suggests here and elsewhere that the occurrence of such moralities may be necessary for, a "precondition" of, moral progress.

personal in us, not offering ourselves "in sacrifice to the state, to science, to the needy as if it [the personal] were something bad which had to be sacrificed" (*HAH*, I, "On the History of the Moral Sensations," 95).

Working for our fellow man is fine, but not if it is a sacrifice. As a result the morality of the mature individual is not an impersonal morality:

> Until now man has taken the true sign of a moral act to be its impersonal nature; and it has been shown that in the beginning all impersonal acts were praised and distinguished in respect of the common good . . . to make a whole person of oneself and keep in mind that person's greatest good in everything one does – this takes us further than any pitying impulses and actions for the sake of others. (*HAH*, I, "On the History of the Moral Sensations," 95)

From these passages one gleans that the morality of the mature egoist is to be contrasted both with forms of immature egoism (that of the unsocialized individual seeking his advantage, and that of him who, having a crude unrefined concept of his own good, seeks "momentary comfort"), and also with the morality of the self-sacrificing altruist who has internalized an impersonal morality.

Aristotle's architectonic of virtue in which a virtue is a mean opposed to vices of excess and deficiency may thus be contrasted to some extent with a Nietzschean architectonic of the virtues of the mature egoist opposed to correlative vices of immature egoism and self-sacrificing altruism. In one respect my account of this contrast is more complex than Brian Leiter's (2002) account of Nietzsche's excellences of the "higher man" in that although the higher man is a mature egoist, not all mature egoists need be higher men. As I shall explicate in the next section, what I regard as the (universal) virtues of mature egoism need to be "differentiated" according to such factors as role, talents, and capabilities of strength. Though higher men are "great" in some way – important leaders, highly talented artists, and so forth, "seeking burdens and responsibilities" (Leiter 2002: 117) – the human excellences of the mature egoist are not restricted to such men. As Leiter rightly claims, "morality" (of the kind criticized by Nietzsche) is harmful because it is harmful to the development of higher men, but on my account of Nietzsche it is seen as harmful more generally because it is also harmful to the development of human virtue in those not destined to become "higher." As we shall see, some qualities will be seen as excessive and thus not virtues if qualities of "lower" men, but will be virtues of mature egoism when possessed by higher men.

Several virtues of the mature egoist and their correlative vices are considered below. Virtues in their order of presentation are:

(1) **Assertiveness**
    contrasted with vices of
    (a) Cruelty
    (b) Excessive passivity
(2) **Justice**
    contrasted with vices of
    (a) Vengefulness and rigorous punitivism
    (b) "Scientific fairness"
(3) **Objectivity**
    contrasted with vices of
    (a) Egocentricity of perspective
    (b) "Hyperobjectivity"
(4) **Mature generosity**
    contrasted with vices of
    (a) (Unhealthy) selfishness
    (b) Self-sacrificing charity
(5) **Independence/self-sufficiency**
    contrasted with vices of
    (a) Excessive independence
    (b) Parasitism
    (c) Disposition to immerse oneself in the collectivity
(6) **Discipline**
    contrasted with a vice of
    (a) Asceticism

(ii) THE STRUCTURE AND NATURE OF VIRTUE

In sections (iii)–(viii) I contrast what Nietzsche regards as virtues of the mature egoist with correlative vices, particularly in relation to *GM*. In order to make the contrasts between virtue and correlative vice I need to give an account of several structural features of virtue: the idea of the field of a virtue; the thin versus thick account of a virtue; and the distinction between basic and differentiated virtue. I need also to outline the central quality of virtue for Nietzsche: the depth-psychological quality of motive, desire, or "instinct."

The field of a virtue is the domain of concern of a virtue. On this conception, virtues are identified according to their domains; thus for example on Aristotle's conception temperance is concerned centrally with the pleasures of food, sex, and drink. The field of a virtue may also be outside the agent, for example friends and potential friends are the field of the virtue of friendship, dangerous situations and potentially dangerous situations at least part of the field of courage as a general virtue, and so on (Nussbaum 1988).

Once virtues are identified according to their fields we can distinguish between the thin and thick accounts of a virtue: a distinction due to Martha Nussbaum (1988). In a thin account of a virtue we identify a virtue and its correlative vices according to the delineation of its field, and define a *virtue* as being *well* disposed in relation to that field in respect of the various aspects of virtue (such as affective states, motivational states, wisdom, and action). Thus temperance as a virtue involves, for example, being wise and knowledgeable about types and amounts of food to be eaten, when, where, and how; having appropriate appetites, excellent motivation in relation to getting, eating, keeping, etc., food; and getting things right in action in relation to those things.[4] Thick accounts of virtue are substantive positions on what constitutes being well disposed in the relevant areas of a virtue, areas such as action and motivation.

Let us turn to the distinction between basic and differentiated virtue. A basic virtue such as generosity or loyalty is a virtue described at a high level of generality or abstraction in its thick account(s). By a high level of generality is meant that the virtue, so specified, does not accommodate, for example, what Nietzsche would regard as the individual qualities of a virtue as it manifests in a particular person. For Nietzsche, individuals cultivate virtues according to their distinctive circumstances, nature, and the narrative particularities of their lives, thereby making virtues *their own*. Nor will an account of a basic virtue be "differentiated" according to the exigencies of a role, or, of particular interest to Nietzsche, the type of individual she is: whether or not she is destined for greatness in leadership or artistic roles for example. If one is an average individual and is thus a member of the "herd," as Nietzsche puts it, one must still avoid the vices of immature egoism: in particular that herd-like vice of being disposed to seek "momentary comfort" with attendant vices of laziness and failing to cultivate one's talents.

Accounts of virtues which are applied to roles, or relativized to cultural or historical situatedness, for example, I call accounts of *differentiated* virtue. Thus we may speak of generosity *qua* chief executive officer of a business firm for example. Such generosity, if virtuous, will be severely constrained

---

[4] I do not intend this last generalization to be universal since I do not believe that necessarily, virtuous agents perform right acts even when acting in character (see further Swanton 2003: chapter 11).

by business imperatives of various kinds, constraints that do not apply to generosity in a private individual. It is a mark of Nietzsche's philosophy that virtues are differentiated according to many features, most importantly, personal strength. For example, the disposition to seek solitude is inadvisable for the many, says Nietzsche, simply because herd-like individuals are not strong enough for solitude. On the other hand, higher types crave and need solitude: the disposition to seek solitude is a virtue in them assuming that they can cope well with the solitude sought. Notwithstanding this claim, I shall argue that Nietzsche's account is consistent with the idea of universal virtues. I describe a number of universal virtues at a basic level of description, virtues which are universal (in that in some form they are virtues for all), but which should be differentiated according to various factors, such as role as leader, and (no doubt controversially) gender (see section (vii)). In this way, Nietzsche's claim in *BGE*, 228, "that the demand for *one* morality for all is detrimental to precisely the higher men" can be seen as compatible with universal virtue.

Central to Nietzsche's thick account of virtue are depth-psychological features. In numerous places, including in *GM*, Nietzsche deplores the shallowness of conventional moral philosophy which rests easy with surface intention and consequences of actions. He implores us to venture into the depths (*BGE*, 23), by which he means the deeper springs of our motivations, including the psychological features of the ascetic ideal, the spirit of sacrifice, resentment, spiritualized cruelty (cruelty "turned inwards"), fear of our "genius," drives to conformity and mediocrity, and other forms of "escape from self." Once we understand the psychological roots of vice we are able to form a less superficial view of virtue. In *BGE*, 214, for example, he implores us not to think of virtue as those "square and simple virtues on whose account we hold our grandfathers in high esteem but also hold them off a little." Rather we have to investigate our "most fervent needs"; we have to look for virtue "within our labyrinths" where "such a variety of things lose themselves" (*BGE*, 214).

Nietzsche is not saying that the "square and simple virtues" are not virtues at all. Rather they need to be understood correctly and non-superficially as virtues (in their thick accounts) in order to distinguish them from apparently resembling correlative vices. He deplores superficial, timid, and boring analyses ("all moral philosophy hitherto has been boring and . . . a soporific"; *BGE*, 228, p. 157). Accordingly, to explore the "labyrinths" we need to employ depth psychology where Nietzsche highlights three types of psychological distortion leading to and constituting vice. These, in broadest terms, are:

(1) The depth analysis of vices of immature egoism in its unsocialized or inadequately socialized form, notably cruelty, where individuals have failed to internalize the importance of respect for others and others' having respect for them. In "noble" morality as described in *GM*, these "others" include "barbarians." As Nietzsche puts it, the nobles require the invention of a category of the outside world: foreigners towards whom they can behave like "uncaged beasts of prey" (*GM*, p. 25). They leave "the concept of 'barbarian' in their traces" (*GM*, p. 25).

(2) The depth analysis of vices of immature egoism in the form of the instant gratification characterizing vices associated with desire for "momentary comfort." These are the classic "herd-animal" vices where the "personal" or the "genius" in one is not cultivated.

(3) The depth analysis of a range of vices associated with the spirit of self-sacrifice, for example pity, self-sacrificing forms of charity, dispositions of envy leading to valorizing the wrong kind of equality, and "scientific fairness."

(iii) ASSERTIVENESS

We turn now to the rich resources of *GM* for a discussion of a range of virtues possessed by the mature egoist and their correlative vices. We begin with what we may call (proper) assertiveness by contrast with the vices of cruelty and (excessive) passivity. The field of the virtue comprises a sphere of feeling and activity that is the domain of the virtue. The sphere of assertiveness with respect to feeling comprises for Nietzsche what he would call an "instinct," namely aggression, which should not be confused with an instinct for cruelty. In the sphere of action, the virtue concerns appropriate expression and deployment of aggression when faced with obstacles to the realization of the goals of the agent.[5] In relation to feeling, on the thin account of the virtue of assertiveness the virtue consists of being *well* disposed in relation to the "instinct" of aggression. In relation to action, it involves a disposition to act well (i.e. properly assertively) when dealing with obstacles to the realization of goals, and satisfaction of desires. Furthermore, being well disposed in this area consists also in having *goals* characteristic of

---

[5] Richard Schacht, properly on my view, describes a "higher morality" as "self-assertive" "in a broad sense," by which he means the morality of the self-affirming creative orientation of what I have called the mature egoist. I here use the term "assertiveness" in a narrower sense to denote a specific virtue contrasted with the vice of cruelty (Schacht 1983: 469).

the mature egoist, as opposed to those of the immature egoist and the self-sacrificing altruist.

Correlative vices whose analyses help provide the thick account of the virtue, are cruelty and excessive passivity. These consist (in their thin accounts) of being ill-disposed with respect to the field of the virtue of (proper) assertiveness. We consider each of these vices in turn.

Cruelty

A major difficulty in the reading of GM is the evaluation of cruelty, and more generally "noble" morality. For many, such as Brian Leiter, Nietzsche has the courage to recognize that cruelty is a basic instinct: "the instinct for cruelty is ... a fundamental human instinct" (2002: 231); "humans are naturally cruel" (232). This interpretation is supported by Leiter with a citation of Freud (1961: 78–79), who claims that "[man's] aggressiveness is introjected, internalized; it is, in point of fact, sent back to where it came from – that is, it is directed towards his own ego."[6] Note, however, that Freud speaks of aggressiveness, not cruelty, and it is the instinct for aggressiveness that I have claimed constitutes part of the field of a virtue of proper assertiveness. In fact I shall argue, for Nietzsche cruelty is a form of aggression characterizing the *immature* egoist, and is a distortion of the basic instinct of aggression.

In GM Nietzsche speaks of cruelty in connection with noble morality, which he appears to valorize. However, he valorizes it by comparison with slave morality which for him is clearly much more dangerous in its tendencies to undermine the development of "higher man" – which Leiter is right to emphasize as being of supreme importance to Nietzsche. However, it does not follow that noble morality is the highest morality to which humans can aspire,[7] and indeed Nietzsche's discussion of the immaturity of cruelty suggests it is not.

Why is cruelty immature? Of central importance for Nietzsche is that it is a form of regression. They "[the nobles] *regress* to the innocence of the predator's conscience"[8] engaging without qualm in a "hideous succession of murder, arson, rape and torture ... as though they had simply played a student prank ..." (GM, p. 25). The goal of cruelty as described by

---

[6] Cited in Leiter 2002: 233, n. 13.
[7] See further Schacht 1983: 466: "Higher morality" is not noble or master morality, or master morality resurrected.
[8] *On the Genealogy of Morals*, I, 11, p. 26 (Smith translation) (Carol Diethe renders the passage as "they *return* to the innocent conscience of the wild beast ..."; p. 25).

Nietzsche clearly characterizes immature egoism insofar as it is based on the pleasures of instant gratification, and has no purpose. The perpetrators experience a "shocking cheerfulness, and depth of delight in all destruction" (*GM*, p. 25). The root cause of this regression is the unbearable frustration caused by "social constraint" (*GM*, p. 25) where the "noble man" is "so strongly held in check by custom, respect, habit, gratitude . . ." (*GM*, p. 24) and in this "checked" state exhibits virtues of "consideration, self-control, delicacy, loyalty, pride and friendship" (*GM*, p. 25). Instead of dealing with the frustration of "being closed in and fenced in" (*GM*, p. 25) in a mature way however, by enduring it or sublimating it, he needs to "compensate for the tension" in other ways. Specifically that frustration leads to regression to "animal" instincts, where it is discharged in the manner of "uncaged beasts of prey" (*GM*, p. 25). In quite Freudian terms Nietzsche claims: "the energy of this hidden core [the predatory animal instincts]" "needs to be discharged from time to time, the animal must emerge again."[9] We have here the energy of the unconscious needing to manifest itself.

It will be claimed that for Nietzsche cruelty is not sick in the sense of being a neurosis. Indeed this is so. However, anticipating Freud's distinction between neurosis and perversion, Nietzsche's analysis treats it as a perversion of aggression, having the following features:

(1) As in neurosis, as a result of psychic conflict, there is regression to and a fixation on immature or infantile modes, which block progress to maturity. Here the individual "move[s] backwards down the path of . . . development" (Wollheim 1971: 140).

(2) At the "fixation" point to which the individual has regressed, the individual gains satisfaction "in the more primitive mode" (Wollheim 1971: 140).

By contrast, a neurotic response at the fixation point would occur only if the individual "forbids himself the untrammelled satisfaction of the primitive desires" (Wollheim 1971: 140). The cruelty of the nobles on this account is an immature "perverted" form of aggression; indeed for Nietzsche, the nobles are described as "exultant monsters" (*GM*, p. 25).

Excessive passivity

We turn now to a vice of self-sacrificing altruism in relation to the domain of the virtue of (proper) assertiveness, excessive passivity. Of considerable

---

[9] I, II, p. 26 (Smith translation). Carol Diethe renders the passage as "this hidden centre needs release from time to time, the beast must out again . . ." (p. 25).

interest is the analysis of the Christian virtue of "turning the other cheek," which at first sight appears to be a vice of self-sacrifice and weakness: excessive passivity, rather than a genuinely loving form of assertiveness. However, on Nietzsche's analysis in *GM* it is not at all clear that this is so. Here is the canonical Christian New Testament text (Matthew 5:38):

> You have heard that it was said, "Eye for an eye and tooth for tooth." But I say do not resist an evil person. If someone strikes you on the right cheek turn to him the other also. And if someone wants to sue you and take your tunic, let him have your cloak as well. If someone forces you to go one mile, go with him two miles.

In *GM* Nietzsche describes a virtue of strong forgetfulness possessed by those societies or individuals who can say: "'What do I care about my parasites' ... let them live and flourish: I am strong enough for all that!" (p. 51). He even goes so far as to say that only in such strong individuals is love of one's enemy possible, though he doubts that such love is instantiated in any humans as they are now. In the first essay (I, 10, p. 24) he claims that a "noble man" has respect for his enemies, but that we can aspire to something higher: "a respect of that sort is a bridge to love" (*GM*, p. 24). Of course such a love cannot be the kind of weak love which Nietzsche claims is part of Christian *culture* (even if it is a strong form of love that is valorized in Christian theology properly understood).

In strong forgetfulness, even illegitimate obstacles to the realization of one's goals are like water off a duck's back: to be forgotten in the sense of not punished or retaliated against. Such strong forgetfulness is part of a broader character trait of a kind of self-sufficiency which does not take insults, misfortunes, or even past misdeeds seriously as things to be dwelt on in a guilt-ridden or wounded way.[10] Such a virtue is closely linked to that of independence (see section (vii)). A distinction should nonetheless be drawn between those who are in a position to be able to achieve their goals despite interferences, and those who are oppressed and live under structured burdens. Even here though, passive resistance in the forswearing of violence or retaliation should be contrasted with two other options for the oppressed: fight or flight. Turning the other cheek is not a form of flight and could be a form of strength.

We need to ask then, whether for Nietzsche:

(a) Turning the other cheek as a virtue of strong assertiveness is a virtue for all, and

---

10 As Nietzsche puts it in *GM*: "to be unable to take his enemies, his misfortunes, and even his misdeeds seriously for long – that is a sign of strong rounded natures with a superabundance of a power which is flexible . . ." (p. 23).

(b) Turning the other cheek is always expressive of virtue.

First, proper assertiveness as a virtue should be seen as differentiated according to an individual's strength. As Nietzsche warns in *Z*, "Do not be virtuous beyond your strength!" (IV, 13, "On the Higher Man," 13). Maybe Gandhi-like passive resistance (a strong form of "turning the other cheek") is not for all of us. So turning the other cheek as a virtue of strong assertiveness is not a virtue for all. It is thus a differentiated form of the basic virtue of assertiveness. Second, passivity in lesser individuals takes on a different cast: it can be understood as weak passivity, the behavior of a "doormat." Here turning the other cheek would be seen as expressive of a vice of excessive passivity, and would not be a form of strength. So turning the other cheek is not always expressive of virtue.

(iv) JUSTICE

The field of justice as a virtue in *GM* consists of such things as keeping promises and repaying debts, and the appropriate enforcement of such rights and duties. Importantly it requires appropriate attitudes to the honoring and enforcement of those rights and duties. For Nietzsche, I shall argue, being well disposed in relation to that field is contrasted with two forms of being ill-disposed: rigorous punitivism and "scientific fairness." The virtue is free of the distorted psychology of those two vices: the one an offshoot of the immature egoism of cruelty, the other a resentment-based obsession with equality characteristic of what Horney (1970) calls the "self-effacing" type.

While the "eye" of the just person is "penetrating" for Nietzsche, that eye is also "mild" as opposed to harsh and vengeful. She is not vengeful for she is impartial. She thus avoids the egocentric vice of the immature egoist, vengefulness, which Nietzsche claims is very difficult for the average individual. Even a "small dose of aggression, malice or insinuation is enough to make the most upright man see red and drive moderation *out of* his sight" (p. 53).[11]

She is not harsh for the "penetrating eye" of justice is tempered with humanity and grace:

Justice, which began by saying: "Everything can be paid off, everything must be paid off," ends by turning a blind eye and letting off those unable to pay, – it ends, like every good thing on earth, by *sublimating itself*. This self-sublimation of justice: we know what a nice name it gives itself – *mercy*; it remains,

---

[11] Rendered by Smith as "to deprive them of an impartial eye" (*GM*, II, 11, p. 55).

of course, the prerogative of the most powerful man, better still, his way of being beyond the law. (pp. 51–52)[12]

Notice that since mercy is the "prerogative of the most powerful man," it is compatible with hardness and severity, virtues of the strong (see below), and to be contrasted with cruelty, callousness, and vengefulness. Mercy and grace are not soft or "cheap," though where the boundaries are to be drawn in this area is of course not subject to formula. Mercy then is not seen by Nietzsche as opposed to the virtue of justice, but rather to the vice of rigorous punitivism sourced in instincts for revenge, where the punished has "forfeited" ... "all mercy" (p. 51). Impartiality combined with "penetration" is not sufficient for justice as a virtue since the impartiality of rigorous "justice" may lack humanity. To the vice of rigorous punitivism we now turn.

Rigorous punitivism

At first sight the distinction between justice and one of the forms of "justice to excess," rigorous punitivism, is difficult to draw since it might appear that for Nietzsche justice in general has its roots in the cruelty of noble morality. He claims indeed that justice has its origin in the aggressive man:

... in what sphere, up till now, has the whole treatment of justice, and the actual need for justice, resided? With men who react perhaps? Not in the least: but with the active, the strong, the spontaneous and the aggressive. (p. 53)

We have already seen, however, that aggression is not to be confused with its perverted form, cruelty, so Nietzsche is not saying here that justice has its roots in cruelty. Nonetheless a distorted form of "justice," the vice of rigorous punitivism, does have its source in a form of cruelty. Here the impartiality of justice is not "mild" but punishing and in excessive ways. Punishment as such for Nietzsche is not itself a value: by increasing fear and helping to master desires, making a person more "prudent," it "*tames* man" "but does not make him 'better'" (p. 60). What then are the roots of excessive punishment?

By contrast with perverted cruelty, rigorous punitivism is described by Nietzsche as a neurotic "sick" form occurring when the individual, unable to simply endure or sublimate frustration, regresses to a more primitive mode. However, instead of venting his frustrations in (overt) cruelty he forbids himself the satisfaction of those primitive instincts. The symptom

---

[12] Smith translates what Diethe translates as "mercy," "grace," and "sublimation" as "cancellation."

of this repression is the expression of those instincts in legitimized but nonetheless cruel forms of punishment whose excesses ("a thorough and prolonged bloodletting"; p. 45) are described by Nietzsche as a "compensation," constituted by "a warrant for and entitlement to cruelty" (p. 45). At bottom then, such punitivism is a form of cruelty turned inwards, cruelty "spiritualized," but then *externalized* in the legitimization of excessive punishment. By contrast the spiritualized cruelty to self of the *self-punishing* (mortification of the flesh and so forth), is not externalized, and is a symptom of the ascetic ideal (see section (viii)).

Scientific fairness

Like rigorous punitivism, what Nietzsche calls "scientific fairness" (p. 52) is a distorted form of justice whose roots lie in repressed anger, but its psychology is different. This is the "justice" of the person of resentment, a person who, unlike the noble type, is driven by a sense of his impotence or inferiority by comparison with others, in talents, strength, power, rewards, or good fortune. He is thus resentment-filled and envy-driven. Such people desire equality "for its own sake" as a form of justice, but really as a way of bringing others down to their level. Nietzsche makes it clear in *GM* that justice is not sourced in resentment:

Now a derogatory mention of recent attempts to seek the origin of justice elsewhere – namely in *ressentiment*. (p. 52)

Resentment is rather the source of a trait masquerading as justice, namely a tendency to compare merits and rewards in others (by comparison with themselves) so that these are in "scientifically" exact proportions. This is the vice of "scientific fairness." Ironically a biblical text illustrates this vice perfectly, the parable of the landowner (Matthew 20:1–15) where the landowner, eschewing payment according to exact principles of merit as normally understood, berates the complainants for resenting the good fortune of the ones who are "overpaid," even though they themselves have received what was agreed upon. He is fair, but not scientifically fair:

Friend, I am being fair to you. You agreed to work for one coin. So take your pay and go. I want to give the man who was hired last the same pay as I gave you. I can do what I want with my own money. Are you jealous because I am good to those people?

It may be replied that what Nietzsche sneeringly refers to in *GM* as "scientific fairness" is exactly justice as we understand it. But it is the point of Nietzsche's critique of morality that what *we* call virtues are often traits admired by the weak and the resentful. Justice proper for Nietzsche is a trait of the strong, what he calls that "rarest of all virtues," an "impossible virtue" (*UM*, II, "On the Uses and Disadvantages of History for Life," 88). For not only are the strong capable of being just without being vengeful or punitive, only the strong forswear narcissistic self-referential comparisons. They do not need to compare with others to derive a sense of their worth.

(v) OBJECTIVITY

In a famous passage in *GM*, Nietzsche claims

There is *only* a perspectival seeing, *only* a perspectival knowing; the *more* affects we allow to speak about a thing, the *more* eyes, various eyes we are able to use for the same thing, the more complete will be our "concept" of the thing, our "objectivity." (p. 92)

The passage provides a clue about the field of objectivity as an intellectual (and I might say moral) virtue, namely possession and deployment of perspective in one's knowledge of the world, and attitudes/emotions in relation to perspective. Being well disposed in this area is contrasted with two vices: egocentricity of perspective (what I have elsewhere called hyper-subjective vice; Swanton 2003) and the tendency to equate impartiality and objectivity with freedom from perspective altogether: "the view from nowhere" of what I have called hyperobjective vice. The third essay of *GM* can be understood as an attack on the "will to (absolute) truth" characterizing hyperobjectivity: an aspect of what Nietzsche calls the ascetic ideal.

To understand a Nietzschean virtue of objectivity, then, we need to understand what it is to be well disposed in relation to perspective.

1. The attempt to be free of all perspective is a philosopher's fiction well described in the third essay of *GM*. The hallmarks of this vice are described below.

2. At the same time objectivity can be gained only by incorporating multiple perspectives (and not just one's own or those about which one feels comfortable or familiar).

3. Recognition of limitations in our perspective does not mean that we ourselves should attempt to attain all perspectives. The passage quoted does not imply that *each individual* should himself cultivate as many feelings about a matter as possible. Indeed that would be a face of hyperobjective vice. All that is required is that as many "affects" as possible be brought to bear on a matter (given constraints of context).

4. The passage quoted does not imply that all perspectives are equally good. This would indeed be antithetical to the whole cast of Nietzsche's philosophy. For him in fact the religious perspective is pernicious:

> Against this theologians' instinct I wage war: I have found its traces everywhere ... This faulty perspective on all things is elevated into a morality, a virtue, a holiness: ... and no *other* perspective is conceded any further value once one's own has been made sacrosanct with the names of "God," "redemption," and "eternity." I have dug up the theologians' instinct everywhere: it is the most widespread, really *subterranean*, form of falsehood found on earth. (*A*, 9)

5. The virtue of objectivity, however, is not simply attained by one with a superior perspective such as that of a virtuous agent. Those with superior perspectives are not objective unless they have considered and integrated a multiplicity of other perspectives (usually with others). How many, and which ones, depends on context of course.

It may be wondered how objectivity as a virtue can be connected with mature egoism. Given that knowledge and objectivity in knowledge in an individual person should not be impersonal for Nietzsche, the kind of knowledge the individual seeks is relative to her own goals and creative purposes. The objective, wise individual recognizes that truth is not sought by a single individual as "the judgement of humanity" but is "the prey joyfully seized by the individual huntsman"; it is an "egoistic possession" (*UM*, 88–89). Nonetheless of course what might be called hypersubjective vice – a vice of the immature egoist who cannot get past her own perspective – has to be avoided if objectivity is to be attained.

Hyperobjectivity

Hyperobjective vice is a vice of resignation from the world, a form of disgust with all its messiness, plurality, particularity, resistance to systematization and codification. It exhibits as a desire for purity, escape, a will to absolutes and simplicity. In *GM*, III, Nietzsche describes a number of hallmarks and manifestations of hyperobjective vice. Here are some of its features as described there.

1. Anticipating Heidegger's attack on science as arrogating to itself the title of THE theory of the real, Nietzsche describes the absolutism of hyperobjective vice as a manifestation of the ascetic ideal of which science is its most recent manifestation (pp. 115–16).

2. Part of this absolutism is the unconditional will to (absolute) truth, characterized by the embracing of such metaphysical fictions as the

"*factum brutum*" (p. 119) the "indifferent substratum" "behind" a person (as self) (p. 28), the "renunciation of any interpretation" (p. 119), and a desire to "stand still before the factual" (p. 119) understood in this absolute, uninterpreted sense.[13]

3. Since such absolutism can only be realized through a perspectiveless orientation where even the artist is seen as "a sort of mouthpiece of the 'in itself' of things" (p. 78), the orientation of the ascetic ideal is that of the disinterested spectator. This orientation is contrasted with the truthfulness and integrity of a person who actively engages with the world.[14]

4. The emotional orientation of hyperobjective vice is essentially one of disgust and a desire to escape both the self and the world as a whole; in short "*to escape from torture!*" (p. 80).

In its moral theoretic manifestation, hyperobjectivity has the above properties of hyperobjectivity in general, plus some of the characteristics of self-sacrificing altruism, namely a valorizing of ideals of the common good and a conception of impartiality demanding self-sacrifice and a downgrading of the self. The self-love of the "mature individual" carries little moral weight. The evil in such systems for Nietzsche lies in three basic features.

1. The "common good" is portrayed in a way which has to be calculable and impersonal, thereby washing over the "personal" in people. In contrast, a person's own "advantage" is something that is not easily discovered, has hidden depths, needs to be worked on, evolves, is to be refined, and is not subject to crude measure.

2. The common good, because necessarily conceived in a crude way, is conceived as something that as a consequence *can* be pursued *as* a common good.

3. Impersonal hyperobjective systems of morality encourage the conception of hyperobjective vice as a moral virtue, creating not only the belief that the common good *can* be pursued but a felt imperative that it morally *must* be pursued. However, given the complex and variable nature of the personal, it can only be pursued in a spirit of self-sacrifice, or in a way which involves self-sacrifice.

---

[13] Note that when Nietzsche claims, famously, that there are no moral facts, only moral interpretations of facts, this is the point he is making. He is giving an account of how a "fact" should properly be understood, not arguing for moral relativism. See e.g. *Twilight of the Idols*, "The Improvers of Mankind," §1, p. 501. Note that here he says: "Morality is ... more precisely a misinterpretation [of certain phenomena]."

[14] For the value of truthfulness and its relation to the value of untruth see May 1999. I do not have space in this paper to discuss truthfulness as a virtue and its correlative vices.

(vi) GENEROSITY

The field of the virtue of generosity is an agent's capacity and willingness to use, and success in using, her resources (material or otherwise) to help, benefit, or sympathize with others. (In the latter case we may speak of generosity of spirit.) This field is shared by what Nietzsche would regard as correlative vices such as self-sacrificing charity, and pity (in Nietzsche's sense). Pity (*Mitleid*) on Nietzsche's conception is sympathizing with others in a way that exhibits vice. It has its roots in a form of immature egoism, but manifests as altruistic sentiment. In pity one is *"very strongly unconsciously"* thinking of oneself, in particular one's own vulnerabilities, and it is thus for Nietzsche a subtle form of revenge, an expression of resentment at being reminded of this (*D*, 133). By contrast, sympathy (*Mitgefühl*) is a form of virtuous sympathizing with others, and is indeed listed as a virtue in *BGE* (284). To be a virtue, sympathy must be free of the narcissism of pity as Nietzsche understands it as a psychological phenomenon.

The distinction between virtue and vice in the general field of generosity is not identical to the distinction between selfishness and unselfishness. Like Maslow (1971) and other psychologists such as Fromm (1975), Nietzsche distinguishes between healthy and unhealthy selfishness. Given that he contrasts mature egoism both with immature egoism and self-sacrificing altruism, the distinction between selfishness and unselfishness *simpliciter* is unsurprisingly seen as crude by Nietzsche. For example in *Z*, I, 22 ("On the Gift-Giving Virtue," 186–87), Nietzsche distinguishes a healthy selfishness from "sick selfishness." The generosity of the mature egoist is characterized by self-love where a neediness to escape into others is absent. On the contrary the virtuously generous person is described as "overflowing." She has a sense of having more than enough for herself so she wants to give something away. In *GM* generosity is not so much described as a virtue as understood through an account of one of its correlative vices, the charity of the weak. To this aspect of self-sacrificing altruism we now turn.

Self-sacrificing charity

In *GM*, III, Nietzsche describes the nature of the *"will to power"* (p. 106) of the charitable individual as the happiness of "smallest superiority" (p. 106). This feature is well known from Nietzsche's discussion of pity in works other than *GM*, such as *Daybreak*, but in *GM* he focuses on another feature, the tendency of the charitable weak to congregate. Nietzsche describes the weak as individuals who, in a "fight against depression" – the depression of those who desire to "shake off dull lethargy and the feeling of weakness" (p. 106) – herd together in "associations for mutual support." Here, they engage in "mutual do-gooding" and make themselves useful as a means of "consolation" for themselves: the "physiologically inhibited." In this way, such a person escapes "his aversion to *himself*" (p. 106).

Nietzsche claims that while the strong seek to disperse, the weak seek to congregate (p. 107) in an effort "to forget oneself" in a "discipline" "to be 'impersonal'" (p. 105). (Hence for Nietzsche, the origins of hyperobjective vice in our ethical comportment lie in weakness.) The sense of weakness of the weak is thus consoled in two ways: (a) the losing of self in congregation and impersonality, and (b) the happiness of "minimal superiority" as one shows "compassion" to another whose vulnerability is at least temporarily seen as worse than one's own.

(vii) INDEPENDENCE

The field of independence as a virtue is attitudes and behavior in relation to one's dependence on others. Independence as a virtue is contrasted with two correlative vices of immature egoism (parasitism and excessive independence) and a vice of self-sacrificing altruism. This vice is characterized by a neediness to submerge oneself in a larger whole to the point where one loses one's sense of self, what is to one's advantage, or at least a sense of the value of one's own projects (by comparison with others' projects or the "common good" in the sense excoriated by Nietzsche).

As we have seen, in *GM* Nietzsche claims that it is a hallmark of the strong to "disperse." This is essential to escape the "contamination" of the sick and excessively needy, and thus to have space to pursue one's goals and projects. Those possessing independence as a virtue are mature, wise, and even profound, rather than trivial and antisocial. At times Nietzsche describes this virtue (with this rationale – a "sublime urge for cleanliness") as "solitude" (*BGE*, 284). Note, however, that independence and (a disposition to crave and seek) solitude as *virtues* must be distinguished from solitude and a resignatory form of independence as ascetic vices of escape from the world, discussed in the third essay of *GM* (see below section (viii)). Nietzsche warns against misunderstanding the virtue of solitude: the creative person is a spirit "whose solitude will be misunderstood by the people, as though it were a flight *from* reality –: whereas it is just his way of being absorbed, buried and immersed in reality . . ." (*GM*, p. 71).

We must also warn against failure to distinguish the virtue of independence in its basic form from its differentiated forms. Certainly the virtue is understood in general as appropriate independence, but it is differentiated according to both role (such as role as leader) and degree of strength. For example in *BGE*, 29, Nietzsche claims:

> Few are made for independence – it is a privilege of the strong. And who attempts it, having the completest right to it but without being *compelled* to, thereby proves that he is probably not only strong but also daring to the point of recklessness.

It does not follow from this passage that for Nietzsche independence *in some form or other* (given my understanding of the field of the virtue of independence and its thin account as being well disposed in relation to it) is not a universal virtue; he is merely claiming that only in the strong should it take the above form. It may be true of course that in the case of the less strong, being well disposed in relation to that field is not what Nietzsche would call *real* independence. This is indeed a problem with the language of virtue as a language of the so-called thick concepts. The problem also occurs *inter alia* with the virtue of honesty: being well disposed in relation to its field may permit on rare occasions lying, but lying can hardly be described as honest.

Excessive self-sufficiency

It may be thought that for Nietzsche what Watson (1984) calls "virtue in excess" is always virtue for Nietzsche.[15] But this is to ignore the importance of differentiated virtue for Nietzsche. What may appear excessive may be virtuous in the strong and not excessive in relation to them, but be genuinely excessive and not virtuous in the weak or convalescent. One of the most controversial examples is his discussion of independence in women. Although vices of excessive independence from aspects of the world are portrayed in *GM* in relation to the ascetic ideal (see below), in the sister work *BGE* another rather different manifestation occurs in an attack on the emancipatory ideal for women:

> Woman wants to be independent: and to that end she is beginning to enlighten men about "woman as such" – *this* is one of the worst developments in the general *uglification* of Europe. (232)

---

[15] Solomon (2003) claims that "the metaphor of 'overflowing' is the key to Nietzsche's conception of the virtues" (158) but I think this is overly simple. Not all virtues are overflowing in their nature for Nietzsche, notably justice, and the claim neglects the differentiation of virtue in the herd, unless one thinks that the "herd" cannot be virtuous even when performing excellently in their roles, in a judicious manner. I do not think Nietzsche claims this; rather for him it is not virtuous to attempt to emulate the strong when you are not yourself really strong.

Wherever the spirit of industry has triumphed over the military and aristocratic spirit woman now aspires to the economic and legal independence of a clerk . . . she thus seizes new rights, looks to become "master" . . . (239)

In section 232 and subsequent passages, Nietzsche takes to task the democratic taste for equality which renders the aspirations and rational qualities of women and men uniform, thus inhibiting the development of "higher man." A drive for equality which demands the independence of self-sufficiency or high levels of power and control, to the detriment of maternal instincts, desire for children and their adequate nurture, is for Nietzsche not only defeminizing but downright degenerating. This for Nietzsche is another manifestation of a desire to be independent of, to escape from, vital aspects of one's nature. An emancipatory spirit of self-sufficiency to the point of doing violence to one's nature is for him another form of frustrated desire resulting in cruelty turned inwards: another form of the desire for mastery and power characterizing immature egoism.

Of course the way in which woman (*Weib an sich*) differs from male nature is controversial, as are views about how (or whether) different aspects of one's nature can *all* be developed in a satisfying way. Much of what Nietzsche says about this in relation to women is offensive,[16] but the essential point about appreciating how virtue can be differentiated, and according to which factors, is a live and controversial issue today.

Parasitism

The form of parasitism most discussed by Nietzsche is the lack of productivity and creativity of the herd. Here we are focusing on the herd as sick (or sick elements of the herd) where the sickness of immature egoism takes the form of a will-less complacency, a focus on "momentary comforts," and a failure to appreciate that there can be *meaningful* suffering in the interests of creative goals. Not only is the vice expressive of weakness, but lazy, unproductive individuals contribute to the mediocritization of society.

Disposition to immerse oneself in the collectivity

Parasitism, as a vice of immature egoism, is to be contrasted with another kind of (nameless) vice of excessive *dependence*, more properly described as a tendency to immerse oneself in a social group, to the point where

---

[16] Much more can be said about this: for different views on the nature of the offensive or apparently offensive remarks see Clark 1994 and Julian Young, forthcoming.

individuality is no longer valued. This is a vice associated with self-sacrificing altruism, tellingly described by Ayn Rand through her character Ellsworth Tooley of *Fountainhead*. In *GM* as we have seen, it is described as a symptom of the weak individual's need to congregate. Not only is there a tendency to congregate, the "disciplining" of oneself towards an impersonal standpoint renders one more likely to subordinate one's goals to those of the needy, and indeed to lose sight of, knowledge of, and interest in, one's advantage altogether.

(viii) DISCIPLINE

The field of discipline as a virtue is dealing with unruly desires, temptations, the impossibility and undesirability of the satisfaction of those desires, and the frustrations and psychic conflict that occur as a result of all these features. To be well disposed in these areas is to possess discipline as a virtue. A chief mechanism for disciplining desire is the alteration and refinement of desire through a process of sublimation, but to be *well* disposed in relation to the field of discipline, as we explore further below, it is not enough to alter and refine one's desires. One must alter and refine them in the right directions. Disciplining oneself towards an impersonal standpoint, as we saw above, is not for Nietzsche manifesting discipline as a virtue.

It may be thought that only what Nietzsche calls the "convalescent" can exhibit discipline, since those whose desires have reached Aristotelian harmony are perfectly virtuous and have no need for discipline. However, as applied to those with Aristotelian virtue, "being disciplined" can be seen as a success term, and there is no need for (further) discipline. Furthermore, on Nietzsche's philosophy of "overcoming," such a state of perfect virtue is a moral philosopher's fiction, as it is indeed for Kant, in the real world of nature. As a result for Kant, virtue is essentially strength of will. For Nietzsche, however, discipline through the psychological processes of endurance and sublimation takes the individual beyond mere strength of will.

Consider first endurance. Enduring such states as pain and frustration, rather than avoiding them in some way, allows the individual to become "hard" and "severe" which, as Solomon (2003: 170–71) notes, are virtues, not to be confused with callousness. Rather it is a prime vehicle for avoiding the "soft" vices of immature egoism, self-indulgence, and a tendency to focus on the comforts and pleasures of instant gratification. The form of discipline, endurance, is most in evidence where the field of discipline as a virtue is to avoid (or be weak in the face of) the unpleasant (such as the fearful and the painful). It is the subject of the following section of *BGE*:

The discipline of suffering, of *great* suffering – do you not know that it is *this* discipline alone which has created every elevation of mankind hitherto? That tension of the soul in misfortune which cultivates its strength, its terror at the sight of great destruction, its inventiveness and bravery in undergoing, enduring, interpreting, exploiting, misfortune . . . (*BGE*, 225)

Related virtues of discipline as endurance are perseverance and courage, as well as wisdom and profundity, for these are all aspects of or results of endurance. Endurance as a virtue of discipline (the disposition to endure appropriately) is the result of endurance as a psychological mechanism (described by Richard Wollheim 1971: 140–41, interpreting Freud). It is contrasted with immature modes of dealing with conflict, frustration, and the unpleasant, namely regressive tendencies.

We turn now to (healthy) sublimation: the second mechanism of virtuous discipline. Sublimation in general, whether healthy or unhealthy, is for Nietzsche a psychological process: a tendency to divert the energy of "lower" desires into strivings towards other ends which are more refined. This feature is not sufficient for sublimation to be part of a process of virtuous discipline, for sublimation may not be healthy. Sublimation may be in the service of goals which are life-affirming, creative, and healthy, but it is clear that for Nietzsche the alteration and refinement of desire characteristic of sublimation may also be a form of life-denial – a form of being ill-disposed in relation to discipline. Discipline of this nature would be a vice, rather than a virtue. Its ascetic form is described below.

Asceticism

Asceticism as a vice is to be contrasted with what Robert Solomon (2003: 163–65) calls aestheticism as a virtue. The contrast is evident in *GM*. In the "religious neurosis" (p. 113) (see also *BGE*, 47) the "dangerous dietary prescriptions" of "solitude, fasting and sexual abstinence" (*BGE*, 47) are forms of asceticism deemed to be virtues through the "ascetic doctrine of sin" (*GM*, p. 113). In *GM* Nietzsche refers to the (supposed) "virtues" of the ascetic ideal in terms of the "three great catch-words of the ascetic ideal" "poverty humility, chastity" (p. 82). The "religious neurosis" is not, however, a form of aestheticization of carnal desire through healthy sublimation, but a form of extirpation constituting a "self-denial, self-annulment" (*GM*, p. 74). Both asceticization and aestheticization involve refinement of desire;

however, only in the latter case does "a certain asceticism" involve "a hard and hearty renunciation with a good will" (*GM*, p. 85). In that severe but hearty manifestation, sensuality is not cancelled out but is "only transfigured and no longer enters the consciousness as a sexual stimulus" (p. 85). Only this latter form of sublimation, the aestheticized form, is an affirmation of life and nature. For it involves a "remarkable sweetness and fullness characteristic of the aesthetic condition" (*GM*, p. 85) rather than an "asceticism of virtue" (*GM*, p. 119) and a "denial of sensuality" (p. 119). Although the plenitude of the "aesthetic condition" as well as the life-denying practice of ascetic "virtue" thus both involve what Nietzsche calls "spiritualization" (the refinement of desire in the process of sublimation), in the ascetic case the spiritualization is a mark of ascetic vice, whereas the "*highest intellectualization*" (*GM*, p. 74)[17] of the aesthetic condition is a form of virtuous "sensualization" (p. 74).

Ascetic vice as a distortion of the disciplining of the carnal impulses has many forms and several psychological features. All have in common the motif of escape: escape from self and the world. In the form of the "dietary prescriptions" of fasting and celibacy, not to mention mortification of the flesh, we have forms of cruelty turned inwards, but not externalized as in the case of cruel punishment discussed above. Another ascetic vice, charity, can also be seen in this kind of light: the form of denial of the self involved in purification of the flesh makes one pure and fit for service to others and God: "only the will to self-violation provides the precondition for the *value* of the unegoistic" (*GM*, p. 64). Contrary to healthy sublimation or "spiritualization" of carnal or other forms of "lower" desire, sublimation involves in this manifestation repression (regression and a forbidding of the satisfaction of certain desires).

In its intellectual form, asceticism takes the form of escape from the world in fictions of the pure will-less intellect. Indeed for such as Schopenhauer, claims Nietzsche, it expresses a wish "to be *freed from a form of torture*" (p. 80). The desire for truthfulness is sublimated into a will for absolute truth where the "scientific conscience" becomes the model for all intellectual endeavor. Its manifestations in ethics are an epistemology of emotionless rationality, impersonality as an ethical ideal of impartiality, and the "will to a system." At bottom these forms of hyperobjectivity are forms of escape from the complexity and intractability of the world, and the drive for refinement in sublimation becomes a form of ascetic distortion: a drive for intellectual purity, certainty, and determinacy.

---

[17] Translated by Smith as "spiritualization" (p. 79).

Depending on their forms, modes of asceticism can constitute self-sacrificing altruistic vice ("charity" as an ascetic vice) or vices of immature egoism where escape from psychic torture takes precedence over mature engagement with the world. Thus in *GM*, Nietzsche contrasts two forms of happiness: that of the engaged active person "bursting with strength" (*GM*, p. 23), and that of the passive powerless type for whom happiness is a disengaged escape: it is "essentially a narcotic, an anaesthetic, rest, peace, 'sabbath' relaxation of the mind . . . in short [it is] something *passive!*" (p. 23).

(ix) CONCLUSION

In this chapter I have understood Nietzsche as endorsing a psychologically based taxonomy of virtue and vice which cuts across the traditional Aristotelian categories of excess, mean, and deficiency. The Aristotelian taxonomy fails to expose the depth-psychological features of virtue: for example, a tendency to turn the other cheek looks like a vice of deficiency but on closer inspection may express a strong kind of assertiveness of a non-encroaching kind. Again certain sorts of independence and wisdom have the appearance of excess but may express an overflowing proper to the strong. What counts as excess and deficiency is relative to the differentiation of virtue appropriate to, for example, role and strength.

I have suggested that in Nietzsche's psychologically based taxonomy it is the "mature egoist" whose characterological features are expressive of virtue. Mature egoism is opposed both to varieties of immature egoism and to weak self-sacrificing altruism where the individual escapes the self in various ways. I have deployed this taxonomy to elucidate a number of Nietzsche's subtle and rich distinctions between several virtues and closely related vices, particularly those in *On the Genealogy of Morality*. As Lester Hunt (1991: 1) points out, however, *On the Genealogy of Morality* and *Beyond Good and Evil* are basically, as Nietzsche claims, "No-saying" works, as opposed to the "Yes-saying" *Zarathustra*, and other works where other virtues are more prominent.

Indeed, many more Nietzschean virtues and vices in both *GM* and other works can be analyzed according to the proposed taxonomy, such as joyfulness, as opposed to weak tendencies to complain; productiveness, as opposed to laziness; proper modesty, as opposed to vanity and weak humility; cheerfulness, as opposed to gloominess; courage and truthfulness as opposed to cowardice and secretiveness.

CHAPTER 14

Une promesse de bonheur? Beauty in the Genealogy

Aaron Ridley

In this chapter I try to make some progress with three interpretive issues and a philosophical question. The first issue concerns section 6 of the *Genealogy's* third essay.[1] Most generally, I want to know what conclusions Nietzsche draws or suggests there about the nature of beauty. More specifically, I want to know why Nietzsche stops short of endorsing Stendhal's conception, according to which beauty is a promise of happiness: he does cite Stendhal with approval, but only as the best of a bad lot. What is the reason for this? The second issue concerns the relations between what Nietzsche says in *GM*, III, 6, and what he says at the other two places in the *Genealogy* where beauty features at all prominently:[2] on the face of it, none of the passages looks as if it has anything to do with the others, and that feels unsatisfactory. The third issue concerns the relation between Nietzsche's remarks about beauty and his more general conception of values and valuing: assuming that the *Genealogy* is minimally self-consistent, we should expect these relata to be mutually illuminating; and I want to see whether, or to what extent, that expectation is borne out. For obvious reasons, these issues are interconnected, and, for most of the paper, I move back and forth between them freely, attempting to make progress across a broad front, as it were. The philosophical question, finally, is whether Nietzsche's thoughts about beauty – as elucidated, I hope, through my treatment of the interpretive issues – deserve to be taken seriously as a contribution to aesthetics: do they help us to understand what beauty is, or in what sense beauty is a value for us? I conclude by suggesting that, as aestheticians at least, we have better reason to accept what Stendhal says

---

[1] With the occasional small adjustments, I have used the following translations of Nietzsche's writings: *On the Genealogy of Morality*, trans. C. Diethe (1994); *Twilight of the Idols*, trans. R. J. Hollingdale (1968); *The Gay Science*, trans. W. Kaufmann (1974); and *The Case of Wagner*, trans. W. Kaufmann (1967b).

[2] These places are sections 7 and 10 of the first essay (considered together) and section 18 of the second essay.

than to go with the alternative that Nietzsche apparently prefers. I also think that this conclusion should be good for Nietzscheans.

I. THE AESTHETIC PROBLEM

GM, III, 6, is set up as a critique of Kant's aesthetics; it turns quite quickly into a critique of Schopenhauer; while Stendhal is mentioned a couple of times along the way as a corrective to both – without, however, receiving Nietzsche's unqualified approval. It will be helpful to begin with an overview of the section, not least so as to identify the questions that it raises but leaves unanswered.

* * *

1.1 Nietzsche opens by offering two criticisms of Kant's account of beauty. The first, which remains largely implicit and is quickly passed over, is that Kant thought – mistakenly, Nietzsche implies – that he was honoring art "when he singled out from the qualities of beauty those which constitute the honour of knowledge: impersonality and universality" (*GM*, III, 6). On the face of it, this leaves it open whether Nietzsche disagrees with Kant that impersonality and universality are indeed "qualities" of beauty, or whether he simply disagrees that giving prominence to them is to the honor of art. (Six sections later, of course, he denies that these predicates apply even to *knowledge*, to its honor or otherwise.) When we note, however, that he appears to regard Kant's mistake here, whatever exactly it is, as symptomatic of a wider failing that he mentions in his second criticism – namely, "that Kant, like all philosophers, instead of envisaging the aesthetic problem from the point of view of the artist (the creator), considered art and the beautiful purely from that of the 'spectator'" (ibid.) – we must conclude that, according to Nietzsche, Kant's emphasis upon impersonality and universality among "the qualities of beauty" is in some way a sign of his misplaced attachment to the spectatorial standpoint. I'll return to this puzzling thought in a moment.

For now, though, let's turn to the second criticism – which is that, because Kant envisaged the "aesthetic problem" from the wrong point of view, he "inadvertently introduced the 'spectator' himself into the concept 'beautiful'" (ibid.). There are clearly at least three interrelated claims here. There is the claim that the "aesthetic problem" should be envisaged from "the point of view of the artist (the creator)" rather than from that of the spectator; there is the claim that, in envisaging the problem from the spectator's point of view, something germane to that point of view is "introduced ... into the concept 'beautiful'"; and there is the claim, or at any rate the implication, that, when this element is introduced, the concept "beautiful" is distorted or misrepresented in some way.[3] And the implicit upshot of these claims, it would seem, is that, because the "aesthetic problem" – "What is beauty?" – is best addressed from the point of view of the artist, the concept "beautiful" is presented correctly only when something germane to *that* point of view is introduced into it.

* * *

1.2 So what, precisely, is supposed to be wrong with envisaging the "aesthetic problem" from the spectator's point of view? What is it, according to Nietzsche, that the Kantian approach illicitly introduces into the concept "beautiful"?

Nietzsche's "answer" to these questions appears to consist, in part, in an echoing of some of Schopenhauer's remarks about Kant. According to Schopenhauer, "art remained very foreign" to Kant, who

> in all probability had little susceptibility to the beautiful, in fact probably never had the opportunity to see an important work of art, and who seems finally to have had no knowledge even of Goethe, the only man of his century and country to be placed by his side as his giant brother . . .[4]

And Nietzsche agrees: Kant lacked "any refined first-hand experience" of beauty, he says – he was unfamiliar with "an abundance of vivid authentic experiences, desires, surprises, and delights in the realm of the beautiful!" (*GM*, III, 6).[5] But this, clearly enough, doesn't amount to an objection to treating the "aesthetic problem" from the spectator's point of view. At most, it is an objection to treating that problem from the point of view of a spectator like Kant, of someone who hasn't had much exposure to beautiful art.

---

[3] It is because these claims are interrelated in this way that a suggestion of Julian Young's won't work. Young wonders why we couldn't simply have an artist's aesthetics (done from the artist's point of view) and a spectator's aesthetics (done from the spectator's point of view): Young 1992: 120. The difficulty with this suggestion, however, is that what is at issue is not just aesthetics in general, as it were, but, rather, the quite specific part of it that Nietzsche calls *the* "aesthetic problem." And that problem is how the concept "beautiful" is to be understood or defined, a question that doesn't obviously invite, and won't easily tolerate, the kind of easy-going pluralism that Young's suggestion would entail.

[4] Schopenhauer 1969: 529. Schopenhauer goes on, incidentally, to say how remarkable it is that, despite these apparent deficiencies, "Kant was able to render a great and permanent service to the philosophical consideration of art and the beautiful" (ibid). Nietzsche would not have concurred.

[5] It might be pointed out that, even if Kant was as ignorant of artistic beauty as Schopenhauer and Nietzsche suggest, he did at least have some experience of natural beauty: he speaks rather warmly of the beauty of tulips, for instance, and of certain crustacea (2007: section 16). But Schopenhauer and Nietzsche were both Hegelian enough to have been unimpressed by this observation: like Hegel, they regard artistic beauty as primary (although, as we will see, in Nietzsche's case this doesn't necessarily amount to a commitment to the priority of the artistic beauty of *works of art*). My thanks to Chris Janaway for this point.

Nor is the impression that Nietzsche doesn't really answer the question undermined by the rest of what he says. He remarks that "[i]t would not have been so bad" had "the philosophers of beauty" – e.g. Kant – "been sufficiently familiar" – i.e. familiar at first-hand – with the "great *personal* fact" that the experience of beauty can be for a "*genuine* 'spectator'" (ibid.; italics added). Not *so* bad, note:[6] which suggests that it would still have been bad – and bad, presumably, because a spectator would still have been introduced into the concept "beautiful," even if the spectator in question was a "genuine" one. And this leaves us none the wiser about what is *wrong* with approaching the matter from the spectator's point of view. At most, it seems, we might hope to gain a sense from it of what is *less* bad about introducing a "genuine" rather than a Kantian spectator into the equation.

***

1.3 Here, the issue swings on the notion of disinterestedness. The "philosophers of beauty," writes Nietzsche, since they are without "authentic experiences . . . in the realm of the beautiful,"

> have offered us, from the beginning, definitions in which, as in Kant's famous definition of the beautiful, a lack of any refined first-hand experience reposes in the shape of a fat worm of error. "That is beautiful," said Kant, "which gives pleasure *without interest.*" Without interest! Compare this definition with another made by a genuine "spectator" and artist – Stendhal, who once called the beautiful *une promesse de bonheur.* At any rate he *rejected* and repudiated the one point about the aesthetic condition which Kant had stressed: *le désintéressement. (GM,* III, 6)

So Kant's mistake, in Nietzsche's view, is to have introduced the notion of disinterestedness into the concept "beautiful," a notion that derives from the standpoint of the (non-genuine) spectator.

In Kant's case, Nietzsche is inclined to attribute the mistake not only to his "lack of refined first-hand experience," but to his "innocence," to his having had "the naïveté of a country parson." It is not, however, his mistake alone: even Schopenhauer, despite standing "much closer to the arts than Kant," and despite, presumably, having had more in the way of "refined first-hand experience," commits the error. But he commits it in his own way. "There are few things," remarks Nietzsche, "which Schopenhauer speaks about with such certainty as the effect of aesthetic contemplation: he says of it that it counteracts *sexual* 'interestedness', rather like lupulin and camphor; he never tired of singing the praises of *this* liberation from the 'will' as the great advantage and use of the aesthetic condition." So in Schopenhauer's case, the notion of

---

[6] This is a point that is wholly obscured by Diethe's translation. Here, as elsewhere, I have amended her phrasing in light of Kaufmann and Hollingdale's (trans., *On the Genealogy of Morals;* 1967).

disinterestedness is introduced into the concept "beautiful" not, as with Kant, out of naïveté, but "out of 'interest'; in fact, out of the strongest, most personal interest possible: that of the tortured person to escape from torture" (ibid.).

For Kant's sort of spectator, then, disinterestedness enters the concept "beautiful" in the form of will-less pleasure; for Schopenhauer's sort of spectator, it enters the concept as one of the *effects* of the beautiful, as a *stilling* of the will. And, for both, what their respective forms of will-lessness underwrite is a certain kind of impersonality, whether of judgment (Kant[7]) or of perception (Schopenhauer[8]). Which is why, to return to the puzzling thought mentioned a moment ago, Nietzsche regards Kant's emphasis upon the "impersonality and universality" of beauty as a sign of his attachment to a (certain sort of) spectatorial standpoint: for impersonality and universality are precisely the qualities that the judgments or perceptions of the disinterested spectator are supposed to exhibit.[9]

This is, however, the upshot of just one possible sort of spectatorial standpoint. For Stendhal, whom Nietzsche counterposes to Kant and Schopenhauer, is no less a spectator than they – even if he is said to be a "genuine" one (and also an "artist"). His proposal, says Nietzsche, "emphasizes another effect of beauty: 'beauty *promises* happiness'; to him, the fact of the matter is precisely the *excitement of the will* ('interestedness')" (*GM*, III, 6)[10] – and this at least disassociates him from the "fat worm of error" to be found in Kant's and Schopenhauer's aesthetics. Perhaps, too, it is Nietzsche's view that Stendhal was only able to appreciate the interestedness of the experience of beauty *because* he was, also, an artist: it may be this that makes him the "genuine" spectator that Nietzsche holds him to be. But it still makes him a spectator. And so it must mean that even *his* "definition" illicitly introduces "the 'spectator' himself into the concept 'beautiful'," even if it might also be true that the "spectator" that he introduces is not "so bad" as the ones introduced by Kant and Schopenhauer.

* * *

1.4 So: we can say that Nietzsche regards Stendhal's conception of beauty as superior to Kant's and Schopenhauer's, and as superior in virtue of the fact that, for him, beauty *excites* "*the will*" ('interestedness')."[11] But this still

---

[7] Aesthetic judgment, in Kant's view, is, because grounded in disinterested pleasure, valid for everyone.

[8] In aesthetic experience, according to Schopenhauer, we perceive the Platonic Ideas (i.e. the essences of the various representations that comprise the phenomenal world).

[9] For helpful further discussion of this point, see Janaway 2007: 188–91.

[10] The idea that beauty is a promise of happiness appears in Stendhal 1857: chapter 17.

[11] Nietzsche remained committed to the thought that this is the least bad thing that can be said about beauty from the spectator's point of view: see e.g. *TI*, "Expeditions of an Untimely Man," 22.

doesn't take us any closer to an understanding of what, precisely, an approach to "the aesthetic problem from the point of view of the artist" might look like or yield, or of what is wrong with approaching that problem from the point of view of the spectator (even of a "genuine" spectator, such as Stendhal) (*GM*, III, 6).

Daniel W. Conway has suggested that the key, here, is to be found in a passage that Nietzsche wrote in the same year as the *Genealogy* (1887).[12] The relevant part of the passage is this:

The first distinction to be made regarding works of art. – All thought, poetry, painting, compositions, even buildings and sculptures, belong either to monological art or to art before witnesses. In the second class we must include even the apparently monological art that involves faith in God, the whole lyricism of prayer. For the pious there is as yet no solitude; this invention was made only by us, the godless. (*GS*, 367)

And Conway's thought appears to be that, because Nietzsche seems to prefer "godless," "monological art" to "art before witnesses" (where "witnesses" equals "spectators"), an understanding of the best works of art must be altogether orthogonal to considerations concerning spectatorship, as must an understanding of the beauty that those works possess.

I think that Conway is on to something here; and I return to *GS*, 367, in section 4, below. But his idea won't do as it stands, for at least two reasons. First, the distinction between "monological art" and "art before witnesses" appears to be one that Nietzsche draws from the standpoint of the spectator; which, if so, would suggest that any insight that that distinction affords into the nature of beauty must itself be spectatorly. And, second, the passage doesn't actually seem to be about beauty – about the "aesthetic problem" – at all: rather, it seems to be about a distinction that spectators might draw between two varieties of artistic creativity, a variety that presupposes witnesses and a variety that does not. In my view, then, we will have to look elsewhere if we are to start to get a grip on Nietzsche's reasons for giving priority to the standpoint of the artist.

2. MODES OF VALUATION

The question of standpoint is a question about how a person *relates* to a given value: how it arises for him, perhaps, or how it is connected to his other values. And this suggests a natural place to turn to for an elucidation of Nietzsche's views about differences between artistic and spectatorial

[12] Conway 2008: 104.

standpoints – namely, his discussion in the first essay of the *Genealogy* of the distinction between noble and slave morality, a discussion devoted, precisely, to the varying ways in which it is possible to relate to one's values.

The relevant passages (*GM*, I, 7–13) are very familiar, so I will offer only a telegraphic summary here. Noble morality, which "is rooted" – as Nietzsche puts it elsewhere – "in a triumphant Yes said to *oneself*" (*CW*, Epilogue), has two distinctive features. First, it springs from an affirmation, from a "Yes": its basic concept ("good") is therefore positive (its secondary concept, the negative, is derived by contrast); and, second, its founding valuation is exclusively self-regarding – the "Yes" is "said to *oneself*." Slave morality differs from noble morality with respect to both features. First, it begins with a rejection – with a "No" said to "what is 'outside'," to "what is 'different'": its basic concept ("evil") is therefore negative (its secondary concept, the positive, is derived by contrast); and, second, its founding valuation is exclusively other-regarding – the "No" is said to "what is 'not itself'" (*GM*, I, 10).[13] Nietzsche associates the noble mode of valuation with psychic health and the slave mode with psychic sickness; and, perhaps not altogether unpredictably, he prefers the former to the latter.[14]

This is, as I say, well-worn ground: it gives a schematic indication of what Nietzsche thinks a proper and healthy relation between a person and his most fundamental values might be like. What is less often noticed, however, is that the scope of his discussion is quite explicitly *not* restricted to the "good"/"bad" opposition of noble morality or the "evil"/"good" opposition of slave morality. Rather, Nietzsche seems to regard the scope of his point as much wider, at least as far as the noble dimension of value is concerned. For example – and most relevantly for our present purposes – he alludes to a specifically *noble* conception of "beauty," a conception that exactly shadows the noble conception of "good." The "noble mode of valuation," he says, "gratefully and triumphantly" affirms itself – "'we noble ones, we good, *beautiful*, happy ones!'" (*GM*, I, 10 – italics added); and he refers to what he

---

[13] Notice that when Nietzsche refers to the slave revolt in morality as a "reversal of the value-positing eye" he is not referring, as one might naturally imagine, to the first of these features (i.e. to slave morality's being rooted in a "No" rather than a "Yes"), but to the second: the "reversal" consists in a "*need* to direct one's view outward instead of back to oneself" – a need, he says, that "is of the essence of *ressentiment*" (*GM*, I, 10).

[14] Of course, as has been widely noted, his attitudes towards both are more complicated than this suggests. For example, he regards the triumph of slave morality as a condition of man's having become "*an interesting animal*" (*GM*, I, 6). But he also describes slave morality as a "blood-poisoning" (*GM*, I, 9) and "a sickness" (*GM*, III, 15); and he thinks it "perhaps . . . the most hopeful of all spectacles" that this "morality will gradually *perish* now" (*GM*, III, 27) – a prospect that he welcomes, surely, at least in part because it might open the way for a newly noble mode of valuation.

calls "the aristocratic value equation," in which "good = noble = powerful = *beautiful* = happy = beloved of God" (*GM*, I, 7 – italics added).[15] So here, it would seem, we have a fully noble way of conceiving of beauty: it is affirmative and self-regarding – it is "a triumphant Yes said to *oneself.*" And this, one might think, should give at least a hint of the sort of conception of beauty by comparison with which Nietzsche regards others, e.g. spectatorly conceptions, as falling short.

3. TAINTS OF SLAVISHNESS

There would appear to be three obvious ways in which a conception of beauty might fall short of the noble version. It might, like slave morality itself, be rooted in an other-regarding "No": here, one would have to imagine somebody first rejecting "what is 'not [the] self'" as "ugly," and then deriving by contrast a secondary, positive term – "beauty" – which he applies to himself. As far as I can see, the *Genealogy* contains nothing that points us in this direction. A second possibility, to which I turn in section 3.2, is that a conception of beauty might be rooted in a *self*-regarding "No." And, finally, a conception might be rooted in an *other*-regarding "Yes" (on which more directly). Either of these latter two possibilities might plausibly be regarded as tainted with the slavish mode of valuation.[16]

* * *

3.1 That Nietzsche is hostile to approaches that conceive of value as rooted in an other-regarding "Yes" can be seen most clearly, perhaps, in his critique of the "English psychologists" in the *Genealogy*'s opening sections (*GM*, I, 1–3). These "psychologists" begin, he says, by equating "good" with "un-egoistic." They begin, that is, with a positive, affirmative concept ("good"). But, in order to make sense of their equation of "good" with "unegoistic," they have to assume that unegoistic actions were first called "good from the point of view of those to whom they were done." But in such a "theory," Nietzsche protests, "the source of the concept 'good' has been sought and established in the wrong place: the judgement 'good' did *not* originate with those to whom 'goodness' was shown! Rather it was 'the good' themselves, that is to say, the noble . . . who saw and judged themselves and their actions as good." That the English psychologists cannot see this is due in part to

---

[15] I return to Nietzsche's apparently rather relaxed "value equation" in section 4.1, below.
[16] I say this – rather than that both are tainted with the noble mode of valuation – because of the health/ sickness contrast noted above: to be half sick or (only) half healthy is to fall short of an ideal of health, not of sickness.

their lack of "*the historical spirit*" (they are blind to the fact that there was once a noble morality) (*GM*, I, 2) . But it is also, and relatedly, due to their being held captive by the picture promoted by slave morality, according to which "good" is indeed to be equated with "unegoistic," and according to which all valuation is primordially other-regarding – i.e. is rooted, as one might put it, in the point of view of the spectator.

It is tempting to conclude from this that Nietzsche's *real* objection in *GM*, III, 6, to the spectatorly conception of "beauty" is that, because it construes "beauty" as a fundamentally other-regarding valuation – as a valuation that originates with those to whom "beauty" *was shown* – it is essentially slavish. Indeed, I will suggest shortly that this *is*, in essence, Nietzsche's objection to Stendhal. But it doesn't appear to be his objection to Kant and Schopenhauer. It doesn't appear, that is, to be his objection to those whom he most explicitly criticizes for their spectatorliness. And this is because, as is indicated by the other place in the *Genealogy* at which Nietzsche talks about the origins of the concept "beauty," it is simply a mistake to equate spectatorly conceptions such as theirs with conceptions rooted in a mode of valuation that is, primordially, other-regarding.

* * *

3.2 The passage in question is buried deep within the notoriously difficult discussion of the relations between internalization, *ressentiment*, and the various forms of "bad conscience" that Nietzsche (apparently) distinguishes (*GM*, II, 16–22).[17] The details of the discussion are hard to unpick; but what we can say with some confidence is that, whatever else is going on, the chief topic is the formation of a distinctively slavish, non-noble – ultimately, a modern – psyche, a psyche for which the unmediated self-celebration characteristic of noble morality is almost inconceivable. And, in the midst of that discussion, we find this:

We must be wary of thinking disparagingly about this whole phenomenon [inter-nalization] merely because it is inherently painful and ugly. Fundamentally, it is the same active force as the one that is at work on a grand scale in those artists of violence and organizers who build states . . . – only here the material on which the formative and violent nature of this force is let loose is man himself, his whole ancient animal self . . . This secret self-violation, this artists' cruelty, this desire to give form to oneself as a difficult, resisting, suffering material and to brand it with a will, a critique, a contradiction, a contempt, a "no" . . . – this whole *active* "bad conscience" has finally – we have already guessed – as true womb of all ideal and imaginative phenomena, brought a wealth of novel, disconcerting beauty and

---

[17] For a far from perfect attempt to clarify this discussion as a whole, see Ridley 1998a: 15–26.

affirmation to light, and perhaps for the first time, beauty itself. – After all, what would be "beautiful" if the contrary to it had not first come to awareness of itself, if ugliness had not first said to itself: "I am ugly"? (*GM*, II, 18)

And Nietzsche suggests that "after this clue, one puzzle will be less puzzling, namely how an ideal, something beautiful, can be hinted at in self-contradictory concepts such as *selflessness, self-denial, self-sacrifice*" (ibid.).

This is a dense passage, but it is at least clear from it that Nietzsche envisages a concept of "the beautiful" that arises from a mode of valuation that is, in the first instance, both *self*-regarding (like noble valuing) *and* negative (like slave valuing). It begins by branding a "No" into the self – it says to itself "'I am ugly'." And it is from this originary valuation that, by contrast, the secondary, positive term, "the beautiful," is derived ("what would be 'beautiful'" if "ugliness had not first said to itself: 'I am ugly'?") – a term that is reserved for what is *not* the self, and so is associated, precisely, with concepts such as "*self-denial.*" So we have here a mode of valuation that is rooted, as the second of the alternatives canvassed earlier had it, in a self-regarding "No."

It seems plausible to say that it is *this* route to the "beautiful" that most closely reflects the one that Nietzsche understands Kant and Schopenhauer to have taken: a route by which an *other*-regarding conception of "beauty" is arrived at only by way of a negative valuation of the self – this latter valuation, we may take it, being associated by Nietzsche with the forms of "*self-denial*" that Kant and Schopenhauer, in their different ways, express through the ideal of "disinterestedness."[18] And, if this is right, then it is false that Nietzsche's real objection to their conceptions of "beauty" lies in the fact that their mode of valuation is primordially other-regarding: for it is not primordially other-regarding. Rather, if their mode of valuation is to be objected to for its slavishness, the objection will have to be that the valuation in question begins with a "No" – not said to the non-self, as in slave morality, but said self-regardingly.

* * *

3.3 I believe that this is correct: Nietzsche's basic objection to Kant's and Schopenhauer's approaches to the "aesthetic problem" is that they are rooted in a self-regarding "No." And this suggests that his objection to these approaches may be only weakly connected to the fact that they are, also, spectatorial – indeed, the objection may seem no longer to be related to that fact in any way.

---

[18] This connection to "*self-denial*" explains why Nietzsche's discussion of Kant and Schopenhauer appears in the third essay of the *Genealogy*: their conceptions of beauty are iterations of the ascetic ideal.

Up to a point this is true. If an investment in the ideal of "disinterested-ness" is a sign or a sufficient condition of a conception of beauty's being grounded in a "No," so that "the beautiful" is merely "an afterthought and pendant" (*GM*, I, 10) derived by contrast from a more "basic concept" (*GM*, I, 11), then a spectatorly stance with no such investment should escape censure. And here we might reinvoke Stendhal, for whom "'beauty *promises* happiness'; to him, the fact of the matter is precisely the *excitement of the will* ('interestedness')": thus "he *rejected* and repudiated the one point about the aesthetic condition which Kant had stressed: *le désintéressement.*" For Stendhal, then, as a "genuine 'spectator' and artist," there seems to be no "No" in sight – a fact not disconnected, perhaps, from his being a "more happily adjusted personality" than (e.g.) Schopenhauer's (*GM*, III, 6), and so someone having that much less about himself to say "No" to. And, if we were to stop there, we might well conclude that there is nothing at all missing from or wrong with a *genuine* spectator's take on "beauty," and so attribute to Nietzsche an unqualified endorsement of Stendhal's conception of it, that "beauty" is "*une promesse de bonheur.*"

But we shouldn't stop there – not least because, as we have already seen, Nietzsche seems to regard even Stendhal's conception as only a *faute de mieux* (as not "so bad" as Kant's or Schopenhauer's). We should, rather, ask (again) what the problem or shortcoming in Stendhal's "definition" of beauty is supposed to be. For now, as I've already intimated, an obvious answer lies at hand: the problem is that his conception is rooted in an *other-regarding* "Yes." His mode of valuation is certainly positive – it seems that he doesn't arrive at "beauty" by way of any sort of negation. But it is also, at least in the first place, *not* focused on the self. It is beauty *out there* that Stendhal's definition affirms; and this returns us to the objection that his way of thinking is still essentially spectatorial (for all that it begins with a "Yes"), and so to the idea that what Nietzsche is really after is a conception of beauty that is free of slavish taints altogether – that is not just affirmative, but is also self-regarding. What he seems to want, in other words, is "beauty" in its fully noble conception.

4. BEAUTY FOR ARTISTS

This ambition may be problematic, however. Nietzsche's original nobles are, literally, history: they are almost inconceivably primitive. The vast majority of modern human beings are simply too complex and conflicted – too "*interesting*" (*GM*, I, 6) – to be at all like them; which means that, as moderns, we may have little access to or use for *their* mode of valuation. A "triumphant Yes said to *oneself*," that is, may lie beyond our repertoire. And Nietzsche, I think, agrees – in general. But he does appear to believe that there is at least one class of person to whom this generalization does not apply; and this is the class "artists."

* * *

4.1 Here we must leave the *Genealogy* for a moment, and turn to *Twilight of the Idols*, written in the following year. For *Twilight* contains Nietzsche's most sustained late discussion, not of artists as such, but of what it is *like* to be an artist, of what is distinctive of the artistic "condition," as he sometimes puts it. Representative remarks include:

Towards a psychology of the artist. – For art to exist, for any sort of aesthetic activity or perception to exist, a certain physiological presupposition is indispensable: *intoxication*. Intoxication must first have heightened the excitability of the entire machine: no art results before that happens. All kinds of intoxication, however different their origin, have the power to do this: above all, the intoxication of sexual excitement, the oldest and most primitive form of intoxication . . . – The essence of intoxication is the feeling of plenitude and increased energy. From out of this feeling one gives to things, one *compels* them to take, one rapes them. (*TI*, "Expeditons of an Untimely Man," 8)

In this condition one enriches everything out of one's own abundance: what one sees, what one desires, one sees swollen, pressing, strong, overladen with energy. The man in this condition transforms things until they mirror his power – until they are reflections of his perfection. This *compulsion* to transform into the perfect is – art. Even all that which he is not becomes for him none the less part of his joy in himself; in art, man takes delight in himself as perfection. (*TI*, "Expeditions of an Untimely Man," 9)

And there is more in a similar vein. Some of the details are complicated, and many of them repay closer attention. But the outlines are clear enough. In the artistic condition, in the moment of creative activity, man's intoxicated sense of his own erotic energy and fullness spills over and projects itself – forces itself – on to the world, so that the world is transformed into a mirror that reflects his "joy in himself" back to him. And here – although Nietzsche doesn't use the word – it seems right to say that he experiences himself not simply as joyful or powerful or perfect, but as *beautiful*; and that what he makes, the world he transforms "into the perfect" – his art – is beautiful in virtue of *his* beauty.[19]

---

[19] *Cf. TI*, "Expeditions of an Untimely Man," 19: "Anyone who tried to divorce [the beautiful] from man's pleasure in man would at once find the ground give way beneath him. The 'beautiful in itself' is not even a concept, merely a phrase. In the beautiful, man sets himself up as the standard of perfection; in select cases he worships himself in it."

On Nietzsche's view, then, the artist is the locus of a terrific, primal moment of self-affirmation – of "a triumphant Yes said to *oneself*" – in which the *non*-self is subsumed under and made valuable by his self-directed joy. And from this – perhaps the ultimate in the noble mode of valuation – we can get a glimpse of why Nietzsche's "aristocratic value equation (good = noble = powerful = beautiful = happy = beloved of God)" (*GM*, I, 7) is so apparently polysemous. The idea, plausibly, is that noble (artistic) valuing originates in a state of such primally intense affirmation that the core experience is one of, as it were, undifferentiated positivity, an inchoate but irresistible upwelling of the "Yes" that only afterwards, or perhaps from a third-person point of view, cools and crystallizes into the discrete values of everyday life. From the point of view of the valuer himself, that is, he no more affirms himself *as* good, specifically, or *as* powerful than he affirms himself *as* happy or *as* beautiful (although he feels himself, inchoately, to be all of these): rather, he just affirms *himself – simpliciter.*[20]

If this is correct, then artistic creativity as Nietzsche understands it is a peculiarly intense form of self-celebration. It may result in objects that are found beautiful; but, if so, those objects are, strictly speaking, only by-products, and their beauty is merely a reflection of a power and an energy – a beauty – that is, in the first place and most authentically, the artist's own. In section 1.4, I touched upon Daniel W. Conway's suggestion that Nietzsche's preference for approaching the "aesthetic problem" from the artist's point of view might be explained by reference to his distinction between "monological art" and "art before witnesses"; and we can now see what is right about that thought. The idea is not, strictly, that there are two sorts of *art*: but, rather, that there are two sorts of *artist*. After drawing the distinction, Nietzsche continues:

I do not know of any more profound difference in the whole orientation of an artist than this, whether he looks at his work in progress (at "himself") from the point of view of the witness, or whether he "has forgotten the world," which is the essential feature of all monological art. (*GS*, 367)

Thus, the monological artist's attention is focused firmly upon himself, and from his own point of view; he *is* his own "work in progress"; and the beauty that he creates attaches, in the first instance, *to him* (perhaps as mirrored in his "art").

* * *

---

[20] I return to some obvious problems with this idea in section 5, below.

4.2 Assuming that the foregoing is tolerably close to what the later Nietzsche thinks about artists and the creative "condition," we now have a decent idea of how an artist's solution to the "aesthetic problem" might look. "Beauty" – it might go – is, primordially, a quality of the self, a quality that it attains in its intensest moments of potency and (self-directed) affirmation; it is, thus, connected to "interestedness" from top to bottom, and so bears no relation to "impersonality" or "universality"; and while "beauty" may, in a secondary sense, like a residue in the world left by the self's over-spilling, be a quality also attributed to objects (such as works of art), its reality is, above all, as "a great *personal* fact," a fact grasped only in the *first* person (*GM*, III, 6). It is, in short, a noble value. And, if this is what an artist's solution to the problem might look like, it allows us – at last – to unpack Nietzsche's response to Stendhal in a perspicuous way.

Stendhal is right, in Nietzsche's view, to have construed "beauty" in terms of "interestedness." And his making this connection is, indeed, a function of his being an artist, and hence "a genuine 'spectator'" (ibid.). For he knows at first-hand what the creative condition is *like*: he has *said* that "triumphant Yes" to himself, has affirmed himself – in an erotic whirl[21] – as good/noble/powerful/beautiful/happy/beloved of God. And yet, in his "definition," he steps back and becomes a spectator (albeit a well-qualified one). He views "the beautiful" from a second- or third-person point of view; and from this perspective, "beauty" – rather than being happiness itself, as it would be in the first person – is, as he himself puts it, and as Nietzsche rather surprisingly doesn't note, *only* a promise of happiness ("La beauté n'est que la promesse du bonheur"[22]). "Beauty" *out there*, that is, can only prompt and recall the "genuine 'spectator'," i.e. the off-duty artist, back to himself, back to his art, back to the real beauty. So Stendhal's definition is deficient in that it contents itself with defining only the symptom or the summons, rather than the condition or the goal. And this is why Nietzsche will go no further than to suggest that his definition is not "so bad" as those offered by Kant and Schopenhauer.

5. THE PHILOSOPHICAL QUESTION

In the preceding sections, I have argued that Nietzsche's remarks about beauty in the *Genealogy* yield three quite separate conceptions of it, two of

---

[21] Cf. *TI*, "Expeditions of an Untimely Man," 23.
[22] Stendhal (1857: §17). A stricter translation might be: "Beauty is only happiness's promise," although I can't see that this makes a difference that matters.

which he rejects, with varying degrees of vehemence, and one that he apparently accepts. Least attractive, in his eyes, is the fundamentally ascetic conception of beauty to be found in Kant and Schopenhauer, a conception rooted in a "No" said to the self, in a form of self-denial that eventuates in "disinterestedness" as an aesthetic ideal. Better, he thinks, although still imperfect, is Stendhal's conception, which is affirmative and "interested" but is also other-regarding, and so holds itself at arm's length from beauty as it really is. The third conception – beauty as, according to Nietzsche, it really is – construes it as one name for, or one dimension of, an erotically intense experience of affirmation, a condition in which value attaches, primordially and essentially, to *the self.* The first two conceptions can, in one way or another, be thought of as slavish: the first is grounded in negation; the second presents the non-self as the originary locus of value. The final conception, by contrast, is *noble*: it is both affirmative and self-regarding.

* * *

5.1 It is clear that one's receptiveness to Nietzsche's views on these matters – one's willingness to treat what he says as a genuine contribution to the theory of beauty, to aesthetics – is going to depend upon how convincing one finds his thoughts about value in general, and how convincing one finds his reasons for privileging certain modes of valuation over others.

   With respect to the first issue, Nietzsche appears to be committed to the claim that value in some sense originates in a "Yes"/"No" said to the self/ non-self. In one way this looks uncontroversial: values are either positive or negative; and the self/non-self dichotomy is exhaustive. But the plausibility of the claim does depend on what one means by "originates." Is the thought that, just by saying "Yes" to something, for example, one brings into existence a value that that thing now instantiates? Surely not. One might say "Yes" to something in virtue of recognizing that it does, in fact, instantiate a given value. Or one might, conceivably, inaugurate a system of values – a system of exchange, for instance – in which certain things are to be said "Yes" to. In the first case, no new value has been brought into being (although something has been newly found valuable); in the second case, new values have perhaps been created, but not by anybody saying "Yes" to anything (although a new reason for "Yes"-saying may now exist). In neither case has saying "Yes" produced or originated a value.

   A more plausible way to take the idea of origination might be to construe it as referring to the manner in which something comes to be, or comes to be acknowledged *as*, a value for someone. So, for example, we might imagine a person (a child) for whom "courage," say, emerges as a value through his experience of reading the Biggles books: the value "originates" in a "Yes" said to the non-self. Or, more complicatedly, we might imagine a person for whom the same value emerges, first, through uncomfortable feelings of hesitancy in the face of the unknown, an experience that leads him to form a certain admiration for those whose behavior appears not to be informed by such feelings: here, the value originates in a "No" said to the self. It is easy, too, to imagine a case in which the value originates in a "No" said to the non-self (in disdain for the hesitancy of others, etc.). What it is not easy to imagine, however, is someone for whom "courage" emerges as a value purely and simply through a self-directed "Yes." Indeed, it is difficult to imagine that *any* value might emerge in this way.

The reason for this is the straightforward one that solipsism can originate nothing. Like every other kind of meaning in our lives, our values are sustained and made possible by a shared social world. Even the person for whom "courage" emerges as a value through a "No" said to the self is not, in the relevant sense, a solipsist: his mode of valuation rests on a contrast between himself and others. And the point goes, I think, even for the species of value that might seem most naturally to be thought of as originating in a self-directed "Yes": I have in mind hedonic value. For either the self-directed "Yes" means merely "I like this," in which case we're dealing with a preference rather than a value; or the "Yes" really does pick out a value, in which case it is being offered as a source of *reasons* (to do this, to refrain from that), which is already to presuppose a shared social world. In neither case does the "Yes" mark the solipsistic emergence of pleasure as a value for someone.

If this is right, and if the present way of construing "origination" is right, then Nietzsche's position is significantly compromised. For it would seem that there is no such thing as the noble mode of valuation – as a value originating purely through a "Yes" said to the self – and so no conceivable reason to privilege this mode of valuation over other (more "slavish") alternatives. And Nietzsche, I think, comes remarkably close to acknowledging the fact. When he first introduces the noble mode of valuation, and insists against the "English psychologists" that it was "the noble" themselves who "saw and judged themselves and their actions as good, that is, of the first rank," he continues: "in contrast to everything lowly, low-minded, common and plebeian. It was from this *pathos of distance* that they first claimed the right to create values" (*GM*, I, 2). So, if Nietzsche is to be believed here, even the noble mode of valuation, because rooted in a "*pathos of distance*" – in a contrast between oneself and others – already presupposes a context that goes *beyond* the self, a context upon which the noble "Yes" depends for its point. Which means that Nietzsche himself has reason to deny that a value can originate *purely* in a self-regarding "Yes."

∗ ∗ ∗

5.2 I think that we should agree with Nietzsche about this, and note three consequences. The first is that the self/non-self dichotomy turns out to be something of a red herring: the non-self is *always* integral to the origination of value. The second consequence is that Nietzsche's erotically self-affirming artist, the artist who "'has forgotten the world'" (*GS*, 367), isn't properly to be understood as creating values or as originating them. Rather, as I noted in section 4.1, his condition appears simply to be one of undifferentiated positivity – a condition which, however intense, falls short of *valuing*, since valuing is always valuing *in some respect*: as good, as noble, as powerful, etc. (a point, incidentally, that may undermine the claim of Nietzsche's "aristocratic value equation" [*GM*, I, 7] to be a *value* equation at all). The final consequence is that Nietzsche no longer has a principled objection to offer to approaches to the "aesthetic problem" – "What is beauty?" – that envisage it from the point of view of the spectator (*GM*, III, 6). Assuming that he *does* have a principled objection to approaches that begin with a "No," he still has grounds to reject Kant's and Schopenhauer's conceptions of beauty (for their "disinterestedness").[23] But he has no reason left to reject Stendhal's conception. Nietzsche gives us no reason, that is, to deny that beauty might, after all, be a promise of happiness.[24,25,26]

---

[23] This assumption is surely reasonable, given Nietzsche's concern, *contra* Schopenhauer especially, with the possibility of an affirmative attitude towards life.

[24] Yet he does, perhaps inadvertently, give us a version of Stendhal's formula (i.e. a version without the "only") that we might prefer to Stendhal's own. (Cf. Nietzsche's remark that "Art is the great stimulus to life"; *TI*, "Expeditions of an Untimely Man," 24].)

[25] For some attractive reasons to think that beauty might indeed be such a promise, see Nehamas 2007.

[26] My thanks to Simon May and Genia Schönbaumsfeld for comments on an earlier draft of this paper.

Bibliography

PRIMARY LITERATURE

German editions

Colli, G., and Montinari, M., eds. (1967–77) *Werke: Kritische Gesamtausgabe*. Berlin: Walter de Gruyter.
  eds. (1980–88) *Sämtliche Werke: Kritische Studienausgabe*, rev. student edn., ed. K. Ansell-Pearson. Berlin: Walter de Gruyter.

Translations

Clark, Maudemarie, and Swensen, Alan, trans. (1998) *On the Genealogy of Morality*. Indianapolis: Hackett.
Diethe, Carol, trans. (1994) *On the Genealogy of Morality*, ed. K. Ansell-Pearson. Cambridge University Press.
  trans. (2007) *On the Genealogy of Morality*. Cambridge University Press.
Faber, Marion, with Stephen Lehmann, trans. (1984) *Human, All Too Human*. Lincoln: University of Nebraska Press.
Hollingdale, R. J., trans. (1968) *Twilight of the Idols*. London: Penguin.
  trans. (1969) *Thus Spoke Zarathustra*. Harmondsworth: Penguin.
  trans. (1982a) *Beyond Good and Evil*. Harmondsworth: Penguin.
  trans. (1982b) *Daybreak*. Cambridge University Press.
  trans. (1983) *Untimely Meditations*. Cambridge University Press.
  trans. (1986) *Human, All Too Human*. Cambridge University Press.
  trans. (1990a) *Beyond Good and Evil: Prelude to a Philosophy of the Future*. London: Penguin.
  trans. (1990b) *Twilight of the Idols and The Anti-Christ*. Harmondsworth: Penguin.
Kaufmann, Walter, trans. (1954a) *The Antichrist*. New York: Viking.
  trans. (1954b) *Thus Spoke Zarathustra*, in *The Portable Nietzsche*, ed. and trans. Walter Kaufmann. New York: Viking.

trans. (1954c) *Twilight of the Idols*, in *The Portable Nietzsche*, ed. and trans. Walter Kaufmann, New York: Viking.

trans. (1966a) *Beyond Good and Evil*. New York: Vintage.

trans. (1966b) *Thus Spoke Zarathustra*. Harmondsworth: Penguin.

trans. (1967a) *The Birth of Tragedy*, in *The Birth of Tragedy and The Case of Wagner*. New York: Vintage.

trans. (1967b) *The Case of Wagner*, in *The Birth of Tragedy and The Case of Wagner*. New York: Vintage.

trans. (1967c) *Ecce Homo*. New York: Vintage.

trans. (1968a) *The Antichrist*, in *The Portable Nietzsche*, ed. and trans. Walter Kaufmann. Harmondsworth: Penguin.

trans. (1968b) *Beyond Good and Evil*, in *Basic Writings of Nietzsche*, ed. and trans. Walter Kaufmann. New York: Modern Library.

trans. (1968c) *On the Genealogy of Morals*, in *Basic Writings of Nietzsche*, ed. and trans. Walter Kaufmann. New York: Modern Library.

trans. (1968d) *Twilight of the Idols*, in *The Portable Nietzsche*, ed. and trans. Walter Kaufmann. Harmondsworth: Penguin.

trans. (1969) *Ecce Homo*. New York: Random House.

trans. (1974) *The Gay Science*. New York: Vintage.

trans. (1976a) *The Antichrist*, in *The Portable Nietzsche*, ed. and trans. Walter Kaufmann. New York: Penguin.

trans. (1976b) *Twilight of the Idols*, in *The Portable Nietzsche*, ed. and trans. Walter Kaufmann. New York: Penguin.

trans. (1989) *Ecce Homo*. New York: Vintage.

Kaufmann, Walter, and Hollingdale, R. J., trans. (1967) *On the Genealogy of Morals*, in *On the Genealogy of Morals and Ecce Homo*. New York: Vintage Books.

trans. (1968) *The Will to Power*, ed. Walter Kaufmann. New York: Vintage.

Smith, Douglas, trans. (1996) *On the Genealogy of Morals*. Oxford University Press.

SECONDARY LITERATURE

Acampora, Christa Davis (2002) "Nietzsche contra Homer, Socrates, and Paul," *Journal of Nietzsche Studies* 24: 25–53.

(2006a) "On Sovereignty and Overhumanity: Why It Matters How We Read Nietzsche's Genealogy II:2," in Acampora (2006b), pp. 147–61.

ed. (2006b) *Nietzsche's* On the Genealogy of Morals: *Critical Essays*. Lanham, MD: Rowan & Littlefield.

Ansell-Pearson, Keith (1991) "Nietzsche on Autonomy and Morality: The Challenge to Political Theory," *Political Studies* 39: 270–86.

ed. (2006) *A Companion to Nietzsche*. Oxford: Blackwell.

Augustine (1961) *Confessions*, trans. R. S. Pine-Coffin. London: Penguin.

Austen, Jane (1980) *Northanger Abbey*. Oxford World's Classics. Oxford University Press.

Austin, J. L. (1979) "Other Minds," in *Philosophical Papers*. 3rd edn., ed. J. O. Urmson and G. J. Warnock. Oxford University Press.

Beauvoir, Simone de (1976) *The Ethics of Ambiguity*, trans. Bernard Frechtman. New York: Kensington Press.

Bentham, Jeremy (2003) *An Introduction to the Principles of Morals and Legislation*, in *Utilitarianism and On Liberty*. Oxford: Blackwell.

Bergman, Frithjof (1988) "Nietzsche's Critique of Morality," in Solomon and Higgins (1988), pp. 29–45.

Bittner, Rüdiger (1994) *"Ressentiment,"* in Schacht (1994), pp. 127–38.

Blumenberg, Hans (1966) *Die Legitimität der Neuzeit*. Frankfurt: Suhrkamp.

Brobjer, Thomas (2008) *Nietzsche and the "English": The Influence of British and American Thinking on His Philosophy*. Amherst, NY: Humanity Books.

Burkert, Walter (1987) *Ancient Mystery Cults*. Cambridge, MA: Harvard University Press.

Byrne, Alex, and Hilbert, David R., eds. (1997) *Readings on Color*. 2 vols. Cambridge, MA: MIT Press.

Cavell, Stanley (2008) "On Nietzschean Perfectionism," paper presented at the American Philosophical Association, Eastern Division Meeting, Philadelphia, PA, December 2008.

Chappell, Timothy, ed. (2006) *Values and Virtues: Aristotelianism in Contemporary Ethics*. Oxford: Clarendon Press.

Clark, Maudemarie (1994) "Nietzsche's Misogyny," *International Studies in Philosophy* 26, no. 3: 3–12.

Clark, Maudemarie, and Dudrick, David (2007) "Nietzsche and Moral Objectivity: The Development of Nietzsche's Metaethics," in Leiter and Sinhababu (2007), pp. 192–226.

(2009) "Nietzsche on the Will: An Analysis of BGE 19," in Gemes and May (2009), pp. 247–68.

Clark, Maudemarie, and Leiter, Brian (1997) Introduction to Nietzsche's *Daybreak*. Cambridge University Press.

Conrad, Joseph (1900) *Lord Jim*. Electronic Text Center, University of Virginia Library. etext.virginia.edu/toc/modeng/public/ConLord.html

Conway, Daniel W. (2008) *Nietzsche's* On the Genealogy of Morals: *A Reader's Guide*. London: Continuum.

Craig, Edward (2007) "Genealogies and the State of Nature," in Thomas (2007), pp. 181–200.

Crisp, Roger (2003) "Socrates and Aristotle on Happiness and Virtue," in Heinaman (2003), pp. 55–78.

Deleuze, Gilles ([1962] 1983) *Nietzsche and Philosophy*, trans. Hugh Tomlinson. New York: Columbia University Press.

Dodds, E. R. (1968) *The Greeks and the Irrational*. Berkeley, CA: University of California Press.

Eliot, T. S. (1934) "Shakespeare and the Stoicism of Seneca," in his *Elizabethan Essays*. London: Faber, pp. 126–40.

Foot, Philippa (2002a) "Nietzsche's Immoralism," in her *Moral Dilemmas*. Oxford University Press, pp. 144–58.

(2002b) "Virtues and Vices," in her *Virtues and Vices and Other Essays in Moral Philosophy*. Oxford University Press, pp. 1–18.

Foucault, Michel (1991) "On the Genealogy of Ethics: An Overview of Work in Progress," in Rabinow (1991), pp. 340–72.

(2001) "Nietzsche, Genealogy, History," in Richardson and Leiter (2001), pp. 341–59.

French, Peter A., Uehling, Theodore E. Jr., and Wettstein, Howard K., eds. (1988) *Ethical Theory: Character and Virtue*. Midwest Studies in Philosophy 13. University of Notre Dame Press.

Freud, Sigmund (1930) *Civilization and Its Discontents*, in J. Strachey, trans., *The Standard Edition of the Complete Psychological Works of Sigmund Freud*. London: The Hogarth Press, vol. XXI, pp. 59–148.

(1961) *Civilization and Its Discontents*, ed. and trans. J. Strachey. New York: W. W. Norton & Co.

Fries, Jakob Friedrich (1982) *Dialogues on Morality and Religion*, ed. D. Z. Phillips, trans. David Wolford. Oxford: Blackwell.

Fromm, Erich (1975) *The Art of Loving*. London: Unwin.

Fuller, Peter (1986) *Marches Past*. London: Chatto & Windus.

Futuyma, Douglas J. (1998) *Evolutionary Biology*. Sunderland, MA: Sinauer Associates.

Gemes, Ken (2008) "Nihilism and the Affirmation of Life: A Review of and Dialogue with Bernard Reginster," *European Journal of Philosophy* 16: 459–71.

(2009) "Nietzsche on Free Will, Autonomy and the Sovereign Individual," in Gemes and May (2009), pp. 33–49.

Gemes, Ken, and May, Simon, eds. (2009) *Nietzsche on Freedom and Autonomy*. Oxford University Press.

Gemes, Ken, and Richardson, John, eds. (forthcoming) *The Oxford Handbook of Nietzsche*. Oxford University Press.

Geuss, Raymond (1981) *The Idea of a Critical Theory*. Cambridge University Press.

(1999) *Morality, Culture and History*. Cambridge University Press.

(2001) "Nietzsche and Genealogy," in Richardson and Leiter (2001), pp. 322–40.

(2002) "Genealogy as Critique," *European Journal of Philosophy* 10: 209–15.

Guay, Robert (2006) "The Philosophical Function of Genealogy," in Ansell-Pearson (2006), pp. 353–70.

Harcourt, Edward, ed. (2000) *Morality, Reflection and Ideology*. Oxford University Press.

Hatab, Lawrence J. (2008) *Nietzsche's* On the Genealogy of Morality*: An Introduction*. Cambridge University Press.

Heinaman, Robert A., ed. (2003) *Plato and Aristotle's Ethics*. Aldershot: Ashgate.

Hick, John (1966) *Evil and the God of Love*. London: Macmillan.

Hill, R. Kevin (2003) *Nietzsche's Critiques: The Kantian Foundations of His Thought*. Oxford: Clarendon Press.

Horney, Karen (1970) *Neurosis and Human Growth: The Struggle Towards Self-Realization*. New York: Norton.

Hoy, David (1994) "Nietzsche, Hume and the Genealogical Method," in Schacht (1994), pp. 251–68.

Hume, David (1960) *A Treatise of Human Nature*. Oxford: Clarendon Press.

Hunt, Lester H. (1991) *Nietzsche and the Origin of Virtue*. London and New York: Routledge.

Hussain, Nadeem J. Z. (2004) "The Guise of a Reason," *Philosophical Studies*, 121: 263–75.

(2007) "Honest Illusion: Valuing for Nietzsche's Free Spirits," in Leiter and Sinhababu (2007), pp. 157–91.

(2008) "Constitution, Inescapability, and Necessity," Keynote Address, Intermountain West Student Philosophy Conference, University of Utah, Salt Lake City, 27–29 March 2008.

Husserl, Edmund ([1938] 1973) *Experience and Judgement*. Evanston: Northwestern University Press.

Irwin, Terence (2009) *The Development of Ethics*, vol. III. Oxford University Press.

Janaway, Christopher, ed. (1998) *Willing and Nothingness: Schopenhauer as Nietzsche's Educator*. Oxford University Press.

(2007) *Beyond Selflessness: Reading Nietzsche's Genealogy*. Oxford University Press.

Jaspers, Karl (1965) *Nietzsche: An Introduction to the Understanding of His Philosophical Activity*, trans. Charles F. Wallraff and Frederick J. Schmitz. Tucson: University of Arizona Press.

Johnston, Mark (1988) "Self-deception and the Nature of Mind," in McLaughlin and Rorty (1988), pp. 63–91.

(1997) "How to Speak of the Colors," in Byrne and Hilbert (1997), vol. I, pp. 137–76.

Kail, Peter (2007) "Understanding Hume's Natural History of Religion," *Philosophical Quarterly* 57: 190–211.

(2009) "Naturalism, Method and Genealogy in *Beyond Selflessness*," *European Journal of Philosophy* 17: 113–20.

Kant, Immanuel (2005) *The Moral Law: Groundwork of the Metaphysic of Morals*, trans. H. A. Paton. London: Routledge.

(2007) *Critique of Judgement*, trans. J. Meredith. Oxford University Press.

Katsafanas, Paul (2011a) "Deriving Ethics from Action: A Nietzschean Version of Constitutivism," *Philosophy and Phenomenological Research* 82. doi: 10.1111/j.1933-1592.2010.00440.x

(2011b) "The Concept of Unified Agency in Nietzsche, Plato, and Schiller," *Journal of the History of Philosophy* 49: 87–113.

Kaufmann, Walter (1974) *Nietzsche: Philosopher, Psychologist, Antichrist*. 4th edn. Princeton University Press.

Kemal, Salim, Gaskell, Ivan, and Conway, Daniel, eds. (1998) *Nietzsche, Philosophy and the Arts*. Cambridge University Press.

Kolakowski, Leszek (1978) *Main Currents of Marxism: Its Rise, Growth, and Dissolution*. Oxford: Clarendon Press.

Lazar, Ariela (1999) "Deceiving Oneself or Self-deceived? On the Formation of Beliefs 'Under the Influence'," *Mind* 108: 265–90.

Leiter, Brian (1992) "Nietzsche and Aestheticism," *Journal of the History of Philosophy* 30: 275–90.

(1998) "The Paradox of Fatalism and Self-Creation in Nietzsche," in Janaway (1998), pp. 217–57.

(2000) "Nietzsche's Metaethics: Against the Privilege Readings," *European Journal of Philosophy* 8: 277–97.

(2002) *Nietzsche on Morality*. London: Routledge.

(2007) "Nietzsche's Theory of the Will," *Philosophers' Imprint* 7 (September): 1–15. www.philosophersimprint.org/007007/ Also reprinted in Gemes and May (2009), pp. 107–26.

(forthcoming) "Nietzsche's Naturalism Reconsidered," in Gemes and Richardson (forthcoming).

Leiter, Brian, and Sinhababu, Neil, eds. (2007) *Nietzsche and Morality*. Oxford: Clarendon Press.

Lukes, Steven (1985) *Marxism and Morality*. Oxford: Clarendon Press; New York: Oxford University Press.

Mackie, John (1977) *Ethics: Inventing Right and Wrong*. Harmondsworth: Penguin.

Marx, Karl ([1871] 1978a) *The Civil War in France*, in Tucker (1978), pp. 618–52.

([1845–46] 1978b) *The German Ideology*, pt. I, in Tucker (1978), pp. 146–200.

([1848] 1978c) "Manifesto of the Communist Party," in Tucker (1978), pp. 469–500.

Maslow, Abraham (1971) *The Farther Reaches of Human Nature*. Harmondsworth: Penguin.

May, Simon (1999) *Nietzsche's Ethics and His War on "Morality."* Oxford University Press.

(2009) "Nihilism and the Free Self," in Gemes and May (2009), pp. 89–106.

McGinn, Colin (1997) *Ethics, Evil, and Fiction*. Oxford University Press.

McLaughlin, Brian, and Rorty, Amélie Oksenberg, eds. (1988) *Perspectives on Self-Deception*. London: University of California Press.

Mele, Alfred (1997) "Real Self-Deception," *Behavioral and Brain Sciences* 20: 91–102.

Migotti, Mark (1998) "Slave Morality, Socrates, and the Bushmen: A Reading of the First Essay of *On the Genealogy of Morals*," *Philosophy and Phenomenological Research* 58: 745–79.

(2006) "Slave Morality, Socrates, and the Bushmen," in Acampora (2006b), pp. 109–29.

Miles, Thomas (2007) "On Nietzsche's Ideal of the Sovereign Individual," *International Studies in Philosophy* 39, no. 3: 5–25.

Mill, John Stuart (2003) *Utilitarianism*, in *Utilitarianism and On Liberty*, ed. Mary Warnock. Oxford: Wiley-Blackwell.

Moore, G. E. (1903) *Principia Ethica*. Cambridge University Press.

Moran, Richard (2001) *Authority and Estrangement: An Essay on Self-Knowledge*. Princeton University Press.

Morgan, George Allen ([1941] 1965) *What Nietzsche Means*. New York: Harper.

Bibliography

Mulhall, Stephen (2009) "Nietzsche's Style of Address: A Response to Christopher Janaway's *Beyond Selflessness*," *European Journal of Philosophy* 17, no. 1: 121–31.

Nehamas, Alexander (1985) *Nietzsche: Life as Literature*. Cambridge, MA, and London: Harvard University Press.

(1998) *The Art of Living*. Berkeley, Los Angeles, and London: University of California Press.

(2007) *Only a Promise of Happiness*. Princeton University Press.

Norton, Robert E. (1995) *The Beautiful Soul: Aesthetic Morality in the Eighteenth Century*. Ithaca and London: Cornell University Press.

Nussbaum, Martha (1988) "Non-relative Virtues: An Aristotelian Approach," in French, Uehling, and Wettstein (1988), pp. 25–53.

O'Shaughnessy, Brian (1980) *The Will: A Dual Aspect Theory*. 2 vols. Cambridge University Press.

Owen, David (2003) "Nietzsche, Re-evaluation and the Turn to Genealogy," *European Journal of Philosophy* 11, no. 3: 249–72.

(2007) *Nietzsche's Genealogy of Morality*. Stocksfield: Acumen; Montreal: McGill-Queen's University Press.

Pears, David (1985) *Motivated Irrationality*. Oxford University Press.

(1991) "Self-Deceptive Belief-Formation," *Synthese* 89: 393–405.

Pippin, Robert (2006) "Lightning and Flash, Agent and Deed (*GM* I:6–17)," in Acampora (2006b), pp. 131–45.

Poellner, Peter (1995) *Nietzsche and Metaphysics*. Oxford: Clarendon Press.

(2003) "Non-conceptual Content, Experience and the Self," *Journal of Consciousness Studies* 10, no. 2: 32–57.

(2009) "Nietzschean Freedom," in Gemes and May (2009), pp. 151–79.

Prinz, Jesse (2007) *The Emotional Construction of Morals*. New York: Oxford University Press.

Rabinow, Paul, ed. (1991) *The Foucault Reader*. London: Penguin.

Reginster, Bernard (1997) "Nietzsche on *Ressentiment* and Valuation," *Philosophy and Phenomenological Research* 57: 281–305.

(2006) *The Affirmation of Life*. Cambridge, MA: Harvard University Press.

Richardson, John (1996) *Nietzsche's System*. Oxford University Press.

(2009) "Nietzsche's Freedoms," in Gemes and May (2009), pp. 127–49.

Richardson, John, and Leiter, Brian, eds. (2001) *Nietzsche*. New York: Oxford University Press.

Richardson, John (2007) *A Life of Picasso: The Triumphant Years, 1917–1932*. London: Jonathan Cape.

Ridley, Aaron (1998a) *Nietzsche's Conscience: Six Character Studies from the Genealogy*. Ithaca: Cornell University Press.

(1998b) "What Is the Meaning of Aesthetic Ideals?" in Kemal, Gaskell, and Conway (1998), 128–47.

(2005) "Nietzsche and the Re-evaluation of Values," *Proceedings of the Aristotelian Society* 105: 155–75.

(2009) "Nietzsche's Intentions: What the Sovereign Individual Promises," in Gemes and May (2009), pp. 181–96.

Risse, Mathias (2001) "The Second Treatise in *On the Genealogy of Morality*: Nietzsche on the Origin of the Bad Conscience," *European Journal of Philosophy* 9: 55–88.

Rutherford, Donald (2009) "Freedom as a Philosophical Ideal: Nietzsche and His Antecedents." University of California, San Diego, Department of Philosophy website. http://philosophyfaculty.ucsd.edu/faculty/rutherford/NietzscheFreedom.pdf

Saars, Martin (2002) "Genealogy and Subjectivity," *European Journal of Philosophy* 10: 231–45.

Sartre, Jean-Paul (1993) *Being and Nothingness*, trans. Hazel Barnes. New York: Washington Square Press.

([1943] 2003) *Being and Nothingness*. London: Routledge.

Schacht, Richard (1973) "Nietzsche and Nihilism," in Solomon (1973b), pp. 58–82.

(1983) *Nietzsche*. London: Routledge & Kegan Paul.

ed. (1994) *Nietzsche, Genealogy, Morality: Essays on Nietzsche's* On the Genealogy of Morals. Berkeley: University of California Press.

Schopenhauer, Arthur (1969) *The World as Will and Representation*, vols. I and II, trans. E. F. J. Payne. New York: Dover.

Shearman, John (1967) *Mannerism*. Harmondsworth: Penguin.

Sinhababu, Neil (2007) "Vengeful Thinking and Moral Epistemology," in Leiter and Sinhababu (2007), pp. 262–80.

Solomon, Robert C. (1973a) "Nietzsche, Nihilism and Morality," in Solomon (1973b), pp. 202–25.

ed. (1973b) *Nietzsche: A Collection of Critical Essays*, New York: Anchor Books.

(2003) *Living with Nietzsche: What the Great Immoralist Has to Teach Us*. Oxford University Press.

Solomon, Robert C., and Higgins, Kathleen M., eds. (1988) *Reading Nietzsche*. New York: Oxford University Press.

Stendhal (1857) *De l'amour*. Paris: Éditions Garnier Frères.

Stevenson, Charles (1938) "Persuasive Definitions," *Mind* 47: 331–50.

Stroud, Barry (2000) *The Quest for Reality: Subjectivism and the Metaphysics of Colour*. Oxford University Press.

Swanton, Christine (2003) *Virtue Ethics: A Pluralistic View*. Oxford University Press.

(2006) "Can Nietzsche Be Both an Existentialist and a Virtue Ethicist?" in Chappell (2006), pp. 171–88.

Taylor, Charles (1982) "Responsibility for Self," in Watson (1982), pp. 111–26.

(1989) *Sources of the Self*. Cambridge, MA: Harvard University Press.

(2007) *A Secular Age*. Cambridge, MA: Harvard University Press.

Taylor, Gabriele (1985) *Pride, Shame, and Guilt: Emotions of Self-Assessment*. Oxford: Clarendon Press.

Thatcher, David (1989) "Zur Genealogie der Moral: Some Textual Annotations," *Nietzsche-Studien* 18: 587–99.

Thomas, Alan, ed. (2007) *Bernard Williams: Contemporary Thinkers in Focus*. Cambridge University Press.

Tucker, Robert C., ed. (1978) *The Marx–Engels Reader*. 2nd edn. New York: Norton.

Velleman, David (2006) "A Rational Superego," in *Self to Self: Selected Essays*. Cambridge University Press, pp. 129–55.

Wallace, R. Jay (2007) "*Ressentiment*, Value, and Self-Vindication: Making Sense of Nietzsche's Slave Revolt," in Leiter and Sinhababu (2007), pp. 110–37.

Watson, Gary, ed. (1982) *Free Will*. Oxford University Press.

(1984) "Virtues in Excess," *Philosophical Studies* 46: 57–74.

West, M. T., ed. (1980) *Delectus ex iambis et elegis graecis*. Oxford Classical Texts. Oxford University Press.

Weston, Michael (1975) *Morality and the Self*. Oxford: Blackwell.

Wilcox, John T. (1974) *Truth and Value in Nietzsche: A Study of His Metaethics and Epistemology*. Ann Arbor: University of Michigan Press.

Williams, Bernard (1976) *Morality: An Introduction to Ethics*. Cambridge University Press.

(1985) *Ethics and the Limits of Philosophy*. London: Fontana.

(1994) "Nietzsche's Minimalist Moral Psychology," in Schacht (1994), pp. 237–47.

(2000) "Naturalism and Genealogy," in Harcourt (2000), pp. 148–61.

(2002) *Truth and Truthfulness*. Princeton University Press.

Wittgenstein, Ludwig (2009) *Philosophical Investigations*. Revised 4th edn., trans. P. M. S. Hacker and J. Schulte. Oxford: Blackwell.

Wollheim, Richard (1971) *Freud*. London: Fontana/Collins.

Young, Julian (1992) *Nietzsche's Philosophy of Art*. Cambridge University Press.

(forthcoming) "Nietzsche and Women," in Gemes and Richardson (forthcoming).

Zahavi, Dan (1999) *Self-Awareness and Alterity*. Evanston: Northwestern University Press.

Index

335